Lecture Notes in Computer Science 12083

More information about this series at http://www.springer.com/series/7407

Fernando Rincón · Jesús Barba ·
Hayden K. H. So · Pedro Diniz ·
Julián Caba (Eds.)

Applied Reconfigurable Computing

Architectures, Tools, and Applications

16th International Symposium, ARC 2020
Toledo, Spain, April 1–3, 2020
Proceedings

 Springer

Editors
Fernando Rincón 🆔
Technology and Information Systems
University of Castilla-La Mancha
Ciudad Real, Spain

Jesús Barba 🆔
Technology and Information Systems
University of Castilla-La Mancha
Ciudad Real, Spain

Hayden K. H. So 🆔
Department of Electrical and Electronic
Engineering
University of Hong Kong
Hong Kong, China

Pedro Diniz 🆔
INESC-ID
Lisbon, Portugal

Julián Caba 🆔
Technology and Information Systems
University of Castilla-La Mancha
Ciudad Real, Spain

ISSN 0302-9743   ISSN 1611-3349   (electronic)
Lecture Notes in Computer Science
ISBN 978-3-030-44533-1   ISBN 978-3-030-44534-8   (eBook)
https://doi.org/10.1007/978-3-030-44534-8

LNCS Sublibrary: SL1 – Theoretical Computer Science and General Issues

This Springer imprint is published by the registered company Springer Nature Switzerland AG
The registered company address is: Gewerbestrasse 11, 6330 Cham, Switzerland

Preface

During its 16 editions, the International Applied Reconfigurable Computing Symposium (ARC) has been an open meeting point for the discussion and dissemination of FPGA-related topics, as evidenced by the fact of having been held in many different countries around the world (Portugal, Brazil, Thailand, Germany, the UK, the USA, etc.) and also the large variety in the country of origin of the submitted papers.

The 16th edition of the symposium was held in Toledo[1], one of the most historic and beautiful cities of Spain, formally the ancient capital of the Visigothic Kingdom, and currently the capital of the Castilla-La Mancha region – recognized as a UNESCO World Heritage site.

The program included the presentation of 18 full papers (acceptance rate of 45%) and 11 poster presentations, selected from over 40 submissions from 10 different countries, after a thorough review process. The program also included three invited talks covering different application fields, such as Space or sustainable development, and a social program that helped the participants to unveil the many treasures of Toledo.

February 2020

Fernando Rincón
Jesús Barba
Julián Caba

---

[1] On the basis of the COVID-19 spreading trend worldwide, it was decided to postpone the conference.

Organization

The Applied Reconfigurable Computing Symposium (ARC 2020) was organized by the Grupo de Arquitectura y Redes de Comunicaciones (ARCo) and the University of Castilla-La Mancha, Spain. The symposium took place at the Faculty of Law and Social Sciences in Toledo, the capital of the Castilla-La Mancha region in Spain.

Sponsors

ARC 2020 was sponsored by:

General Chair

Fernando Rincón — University of Castilla-La Mancha, Spain

Program Committee Chairs

Jesús Barba — University of Castilla-La Mancha, Spain
Hayden K. H. So — University of Hong Kong, Hong Kong

Steering Committee

Hideharu Amano — Keio University, Japan
Jürgen Becker — Universität Karlsruhe (TH), Germany
Mladen Berekovic — Braunschweig University of Technology, Germany
Koen Bertels — Delft University of Technology, The Netherlands
João M. P. Cardoso — University of Porto, Portugal
Katherine (Compton) Morrow — University of Wisconsin-Madison, USA
George Constantinides — Imperial College of Science, UK
Pedro C. Diniz — INESC-ID, Portugal
Philip H. W. Leong — University of Sydney, Australia
Walid Najjar — University of California Riverside, USA
Roger Woods — The Queen's University of Belfast, UK

Program Committee

Hideharu Amano	Keio University, Japan
Zachary Baker	Los Alamos National Laboratory, USA
João Bispo	University of Porto, Portugal
Marcelo Brandalero	Brandenburg University of Technology Cottbus, Germany
João Canas Ferreira	University of Porto, Portugal
João Cardoso	University of Porto, Portugal
Luigi Carro	UFRGS, Brazil
Ray Cheung	City University of Hong Kong, Hong Kong
Daniel Chillet	CAIRN, IRISA, ENSSAT, France
Steven Derrien	Université de Rennes, France
Giorgos Dimitrakopoulos	Democritus University of Thrace, Greece
António Ferrari	University of Aveiro, Portugal
Ricardo Ferreira	Universidade Federal de Viçosa, Brazil
Mohammad Ghasemzadeh	Apple Inc., USA
Roberto Giorgi	University of Siena, Italy
Diana Goehringer	TU Dresden, Germany
Frank Hannig	Friedrich-Alexander University Erlangen-Nürnberg, Germany
Jim Harkin	University of Ulster, UK
Christian Hochberger	TU Darmstadt, Germany
Michael Huebner	Brandenburg University of Technology Cottbus, Germany
Kimon Karras	Think Silicon S.A., Greece
Krzysztof Kepa	GE Global Research, USA
Georgios Keramidas	Technological Educational Institute of Western Greece, Greece
Andreas Koch	TU Darmstadt, Germany
Tomasz Kryjak	AGH University of Science and Technology, Poland
Konstantinos Masselos	University of Peloponnese, Greece
Cathal Mccabe	Xilinx, UK
Antonio Miele	Politecnico di Milano, Italy
Takefumi Miyoshi	e-trees.Japan, Inc., Japan
Walid Najjar	University of California, Riverside, USA
Brent Nelson	Brigham Young University, USA
Horácio Neto	INESC-ID/IST, University of Lisbon, Portugal
Dimitris Nikolos	University of Patras, Greece
Andrés Otero	Universidad Politécnica de Madrid, Spain
Kyprianos Papadimitriou	Technical University of Crete, Greece
Monica Pereira	Universidade Federal do Rio Grande do Norte, Brazil
Thilo Pionteck	Otto-von-Guericke Universität Magdeburg, Germany
Mihalis Psarakis	University of Piraeus, Greece
Yukinori Sato	Toyohashi University of Technology, Japan
António Carlos Schneider	Universidade Federal do Rio Grande do Sul, Brazil

Yuichiro Shibata	Nagasaki University, Japan
Dimitrios Soudris	National Technical University of Athens, Greece
Gustavo Sutter	Universidad Autónoma de Madrid, Spain
Theocharis Theocharides	University of Cyprus, Cyprus
George Theodoridis	University of Patras, Greece
David Thomas	Imperial College London, UK
Chao Wang	University of Science and Technology of China, China
Roger Woods	Queen's University Belfast, UK

Additional Reviewers

Pedram Amini	Vasileios Leon
Muhammad Ali	Spiridon Likothanassis
Julin Caba	Dimosthenis Masouros
Anna Drewes	Umar Minhas
Marek Gorgon	Daniele Passareti
Christian Heidorn	Marco Procaccini
Carsten Heinz	Alexander Schwarz
Jaco Hofmann	Kostas Siozios
Ahmed Kamal	Lukas Sommer
Farnam Khalili	Ioannis Stamoulias
Gerald Krell	Jacob Wenzel

Contents

Architectures

Applications

Design Methods and Tools

Improving Performance Estimation for FPGA-Based Accelerators for Convolutional Neural Networks

Martin Ferianc[1]([✉]), Hongxiang Fan[2], Ringo S. W. Chu[3], Jakub Stano[4], and Wayne Luk[2]

[1] Department of Electronic and Electrical Engineering,
University College London, London, UK
martin.ferianc.19@ucl.ac.uk

[2] Department of Computing, Imperial College London, London, UK
{h.fan17,w.luk}@imperial.ac.uk

[3] Department of Computer Science, University College London, London, UK
ringo.chu.16@ucl.ac.uk

[4] Department of Information Technology and Electrical Engineering,
ETH Zurich, Zurich, Switzerland
jstano@ethz.ch

Abstract. Field-programmable gate array (FPGA) based accelerators are being widely used for acceleration of convolutional neural networks (CNNs) due to their potential in improving the performance and reconfigurability for specific application instances. To determine the optimal configuration of an FPGA-based accelerator, it is necessary to explore the design space and an accurate performance prediction plays an important role during the exploration. This work introduces a novel method for fast and accurate estimation of latency based on a Gaussian process parametrised by an analytic approximation and coupled with runtime data. The experiments conducted on three different CNNs on an FPGA-based accelerator on Intel Arria 10 GX 1150 demonstrated a 30.7% improvement in accuracy with respect to the mean absolute error in comparison to a standard analytic method in leave-one-out cross-validation.

Keywords: Field-programmable gate array · Deep learning · Convolutional neural network · Performance estimation · Gaussian process

1 Introduction

Field-programmable gate arrays (FPGAs) are becoming increasingly popular in the deep learning community, particularly in the acceleration of convolutional neural networks (CNNs) [4,5,11]. This acceleration is achieved by parallelising the extensive concurrency exhibited by CNNs. As such, FPGA is ideal as the

© Springer Nature Switzerland AG 2020
F. Rincón et al. (Eds.): ARC 2020, LNCS 12083, pp. 3–13, 2020.
https://doi.org/10.1007/978-3-030-44534-8_1

platform allows implementation of fine-grain parallelisations. To do an architectural exploration and determine the optimal hardware configuration, it is necessary to estimate the performance with respect to multiple different hardware specifications.

There are several performance estimation frameworks for reconfigurable FPGA-based accelerators [2,3,19], however, estimating the performance without knowing about scheduling is still a very challenging task because of two main reasons. First, the explicit time to execute a certain operation on hardware varies by on/off-chip communication, synchronisation, control signals, I/O interruptions and in particular for the CNN accelerators - the CNN's architecture, which complicate analytic estimation. Second, it is difficult to accurately select the most representative design features for all hardware specifications during the performance estimation.

In this paper, we propose a novel approach for performance estimation for FPGA-based CNN accelerators [11]. This method constitutes a Gaussian process (GP) [18] coupled with a standard analytic method and statistical data. Gaussian process is a stochastic process, such that every finite collection of random variables has a multivariate normal distribution [15]. Experiments were conducted on three different CNNs on Intel Arria GX 1150 FPGA and we compared the method to linear regression (LR), GP with zero mean function, GP with an artificial neural network (ANN) mean function [6], gradient tree boosting (GTB) and ANN in estimating latency. We show that the proposed method achieved the top result among all compared methods.[1]

In Sect. 2 we demonstrate the standard approach for analytic performance estimation. Afterwards, in Sect. 3 we introduce the proposed method, followed by Sect. 4 where we describe the accelerator as well as the dataset on which we benchmarked the method. Then we present the evaluation in Sect. 5 followed by a conclusion in Sect. 6.

2   Background

The most accurate method of determining the performance is escalating the CNN onto the hardware. One major drawback of this method is requiring re-synthesis and re-implementation for different hardware specifications. Therefore, it is more feasible and practical to perform the design space exploration (DSE) [9] with respect to an estimate of the performance in a software level, rather than running the CNN each time for a different hardware configuration.

Even with a more advanced option of performance estimation, high irregularity within a complex accelerator results in case-by-case estimation. Therefore, this approach is unfeasible in general case, as it is usually constrained to a single hardware configuration. In our work, we are focused on estimating one particular aspect of performance - latency for a CNN reconfigurable accelerator.

The standard 2D convolution layers, from which the CNN is constructed, occupy over 90% of the overall processing time [17] and their latency T_i on the

---

[1] A tutorial code is available at https://git.io/Jv31c.

accelerator needs to be estimated to determine the best hardware configuration through DSE. For 2D convolution, there are several categories of parallelism including filter parallelism (PF) or channel parallelism (PC) in addition to spatial and kernel parallelisms. These are the parameters that usually need to be determined during the DSE.

A performance estimation framework for reconfigurable dataflow platforms was proposed by Yasudo et al. [19] that can analytically determine the number of accelerators suitable for the application. Dai et al. [2] proposed an estimation method based on a GTB and a high-level synthesis report and they compared it with LR and ANN. However, their method requires a significant amount of data and features from the synthesis report, which might not be available, especially when high-level synthesis is not being used to describe the accelerator. Enzler et al. proposed a general heuristic-based method [3] for estimating the performance of accelerator designs, which can be modified for CNN accelerators and is now used as the standard method.

Table 1. Notation used for performance estimation in an FPGA-based accelerator for convolutional neural networks.

Parameter	Description
H	Height of input feature map
W	Width of input feature map
H_O	Height of output feature map
W_O	Width of output feature map
K	Kernel size
F	Number of filters
C	Number of channels
PF	Parallelism in filter dimension
PC	Parallelism in channel dimension
M_{CLK} [MHz]	Memory access clock cycle time
L_{CLK} [MHz]	Logic clock cycle time
M_{EFF} [%]	Memory transfer efficiency
S [bits]	Memory transfer size
DW [bits]	Processing data width
M	Number of input features
N	Number of layers in a CNN
P	Number of training samples

The simplest form of a heuristic for estimating latency on a hardware accelerator consists of dividing the overall processing time for a single input T into time steps T_i which correspond to the time to perform one 2D convolution in a

Table 2. Number of operations and a data size for a 2D convolution i.

Sizes	Number of operations/Data size
Number of compute operations	$F_i \times C_i \times H_i \times W_i \times K_i \times K_i$
Input size	$H_i \times W_i \times C_i$
Weights size	$F_i \times C_i \times K_i \times K_i$
Output size	$H_{O_i} \times W_{O_i} \times F_i$

feed-forward CNN consisting of N 2D convolutions. The total estimated latency for the CNN in that given configuration is then simply added as $T = \sum_{i=1}^{N} T_i$.

The time T_i is being split into three different terms: (1) On-chip memory loading time T_{load_i}, (2) Computation time $T_{compute_i}$ and (3) Off-chip memory storing time T_{store_i}. Assuming the design is pipelined, the runtime T_i is then decided by the slowest path which is chosen by the maximum among T_{load_i}, $T_{compute_i}$ and T_{store_i}. Each of these terms depends on a mixture of parameters that are specified by the 2D convolution: *Input size, Output size, Number of compute operations*, device specific settings: *Memory bandwidth, Clock cycle time* or the hardware architecture: *Parallelism*, which are known prior to making a prediction. The estimated latency per layer is then computed as shown in Eq. 1 below

$$T_{load_i} = \frac{\text{Input size}}{\text{Memory bandwidth}} \quad T_{compute_i} = \frac{\text{Number of compute operations}}{\text{Clock cycle time} \times \text{Parallelism}}$$

$$T_{store_i} = \frac{\text{Output size}}{\text{Memory bandwidth}} \quad T_i = max\left(T_{load_i}, T_{compute_i}, T_{store_i}\right) \qquad (1)$$

The heuristic approach does not depend on any statistical data to perform the estimation and it is simple to implement since it relies only on the features that can be easily read from the respective datasheets. Nevertheless, this general estimation method usually computes the most optimistic estimate and it does not leave room for delays caused by communication, synchronisation or control. One way to refine the estimation is that we can collect runtime data and use this data to improve the estimate. Therefore, in our work, we are proposing to use the standard analytic method as a mean function inside a GP together with the profiling data collected by running the CNN on real hardware to train the GP to model the observed misestimation.

3 Gaussian Process with an Analytic Mean Function

GP is a modelling function built around Bayesian modelling which can embody our prior knowledge/model into our target [15]. A GP is specified by a mean function $m(.)$ and a covariance function (kernel) $k(.,.)$. The mean function represents the supposed average of the estimated data. The kernel computes correlations between inputs and it encapsulates the structure of the hypothesised function.

The main benefit of using a GP over other methods such as LR, GTB or ANN is that it can use the developed analytic foundations, such as the standard analytic performance estimation, as prior knowledge in a form of $m(.)$.

The predictive distribution of the GP, $p(\mathbf{y_T}|\mathbf{X}, \mathbf{y}, \mathbf{X_T})$ for the targets $\mathbf{y_T}$ given the corresponding features $\mathbf{X_T}$ and the training data $\mathbf{X}, \mathbf{y}$ is defined as a multivariate Gaussian distribution $\mathcal{N}$ with a predictive mean $\mathbb{E}[\mathbf{y_T}|\mathbf{X}, \mathbf{y}, \mathbf{X_T}]$ and a predictive variance $\mathbb{V}[\mathbf{y_T}|\mathbf{X}, \mathbf{y}, \mathbf{X_T}]$.

The $\mathbf{X} \in \mathcal{R}^{P \times M}$ and $\mathbf{X_T} \in \mathcal{R}^{N \times M}$ are the sets of M features for P samples for training and N samples for testing. The $\mathbf{y} \in \mathcal{R}^P$ and $\mathbf{y_T} \in \mathcal{R}^N$ are the target objectives corresponding to the number of samples per dataset respectively. The $\mathbb{E}[\mathbf{y_T}|\mathbf{X}, \mathbf{y}, \mathbf{X_T}]$ is defined in Eq. 2 below as

$$\underline{m(\mathbf{X_T}) \frown T_i(\mathbf{X_T})} + k(\mathbf{X_T}, \mathbf{X})(k(\mathbf{X}, \mathbf{X}) + \sigma^2 \mathbf{I})^{-1}(\mathbf{y} - \underline{m(\mathbf{X}) \frown T_i(\mathbf{X})}) \qquad (2)$$

and $\mathbb{V}[\mathbf{y_T}|\mathbf{X}, \mathbf{y}, \mathbf{X_T}]$ is defined in Eq. 3 below as

$$k(\mathbf{X_T}, \mathbf{X_T}) - k(\mathbf{X_T}, \mathbf{X})(k(\mathbf{X}, \mathbf{X}) + \sigma^2 \mathbf{I})^{-1}k(\mathbf{X_T}, \mathbf{X})^T \qquad (3)$$

where the σ^2 represents the noise amplitude and $\mathbf{I}$ is the identity matrix[2]. In the formulas above, GP possesses a set of hyperparameters associated with both the mean function and the choice of the kernel. The hyperparameter values can be found by maximising the marginal likelihood. The optimal hyperparameters are then chosen by observing the likelihood or by cross-validation.

The GP is usually used with an agnostic mean function centred at zero. However, we propose to use the previously developed latency model T_i, for each 2D convolutional layer i in a CNN, as a mean function $m(.)$ inside the predictive mean to encapsulate the known analytic model of the accelerator into the proposed method. It uses the collected data $\mathbf{X}$, which in this case are the parameters, and the hardware configuration of the accelerator for each convolution, which would normally be used in the standard analytic estimation. By also recording our past measurements from our past implementations $\mathbf{y}$, we can form a training set on which we can learn the nonlinearities that cannot be analytically modelled. The $\mathbf{X_T}$ represents the set of test features corresponding to the 2D convolutions for which we would like to estimate their target performance $\mathbf{y_T}$, in this case, latency.

Therefore, the advantage of this method in comparison to other machine learning (ML) inspired methods is that it avoids completely relying on the data while estimating the performance. Additionally, this method does not need to extract any features from the data because the features for the estimation are already known and they are the ones used in the standard analytic estimation. Hence, this method reuses previously developed knowledge by incorporating the standard method into the model as the mean function of the GP to anchor the estimate within reliable bounds. By anchoring the estimate, the model is also more interpretable in comparison to purely data-reliant methods which depend completely on the learnt features which are usually not human-readable. Additionally, by specifying the mean function and combining it with the collected

---

[2] For a detailed derivation please refer to [15].

data, the proposed method can give a prediction outside the observed data sample without collapsing.

In the next Section, we present the FPGA-based accelerator from which we have collected the data and onto which we have evaluated our proposed method.

4   Accelerator and Dataset

4.1   Accelerator's Architecture

The per-layer latency of an implemented FPGA-based CNN accelerator is characterised according to the standard method into three parts: (1) Loading time for loading the input, (2) Computation time, (3) Storing time for storing the results.

The input has to be loaded into the on-chip memory only once for the first layer, similarly to the output being stored only once from the on-chip memory to the off-chip memory. The output of intermediate layers is buffered in the on-chip memory.

The notation is shown in Table 1 and the size of the weights and input/output for convolution is shown in Table 2. Following the standard method, the per-layer latency T_i for a single input is shown in Eqs. 4, 5 and 6 as follows

1. Loading time i.e., the time to load the input into the on-chip memory

$$
\begin{aligned}
T_{weights_i} &= \frac{K_i \times K_i \times F_i \times C_i \times DW}{PF \times M_{CLK} \times S \times M_{EFF}} \\
T_{data_i} &= \frac{H_i \times W_i \times C_i \times DW}{PF \times M_{CLK} \times S \times M_{EFF}} \\
T_{load_i} &= T_{weights_i} + T_{data_i}
\end{aligned}
\tag{4}
$$

2. Computation time i.e., the time to compute $PC \times PF$ parallel channels and filters respectively

$$
T_{compute_i} = \frac{F_i \times C_i \times H_i \times W_i \times K_i \times K_i}{PF \times PC \times L_{CLK}}
\tag{5}
$$

3. Storing time i.e., the time to store the output back to the off-chip memory

$$
T_{store_i} = \frac{H_{O_i} \times W_{O_i} \times F_i \times DW}{PF \times M_{CLK} \times S \times M_{EFF}}
\tag{6}
$$

Therefore, the time required to process a single 2D convolutional layer can be written as in Eq. 7 below as

$$
T_i = \begin{cases}
T_{i=1} & = T_{load_i} + T_{compute_i} \\
T_{i \neq 1 \vee N} & = max(T_{weights_i}, T_{compute_i}) \\
T_{i=N} & = max(T_{weights_i}, T_{compute_i}) + T_{store_i}
\end{cases}
\tag{7}
$$

4.2   Dataset

The evaluation dataset comprises of several different configurations of 2D convolutional layers which are the building blocks of three different CNNs, namely SSD [12] with 24 2D convolutions, Yolo [16] with 75 2D convolutions and ResNet-50 [8] with 57 2D convolutions. SSD and Yolo are characteristic for their irregularities, which results in the output being produced at different times, while the ResNet is known for its residual blocks. Each network was trained in 32-bit floating-point representation and then linearly quantised into 8-bit integer representation [4]. In total giving P training samples $\mathbf{X}$ as 156 and the input feature size M being 15 corresponding to the first 15 parameters in the Table 1. The recorded latency per each convolution represents the targets $\mathbf{y}$.

Each network was executed on the implemented accelerator on Intel Arria GX 1150 FPGA. The analysis of the dataset together with the evaluation parameters can be found in Tables 3 and 4.

Table 3. Dataset for evaluation.

Parameter	Min	Mean	Max
H/W	1	42	418
H_O/W_O	1	37	416
K	1	2	7
C	3	360	2048
F	64	371	2048
Latency [ms]	0.018	0.841	11.727

Table 4. Evaluation parameters.

Parameter	Value
PC	64
PF	64
M_{CLK}	200 MHz
L_{CLK}	200 MHz
M_{EFF}	70%
S	64-bit
DW	8-bit

5   Evaluation

In evaluation, the proposed method is compared with the standard method, including a GP with a zero mean function, a GP with the ANN mean function [6], LR, GTB and ANN. The dataset described in Sect. 4.2 is being used to evaluate all these methods.

For a more comprehensive evaluation, leave-one-out cross-validation (LOO-CV) with respect to the mean absolute error (MAE) is used to compare the estimators. LOOCV is a particular case of leave-k-out cross-validation where $k = 1$, which means that a model is trained on all samples except one, onto which the performance is then evaluated. In this instance, the performance of the predictor is measured by the absolute error between the prediction and the target value. The error is accumulated for all samples from which the mean is then calculated by dividing the total summed error by the number of samples.

This approach was also used to determine the best hyperparameters for each regressor with respect to the LOOCV MAE. The results, as well as the individual properties and implementation details for the estimators, are summarised in Table 5. We considered several hyperparameters for the proposed GP-based

Table 5. Evaluation of latency estimation for different methods.

Methods	LOOCV MAE [ms]	Implementation and optimiser	Properties
Standard method	0.450	None	None
Gaussian process	0.521	GPFlow [13] - Adam [10]	*Mean function:* Zero *Learning rate:* 0.001 *Best kernel:* Matérn 3/2
Our method	**0.312**	GPFlow [13] - Adam [10]	*Mean function:* T_i *Learning rate:* 0.001 *Best kernel:* Matérn 3/2
Gaussian process with Artificial neural network mean function	0.692	GPFlow [13] - Adam [10]	*Mean function:* Artificial neural network 15, 64, 1 nodes and tanh activations *Learning rate:* 0.00001 *Best kernel:* Matérn 3/2
Linear regression	0.450	sklearn [14]	Default
Gradiet tree boosting	0.607	sklearn [14] - AdaBoost [7]	*Learning rate:* 0.1 *Number of trees:* 10 *Maximum depth:* 3
Artificial neural network	1.257	Tensorflow [1] - Adam [10]	*Batch size:* 8 *Learning rate:* 0.1 *Regulariser:* L2, 0.001 *Number of nodes:* 10, 10, 1 *Activations:* ReLU

method such as the learning rate, ranging from 0.1 to 0.000001 on a logarithmic scale and the kernel, ranging from linear, Gaussian to Matérn kernels [15] and their combinations. The best parameters were found by a grid search with respect to the LOOCV MAE.

In case of the GP with the ANN mean function, it was necessary to find hyperparameters for the ANN such as the number of nodes in the hidden layers, between 16, 32 and 64 and the number of hidden layers, ranging from 1 to 3. For the activation function, we considered tanh, ReLU and sigmoid. For GTB and ANN, we needed to determine the most influential parameters such as the learning rate, ranging from 0.01 to 0.0001 on a logarithmic scale or for the GTB, the number of trees or the tree depth that was determined by gradual pruning. For the ANN we needed to decide the number of hidden nodes, between [10, 1], [10, 10, 1] and [10, 10, 10, 1] and for the activation function, we again considered tanh, ReLU and sigmoid. The hyperparameters were similarly found through a grid search with respect to the LOOCV MAE. For the standard method and LR, it was not necessary to determine any hyperparameters.

Overall, the best method proved to be the combination of the standard method and the collected data in the form of the GP with an analytic mean function. In comparison to other approaches, the proposed method achieved approximately a 30.7% improvement in LOOCV with respect to MAE decreasing to 0.312 ms in comparison to the second best-performing methods, which were LR and the standard method with 0.450 ms MAE.

The main advantage of the method lays in its implementation simplicity, as it reuses the analytic approximation that is commonly used for DSE, combined with recorded measurements. The method can be improved by recording more measurements and simple fine-tuning of the hyperparameters related to the kernel k or the analytic mean m.

A potential limitation of this method stems from the kernel computation which scales with the complexity of $O(P^3)$, which means that the inference time can be prolonged if there are many training samples. One possible solution to overcome this problem is using k-Means clustering to determine the k most important points that have to be included in the kernel. Nevertheless, the inference time is much less than the time needed for synthesis and then running the design on hardware.

6   Conclusion and Future Work

In this paper, we proposed an accurate method for estimating the performance of an field-programmable gate array-based accelerator for convolutional neural networks and compared it with the standard method and variations of the Gaussian process, linear regression, gradient tree boosting and an artificial neural network. The evaluation demonstrated that the innovative Gaussian process paired with the domain-specific knowledge and collected data can provide an approximately 30.7% accuracy improvement with respect to the standard method or the linear regression.

In the proposed method, users need to decide what are the relevant software/hardware features M together with an analytic approximation for the modelled performance that will be used as the mean function $m(.)$ in the Gaussian process. Afterwards, they need to supply the profiling data for training $\mathbf{X}, \mathbf{y}$, $\mathbf{X}$ is the feature matrix and $\mathbf{y}$ are the targets, in this case, the per-layer latency. In the end, the user needs to decide what is going to be the best kernel $k(.,.)$ and use it to train the Gaussian process to obtain the best values for the hyperparameters (see footnote 1).

In the future, we will validate the method on more configurations on different hardware boards. Furthermore, we will formulate similar analytic approximations for other potential objectives, for example, the resource usage or power consumption and use them as priors for estimating these objectives through our proposed Gaussian process-based method.

Acknowledgments. We thank Yann Herklotz, Alexander Montgomerie-Corcoran and ARC'20 reviewers for insightful suggestions.

References

1. Abadi, M., et al.: TensorFlow: large-scale machine learning on heterogeneous systems (2015). https://www.tensorflow.org/
2. Dai, S., Zhou, Y., Zhang, H., Ustun, E., Young, E.F., Zhang, Z.: Fast and accurate estimation of quality of results in high-level synthesis with machine learning. In: Proceedings of the 2018 IEEE 26th Annual International Symposium on Field-Programmable Custom Computing Machines (FCCM), pp. 129–132. IEEE, Boulder (2018)
3. Enzler, R., Jeger, T., Cottet, D., Tröster, G.: High-level area and performance estimation of hardware building blocks on FPGAs. In: Hartenstein, R.W., Grünbacher, H. (eds.) FPL 2000. LNCS, vol. 1896, pp. 525–534. Springer, Heidelberg (2000). https://doi.org/10.1007/3-540-44614-1_57
4. Fan, H., et al.: A real-time object detection accelerator with compressed SSDLite on FPGA. In: Proceedings of the 2018 International Conference on Field-Programmable Technology (FPT), pp. 14–21. IEEE, Sakura (2018)
5. Fan, H., et al.: F-E3D: FPGA-based acceleration of an efficient 3D convolutional neural network for human action recognition. In: Proceedings of the 2019 IEEE 30th International Conference on Application-Specific Systems, Architectures and Processors (ASAP), vol. 2160, pp. 1–8. IEEE, New York (2019)
6. Fortuin, V., Rätsch, G.: Deep mean functions for meta-learning in Gaussian processes. arXiv preprint arXiv:1901.08098 (2019)
7. Friedman, J.H.: Stochastic gradient boosting. Comput. Stat. Data Anal. **38**, 367–378 (2002)
8. He, K., Zhang, X., Ren, S., Sun, J.: Deep residual learning for image recognition. In: Proceedings of the 2016 IEEE Conference on Computer Vision and Pattern Recognition (CVPR), vol. 2016, pp. 770–778. IEEE, Las Vegas (2016)
9. Holland, B., George, A.D., Lam, H., Smith, M.C.: An analytical model for multi-level performance prediction of multi-FPGA systems. ACM Trans. Reconfig. Technol. Syst. (TRETS) **4**(3), 27 (2011)

10. Kingma, D.P., Ba, J.: Adam: a method for stochastic optimization. arXiv preprint arXiv:1412.6980 (2014)
11. Lian, X., Liu, Z., Song, Z., Dai, J., Zhou, W., Ji, X.: High-performance FPGA-based CNN accelerator with block-floating-point arithmetic. IEEE Trans. Very Large Scale Integr. VLSI Syst. **27**, 1874–1885 (2019)
12. Liu, W., et al.: SSD: single shot MultiBox detector. In: Leibe, B., Matas, J., Sebe, N., Welling, M. (eds.) ECCV 2016. LNCS, vol. 9905, pp. 21–37. Springer, Cham (2016). https://doi.org/10.1007/978-3-319-46448-0_2
13. Matthews, D.G., et al.: GPflow: a Gaussian process library using TensorFlow. J. Mach. Learn. Res. **18**, 1299–1304 (2017)
14. Pedregosa, F., et al.: Scikit-learn: machine learning in Python. J. Mach. Learn. Res. **12**, 2825–2830 (2011)
15. Rasmussen, C.E.: Gaussian Processes in Machine Learning. The MIT Press, Cambridge (2005)
16. Redmon, J., Divvala, S., Girshick, R., Farhadi, A.: You only look once: unified, real-time object detection. In: Proceedings of the 2016 IEEE Conference on Computer Vision and Pattern Recognition (CVPR), vol. 3, pp. 779–788. IEEE, Las Vegas (2016)
17. Venieris, S., Kouris, A., Bouganis, C.S.: Toolflows for mapping convolutional neural networks on FPGAs: a survey and future directions. ACM Comput. Surv. (CSUR) **51**, 1–39 (2018)
18. Williams, C.K., Rasmussen, C.E.: Gaussian processes for regression. In: Advances in Neural Information Processing Systems, pp. 514–520 (1996)
19. Yasudo, R., Coutinho, J., Varbanescu, A., Luk, W., Amano, H., Becker, T.: Performance estimation for exascale reconfigurable dataflow platforms. In: Proceedings of the 2018 International Conference on Field-Programmable Technology (FPT), pp. 314–317. IEEE, Sakura (2018)

Judiciously Spreading Approximation Among Arithmetic Components with Top-Down Inexact Hardware Design

Giovanni Ansaloni$^{(\boxtimes)}$, Ilaria Scarabottolo, and Laura Pozzi

Università della Svizzera Italiana, Lugano, Switzerland
{giovanni.ansaloni,ilaria.scarabottolo,laura.pozzi}@usi.ch

Abstract. Approximate logic synthesis is emerging as a promising avenue towards the development of efficient and high performance digital designs. Indeed, effective methodologies for the inexact simplification of arithmetic circuits have been introduced in recent years. Nonetheless, strategies enabling the integration of multiple approximate components to realise complex approximate hardware modules, able to maximise gains while controlling ensuing Quality-of-Service degradations, are still in their infancy. Against this backdrop, we herein describe a methodology to automatically distribute the error leeway assigned to a hardware design among its constituent operators. Our strategy is able to identify high-quality trade-offs among resource requirements, performance and exactness in digital implementations, across applications belonging to different domains, and without restrictions on the type and bit-width of their approximable arithmetic components.

Keywords: Inexact computing · Approximate logic synthesis · Electronic design automation

1 Introduction

Established methodologies for hardware development explore trade-offs between performance (latency, throughput) and cost (area, energy) of a target design. Approximate Logic Synthesis challenges this paradigm by also considering a further dimension: that of the desired degree of *exactness*. ALS frameworks simplify those parts of a design that have a small impact on the performed computation, deriving inexact, but more efficient, implementations. ALS can be effectively applied in domains ranging from signal processing to machine learning [9], where careful approximation-induced perturbations lead to graceful Quality-of-Service (QoS) degradations.

This work has been partially supported ML-edge (grant no. 200020_182009 - 156397) project funded by the Swiss NSF and the MyPreHealth (grant no. 16073) project funded by Hasler Stiftung.

F. Rincón et al. (Eds.): ARC 2020, LNCS 12083, pp. 14–29, 2020.
https://doi.org/10.1007/978-3-030-44534-8_2

ALS has been the focus of an increasing number of research efforts in recent years [14,15,18]. Nonetheless, most works in this field target the simplification of single arithmetic circuits. To fully realise the potential of ALS, it is instead critical to establish strategies that integrate multiple, individually-tailored, inexact elements to realise complex (inexact) hardware modules. Against this backdrop, we here introduce a methodology, named TDApprox, that automatically distributes the error tolerable at the output of a hardware design among its constituent operators, hence driving their inexact synthesis.

Other recent works addressing this challenge assume, as a required input to their frameworks, the availability of a library of approximated components, which are then selected and integrated [1,2,6,10,16]. As illustrated on the left side of Fig. 1, such bottom-up stance (in which the characterisation of operators is performed a-priori, independently from the design implementation) poses a limit on flexibility, because (a) for a given operator, library instances could expose approximation levels which are not compatible with the ones required by a target design, or (b) the accelerator to be simplified may require input/output bitwidths not available in characterised components. Finally (c), and most importantly, an operator could even be entirely missing from the employed library.

To avoid these pitfalls, TDApprox instead embodies a top-down strategy (hence its name). As described on the right side Fig. 1, in our approach the ALS of operators is only performed *after* assessing their approximability, i.e.: the impact of operators-level approximations on the overall design Quality-of-service

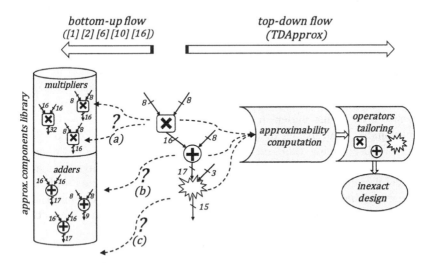

Fig. 1. Comparison between a bottom-down approach (left), selecting approximated components from a library, and the top-down stance embodied by TDApprox (right), in which the evaluation of the approximability of arithmetic operators is precursory to their synthesis.

(QoS). TDApprox is therefore not limited to a pre-determined set of operators and I/O bitwidth, and can consider arbitrary degrees of approximation.

TDApprox interfaces to state-of-the-art methods for the ALS of single arithmetic circuits, automatically deriving synthesisable hardware netlists of complex inexact accelerators, from C code and an error bound on the design output.

In summary, our contribution is three-fold:

– We introduce a top-down methodology for distributing a user-defined approximation leeway among the arithmetic operators comprising a hardware design.
– We detail how TDApprox is integrated in an ALS framework for the synthesis of inexact designs, starting from a high-level (C) description of their functionality.
– We showcase the effectiveness of TDApprox on applications from diverse error-resilient fields, considering both combinatorial and sequential implementations.

The paper proceeds as follows: Sect. 2 further places our contribution in the context of related works. Section 3 details the TDApprox methodology, while Sect. 4 assesses its performance. Section 5 concludes the paper.

2   State of the Art

Various automated strategies for the inexact synthesis of generic arithmetic circuits have been proposed in literature. Notably, Venkataramani et al. proposed in [19] to approximate logic cones based on don't care analysis, while in [18] introduced an algorithm to identify and merge sub-circuits performing similar functions. Schlachter et al. [15] instead adopt a significance and an activity metric to guide logic simplification, Ranjan et al. [13] is based on model checking, and Nepal et al. [12] enumerate inexact transformations modelled as abstract syntax trees. Finally, Scarabottolo et al. [14] base their approach on a branch-and-bound algorithm, identifying the largest sub-circuit that can be simplified from a gate-level netlist under an error constraint.

Occasionally, the authors of these works provide examples of how inexact operators realised using their methodologies can be integrated: [15] and [13] study the performance of a DCT accelerator implemented using their approximated components, while [12] consider a perceptron classifier and a block matcher. Nonetheless, in all those cases the accelerators implementations are had-hoc, and no strategy is suggested to systematically compose inexact building blocks.

The few works that aim at addressing the ensuing integration problem do so, as opposed to our methodology, from a bottom-up perspective: Du et al. [2] rely on a pre-characterised set of seven inexact multipliers to drive their heuristic, Li et al. [6] consider five inexact adders and multipliers, which are selected by either a knapsack algorithm or an ILP formulation. Sengupta et al. [16] and Chan et al. [1] analytically derive the errors and resource requirements of simplified adders and multipliers. Mrazek et al. [10] adopts a machine learning approach to compose the inexact operators included in the EvoApprox8b library [11], which provides three adders and eight multipliers at varying approximation levels.

3   Methodology

Input to TDApprox is a directed and acyclic Data Flow Graph (DFG) $G(N, E)$, representing the exact functionality to be approximated. Nodes n_i represents arithmetic operations and edges $e(n_i, n_j)$ data dependencies among them. Additionally, the edge set E_{in} accounts for the DFG inputs; e_{out} for its output[1]. Furthermore, input edges are annotated with the lower and upper bounds of their admissible values: $x_i = [l_i, u_i]$. As and example, $x_i = [0, 255]$ for an 8-bit unsigned value.

The DFG is traversed to analyse the effect, as seen by e_{out}, of perturbations induced by each node. As an illustrative example, consider the simple case in Fig. 2a, where the output of an approximate adder is connected to one input of an exact multiplier. If the adder output differs from that of an exact addition by δ_A, the error at the DFG output is, in the worst case, $\delta_A \times \max(|x_3|)$, hence magnifying the approximation degradation if $\max(|x_3|) > 1$. Note that $\max(|x_3|)$ can be either $-l_3$ or u_3 depending on the bounds on its admissible values.

As detailed by Misailovic et al. [8], if a node $n_i \in N$ performing a generic arithmetic operation f with input edges $e_{1,i}(n_{j1}, n_i)$ and $e_{2,i}(n_{j2}, n_i)$ has inexact predecessors, and it is itself inexact, the error at its output is bounded as follows:

$$|f_i(x1, x2) - \hat{f}_i(\hat{x1}, \hat{x2})| \leq k_{1,i}|err(e_{1,i})| + k_2|err(e_{2,i})| + |\delta_i| \qquad (1)$$

where $f(x1, x2)$ and $\hat{f}(\hat{x1}, \hat{x2})$ are the node output values in the exact and the inexact case (respectively), $err(e_1)$ and $err(e_2)$ represent the impact of approximating the predecessors of n_i, and δ_i is the approximation introduced by n_i itself. Moreover, the propagation coefficients k_1 and k_2 indicate how the inexactness at the input of the node are magnified or dampened by the performed function f, and are defined as:

$$k_1 = \max_{x1,x2} |\frac{\partial f(x1, x2)}{\partial x1}| \qquad k_2 = \max_{x1,x2} |\frac{\partial f(x1, x2)}{\partial x2}| \qquad (2)$$

The solution of Eq. 2 for common arithmetic operations is presented in Table 1.

We apply such formulation in a different context with respect to Misailovic et al. [8] [2] i.e., the approximate synthesis of hardware accelerators. In our scenario, the error caused by an approximate node n_i (with approximation bound δ_i) must be evaluated at the DFG output e_{out}. Therefore, we define the induced

---

[1] For simplicity, we focus on single-output DFGs. Multiple-outputs cases can nonetheless be addressed by considering each output in isolation, and then selecting the most stringent approximation constraint for each operation.

[2] The authors of [8] aim to bind approximable operations (with known approximability) to inexact functional units.

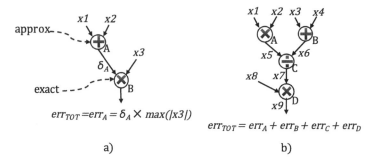

Fig. 2. Right: DFG with one approximated node. Left: DFG having all nodes implemented as approximate operators.

error bound of an operation as err_i, which is the product of the propagation coefficients along the path connecting n_i to e_{out}, if only one such path exist:

$$err_i = \delta_i \times \prod_{n_j \in succ(n_i)} k(n_j) \tag{3}$$

where $succ(n_i)$ are the successor nodes of n_i in G, considered recursively.

When instead several paths between n_i and e_{out} are present, err_i is bounded by the sum of the errors induced along the different paths:

$$err_i = \delta_i \times \sum_{p \in paths} (\prod_{n_j \in succ(n_i)} k(n_j)) \tag{4}$$

Finally, when *all* nodes in G are inexact to a degree, the deviation from an exact formulation is the super-position of the errors due to the approximation of each operation:

$$err_{TOT} = \sum_{n_i \in G} err_i = \sum_{n_i \in G} [\delta_i \times \sum_{p \in paths} (\prod_{n_j \in succ(n_i)} k(n_j))] \tag{5}$$

err_{TOT} is the bound to the overall quality degradation at the DFG level, set according to the application constraint. This leeway can then be distributed among the err_i coefficients.

Table 1. Propagation coefficients for common operations.

Operation	k_1	k_2
Addition/subtraction $(+/-)$	1	1
Multiplication $(\times)$	$\max(|x_2|)$	$\max(|x_1|)$
Division $(\div)$	$\max(1/|x_1|)$	$\max(|x_1/x_2^2|)$

If $err_1 = ... = err_N = err_{TOT}/card(N)$, the error induced by each approximate operation equally affects the output QoS degradation. While this may seem a sensible choice, operators may have different resource requirements e.g.: a high bit-width multiplier being much more area- and power-hungry than a small-bitwidth adder. Consequently, TDApprox assigns more error slack to the operators having a higher Energy-Area-Delay Product (EDAP) in their exact implementation:

$$err_i = err_{TOT} \times \frac{EDAP(i)}{\sum_{n \in N} EDAP(n)} \qquad (6)$$

Fixing the values of the err_i coefficients allows to solve the Eq. 4 for $\Delta = \{\delta_1, ..., \delta_N\}$, i.e., to compute the error bound for each operation in G. As shown below, such equations are not independent from each other, because the propagation factors k pertaining to a DFG node depend on the admissible intervals of its inputs (as defined in Table 1), themselves influenced by the perturbation introduced by the node predecessors.

Example. Consider the DFG in Fig. 2b, composed of 4 nodes (n_A, n_B, n_C, n_D), and whose inputs are bounded in the intervals $x1, x2, x3, x5, x4, x8$. The first input of each operation is depicted as the left edge, the second input as the right edge. For each node, Eq. 4 is as follows:

$$\begin{cases} err_A = \delta_A \times k_{1,C} \times k_{2,D} \\ err_B = \delta_B \times k_{2,C} \times k_{2,D} \\ err_C = \delta_C \times k_{2,D} \\ err_D = \delta_D \end{cases} \qquad (7)$$

Using the propagation rules in Table 1 for all k values:

$$\begin{cases} err_A = \delta_A \times \max\left(|1/x6|\right) \times \max|x8| \\ err_B = \delta_B \times \max\left(|x5/x6^2|\right) \times \max|x8| \\ err_C = \delta_C \times \max|x8| \\ err_D = \delta_D \end{cases} \qquad (8)$$

$$\text{out} = \sum_{i=1}^{3}(a[i] \times b[i])$$

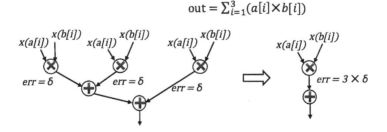

Fig. 3. Coalescing iterations in an accumulation loop.

The intermediate values x5 and x6 can be expressed as a function of DFG inputs and errors induced by the approximation of operators proceeding them, back-traversing the DFG:

$$x5 = (x1 \times x2) + \delta_A \qquad x6 = (x3 + x4) + \delta_B \qquad (9)$$

Substituting these expressions in Eq. 8 gives the final form of a system of equations, with err_i parameters and δ_i unknowns:

$$\begin{cases} err_A = \delta_A \times \max\left(|1/(x3 + x4 + \delta_B)|\right) \times \max|x8| \\ err_B = \delta_B \times \max\left(|(x1 * x2 + \delta_A)/(x3 + x4 + \delta_B)^2|\right) \times \max|x8| \\ err_C = \delta_C \times \max|x8| \\ err_D = \delta_D \end{cases} \qquad (10)$$

Solving the unknowns provides the approximation leeway for each DFG node.

Applicability. The TDApprox approach can be applied to all cases where a DFG, representing the computation in an approximate hardware datapath, can be obtained. Such representation is derived straightforwardly from a software description when no control statements are present, or when these are flattened (e.g.: fully unrolling every loop) [5,17]. An equivalent DFG can also be constructed when statically-defined (e.g.: for) loops are employed to update an accumulator register, as exemplified in Fig. 3. This case, common in approximable applications (as the one investigated in Sect. 4.3), is addressed by only considering the operations in a single iteration of the loop bodies, with the maximum input/output bitwidths required considering all iterations. Since the accumulator variables also accumulate the error due to the inexactness of their predecessors, the *err* value at their inputs must then be multiplied by the number of loop iterations.

4 Experimental Evaluation

4.1 Experimental Setup

We interfaced the error distribution algorithm described in Sect. 3 with a front-end deriving the DFG of the targeted applications, and a back-end performing the approximation of operators according to the identified leeways. A block scheme of such experimental environment is illustrated in Fig. 4.

The framework processes the source code description of an accelerator functionality, expressed in C and containing annotations that specify the maximum and minimum admissible value of the accelerator inputs. The corresponding DFG, as well as the DFG nodes types and their input/output bitwidths, are extracted employing dco-scorpio [17]. We leveraged this information to automatically generate a behavioural verilog descriptions of the DFG nodes, which are then synthesised to obtain (a) the operators EDAP required by the TDApprox algorithm and (b) the operators gate level netlists to be simplified.

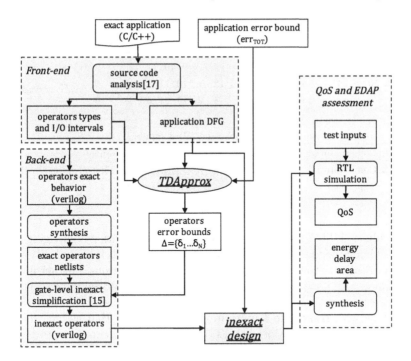

Fig. 4. Experimental framework. The front-end provides a DFG representation of the source code, while the back-end individually tailors the operators according to the Δ bounds retrieved by TDApprox, and perform the synthesis of the resulting inexact design.

Output of TDApprox are error bounds for each operation. They are employed in the framework back-end to individually tailor each corresponding netlist by removing their least critical gates. For this step, we re-implemented the Gate Level Pruning (GLP) strategy illustrated in [15], but any equivalent methodology (e.g., [14,18]) could be similarly used. Output of our GLP implementation are inexact hardware arithmetic operators, described (again, in verilog), as a series of statements expressing bit-wise operations.

Finally, these are integrated and synthesised to evaluate their area, critical path delay, and energy. Moreover, they are simulated to gauge their Quality-of-Service. We employed Synopsys Design Compiler (considering a 40 nm technology library) as a synthesis tool, and Menthor Graphics Moldesim for simulations. The generation of test benches is not automated at this time; nonetheless, since simplification does not affect the operators interface (but only their internal structure), the same test bench can be employed for both exact and inexact implementations, or to compare different inexact variants of the same design.

Table 2. Benchmarks characteristics.

B.mark	#ops	#mults	mult bit-width	#adds	adds bit-width	#divs	divs bit-width
Sobel	45	0	-	26	9, 10, 11, 12	9	8
mult-FIR	50	24	9, 10, 13, 14, 16	12	10, 11, 13, 15, 16	0	—
SVM	9	3	16, 27, 30	4	14, 21, 37, 38	0	—

B.mark	Implementation	Timing constraint	Test inputs
Sobel	Combinatorial	2 nS	100×100 RGB image
mult-FIR	Combinatorial	1 nS	2×256 points signals: $\sin(at)$, $\sin(bt^2)$
SVM	Sequential	2 nS	ECG features

We evaluated TDApprox on three benchmark applications belonging to the domains of image/signal processing and classification, fields that typically exhibit a degree of resilience towards judicious exactness degradations. Further illustrating our framework flexibility, we considered both combinatorial implementations and sequential ones. Similarly to [11,16], we assessed the performance of our methodology with respect to a uniform baseline strategy that assigns the same error (δ_i) to all operators. More details describing the benchmarks are provided in Table 2; for brevity, only the output widths of operators are reported, even if in all cases input widths also vary widely, and are not symmetric. This characteristic, along with the presence of operations other than multiplications and additions, makes these applications ill-suited for bottom-up methods relying on pre-characterised inexact components. As an example, [11] also considers a Sobel accelerator, but the implementation described therein misses the RGB averaging step, because the required operator (divide-by-3) is not available in their employed library [10].

4.2   Combinatorial Designs

The Sobel benchmark averages the red, green and blue components of 3×3 neighbourhoods of pixels in an input image, and convolves them with a kernel matrix to obtain a blurred greyscale output:

$$out = (R_{3\times3} + G_{3\times3} + B_{3\times3})/3 * (\frac{1}{16} \begin{bmatrix} 1 & 2 & 1 \\ 2 & 4 & 2 \\ 1 & 2 & 1 \end{bmatrix}) \tag{11}$$

The mult-FIR benchmark instead operates on sliding windows of 12 elements, multiplying element-wise the samples of two input signals, which are then fed to a 12-taps low-pass FIR filter:

$$out = ((sig1_{12\times1} \odot sig2_{12\times1})/128)$$
$$\cdot (\frac{1}{256}[-2, -2, 3, 18, 42, 61, 61, 42, 18, 3, -2, -2]) \tag{12}$$

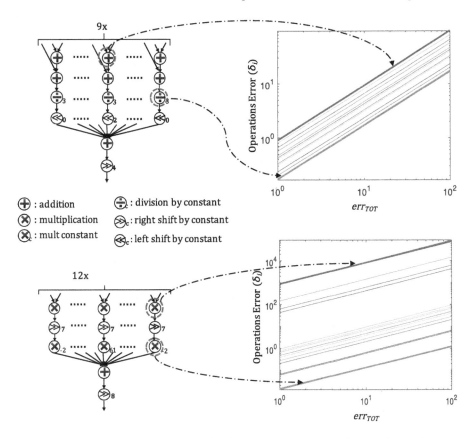

Fig. 5. Left: Schemes of the `Sobel` (top) and the `mult-FIR` (bottom) benchmarks. Right: Respective operations errors δ_i computed by TDApprox, varying the output error bound err_{TOT}.

In both cases, inputs are represented as 8-bit values. The structure of the resulting datapaths are depicted on the left side of Fig. 5. Moreover, the right side of the figure reports the inexactness bounds $\Delta = \{\delta_1, ..., \delta_N\}$ assigned by TDApprox to each arithmetic operator for varying datapaths error bounds err_{TOT}, obtained by solving Eqs. 4 and 6 for the two DFGs.

In the case of the `Sobel` benchmark (top), one order of magnitude separates the δ of the least and the most critical operations i.e., the ones assigned the highest and lowest leeway for approximation (highlighted in the figure). As expected, the operations averaging RGB components at the corners of the input neighbourhood, which are multiplied by 1 using the kernel matrix, are assigned a higher δ with respect to the ones averaging the central pixel, which is multiplied by 4, hence magnifying any perturbation.

A similar observation can be made for the `mult-FIR` case (bottom of Fig. 5): TDApprox assigns a higher δ to the multipliers operating on the extremes of the sliding window, which correspond to smaller FIR coefficients. Moreover, when

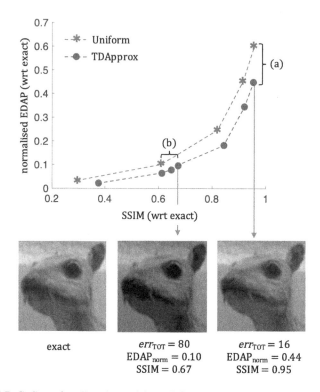

Fig. 6. EDAP-QoS trade-offs achieved by TDApprox and uniform error distributions when approximating the `Sobel` datapath.

examining the adder chain accumulating the final output, a smaller δ is assigned to the first stages (which require a smaller bit-width, hence fewer resources) with respect to the latter ones. In the case of `mult-FIR`, the most approximable operation is assigned 900X more slack than the least approximable one.

Such non-uniform error distribution results in high-quality resource-QoS trade-offs at the application level, showcased in Fig. 6 for the `Sobel` benchmark. Exact and approximated outputs (for two approximation levels) are depicted at the bottom of the figure, highlighting that a normalised Energy-Delay-Area Product of 0.1 (a 10X reduction) can be achieved with little impact on the perceived output quality. In its upper part, the figure reports the Pareto curve of the best performing inexact implementations retrieved using TDApprox, plotting their EDAP on the x axis and their QoS on the y axis. The latter is expressed as achieved Structural Similarity Index (SSIM) with respect to the exact output. The characteristics of the best performing implementations employing the same error bound in all operators are also presented. Compared with this baseline strategy, TDApprox achieves (a) 34% higher reduction in EDAP for an SSIM of 0.95, and (b) 10% higher SSIM for a normalised EDAP of 0.1.

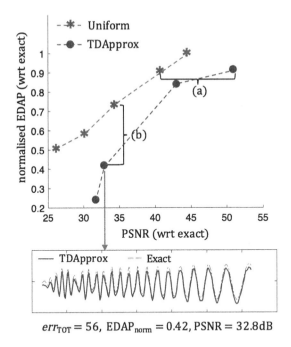

Fig. 7. EDAP-QoS trade-offs achieved by TDApprox and uniform error distributions when approximating the `mult-FIR` datapath.

The effectiveness of TDApprox is even more apparent for the `mult-FIR` benchmark (Fig. 7), because it presents higher variations in the approximability of operators. In this case, we considered the Peak Signal-to-Noise Ratio (PSNR) between exact and inexact outputs as a QoS metric. Indeed, when compared to a uniform distribution of error leeways among DFG operations, the bounds computed by TDApprox result in implementations having (a) a 41% increase in PSNR for the same EDAP, or alternatively (b) an increase in EDAP savings of 44% for a PSNR difference of only 3%.

4.3 Sequential Design

As an example of a sequential design, we targeted the inference calculation of a quadratic SVM machine. The SVM determines which features set, extracted from 2-min electrocardiogram (ECG) windows, were acquired during epileptic episodes. Features were derived according to the methodology described in [4]. The clinical data processed in this set of experiments, provided by CHUV university hospital (Lausanne, Switzerland), is divided in 24 folds, containing 10 seizure and 10 non-seizure windows. Cross-fold validation was performed, employing in each round one fold for test and the rest of the database for training, then averaging the results.

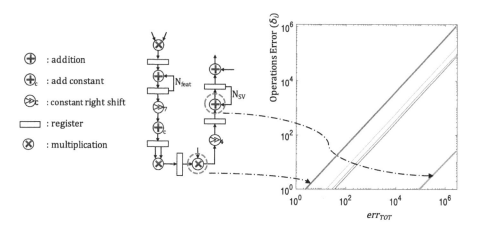

Fig. 8. Left: Block scheme of the SVM datapath. Right: Operations errors δ_i computed by TDApprox, varying the output error bound err_{TOT}.

The inference formula for quadratic SVMs is as follows:

$$Y = \sum_{i \in SVs} \left(\alpha_i y_i \left(\mathbf{x}_T \cdot \mathbf{x}_i + 1 \right)^2 \right) + b \tag{13}$$

where the sign of Y discriminates among classes.

As an exact baseline, we consider an aggressively tailored design employing reduced bitwidths in all datapath stages, with the aim to explore the *further* savings attainable by TDApprox, beyond the ones deriving from the truncation of Least Significant Bits (LSBs). In the baseline implementation, inputs are quantised to 8 bits, while 7 LSBs are dropped after the dot-product stage and 4 LSBs before the summation stage. As reported by the authors of [7] such setting, with respect to a floating-point equivalent, resulted in a negligible ($< 1\%$) impact on QoS, defined for the SVM benchmark as the geometric mean of the achieved Sensitivity (Se) and Specificity (Sp) [3]: $GM = (Se \times Sp)^{1/2}$.

The datapath, whose block scheme is provided in Fig. 8, presents a first feedback loop to accumulate the dot-product between the test feature vector $\mathbf{x}_T$ and a support vector $\mathbf{x}_i$, and a second one to accumulate the terms of the summation in Eq. 13. The figure also plots the Δ thresholds of its operations inexactness in dependence of the error bound at the datapath output Y. Again, orders of magnitude separate the most and the least approximable operation.

In our implementation, 15% of the hardware real estate is devoted to the control logic, which is not amenable to approximation. Even when this overhead is accounted for, approximate logic synthesis driven by TDApprox leads to tangible gains. As shown if Fig. 9, a 21% reduction in EDAP is attainable for a negligible GM degradation of 0.5% (a). The quality of the obtained approximated implementations dwarves the one attainable with a homogeneous distribution of errors: by smartly assigning error bounds, TDApprox achieves both a better

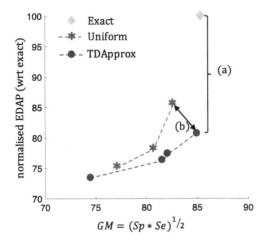

Fig. 9. EDAP and QoS of TDApprox-driven implementations with respect to an exact one, and alternatives assigning the same error to all operators.

Table 3. Performance of inexact implementations, using TDApprox vs. a uniform distribution of error bounds.

TDApprox	err_{TOT}	$EDAP_{norm}$	Sp	Se	GM
	1000	81.02	81.99	88.04	84.96
	2000	83.78	80.43	85.87	83.11
	5000	76.42	73.91	89.86	81.50
	10000	73.51	60.25	92.03	74.46
Uniform	δ_i	$EDAP_{norm}$	Sp	Se	GM
	100	85.6	83.23	81.88	82.55
	200	78.24	82.30	78.99	80.62
	300	75.13	74.53	79.71	77.08

classification performance ($+2.5\%$ GM between the points marked as (b) in the figure) and lower resource requirements (-6% EDAP). Table 3 further details the experimental outcomes, reporting the achieved performance for varying err_{TOT} bounds (in the case of TDApprox) and for different assignment of δ_i inexactness level (for the baseline uniform methodology).

5   Conclusion

We presented TDApprox, a top-down methodology for the design of complex inexact hardware modules. By distributing approximation leeways to arithmetic operators based solely on a description of the intended functionality and on a threshold to the overall exactness, TDApprox can effectively drive their automated synthesis. Hence, our methodology is not bound by a pre-determined library of approximable operators nor an a-priori choice of approximation levels.

Such approach seamlessly enables to target diverse application fields and QoS metrics, identifying highly effective resource/quality trade-offs.

References

1. Chan, W.T.J., Kahng, A.B., Kang, S., Kumar, R., Sartori, J.: Statistical analysis and modeling for error composition in approximate computation circuits. In: Proceedings of the International Conference on Computer Design, pp. 47–53, October 2013
2. Du, Z., Palem, K., Lingamneni, A., Temam, O., Chen, Y., Wu, C.: Leveraging the error resilience of machine-learning applications for designing highly energy efficient accelerators. In: Proceedings of the Asia and South Pacific Design Automation Conference, pp. 201–206, January 2014
3. Fleming, P.J., Wallace, J.J.: How not to lie with statistics: the correct way to summarize benchmark results. Commun. ACM **29**(3), 218–221 (1986)
4. Forooghifar, F., et al.: A self-aware epilepsy monitoring system for real-time epileptic seizure detection. Mob. Netw. Appl. 1–14 (2019)
5. Lattner, C., Adve, V.: LLVM: a compilation framework for lifelong program analysis & transformation. In: Proceedings of the 2nd International Symposium on Code Generation and Optimization, pp. 75–88, March 2004
6. Li, C., Luo, W., Sapatnekar, S.S., Hu, J.: Joint precision optimization and high level synthesis for approximate computing. In: Proceedings of the 52nd Design Automation Conference, pp. 1–6, June 2015
7. Ferretti, L., et al.: Tailoring SVM inference for resource-efficient ECG-based epilepsy monitors. In: Proceedings of the Design, Automation and Test in Europe Conference and Exhibition, pp. 1–4, March 2019
8. Misailovic, S., Carbin, M., Achour, S., Qi, Z., Rinard, M.C.: Chisel: reliability-and accuracy-aware optimization of approximate computational kernels. In: SIGPLAN Notices, vol. 49, pp. 309–328. ACM, October 2014
9. Mittal, S.: A survey of techniques for approximate computing. ACM Comput. Surv. (CSUR) **48**(4), 62:1–62:33 (2016)
10. Mrazek, V., Hanif, M.A., Vasicek, Z., Sekanina, L., Shafique, M.: autoAx: an automatic design space exploration and circuit building methodology utilizing libraries of approximate components. In: Proceedings of the 56th Design Automation Conference, p. 123, June 2019
11. Mrazek, V., Hrbacek, R., Vasicek, Z., Sekanina, L.: EvoApproxSb: library of approximate adders and multipliers for circuit design and benchmarking of approximation methods. In: Proceedings of the Design, Automation and Test in Europe Conference and Exhibition, pp. 258–261, March 2017
12. Nepal, K., Li, Y., Bahar, R., Reda, S.: ABACUS: a technique for automated behavioral synthesis of approximate computing circuits. In: Proceedings of the Design, Automation and Test in Europe Conference and Exhibition, pp. 1–6, March 2014
13. Ranjan, A., Raha, A., Venkataramani, S., Roy, K., Raghunathan, A.: ASLAN: synthesis of approximate sequential circuits. In: Proceedings of the Design, Automation and Test in Europe Conference and Exhibition, pp. 1–6, March 2014
14. Scarabottolo, I., Ansaloni, G., Pozzi, L.: Circuit carving: a methodology for the design of approximate hardware. In: Proceedings of the Design, Automation and Test in Europe Conference and Exhibition, pp. 545–550, March 2018

15. Schlachter, J., Camus, V., Palem, K.V., Enz, C.: Design and applications of approximate circuits by gate-level pruning. IEEE Trans. Very Large Scale Integr. VLSI Syst. **25**(5), 1694–1702 (2017)
16. Sengupta, D., Snigdha, F.S., Hu, J., Sapatnekar, S.S.: SABER: selection of approximate bits for the design of error tolerant circuits. In: Proceedings of the 54th Design Automation Conference, p. 72, June 2017
17. Vassiliadis, V., et al.: Towards automatic significance analysis for approximate computing. In: Proceedings of the 14th International Symposium on Code Generation and Optimization, pp. 182–193. IEEE, March 2016
18. Venkataramani, S., Roy, K., Raghunathan, A.: Substitute-and-simplify: a unified design paradigm for approximate and quality configurable circuits. In: Proceedings of the Design, Automation and Test in Europe Conference and Exhibition, pp. 1367–1372, March 2013
19. Venkataramani, S., Sabne, A., Kozhikkottu, V., Roy, K., Raghunathan, A.: SALSA: systematic logic synthesis of approximate circuits. In: Proceedings of the 49th Design Automation Conference, pp. 796–801, June 2012

Optimising Operator Sets for Analytical Database Processing on FPGAs

Anna Drewes[1]([⊠]), Jan Moritz Joseph[1], Bala Gurumurthy[2], David Broneske[2], Gunter Saake[2], and Thilo Pionteck[1]

[1] Institute of Information Technology and Communications, Otto-von-Guericke University, 39106 Magdeburg, Germany
anna.drewes@ovgu.de

[2] Institute of Technical and Business Information Systems, Otto-von-Guericke University, 39106 Magdeburg, Germany

Abstract. The high throughput and partial reconfiguration capabilities of modern FPGAs make them an attractive hardware platform for query processing in analytical database systems using overlay architectures. The design of existing systems is often solely based on hardware characteristics and thus does not account for all requirements of the application. In this paper, we identify two design issues impeding system integration of low-level database operators for runtime-reconfigurable overlay architectures on FPGAs: First, the granularity of operator sets within each processing pipeline; Second, the mapping of query (sub-)graphs to complex hardware operators. We solve these issues by modeling them as variants of the subgraph isomorphism problem. Via optimised operator fusion guided by a heuristic we reduce the number of required reconfigurable regions between 30% and 85% for relevant TPC-H database benchmark queries. This increase in area efficiency is achieved without performance penalties. In 86% of iterations of the operator fusion process, the proposed heuristic finds optimal candidates, which is 3.6× more often than for a naive greedy approach.

Keywords: Query processing · Database operators · Operator fusion · Graph modeling · Heuristic · FPGA · Overlay architecture

1 Introduction

In order to address growing concerns regarding scaling and power efficiency, database research strives to include heterogeneous compute devices as accelerators [5]. In addition to a variety of GPU-based systems [3,13,30], FPGAs are also considered for their special capabilities: Their massive I/O-bandwidths, spatial parallelism, and deeply pipelined processing capabilities are all indicators for high performance in analytical database query processing. FPGAs have been

This work is funded by the German Research Foundation (DFG) projects PI-447/9 and SA-465/51-1.

used both as static accelerators for single database operations [2,12,18,24,27] and also as more general reconfigurable platforms [1,9,28,31]. These examples show large performance enhancements due to the use of heterogeneous hardware.

Despite the advantages of heterogeneous hardware, systems integration issues resulting from a bottom-up design process (cf. Fig. 1) impede their practical applicability. Thus, new optimisation techniques, operator representations, and memory management strategies have been introduced. Mapping queries to vastly differing processing architectures can be accomplished by converting SQL statements into sequences of simple, data-parallel operations [13]. Using this concept of primitive-based query processing, all operations besides pipeline breakers such as *Sort* can be evaluated as data flow graphs. For CPUs, evaluating these sequences of operations is possible via just-in-time compilation of optimised primitive implementations from intermediate representation (IR) [4,20]. This is not viable for FPGAs, as synthesis and place-and-route are very time-consuming compared to software compilation and can take from minutes to hours depending on the complexity and size of the target design. An alternative is sequential execution of pre-synthesised compute kernels, achieving high throughput through massive data parallelism. For FPGAs, implementing the basic database operations as OpenCL kernels follows this paradigm. In contrast to GPUs, where each kernel has access to the full hardware, the resources of an FPGA are either shared between a fixed set of static accelerators, or kernels have to be exchanged at runtime via costly reconfiguration of nearly the complete device [15,28,29]. Thus, both standard solutions for high performance integration of CPUs and GPUs are not targeting the special requirements of FPGAs.

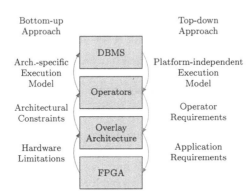

Fig. 1. Two standard approaches to system design/integration.

A better concept for FPGAs is an *overlay architecture*, where the logic resources of the FPGA are spatially divided into interconnected partitions which fit one hardware operator each. The exemplary design shown in Fig. 2 consists of 9 reconfigurable regions (RR) and a static partition, which is shown in blue and contains supporting logic such as bus systems, memory controllers, and the host interface. Specially synthesized hardware operators (compute unit, CU) for data processing or interconnect bridges for data movement can be loaded into the reconfigurable regions via dynamic partial reconfiguration (DPR) of parts of the FPGA fabric. This is shown in red in Fig. 2. Thus, an overlay architecture is an abstraction of the raw FPGA into a set of interconnected compute units and exposes the spatial parallelism inherent to FPGAs in a practical way [6,31]. While this top-down design approach (cf. Fig. 1) solves the problem of synthesis at runtime, it leaves a whole new set of problems to be addressed. The main issue is that most of the database primitives require only a rather small amount of resources (cf. Sect. 5). At the same time even simple queries can require evaluation of a dozen operations in a single pipeline. This leads to the requirement that the FPGA has to be broken up into a very large number of small, but tightly interconnected, reconfigurable regions. This is highly resource-inefficient.

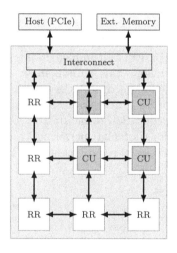

Fig. 2. Example of an FPGA overlay architecture. (Color figure online)

In order to address these urgent design issues, we propose an optimised operator fusion method for database primitives implemented for FPGAs targeting reconfigurable overlay architectures. We improve resource efficiency by reducing the number of reconfigurable regions occupied for executing a query. Specifically, we present an analysis of operators for analytical database query processing on FPGAs using overlay architectures. We reach an application-centered view of the design and integration process by formalising the apparent problems and reducing them to optimisation tasks based on known graph problems. This allows us to reduce the number of reconfigurable regions required for evaluating the considered analytical database queries by 52% on average, with only a slight increase RR size and most importantly, without performance penalties.

This paper is structured as follows: After discussing related work in Sect. 2, we provide an overview on primitives for analytical database query processing for heterogeneous hardware in Sect. 3. Section 4 contains definitions and our proposed optimisation process for the two problems of operator granularity and matching of composed operators. Results for relevant benchmark queries are presented in Sect. 5. Finally, we conclude the paper in Sect. 6.

2 Related Work

The problem addressed in this paper has no exactly matching related work where a direct comparison of results is possible in a meaningful way, but conceptually similar approaches with different optimisation criteria have been used in other application fields. Thus, in this section, we discuss related work on code fusion for heterogeneous hardware in general and optimisations regarding sets of operators for FPGAs.

Data-centric query compilation is important to achieve high performance on CPUs and GPUs [20]. While the problem of query compilation for CPUs and GPUs during runtime is structurally similar to our work, for FPGAs we have to focus on optimisations at design-time and can therefore improve and adapt not only the operator library, but also the static FPGA design. Menon et al. [19] describe a model for operator fusion during query planning in order to better exploit CPU caches. Apart from the lack of caches on FPGAs, their differing architecture requires custom models.

OpenCL can be used as a target platform for custom code generation for heterogeneous hardware. For example, Hawk [4] and Voodoo [22] generate optimised OpenCL code. These approaches not only cover code optimisations, but also address parallelism, both of which are orthogonal to the problems addressed in this paper, which deal with optimisation of the library of operators and reducing the number of discrete hardware operators required.

The model and optimisation approach for Code Fusion on GPUs presented by Wahib et al. [26] is, just as our approach, based on data dependencies between kernels. The authors propose a variation of genetic algorithms to solve the optimisation problem, while we propose a much more simple greedy constructive optimisation process. The results are not comparable to our results due to fundamental differences in optimisation goals: GPUs fuse kernels to reuse data fetched from memory, while we try to achieve better FPGA resource efficiency. Another, completely different problem for database operators on FPGAs involves fitting independent kernels into one large reconfigurable region covering most of the FPGA. Wang et al. [28] use dynamic programming to generate sequential query execution plans, and to partition sets of OpenCL kernels too large to fit into the singular reconfigurable region into several bitstream images based on a cost model. Since we build up queries from small, individually reconfigurable base primitives, this problem does not apply to our system.

Finally, RENO [21] is a data-dependency-driven optimiser implemented in hardware inside a CPU core, enabling the elimination or fusion of certain instructions directly from the instruction stream. Similarly, there exists work on hardware-based fusion of simple instructions into larger macro-operations in order to allow for a more efficient CPU microarchitecture [7,17]. All three works employ mechanisms similar to our work, but focus on the design of efficient high performance hardware implementations of code fusion engines, which are unnecessary in our work, since we do not use instruction-driven processing elements, but assemble pipelines of specialised hardware operators.

3   Database Primitives

Using *database primitives* to split up queries into small highly optimised base operations enables high-performance query processing on heterogeneous hardware architectures. For FPGAs, mapping primitives to reconfigurable regions of an overlay architecture makes construction of deep hardware pipelines possible at runtime. As *database primitives* is a widely used term in various contexts, we begin with a brief introduction and definition of the usage of this term in the scope of this paper.

After a database management system (DBMS) has parsed and optimised a query submitted by a user, it generates a query execution plan. This is necessary since SQL is a declarative language, and thus only describes the desired result and not a sequence of operations [16]. While large parts of parsing and optimisation can be similar for different execution techniques, the actual query execution plan is inherently architecture-specific. One technique for evaluating analytical database queries in heterogeneous systems is the use of database primitives [11,13,22]. These primitives represent the basic operations of parallel programming and can thus be directly implemented on a variety of compute architectures.

We consider *five types of Atomic Primitives*, some of which can be composed to form more complex operations required for evaluating queries.

1. Using the *Map* primitive, a function is applied to all values of one or more input vectors producing an output vector with the same number of tuples. A special case is the pairing of a scalar with each element of a vector. Since there are no dependencies between individual vector elements, *Map* can be parallelised trivially.
2. A *Reduce* operation takes in a vector and aggregates all elements into a single scalar. This primitive can be parallelised using reduction tree approaches, both in coarse- and fine-grained fashions, depending on the target architecture. Analytical database query processing requires a specialised variant of this primitive: *Grouped Aggregation*, which, instead of performing one reduction over the entire input vector, uses another input vector of group IDs to split the data input vector into multiple ranges. This operation can also use a tree-like task structure for parallelisation [14,23].
3. The *Prefix Scan* primitive is mostly used to generate index vectors for other primitives. Thus, probably the most common operation is prefix sum. Parallelising *Prefix Scan* is challenging. A standard approach is to split the input data into multiple chunks, each processed independently. Then the singular result values are aggregated by a single task to generate offsets that can be applied to the chunks in a final step using *Map* [23].

4. *Scatter/Gather* do not provide computation by themselves, but instead rearrange data by using indexed reads or writes. These primitives can exhibit widely varying memory access patterns. The impact of highly parallel *Scatter/Gather* on the memory system has to be carefully considered during implementation.
5. *Sort* is used in various ways in database systems. While preprocessing parts of the input vector is possible, the whole input vector has to be available before any output can be computed. This means that *Sort* is a pipeline breaker. Thus, interaction with other primitives is limited.

Some database operations cannot be captured fully by any one of these categories. They may be described as *Composed Primitives*, consisting of base primitives and special additional functionalities. A common example is construction of hash tables: While the computation of the hash function(s) is described by *Map*, modeling the insertion process using the base primitives is not sensible. Since the behaviour of different hash table variants is highly dependent on data distribution, fusing these operations with other primitives may result in inflexible and slow designs or require a vastly higher number of pre-synthesised operations. Thus, both sorting and hash table-manipulation operations are not considered in this work.

Mapping operators to DPR regions at runtime is a considerable problem, that has been addressed by other works [6], and thus is not detailed in this paper.

4   Optimisation Targets

As already introduced, we achieve more resource-efficient database query processing on FPGAs by targeting two objectives: *Hardware Operator Granularity* optimisation reduces resource requirements by lowering the number of reconfigurable regions required for executing a query, while optimised *Matching of Composed Operators* allows for reduced operator library size and thus improves synthesis time and the required storage space for the operators. In the following subsections, we use standard graph approaches for these optimisation targets.

4.1   Hardware Operator Granularity

Our first optimisation target is hardware operator granularity. In detail, we will present hardware constraints, describe the problem model, introduce operator fusion, and propose a greedy optimisation process.

For the purpose of modeling, we adopt an abstraction of a generalised overlay architecture for FPGAs, where the FPGA is partitioned into a static design and dynamically reconfigurable regions. Memory controllers, as well as an interconnect and various management logic forms the static partition, while hardware operators can be loaded into reconfigurable areas at runtime. The FPGA is thus abstracted into a set of directly interconnected compute units. To keep the amount of constraints low, we assume that each operator can be mapped to every reconfigurable region. For effective hardware pipeline processing, the links between reconfigurable regions are designed to stream data at the bandwidth required by the operators. Only data transfers to and from off-chip memory are assumed to be handled by DMA engines in the static partition.

We model query execution plans as directed, acyclic, coloured graphs $G = (V, E)$. Database primitives, as well as data sources and sinks form nodes $v \in V$. Their colouring (tag) is based on the underlying operator and data types. We define this colouring as *operators*. An operator node in G is defined as an *instance* and needs to be mapped to a reconfigurable region for execution. The directed edges $e \in E$ represent the data dependencies present in the query execution plan. Note that the size of data transfer that is represented by an edge may not necessarily be identical for all edges of a query, as in many cases the actual amount of data transferred is determined by characteristics of the input data. An example query execution plan generated from the TPC-H analytical database benchmark query Q6 is shown in Fig. 3 [25]. It contains a typical amount and complexity of operations, except for joins, which are explicitly not covered in this work. Data flows from bottom to top and the different data transfer sizes are highlighted at the edges. After evaluating the selection criteria via *Map less-than/greater-than (map-s-lt/map-s-gt)* comparison operations, the results are combined via *map-and*. Then, the *filter* operation eliminates all elements of the input vectors that do not meet the selection criteria. The filtered input columns are multiplied element-wise *(map-mul)*. Finally the result is computed by aggregating the result vector of the multiplication operation *(red-add)*.

In general, non-parallelised database primitives that are synthesised as streaming hardware operators have rather small resource requirements. This is especially relevant for runtime-reconfigurable implementations on FPGAs using a multitude of DPR regions, as there is a high degree of area overhead associated with each runtime-reconfigurable region. This overhead is due to the need to provide communications infrastructure and isolation of the reconfigurable region from the rest of the system during reconfiguration. This leads to the goal of fusing database primitives that commonly occur together into larger units, thus reducing the number of DPR regions required for evaluating a query. While the base query Q6 shown in Fig. 3 would require 15 distinct hardware operators, the optimised query shown in Fig. 6 reduces the number of required DPR regions to 4 (cf. Table 1). Operator fusion also relieves some amount of load from the interconnect of the overlay architecture because in many cases fused primitives share input vectors. Data transferred between fused operators are removed from the system interconnect as well. In addition, area efficiency is improved in general, as scheduling can be optimised by the design tools if the operators are synthesized in a fixed combination inside a single reconfigurable region. Of course, the DPR regions have to be sized according to the single largest primitive or fused operator. As FPGA synthesis and place-and-route are time-consuming and resource-intensive tasks, it is generally not feasible for a database management system to synthesize custom hardware accelerators for each query at runtime. Thus, there remains the problem of deciding which combinations of primitives

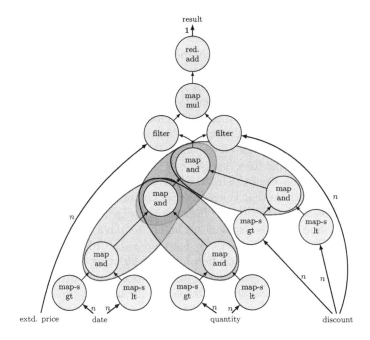

Fig. 3. Query execution plan of TPC-H Query 6. (Color figure online)

should be fused into composed operators. These decisions are relevant, as the size of the operator library is limited by both the available storage space and the time overhead at runtime for finding fitting operators.

In order to optimise the set of required primitives to generate fused operators, we start with a set of query execution plans S_{base}. This set can be either extracted from logs or traces of a running system or generated from database benchmark suites. S_{base} induces a set of operators O_{base}, which describes the set of database primitives used across all queries of S_{base}. The formal goal is to identify the maximum common induced subgraph J for each possible tuple of these graphs (G, H) with $G \in S_{\text{base}}, H \in S_{\text{base}}$ and $G \neq H$. Since the decision problem whether two graphs G, H have a common subgraph J of size k is NP-complete [10], in practice this problem cannot be expected to be solved in an optimal way.

We propose a greedy, constructive algorithm for generating fused operators from a base set of queries. Our iterative process can be summarised as follows: First, we identify the most common combination of operators $(a, b) \in O_i \times O_i$, where O_i is the induced set of operators O after iteration i with $O_0 = O_{\text{base}}$. Second, fuse the identified fusion candidate into a new operator $o = (a, b)$. Third, generate query graphs $G' \in S_{i+1}$ from the graphs $G \in S_i$ by replacing instances of (a, b) with o. This also updates the induced set of operators O_i to the updated set O_{i+1} used in the next iteration. This process can continue until all possible primitives have been fused.

The main problem with this algorithm is the fact that the most commonly occurring operator combination may not be the operator combination that can be replaced most often. This happens because primitives in query execution plans graphs are often arranged in tree or chain-like shapes, thus influencing their neighbours. This is illustrated in Fig. 3: Fusion candidates consisting of two *map-and* operations can be found four times within the graph. They are highlighted using the red, violet, and blue ellipses. As the ellipses are overlapping each other, the fused operator cannot be instantiated four times. It is only possible to replace the right blue ellipse and either the violet or the other blue one resulting in two uses of the fused operator. If the red ellipse were to be replaced, all other possible instances of the fused operator would be blocked. Generalising this example, we conclude that the number of coloured edges, which describe an operator fusion candidate, does not indicate the expected optimisation potential adequately. Solving this problem optimally requires frequent identification of maximum independent edge sets, or matchings. In order to avoid expensive calculation of such an optimal solution for every existing combination of operators in every iteration of the operator fusion process, we introduce a heuristic to select operator fusion candidates. Instead of the naive approach of using the number of edges of each colour to select fusion candidates, we propose to count the number of distinct nodes attached to edges of each colour. Divided by two, this heuristic provides a direct estimate of the target function, i.e. the number of expected possible instances of the potential fused operator. We evaluate the proposed heuristic in Sect. 5.

4.2   Matching of Composed Operators

At runtime, the problem of actually using the previously generated fused operators remains. This problem is especially relevant if the DBMS front end and logical optimisation stages are architecture-oblivious in order to support heterogeneous hardware other than overlay architectures of FPGAs. In this case an FPGA-specific optimiser has to identify (match) subgraphs H describing fused operators in an input query execution plan G, thus needing to repeatedly solve the subgraph isomorphism problem, which is NP-complete [8].

We suggest an approximation by following a greedy steepest gradient descent approach: Since G is a directed acyclic graph, match the largest fitting composed operator following the topological ordered query execution plan. After replacing the matched subgraph with the fused operator, the next matching is constructed.

In addition to the remaining high complexity of the approximation algorithm, sometimes the most appropriate fused operator is not an exact match. An example can be taken from the benchmark queries used in Sect. 5 and is shown in Fig. 4. This is a sequence of two primitives that commonly occurs as last processing step of queries. Data are aggregated according to a vector of group IDs (*gagg-add*). In addition to the sum, this sequence also computes an average value for each group (*map-div*). This requires information about the sizes of the distinct groups (*count*). In general, it is only necessary to count the group sizes once. In contrast, duplicating the *gagg-count* operator for each composed grouped aggregation operation, as depicted in Fig. 5, eliminates the input vector *count* from the fused operator. Since this additional fused primitive is not complex, this is a better optimisation of the query execution plan, but much more difficult to realise, as it requires a fuzzy approach to subgraph matching.

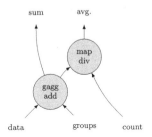

Fig. 4. Default replacement candidate for exact matching.

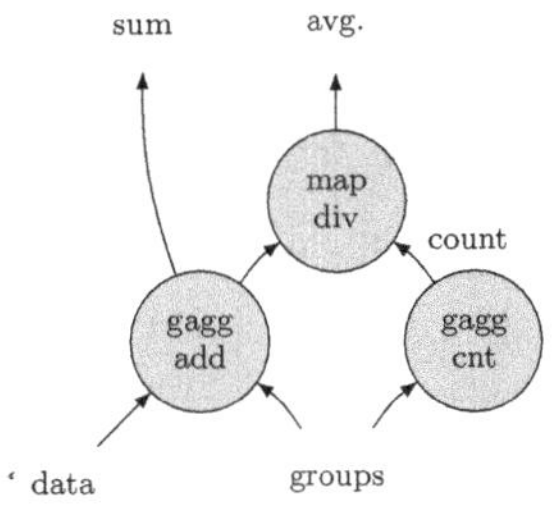

Fig. 5. Candidate for fuzzy matching.

5   Results

To evaluate our proposed optimisation process and heuristic, we applied our algorithm to relevant analytical benchmark queries from TPC-H [25], and also synthesized both the required primitives and fused operators.

5.1   Evaluation Setup

Table 1 lists the considered queries. As sorting and table join operations are pipeline-breaking operators and require implementations tailored to specific data distributions, fusing them will result in either inflexible operators or a large operator library. Thus, we do not consider those parts of the queries. Due to pipeline breakers within their query execution plan, many queries cannot be evaluated using a single continuous processing pipeline. These queries have to be split up into multiple processing pipelines. The partial query execution plans tagged *begin* contain the first operations, usually applying of selection criteria. The partial query execution plans tagged *end* cover final processing steps, such as grouped aggregation. The query execution plans are generated from the SQL statements using standard textbook concepts.

All primitives and optimised fused operators are written in C as single-tuple-per-cycle compute kernels with a data width of 32 bit. They are synthesised using Vivado HLS 2018.1. The directives HLS_DATAFLOW and HLS_PIPELINE are used to generate efficient streaming compute components. Throughout the whole project AXI Stream ports are used. We try to achieve the highest possible clock rate while maintaining a loop initiation interval of one clock cycle, with a starting frequency of 300 MHz. Operators failing to meet this requirement are synthesised

Table 1. Results

Query	Throughput GB s^{-1}		Reconf. Regions (RR Instances)			Resources				
						CLB		DSP		Savings
	Base	Opt.	Base	Opt.	Savings	Base	Opt.	Base	Opt.	
Single RR			1	1		400	450	10	10	–12%
Q1 (begin)	2.30	2.30	4	2	50%	1600	900	40	20	44%
Q1 (end)	14.33	14.33	13	9	30%	5200	4050	130	90	22%
Q4 (begin)	4.60	4.60	6	4	33%	2400	1800	60	40	25%
Q6 (complete)	–	4.60	15	4	73%	6000	1800	150	40	70%
Q12 (begin)	5.75	5.75	12	6	50%	4800	2700	120	60	44%
Q12 (end)	4.41	4.41	3	4	25%	2400	1800	60	40	25%
Q16 (begin)	–	4.60	20	6	70%	8000	2700	200	60	66%
Q19 (complete)	–	9.20	76	12	**84%**	30400	5400	760	120	**82%**
Average improvement					**52%**					**47%**

at lower frequencies. Only the division and grouped aggregation operators require a lowered clock frequency of 250 MHz.

The Xilinx Zynq ZC706 evaluation board is used as the design target. The FPGA part of the Zynq 7Z045 system-on-chip (SoC) has access to 2 GiB of external DDR3 memory with a maximal theoretical bandwidth of 19.2 GB s^{-1}. Its FPGA resources comprise lookup tables (LUT) and flipflops (FF) for implementing logic circuits, which are combined into Configurable Logic Blocks (CLB) that are tiled across the FPGA fabric. The FPGA also contains multiply-accumulate units (DSP) to simplify implementation of certain arithmetic operations. The considered FPGA contains a total of 27 325 CLBs and 900 DSP slices. The reconfiguration granularity for logic resources is a column of 50 CLBs, each consisting of 2 slices of 4 LUTs, while the reconfiguration granularity for DSP slices is 10. Therefore, the size of 2489 LUTs and 2950 FFs of the division operator mandates a minimum reconfigurable region size of 8 columns, which corresponds to 400 CLBs, or 3200 LUTs. Due to the layout of the clock regions within the FPGA fabric, up to 14 completely independent reconfigurable regions can be instantiated. Please note that only those queries with a small number of primitives can be processed in a single compute pipeline in the baseline.

5.2 Optimisation Process

Running the optimisation process until all reused operator combinations were found generates 12 fused operators within 21 fusion steps. The optimisation process is terminated when there are no more duplicated subgraphs. The average fused operator is composed from five base primitives, while the smallest fused operators contains only two. Because TPC-H Query 19 makes use of an identical set of extensive selection criteria three times, the largest fused operator maps to one of these sub-trees and consists of 23 primitives. As an illustrative example,

Fig. 6 shows the optimised query execution plan for the baseline query as shown in Fig. 3 utilising the fused operators shown in Figs. 7, 8, and 9. The primitives and fused operators are highlighted in violet, while the base primitives are shown in green. Figure 4 shows another example of a fused operator.

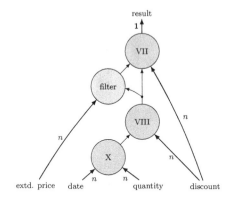

Fig. 6. TPC-H Query 6 using fused operators. (Color figure online)

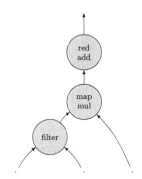

Fig. 7. Fused operator VII. (Color figure online)

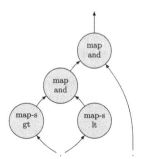

Fig. 8. Fused operator VIII. (Color figure online)

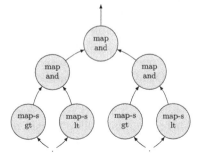

Fig. 9. Fused operator X. (Color figure online)

5.3 Discussion

In order to test the accuracy of our heuristic, we also computed optimal results. Our proposed heuristic correctly identified optimal fusion candidates in 18 out of 21 iterations of our algorithm. This estimation accuracy of 86% is over three times larger than the accuracy of the naive approach.

The reductions in resource requirements achieved by our operator fusion optimisation process are illustrated in Fig. 10: Fusing small database primitives significantly improves resource efficiency for overlay architectures in database query

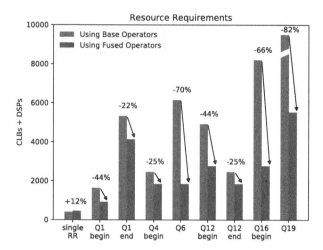

Fig. 10. Comparison of resources requirements using base primitives and fused operators for relevant TPC-H benchmark queries.

processing on FPGAs. Resource requirements for complete queries are reduced by up to 82%. This is an impressive result that shows that FPGA-enabled implementations of primitive-based analytical database management systems require architecture-specific optimisation of operators at design time. As the largest primitive, namely division, is part of the fused operator shown in Fig. 4, the size of each reconfigurable region increases slightly to 450 CLBs, as is shown in the first line of Table 1. This increase in size reduces the savings achieved by use of the fused operators, as can be seen when comparing columns six and eleven of Table 1. On average, the number of reconfigurable regions used for a single query is reduced by 52%, which leads to an average reduction in resource requirements of 47%.

There is no immediate impact on performance, as the maximum clock speed of the operators was not reduced by the fusion process, but due to the lowered number of reconfigurable regions, all queries can now be executed in a single pass. In contrast, the reconfiguration time between queries is reduced, as even with the slightly larger partitions, each query requires a significantly lower number of (re-)configured tiles. The throughput numbers shown in Table 1 refers to the total amount of data being read into and written out of the processing pipeline. Also, as communication between primitives within one fused operator is handled entirely within the operator, the interconnect in the static partition is relieved.

Due to the significant improvement in resource efficiency, our proposed approach improves the feasibility of integration of FPGAs using overlay architectures into analytical database systems. Our approach can also be applied to other application areas, such as network traffic analysis, digital signal processing, and software-defined radio, where data flow graphs generated at runtime are processed using a fixed library of operators.

6   Conclusion

In this paper we analyse the problem of automated fusion of commonly occurring combinations of basic database operators for FPGAs and propose solutions based on standard graph problems. While the underlying problem of identifying commonly occurring subgraphs in a set of graphs is very difficult and in the general case even hard to approximate, the special instance discussed here allowed for good approximation results after developing a heuristic. For the set of standard benchmark queries considered, the proposed optimisation process reduces the number of required reconfigurable regions by about 52% on average with a maximum reduction of 84%. As the size of each reconfigurable region increases slightly due to fusing of operators, the overall resource savings are smaller: Executing a query using fused operators requires between 22% and 82% less FPGA resources than using base primitives. The proposed optimised operator fusion process enables practical applicability of FPGA-based accelerators in query processing, thus increasing efficiency in handling large-scale database systems. Further constraining of the search space may be an interesting direction for future research.

References

1. Backasch, R., Hempel, G., Pionteck, T., Groppe, S., Werner, S.: An architectural template for composing application specific datapaths at runtime. In: ReConFig (2015)
2. Becher, A., Ziener, D., Meyer-Wegener, K., Teich, J.: A co-design approach for accelerated SQL query processing via FPGA-based data filtering. In: FPT, pp. 192–195 (2015)
3. Breß, S., Heimel, M., Saecker, M., Köcher, B., Markl, V., Saake, G.: Ocelot/HyPE: optimized data processing on heterogeneous hardware. PVLDB **7**(13), 1609–1612 (2014)
4. Breß, S., Köcher, B., Funke, H., Zeuch, S., Rabl, T., Markl, V.: Generating custom code for efficient query execution on heterogeneous processors. VLDB J. **27**(6), 797–822 (2018). https://doi.org/10.1007/s00778-018-0512-y
5. Broneske, D., Breß, S., Heimel, M., Saake, G.: Toward hardware-sensitive database operations. In: EDBT, pp. 229–234 (2014)
6. Capalija, D., Abdelrahman, T.S.: A high-performance overlay architecture for pipelined execution of data flow graphs. In: FPL, pp. 1–8 (2013)
7. Celio, C., Dabbelt, P., Patterson, D.A., Asanovic, K.: The renewed case for the reduced instruction set computer: avoiding ISA bloat with macro-op fusion for RISC-V. CoRR abs/1607.02318 (2016). http://arxiv.org/abs/1607.02318
8. Cook, S.A.: The complexity of theorem-proving procedures. In: ACM STOC, pp. 151–158 (1971)
9. Dennl, C., Ziener, D., Teich, J.: On-the-fly composition of FPGA-based SQL query accelerators using a partially reconfigurable module library. In: FCCM, pp. 45–52 (2012)
10. Garey, M.R., Johnson, D.S.: Computers and Intractability: A Guide to the Theory of NP-Completeness. W. H. Freeman, New York (1979)

11. Gurumurthy, B., Broneske, D., Drewes, T., Pionteck, T., Saake, G.: Cooking DBMS operations using granular primitives - an overview on a primitive-based RDBMS query evaluation. Datenbank-Spektrum **18**(3), 183–193 (2018). https://doi.org/10. 1007/s13222-018-0295-8
12. Halstead, R.J., et al.: Accelerating join operation for relational databases with FPGAs. In: FCCM, pp. 17–20 (2013)
13. He, B., et al.: Relational query coprocessing on graphics processors. ACM TODS **34**(4), 21:1–21:39 (2009)
14. Heimel, M., Saecker, M., Pirk, H., Manegold, S., Markl, V.: Hardware-oblivious parallelism for in-memory column-stores. PVLDB **6**(9), 709–720 (2013)
15. Intel Corp.: Intel FPGA SDK for OpenCL Programming Guide (2017)
16. International Organization for Standardisation: ISO/IEC 9075 Information Technology - Database Languages - SQL (2016)
17. Kim, I., Lipasti, M.H.: Macro-op scheduling: relaxing scheduling loop constraints. In: MICRO, pp. 277–290 (2003)
18. Koch, D., Tørresen, J.: FPGASort: a high performance sorting architecture exploiting run-time reconfiguration on FPGAs for large problem sorting. In: ACM SIGDA, pp. 45–54 (2011)
19. Menon, P., Pavlo, A., Mowry, T.C.: Relaxed operator fusion for in-memory databases: making compilation, vectorization, and prefetching work together at last. PVLDB **11**(1), 1–13 (2017)
20. Neumann, T.: Efficiently compiling efficient query plans for modern hardware. PVLDB **4**(9), 539–550 (2011)
21. Petric, V., Sha, T., Roth, A.: RENO - a rename-based instruction optimizer. In: ISCA, pp. 98–109 (2005)
22. Pirk, H., Moll, O., Zaharia, M., Madden, S.: Voodoo - a vector algebra for portable database performance on modern hardware. PVLDB **9**(14), 1707–1718 (2016)
23. Roosta, S.H.: Parallel processing and parallel algorithms - theory and computation. Springer (2000). http://www.springer.com/computer/swe/book/978-0-387-98716-3
24. Teubner, J., Woods, L.: Data Processing on FPGAs. Synthesis Lectures on Data Management. Morgan & Claypool Publishers, San Rafael (2013)
25. Transaction Processing Performance Council (TPC): TPC BENCHMARK H (Decision Support) Standard Specification (2017)
26. Wahib, M., Maruyama, N.: Scalable kernel fusion for memory-bound GPU applications. In: SC, pp. 191–202 (2014)
27. Wang, Z., He, B., Zhang, W.: A study of data partitioning on OpenCL-based FPGAs. In: FPL, pp. 1–8 (2015)
28. Wang, Z., Paul, J., Cheah, H.Y., He, B., Zhang, W.: Relational query processing on OpenCL-based FPGAs. In: FPL, pp. 1–10 (2016)
29. Xilinx Inc: SDAccel Development Environment User Guide (2016)
30. Zhang, S., He, J., He, B., Lu, M.: OmniDB: towards portable and efficient query processing on parallel CPU/GPU architectures. PVLDB **6**(12), 1374–1377 (2013)
31. Ziener, D., et al.: FPGA-based dynamically reconfigurable SQL query processing. ACM TRETS **9**(4), 25:1–25:24 (2016)

Automated Toolchain for Enhanced Productivity in Reconfigurable Multi-accelerator Systems

Alberto Ortiz[ORCID], Rafael Zamacola[✉][ORCID], Alfonso Rodríguez[ORCID], Andrés Otero[ORCID], and Eduardo de la Torre[ORCID]

Universidad Politécnica de Madrid, Madrid, Spain
{alberto.ortiz,rafael.zamacola,alfonso.rodriguezm,
joseandres.otero,eduardo.delatorre}@upm.es

Abstract. Ease-of-use and faster implementation times are key challenges that the community has to face to extend the use of FPGAs to non-hardware experts. In this paper, these challenges are tackled by integrating ARTICo^3 and IMPRESS tools to provide the users with a transparent way to build reconfigurable multi-accelerator systems. ARTICo^3 is an integrated framework that provides an automated toolchain to generate a hardware-based processing architecture to transparently manage custom-made accelerators at runtime. IMPRESS is a reconfiguration tool for building highly-flexible reconfigurable systems. The integration of both tools results in an efficient reconfigurable design flow that decouples the implementation of reconfigurable accelerators from the implementation of an ARTICo^3 static architecture that transparently distributes data to the accelerators. This static architecture is generated only once and reused in consecutive kernel implementations. This way, the user only needs to design the accelerators that are automatically implemented using interfaces compatible with the static architecture. From the user point of view, the reconfigurable fabric is a set of slots where accelerators can be transparently offloaded to decrease the workload on the processor. The integration of ARTICo^3 and IMPRESS also allows building relocatable accelerators, thus reducing the overall memory footprint required for the partial bitstreams. Moreover, model-based design of accelerators using Simulink has also been included as an additional option for users with no hardware background to further simplify the use of reconfigurable systems. Experimental results show that the implementation time is improved by up to 2.96× for a 4-slot reconfigurable system implementation with a memory footprint reduction of 4.54×.

Keywords: FPGAs · Dynamic and Partial Reconfiguration · Relocation · Productivity · Linux

1 Introduction

The fear of the end of Moore's law [18] threatens to change the current processor-based computing paradigm. One way to improve computation efficiency, aside

© Springer Nature Switzerland AG 2020
F. Rincón et al. (Eds.): ARC 2020, LNCS 12083, pp. 45–60, 2020.
https://doi.org/10.1007/978-3-030-44534-8_4

from scaling the number of general-purpose processors, is building heterogeneous systems with devices specialized in certain domain-specific computations [19]. One example that has been extensively used in personal computers is coupling a processors with GPUs. While HPC-oriented (High-Performance Computing) GPUs are great devices for computing highly parallel algorithms, they tend to consume power in the order of hundreds of watts [15]. FPGAs are a great alternative to reduce power consumption while still providing great performance for computing parallel algorithms. As an example, Microsoft has opted for the use of FPGAs in their datacenters over GPUs due to its power consumption and after having found unclear that some latency-sensitive ranking stages (such as feature extraction) would map well to GPUs. As stated by [8], the use of FPGAs in Microsoft datacenters increased throughput up to 95% with only a 10% increase in power consumption. Moreover, the acquisition of Altera by Intel makes it foreseeable that greater use will be made of heterogeneous systems with multi-core processors coupled with FPGAs, GPUs and even dedicated ASICs for specific domains such as artificial intelligence. One example of this type of devices will be Xilinx ACAP family [5] that promises having dramatic performance improvements of up to 20× over today's fastest FPGA implementations and over 100× over today's fastest CPU implementations for Data Centers, wired networks, 5G wireless, and automotive driver assist applications. To ensure that the mainstream community adopts heterogeneous systems, it is mandatory to improve the ease of design and the overall productivity.

The main challenges for the FPGA landscape have evolved over the years since they were first introduced by Xilinx in 1984 [17]. FPGA size and efficient CAD design tools are no longer concerns for most applications. However there are still many challenges, such as ease-of-use, ease-of-debug, accessibility, and slow edit-compile-debug cycles [16], that the community has to face for making FPGAs more attractive to a wider number of people with different backgrounds. In the last few years, the FPGA community has focused on new ways to configure the FPGAs from high-level descriptions in order to solve some of these issues. High-Level Languages (HLL) [9,13] produce HDL (Hardware Description Language) code from high-level algorithmic description languages. Although HLL aim at being used by people without an specific hardware background, it is still necessary to have in-depth knowledge of the underlying hardware to build efficient systems. Model-based design [10] is a great alternative to HLL as it reduces the required hardware expertise. In model-based design, systems are described as a combination of blocks that have a predefined functionality.

In order to build efficient heterogeneous systems, it is not enough with having efficient ways to program each device, but it is also important to view the system as a whole. To that end, it is critical that devices are tightly connected to each other and to have efficient techniques to partition an algorithm so each part of the algorithm is executed in the most suitable device. Main FPGA manufacturers, Xilinx and Intel, have already focused their efforts in bringing to the market Systems on Chip (SoCs) that incorporate a processor tightly coupled with a reconfigurable fabric [2,6]. Moreover, Xilinx and Intel provide design tools to effectively program together both the processor and the FPGA [3,4].

Dynamic Partial Reconfiguration (DPR) is a technique to reconfigure part of the FPGA at runtime while the rest of the system is unaltered. It is possible to leverage DPR in heterogeneous systems so that the reconfigurable fabric is always accelerating parallel sections of an algorithm without being limited by the overall amount of resources. This form of heterogeneous computation, where a processor offloads at runtime sections of an algorithm to an FPGA, is called dynamic reconfigurable computing. Several academic tools aim at enhancing the ease of design in the field of reconfigurable computing. One example is ReconOS [7], an operating system that offers a unified multithreaded programming model and OS services to combine both hardware and software threads. Another example is ARTICo^3 [14], an integrated framework that provides a hardware-based processing architecture, an automated toolchain, and a runtime to transparently generate and manage reconfigurable multi-accelerator systems.

The main goal of this work is to increase the productivity and ease of design of reconfigurable multi-accelerator systems. To that end, the ARTICo^3 framework[1] has been integrated with the reconfiguration tool IMPRESS[2] (IMplementation of Partial REconfigurable SystemS) [20]. The integration of both results in an extended framework for reconfigurable systems which has the architecture infrastructure decoupled from the accelerators provided by the users. This way, the user only has to focus on specifying accelerators with a compatible interface to be automatically implemented with ARTICo^3. The productivity is greatly improved as the ARTICo^3 architecture implementation is only performed once. IMPRESS also provides relocation capabilities to ARTICo^3, thus reducing the memory needed to store the partial bitstreams of the accelerators. Moreover, to ease the design of reconfigurable computing systems for people without a hardware background, and to reduce accelerator design times, the ARTICo^3 framework has been extended to support model-based design of accelerators using Simulink.

The main contributions of this paper, together with their associated benefits can be enumerated as:

- An integrated toolflow that improves design productivity and further simplifies runtime support for reconfiguration.
- Support for multiple grains of reconfiguration, widening the applicability of the tools.
- A relocatable bitstream method for compatible routing regions that reduces memory footprint for bitstream storage.
- Support for accelerator generation from Simulink model-based design descriptions.

The rest of this paper is divided as follows. Section 2 provides background information on IMPRESS and ARTICo^3 tools. The benefits obtained from the combination of both tools are discussed in Sect. 3, while the details of the integration are explained in Sect. 4. Section 5 describes how reconfigurable ARTICo^3-compliant accelerators can be generated from Simulink model-based designs.

---

[1] https://des-cei.github.io/tools/artico3.
[2] https://des-cei.github.io/tools/impress.

The integration is evaluated in Sect. 6 to finally extract the conclusions of this work in Sect. 7.

2   Technical Background

The next subsections provide background information on the main reconfiguration-related concepts, the reconfiguration tool IMPRESS, and the ARTICo^3 toolchain.

2.1   Basic Concepts on Reconfiguration

In order to build partially dynamic reconfigurable hardware, it is necessary to differentiate between the static system, i.e, the circuits that are unchanged during the device lifetime, and the Reconfigurable Modules (RMs), which are the circuits that can be exchanged in the system at runtime. The static system contains special components, called Reconfigurable Partitions (RPs), that are floor-planned in certain regions of the FPGA, called Reconfigurable Regions (RRs). The RPs can be initially implemented as dummy RMs (i.e., a non-functional RM) or they can be implemented using any of the available RMs. At runtime, RMs can be allocated in RRs as long as they share the same interface with the static system.

Another key concept in reconfigurable systems is the Virtual Architecture (VA). The VA defines how the RRs are distributed over the FPGA (i.e., floor-planning) and the physical interfaces between the static system and each RR. The most efficient way to define interfaces is using partition pins [1], as they do not contain any logic and therefore do not have any resource or latency overhead. VAs can be floorplanned using three different styles (island, slot and grid) [11]. The most basic style is the island-based VA which has the RRs isolated from each other. In contrast, the slot and grid styles are composed of contiguous RRs that can be connected to each other. The main advantage of the slot and grid styles over the island style is that an RM can be implemented combining several contiguous RRs depending on the RM size. Thus, if the granularity of the slots or grid elements are small enough, the amount of unused resources decreases.

Partial bitstreams contain the configuration of RMs. They are composed of a series of frames (i.e., the minimum reconfigurable unit in Xilinx FPGAs) that span the height of a clock region. When using Xilinx reconfiguration flow, if one RM is implemented in m RRs, it is necessary to generate m partial bitstreams. This can lead to a considerable memory footprint in systems where RMs are implemented in several RRs, which is often the case in systems with slot- and grid-based VAs. When RRs have the same logic resources distributed in the same way, it is possible to have relocatable RMs where the same partial bitstream can be used for each RR. Thus, significantly reducing the memory footprint required to store partial bitstreams.

2.2   IMPRESS

IMPRESS (IMplementation of Partial REconfigurable SystemS) [20] is a Tcl script-based tool for implementing highly flexible reconfigurable systems using any VA style in Xilinx series 7 FPGAs. Both the slot- and grid-based VAs share the property of having different RRs in the static system and the RMs implementation (i.e., the RM can span several slots or grid elements). In order to implement systems with these VAs, IMPRESS decouples the implementation of the static system and each RM design. To ensure that RMs and the static system can connect to each other, it is necessary to use compatible interfaces. Similar to Xilinx reconfiguration flow [1], IMPRESS uses partition pins to implement the interface of the RRs, thus avoiding any resource and latency overhead. However, IMPRESS only uses one-hop nodes (i.e., nodes that connect adjacent tiles) placed at the border of the RRs. The user can easily define which borders are used for interfacing an RR by specifying the border (e.g., north) or part of the border (e.g., north_0:3 to select only the first four tiles of the north border). This interface style is called virtual interface in IMPRESS terminology. One of the great advantages of IMPRESS virtual interfaces is that they allow connecting neighboring RMs without any static logic or routing. Thus, whenever two adjacent RMs share a common border they can communicate to each other without using any static system resource.

One key feature of IMPRESS is that it is capable of generating relocatable RMs; thus reducing the memory footprint of partial bitstreams. The generation of relocatable RMs has three requirements. The first requirement to relocate one RM into different RRs is that each RR must have the same distribution of logic resources. In IMPRESS the user is held responsible for ensuring this requirement. The second requirement is that each RR must have the same physical interface. This is automatically done by IMPRESS when the user marks different RRs as relocatable. The third and last requirement is ensuring that the static logic and all the module nets cannot enter the RR. To that end, in the routing phase IMPRESS generates a blocker net [12] that acts as a fence so that the routing from the static system cannot enter inside the RR.

When using slot- and grid-based VA styles, it is usually desirable to stack several RMs in the same clock region. As explained in Subsect. 2.1, the minimum reconfigurable unit in Xilinx FPGAs is a frame, that spans the whole height of a clock region. Therefore, when using Xilinx reconfiguration flow is not possible to reconfigure one RM in one clock region without affecting RMs placed on top or below the targeted RM. IMPRESS includes a software-based Reconfiguration Engine (RE) in charge of downloading the partial bitstreams into the FPGA. The RE can perform sub-clock region reconfiguration by doing three steps. First, it performs a readback of the region to be reconfigured, then it recombines it with the desired partial bitstream and lastly, it downloads the recombined bitstream into the FPGA.

2.3   ARTICo[3]

ARTICo[3] [14] is a hardware-based high-performance embedded processing architecture that enables user-driven adaptation at runtime, creating a dynamic 3-D space of solutions with dynamic tradeoffs between computing performance, energy consumption, and fault tolerance. This architecture provides software-like flexibility by the use of Dynamic and Partial Reconfiguration (DPR), maintaining hardware-like performance during execution in a multi-accelerator approach.

In addition to the hardware architecture, a toolchain is provided as part of the ARTICo[3] framework, enabling users to transparently generate dynamically reconfigurable systems from the descriptions of both hardware accelerators and a host application. Users only need to provide the toolchain with an already partitioned hardware/software system, where host code is specified in C/C++ and kernels are specified in low-level HDL (VHDL, Verilog) or C/C++ to be processed with High-Level Synthesis (HLS) tools.

The static architecture of ARTICo[3] transparently distributes data to be processed by the hardware accelerators, with no user intervention. Taking the user-defined system and kernels as inputs, the toolchain automatically performs three tasks: instantiating the user-defined kernel logic in a standard wrapper, generating the on-chip DMA-powered communication infrastructure, and building both hardware and software components to obtain the required binaries that are used in the target platform. As the ARTICo[3] architecture follows a slot-based floorplanning style, as shown in the top-level block design in Fig. 1, and relies on the Xilinx reconfiguration flow, the toolchain will generate the same number of hardware binaries as slots together with the static system. These binaries are used by the software application to transparently configure the FPGA making use of the drivers provided by Xilinx for DPR in supported Linux-based SoPCs.

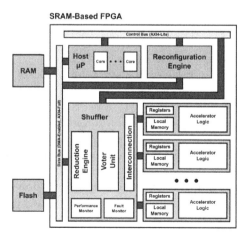

Fig. 1. ARTICo[3] architecture top-level block design

3 Enhancing Productivity with Advanced Reconfiguration Features

The ARTICo^3 toolchain can be leveraged to improve the productivity of heterogeneous SW/HW systems as it provides the means to communicate a processor with custom accelerators. Users just have to focus their efforts on deciding the SW/HW partitioning (i.e., which parts are implemented in SW or HW) and implementing the desired accelerators using HDLs (Hardware Description Language) or HLS (High-Level Synthesis). However, ARTICo^3 still presents some barriers that hinder an enhanced productivity. The integration of ARTICo^3 with IMPRESS breaks these barriers, improving overall productivity.

The main barrier affecting productivity in ARTICo^3 is that the toolchain reimplements the static part whenever a user builds a system with a new set of accelerators. As explained in Subsect. 2.2, IMPRESS decouples the design of the static system and the RMs. Therefore, the integration of both tools allows users to generate the static system once and to reuse it for every design, which reduces the synthesis and implementation times. Different static architecture implementations for different devices are distributed as templates within ARTICo^3. The users can use an available template or build new templates to support more devices, by modifying the number of RRs or adding ARTICo^3 as a subcomponent in a bigger design. Once the user selects a template, the accelerators are automatically built with a compatible interface.

Another advantage that results from the integration of IMPRESS and ARTICo^3 is the reduction in memory footprint. When using the Xilinx standard reconfiguration flow, ARTICo^3 generates one partial bitstream for each RR while IMPRESS generates one RR for a group of compatible RRs (i.e., RRs with the same resource distribution). Therefore, it is important to select RRs as homogeneous as possible to reduce as much as possible the number of partial bitstreams. Another feature of IMPRESS that can be used in ARTICo^3 designs is sub-clock region reconfiguration. Sub-clock region reconfiguration allows having more than one RR in the same clock region. This feature can be used to reduce the granularity of the RRs or to have RRs that span one and a half clock regions.

Another key aspect to increase productivity and to reduce the complexity of building reconfigurable systems is simplifying the design of hardware accelerators. ARTICo^3 already includes the possibility of designing accelerators using HLS languages. Although HLS languages reduce the time and complexity of the hardware design process, it still requires having some understanding of hardware design to build efficient systems. To further simplify the design of the accelerators we have included the possibility of designing accelerators using model-based descriptions with Simulink. Therefore, users with little experience designing hardware can build accelerators by combining blocks with predefined functionalities.

4   Integrating IMPRESS in ARTICo³

After having described the features, the modifications introduced in both tools to achieve the integration are now explained.

4.1   Modifications in ARTICo³ Design Flow

The ARTICo³ toolchain relies on a set of python and Tcl scripts to automatize the implementation of the desired project. These scripts define the design flow and, as such, have been modified to introduce IMPRESS within this flow. Apart from the design flow, the ARTICo³ toolchain provides a modular structure based on the use of system templates to contain information common to all projects targeting the same platform and implementation description. The IMPRESS design flow relies on three files with information relevant to all projects. A new template has been created to contain two of these files, which do not change between projects targeting the same platform implementation. The third file always has the same structure but contains information like project routes that is not common to all projects and, as such, needs to be generated by the toolchain at design time. The description of the information provided by the three files is as follows:

- Virtual Architecture: Includes information regarding the group of reconfigurable slots (that form a relocatable reconfigurable group), such as the FPGA coordinates of every slot in the group. A single relocatable bitstream is generated for every group of relocatable slots. These bitstreams are generated taking into account the interface distribution described in the next file.
- Virtual Interface: Describes the distribution of the interfaces to use with the static system in the boundaries of all the slots in a relocatable reconfigurable group. For every relocatable group, a virtual interface file is needed.
- Project info: This file includes all relevant information needed in a Vivado Project, such as the project name and location, and the root of all relevant files of every kernel and static system.

The first two files above described are project-independent and can be included in the template as they rely only on the platform and floorplanning description, being reusable in every hardware project. For the last file, the project info file, the information needed is extracted from the project configuration file the user has to provide in ARTICo³ using python scripts and written to the project info file of IMPRESS.

Having covered the integration at design level, modifications in the toolchain have been made to create a last extra file at design-time which is needed by IMPRESS during the runtime for correct slot placement when reconfiguring with relocatable bitstreams. This file includes the FPGA coordinates in a CSV style of every slot in every relocatable group. Finally, the ARTICo³ design flow has been modified by replacing the original placement and routing scripts with the scripts provided in IMPRESS.

With the aforementioned modifications, ARTICo^3 will generate and provide the user with:

- A single relocatable binary bitstream (.bin file) for every relocatable reconfigurable group, with the required endianness to be loaded from an SD card to the FPGA.
- The CSV file containing the FPGA coordinates of every slot.
- One symbolic link file per slot that redirects to the correct relocatable bitstream. These files are needed to provide compatibility with previous ARTICo^3 runtime libraries, which expect one partial bitstream file per hardware accelerator.
- The binary of the cross-compiled software application to be used in a Linux-based system.

4.2   Run-Time Reconfiguration Management of Relocatable Bitstreams

The ARTICo^3 runtime relies on a driver provided by Xilinx (FPGA manager) for their Linux distributions, designed to be used with full or partial bitstreams generated with Xilinx reconfiguration flow. However, the bitstreams generated by IMPRESS follow a custom-like composition with the intention of reducing bitstream sizes and augment relocability [20]. Differences with Xilinx-generated bitstreams include no commands, no clock information and no non-used configuration data. Therefore, changes in the driver become a necessity to adapt IMPRESS-generated bitstreams to the format expected by the Xilinx driver.

To begin with, depending on the size of the slots for which a relocatable bitstream is generated, these can occupy a certain number of full clock regions or end up occupying a clock region partially. In this last case, it is important, when configuring the FPGA, to not change the content of the remaining space in the clock region, as it could be in use by the static system. Moreover, in order to augment the relocability of the reconfigurable modules, no clock words are included in the bitstreams, as they introduce possible discontinuities in the design, so this information has to be extracted and composed at runtime. Finally, bitstreams generated by IMPRESS do not include the commands necessary by the reconfiguration flow and, as such, they have to be included by the driver at run-time. All these differences with a Xilinx full partial bitstream can be seen in Fig. 2.

To bridge the gap between Xilinx partial bitstreams and IMPRESS bitstreams, the reconfiguration instructions included in the driver have been modified to load a relocatable bitstream to a hardware accelerator slot:

1. Slot coordinates are passed as arguments to the driver in order to know where to place the bitstream.
2. A readback of the whole clock region is performed in order to obtain the configuration information of the remaining clock region space (not covered by the slot) and the clock configuration words of the whole region.

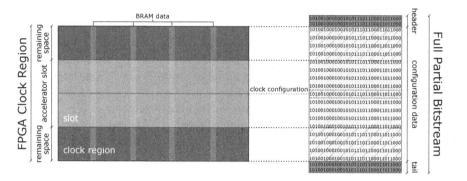

Fig. 2. Reconfigurable clock region with the partial bitstream extracted with IMPRESS

3. Another readback is performed in order to obtain the content of the BRAM memories for the whole clock region.
4. A new partial bitstream is composed for the whole clock region combining the to-be-loaded relocatable bitstream and the configuration and the content of the BRAMs obtained in the readbacks.
5. The needed commands for FPGA partial configuration for the desired reconfigurable region are added to the bitstream, which are the synchronization, configuration, and desynchronization commands (header and tail in Fig. 2).
6. The fully prepared bitstream is sent to the previous Xilinx driver reconfiguration flow for FPGA reconfiguration.

5   Model-Based Design of Hardware Accelerators

Model-based design is an efficient way to design complex embedded systems, supporting all the required steps from requirements specification to hardware implementation. Model-based design methodologies rise the level of abstraction during the whole design process, eliminating the use of handwritten text documents, such as source code or technical reports, as the basic mechanism to transfer project information. Instead, Model-based design substitute them with visual inspection, simulation of models and formal verification techniques, which are easier to understand, update and maintain.

Model-based design methodologies are supported by tools, such as Matlab-Simulink, which have been extended together with FPGA vendors with support for the design of hardware accelerators, directly from block-based descriptions. *System Generator* and *Model Composer* are good representatives of this approach. However, none of these commercial tools provide support for the generation of dynamically reconfigurable accelerators. This enforces developers to combine these technologies manually, which is translated in an increased complexity and cost.

For these reasons, an integrated solution is provided in this paper offering support for the direct generation of hardware accelerators, from Simulink, to

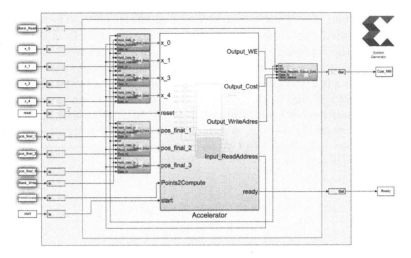

Fig. 3. Structure of the ARTICo^3 Accelerators with the automatic wrapper created in Simulink

ARTICo^3, in such a way that the input/output memory banks required when creating ARTICo^3 compliant accelerators are automatically created by a Matlab script integrated in Simulink, given two parameters describing the required number of input and output ports for the accelerator. The resulting architecture is shown in Fig. 3. The proposed script also creates both input and output Finite State Machines (FSM) controlling the data transference between the accelerators and the ARTICo^3 data delivery infrastructure.

Once the ARTICo^3 wrapper logic is automatically created, they can describe the user logic of the accelerator by using Simulink modules. Once the design has been implemented and verified within the Matlab framework, System Generator automatically provides the VHDL files including all the interface and control logic, in a transparent way to the user. From these files, the logic of the accelerator can be automatically extracted and integrated with the IMPRESS plus ARTICo^3 toolchain described in this paper. This integrated effort provides new ways to increase the efficiency when designing reconfigurable systems.

6   Experimental Results

To evaluate the productivity gain obtained by the advanced features for reconfigurable multi-accelerator systems, several experiments have been carried out targeting the xc7z020clg400-1 SoC (Digilent Pynq board). These experiments have been carried out using the design implementation example shown in Fig. 4, with the matmul kernel provided as an ARTICo^3 example in its open-source repository as the accelerator.[3] In this design, only four slots are available to

---

[3] https://github.com/des-cei/artico3.

allocate up to four reconfigurable accelerators simultaneously. The advantage of having generated this system with IMPRESS is that slots from 0 to 2 are relocatable, so the bitstream generated from Fig. 4b can be allocated in any of them. As a consequence, the memory footprint is reduced in two ways: 2× (1 bitstream for slots 0–2 and 1 bitstream for slot 3, instead of 4 bitstreams) due to relocation, and 2.27× due to the runtime composition approach (Subsect. 4.2), reducing the total memory footprint by 4.54×. Using this design, the experiments carried out are divided into design implementation (bitstream generation for each hardware kernel) and FPGA reconfiguration (using the new run-time reconfiguration management).

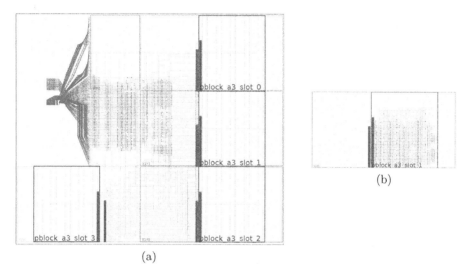

Fig. 4. (a): ARTICo^3 static design implementation for the xc7z020clg400-1 chip. (b): matmul IMPRESS-generated accelerators.

Implementation time has been measured with four different kernels taking into account the time elapsed by the toolchain to generate the necessary bitstreams. These results can be found in Table 1, which compares ARTICo^3 implementation with the integration of IMPRESS and ARTICo^3. ARTICo^3-only implementations can be divided into the generation of the static system bitstream and the partial bitstreams, even though the static system has to be always generated together with the partial bitstreams. This is not the case when using IMPRESS. The static system has to be generated only once for a given platform and floorplanning (i.e., ARTICo^3 template), and afterwards only the relocatable partial bitstreams need to be generated, regardless of the kernel to implement. As such, time improvements in Table 1 have been calculated taking into account the full design time with ARTICo^3 and the time elapsed only to generate the relocatable slots for each kernel with IMPRESS and ARTICo^3. It is important to highlight that ARTICo^3 total time also takes into account the static architecture block design (BD) generation corresponding to the template in use (i.e., the total number of slots), which is not included in the static and slots implementation times.

Table 1. Design implementation time (s) for Zynq-7000 using Xilinx Vivado 2017.3. and ARTICo^3 open-source kernels.

Kernel	ARTICo^3				IMPRESS + ARTICo^3		Speed-up
	BD	Static	Slots	Total	Total	Kernel design	
addvector	30.841	336.974	103.790	**471.605**	419.997	**175.691**	**2.68×**
inout	28.922	326.650	111.435	**467.007**	406.473	**160.793**	**2.90×**
matmul	31.102	347.929	171.727	**550.758**	453.977	**207.430**	**2.66×**
matmul_fp	29.604	474.484	272.199	**776.287**	511.016	**262.333**	**2.96×**

Table 2. Partial bitstreams reconfiguration times (ms) for Zynq-7000.

	ARTICo^3	IMPRESS + ARTICo^3	Improvement
1 acc	25.223	23.147	9.0%
2 acc	49.937	47.088	6.1%
3 acc	75.403	74.819	0.8%
4 acc	101.412	98.926	2.5%

The second round of experiments aims to compare bitstream programming times to the FPGA at runtime, which have been obtained different amounts of hardware accelerators (from 1 to 4). These results can be found in Table 2 together with the slight improvements provided by the new reconfiguration flow. These improvements are a consequence of the lower memory usage of IMPRESS bitstreams. Even though configuration and BRAM readbacks are necessary to complete the bitstreams, the amount of memory, and therefore bits to send to the FPGA, is less than half of Xilinx-generated partial bitstreams, as these last bitstreams also include a first erasing of configuration and BRAM memory data.

Finally, to illustrate the flexibility gained in the slot distribution by the usage of IMPRESS, a design is shown in Fig. 5. The higher flexibility enables the user to configure FPGA slots to fit more than one per clock region (two slots per clock region in this case), thus adapting the granularity of the RRs to the size of the accelerators. Notice that only two relocatable bitstreams are needed for this design, one for slots 0 to 5, and another one for slots 6 and 7. Therefore, the total bitstream memory footprint is less than a Xilinx-generated partial bitstream spanning a single clock region.

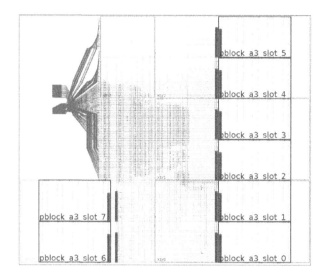

Fig. 5. FPGA slot distribution with two slots per clock region

7 Conclusions

This paper shows an efficient reconfiguration framework for building reconfigurable multi-accelerator systems in Xilinx series 7 FPGAs resulting from the integration of ARTICo[3] and IMPRESS. The integration of both tools decouples the implementation of reconfigurable accelerators from the static architecture, which is pre-implemented once. This way, the user just has to build the reconfigurable accelerators, which results in implementation times that are up to 2.96× times better in a Zynq xc7z020clg400-1 with four reconfigurable regions. Moreover, relocation capabilities provided by IMPRESS reduce the memory footprint up to 4.54× times. The flexibility of the design has also been enhanced, allowing to stack reconfigurable regions in the same clock region. A new reconfiguration engine has been implemented as a Linux driver for downloading IMPRESS-generated partial bitstreams to the FPGA. Despite having to perform a readback of the resources and bitstream recombination before downloading it to the FPGA, the reconfiguration time has been slightly reduced. Moreover, to ease the design of reconfigurable systems, model-based design of ARTICo[3] accelerators with Simulink is now supported. Therefore, the new reconfiguration framework improves key issues of FPGA development as long implementation times and ease-of-design.

Acknowledgment. This work has received funding from the European Union's Horizon 2020 research and innovation programme under grant agreement No. 732105 (CERBERO Project).

References

1. Partial Reconfiguration User Guide. Technical report UG909, Xilinx, April 2018
2. Intel Stratix 10 Hard Processor System Technical Reference Manual. Technical report s105_v4, Intel, May 2019
3. Intel® FPGA SDK for OpenCL™ Pro Edition. Technical report, Version 19.3, Intel, September 2019
4. SDAccel Environment User Guide. Technical report UG1023, Xilinx, January 2019
5. Versal: The First Adaptive Compute Acceleration Platform (ACAP). Technical report, Xilinx, September 2019
6. Zynq UltraScale+ Device Technical Reference Manual. Technical report UG1085, Xilinx, Rev. 1.9, January 2019
7. Agne, A., et al.: ReconOS: an operating system approach for reconfigurable computing. IEEE Micro **34**(1), 60–71 (2014). https://doi.org/10.1109/MM.2013.110
8. Putnam, A., et al.: A reconfigurable fabric for accelerating large-scale datacenter services. SIGARCH Comput. Archit. News **42**(3), 13–24 (2014). https://doi.org/10.1145/2678373.2665678. http://doi.acm.org/10.1145/2678373.2665678
9. Canis, A., et al.: LegUp: an open-source high-level synthesis tool for FPGA-based processor/accelerator systems. ACM Trans. Embed. Comput. Syst. **13**(2), 24:1–24:27 (2013). https://doi.org/10.1145/2514740. http://doi.acm.org/10.1145/2514740
10. Kintali, K., Gu, Y.: Model-based design with Simulink, HDL coder, and Xilinx system generator for DSP (2012). Mathworks white paper
11. Koch, D., et al.: Partial reconfiguration on FPGAs in practice - tools and applications. In: ARCS 2012, pp. 1–12 (2012)
12. Koch, D.: Partial Reconfiguration on FPGAs: Architectures, Tools and Applications. LNEE, vol. 153. Springer, New York (2012). https://doi.org/10.1007/978-1-4614-1225-0
13. Nane, R., et al.: A survey and evaluation of FPGA high-level synthesis tools. IEEE Trans. Comput. Aided Des. Integr. Circuits Syst. **35**(10), 1591–1604 (2016). https://doi.org/10.1109/TCAD.2015.2513673
14. Rodríguez, A., Valverde, J., Portilla, J., Otero, A., Riesgo, T., De la Torre, E.: FPGA-based high-performance embedded systems for adaptive edge computing in cyber-physical systems: the ARTICo^3 framework. Sensors **18**(6) (2018). https://doi.org/10.3390/s18061877. http://www.mdpi.com/1424-8220/18/6/1877
15. Sundararajan, P.: High performance computing using FPGAs. Technical report, Xilinx, September 2010
16. Tessier, R., Pocek, K., DeHon, A.: Reconfigurable computing architectures. Proc. IEEE **103**(3), 332–354 (2015). https://doi.org/10.1109/JPROC.2014.2386883
17. Trimberger, S.M.S.: Three ages of FPGAs: a retrospective on the first thirty years of FPGA technology: this paper reflects on how Moore's law has driven the design of FPGAs through three epochs: the age of invention, the age of expansion, and the age of accumulation. IEEE Solid-State Circuits Mag. **10**(2), 16–29 (2018). https://doi.org/10.1109/MSSC.2018.2822862
18. Waldrop, M.M.: The chips are down for Moore's law. Nat. News **530**(7589), 144 (2016)

19. Williams, R.S.: What's next? [The end of Moore's law]. Comput. Sci. Eng. **19**(2), 7–13 (2017). https://doi.org/10.1109/MCSE.2017.31
20. Zamacola, R., Martínez, A.G., Mora, J., Otero, A., de La Torre, E.: IMPRESS: automated tool for the implementation of highly flexible partial reconfigurable systems with Xilinx Vivado. In: 2018 International Conference on ReConFigurable Computing and FPGAs (ReConFig), pp. 1–8, December 2018. https://doi.org/10.1109/RECONFIG.2018.8641703

Chisel Usecase: Designing General Matrix Multiply for FPGA

Bruno Ferres$^{(\boxtimes)}$, Olivier Muller, and Frédéric Rousseau

Univ. Grenoble Alpes, CNRS, Grenoble INP, TIMA, 38000 Grenoble, France
{bruno.ferres,olivier.muller,frederic.rousseau}@univ-grenoble-alpes.fr

Abstract. To ease developers work in an industry where FPGA usage is constantly growing, we propose an alternative methodology for architecture design. Targeting FPGA boards, we aim at comparing implementations on multiple criteria. We implement it as a tool flow based on Chisel, taking advantage of high level functionalities to ease circuit design, evolution and reutilization, improving designers productivity.

We target a Xilinx VC709 board and propose a case study on General Matrix Multiply implementation using this flow, which demonstrates its usability with performances comparable to the state of the art, as well as the genericity one can benefit from when designing an application-specific accelerator. We show that we were able to generate, simulate and synthesize 80 different architectures in less than 24 h, allowing different trade-offs to be quickly and easily studied, from the most performant to the less costly, to easily comply with integration constraints.

Keywords: Chisel · FPGA · GEMM · Methodology

1 Introduction

As FPGA usage for application acceleration increases in the industry, notably in the domain of Cloud computing [3,7], RTL based design methodology - *i.e.* the standard methodology in industry - can be questioned on criteria such as efficiency, reusability, or accessibility.

The last decade has witnessed the appearance of new technologies easing hardware development, with higher levels of abstraction. The most known of those are High Level Synthesis, which goal is to bring the power of dedicated hardware acceleration to hardware-agnostic software developers. Nevertheless, HLS still has to cope with some flaws, including fine tuning on the code to infer efficient hardware, as well as lack of control on the generated hardware.

On the other hand, more hardware aware initiatives have appeared in the scientific community, like Chisel [2]. Chisel (Constructing Hardware In a Scala Embedded Language) is an open source Scala based language dedicated to hardware generation, with high level programming functionalities, and an ever growing community. It can be used to generate Verilog code, insuring compatibility

Grenoble INP—Institute of Engineering Univ. Grenoble Alpes.

© Springer Nature Switzerland AG 2020
F. Rincón et al. (Eds.): ARC 2020, LNCS 12083, pp. 61–72, 2020.
https://doi.org/10.1007/978-3-030-44534-8_5

with the standard flow, and ease design reutilisation thanks to the software constructs it embeds.

Google used `Chisel` for the design of their Edge TPU [1], and two RISC-V implementations have been proposed - **Rocket Chip** and **BOOM** - showing that the initiative can be integrated in both industrial and academic worlds. Works like [8] showed that `Chisel` can be used to explore different implementations of a circuit, here designed for BLAS (Basic Linear Algebra Subroutines) dot product acceleration.

BLAS introduces a set of linear algebra operations that can be used to evaluate implementation performances on this kind of applications [5]. In particular, it includes the General Matrix Multiply (GEMM) algorithm, a highly indicative application for all algebra computations [9], which has been deployed to various platforms before, including FPGA [4] and GPU [6]. GEMM is usually implemented with variations on the type and length of elements used, SGEMM and DGEMM respectively representing simple and double precision floating points, and other implementations targeting fixed point or integer representations.

This paper introduces a methodology for designing, testing and evaluating an application using `Chisel`, demonstrating its usage on a GEMM case study. Through this usecase, we show that our methodology allows to deeply control the generated hardware, producing accelerators that are not only comparable to the state of the art, but behave as they are designed to. Resource usage can be fully explained by targeted architecture, as no hardware inference has to be made by the compile pass. On the other hand, this flow allows to easily explore multiple architectures, studying the influence of application and target parameters on the produced designs. It enables changing the type and width of the operands, the capacities of communication or even the dimension of the applicative problem. Section 2 introduces the aim and steps of this methodology, while Sect. 3 demonstrates its usage on a GEMM usecase. Section 4 presents the results of this usecase, as well as the functionalities of our tool flow, and Sect. 5 discusses the contribution of our work.

2   High Level Methodology

To efficiently implement an application, one must take into account the application temporal behavior, as well as the environment target, in order to take advantage of the available resources. For example, targeting a FPGA requires the developer to consider the different kind of memory and computational resources embedded, the communication links, the reachable clock frequency, and other factors that will impact the choices of implementations.

On the other hand, to maximize the reusability of the developed design, you need to think about genericity before implementation, so generated designs can be adapted to new implementation constraints if needed, including target change.

This section describes the chosen technology for our methodology, as well as its steps, from application and target specificities to implementation.

2.1   High Level Description

To improve productivity when it comes to hardware development, developers must be able to define architectures in a generic way, to be able to generate different implementations by varying application specific and non-specific parameters (*e.g.* I/O size, element type, ...). Such generic implementation would allow to explore different trade-offs, and be able to suggest the most efficient architecture, the most performant or the less costly, for example.

To do so, we choose to use `Chisel` in our architecture generator flow, since the language offers higher level generic features, compared to the ones proposed by standard RTL languages (such as Verilog, SystemVerilog or VHDL).

Replacing RTL. Although `Chisel` remains a RTL language, we identified three main features of it that can ease the development of such generator, compared to standard RTL languages such as VHDL or Verilog.

Table 1 compares `Chisel` and standard RTL features when it comes to parametrized design generation. We can notice that the third feature - high level generation - is also available in both Verilog and VHDL languages, but that the two other features require external tools and complex constructs to be included in these languages.

Table 1. Feature comparison between `Chisel` and standard RTL languages for design generation

Chisel programming feature	RTL equivalent (Verilog and/or VHDL)
Type genericity	Black boxing type specific operators + string replacement in RTL code (*i.e.* using `sed`) *N.B.* `generic` can be used for width genericity only
Procedural programming	Multiple version of the same code to change functionalities and/or behavior
High level generation	`for` or `generate` loops `if` statements

HLS vs `Chisel`. Choosing `Chisel` over standard RTL languages for design implementation can thus be motivated by a need for higher abstraction level when it comes to hardware development.

However, as stated in introduction, High Level Synthesis technology aims at easing accelerators development by synthesizing algorithmic description to hardware circuit, meaning that it is a good candidate for increasing developers productivity, as well as easing design reusability. Yet, HLS requires, by design, inference from the compilation tool to generate functioning circuits. This means that one can not control easily the hardware generated, which allows software or application developers to use it with no hardware knowledge, but also means that experienced hardware developers can not directly control the generation flow, and can only try to tune the code and the tool to orientate the compilation toward an acceptable architecture.

Zhao et al. [11] state that HLS generated circuits can be compared to RTL written ones, but only with hard code discipline and fine pragma tuning. It can be complex, and might need to be repeated each time you change the generation constraints, meaning that evolving your design can be time consuming.

Since we aim at reusing code and generating multiple accelerators with different constraints, we chose to use the open-source, highly promising technology of `Chisel`.

2.2   From Application to Architecture

Using a language like `Chisel`, we propose a more generic development methodology, relying on hardware knowledge about the chosen target family (*e.g.* does it propose external memory, which kind of computing units are available, ...), and an architectural study of the application. This methodology does not require specific adjustment of code for a particular target board, but rather a generic design for a class of target, making it more **target-agnostic**.

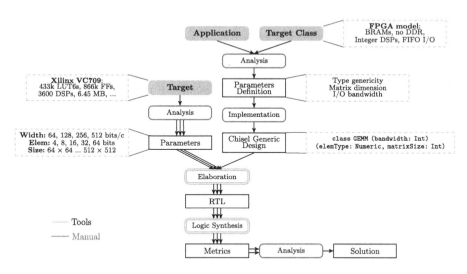

Fig. 1. Proposed methodology for design development. Dashed rectangles presents an example of application to the GEMM usecase.

Figure 1 presents this methodology. As can be observed, we consider three entry points when implementing an application to dedicated hardware: obviously, the **target** and the **application** itself, but also the **target class**, which is defined by generic characteristics we aim at using for this specific application (*e.g.* memory type and capacity, available operators, communication links, ...).

To use this methodology, one has to distinguish two main steps: implementing a generic design of the application using `Chisel`, and instantiating this design with parameter variations for a particular target. Doing this, the generic design - that uses some particular constructs, like embedded memory or DSP units - can be used to implement the application on various boards which includes those constructs. The methodology needs 3 main manual steps:

- Analysis of both application and target class, to define the parameters used for circuit parametrization
- Implementation of a generic architecture using `Chisel`
- Analysis of the target board, to define the parameter sets used for architecture instantiation, with respect to the target characteristics (*e.g.* the band width, the problem dimension, ...)

Elaboration and logic synthesis steps are done automatically, for each parameter set defined in this third step.

3 Methodology Usecase

In order to demonstrate both usability and advantages of the proposed methodology, we defined and implemented a generic GEMM architecture. It illustrates how preliminary reflexions on application and target class - communication model, available memory and computing units, temporal behavior, ... - can, with the help of `Chisel`, improve both productivity and code reusability with generic designs.

GEMM. The General Matrix Multiply (GEMM) algorithm is a generalization of the matrix product algorithm. Let A, B and C be square matrices of dimension $n \times n$ ($\mathcal{M}_n$), and $(\alpha, \beta) \in \mathbf{N}^2$. GEMM is defined as the following f function:

$$\begin{aligned} f : \mathbf{N} \times \mathbf{N} \times \mathcal{M}_n \times \mathcal{M}_n \times \mathcal{M}_n &\to \mathcal{M}_n \\ (\alpha, \beta, A, B, C) &\mapsto \alpha \cdot A \times B + \beta \cdot C \end{aligned} \tag{1}$$

Target Characteristics. For this implementation, we assume that the developer is targeting Xilinx FPGA technology. More precisely, this means that the developed design can take advantage of embedded operators for multiplication (*DSP block*) and **only** embedded memory (*Block RAMs*).

Application Study. GEMM computation complexity is $O(n^3)$ while its communication complexity is only $O(n^2)$. Since, in a generic context, matrices need to be sent to the design anyway, we can assume that $O(n^2)$ - *i.e.* the communication complexity - is a temporal complexity bound.

If one wants to reach this bound, it means that the implemented design needs to be able to compute matrix product in a temporal complexity of n^2. This defines the architecture parallelism level, as it requires to compute n scalar products ($\sum_{k=0}^{n} a_{i,k} \times b_{k,j}$ for $j \in [\![0; n-1]\!]$) in parallel to comply with it.

Figure 2 introduces the targeted temporal behavior for the implementation. It has been defined with respect to software considerations, as matrices are not interleaved nor transformed, except for B which has to be transposed for by-column access. Matrices are sent by blocks of size b (as defined in Sect. 3).

As one can observe on the Fig. 2, the input bus utilization is almost optimal (*i.e.* the input bus is almost used for the whole computation time), as results can be computed on-the-fly while A matrix is being streamed. This way, we can ensure that the induced design will be communication efficient.

Fig. 2. Targeted chronogram for GEMM efficient implementation (Eq. 1)

Application-Specific Parameters. With such temporal behavior, we can compute the maximum throughput of a design implementing it, as a function of

- b the input (or output) bandwidth (in bits/cycle)
- f the clock frequency (in Hz)
- e the matrix element size (in bits)
- n the matrix dimension

We assume that a GEMM kernel performs $\rho = 2 \times n^3$ operations [10].

Let Δ_c be the number of cycles needed to compute the result of the GEMM algorithm - *i.e.* the delta cycle between sending α coefficient and receiving the last bit of the result matrix. We can state that $\Delta_c \geq 3 \times n^2 \times \frac{b}{e}$, $\frac{b}{e}$ being the number of elements sent per cycle, as three matrices must be sent.

Thus, the theoretical maximum throughput T, in number of operation per second (OPs), is given by

$$T = \frac{\rho \times f}{\Delta_c} \leq \frac{2 \times n^3 \times f}{3 \times n^2 \times \frac{b}{e}} = \frac{2}{3} \times \frac{f \times n \times e}{b} \qquad (2)$$

GEMM Parametrization. As specified in Sect. 2, the developer must think its architecture genericity before starting the implementation, to allow both exploration and design reutilization.

For GEMM application, we decided, after application and target class analysis, to define three parameters according to Sect. 3:

- b – bus bandwidth for input/output
- n – size of matrices
- type of elements (which bitwidth is defined as e).

4 Results

To study the usability and performances of our methodology, we implemented it as a tool flow, and used it to analyze and compare multiple GEMM architectures. This way, we can illustrate both hardware controlability and generation abilities of our methodology. We generate 80 different architectures, varying input bandwidth b (64, 128, 256 and 512 bits/cycle), element bitwidth e (4, 8, 16, 32 and 64 bits) and matrix dimension n (64×64, 128×128, 256×256 and 512×512), and we study the impact of those parameters on the performance and resource usage of generated designs. The architectures are generated, simulated and synthesized in less than 24 h, thanks to our tool flow (see Fig. 1).

4.1 Experimental Setup

For the experimentation, we targeted a **Xilinx VC709** board which includes Block RAMs and integer DSPs, as specified in Sect. 3. It embeds a xc7vx690 FPGA with 433k LUT6s, 866 FFs, 3600 DSPs and 1470 BRAMs (6.45 MB).

We developed a tool flow implementing the methodology proposed in Sect. 2, based on Chisel (latest 3.2 version) as entry point to generate multiple Verilog designs with respect to the parameters defined in Sect. 3. The flow simulates generated designs behavior using verilator to ensure functionality, comparing it to a software reference defined in Scala. It also uses simulation to extract design latency Δ_c as defined in the temporal behavior model (Fig. 2). After generation and simulation steps, we use Xilinx vivado (2017.3 version) to synthesize designs and extract performance and resource metrics. For performance evaluation, we use the estimated post-synthesis clock frequency and the simulation latency. We evaluate resource usage (LUT, Flip Flop, DSP and BRAM usage) thanks to post-synthesis resource report. All results presented in this section are given after vivado synthesis step.

Remark: We are only considering designs that can physically fit for this section, implying that Tables 2, 3 and Fig. 3a only include those designs. Figure 3b represents non-fittable designs as hatched.

4.2 Control of Generated Hardware

This section presents our designs achieved performance, demonstrating that this methodology allows to control generated accelerators composition.

GEMM Implementation. As stated in Sect. 1, GEMM algorithm can be implemented using various types and precision, SGEMM and DGEMM (using respectively IEEE-754 simple and double precision) are the most used version, as it has been widely used for performance comparison.

However, since we are targeting Xilinx FPGAs, which does not include dedicated floating point units, we chose to implement a fixed-point GEMM version here. Since the design generator includes type parameters, one could - with few changes to the control flow - target SGEMM and/or DGEMM variants once he implemented basic floating operations on Xilinx boards, as stated in Sect. 2.1.

Impact of Type Precision. Table 2 presents the influence of type precision on achieved throughput for GEMM implementation. For each element bitwidth e, we selected the most performant generated design, $i.e.$ the design that offers the higher throughput, with the generation parameters (b, n) associated. We compared the throughput estimation (based on simulation) with the maximal theoretical throughput as defined in Eq. (2), indicating the functioning frequency of the generated designs in the last column, for information purpose.

By computing the theoretical differentials between achieved and theoretical throughput, we can note that generated designs achieve at least 92% of maximal throughput - for the 8 bits version - meaning that the input bus utilization is almost maximal, and that the behavior can be finely controlled from architecture design to generation.

We showed that our flow can be used to design, implement and analyze designs with high controlability on generated hardware, and demonstrated it on an analysis of type precision influence on the performances of GEMM implementations.

Table 2. Impact of element bitwidth on GEMM throughput.

Element (e)	I/O (b)	Size (n)	Throughput (GOps)		Frequency (MHz)
			Achieved	Theoretical (2)	
4	512	128	3680	3844	352.00
8	512	64	934	1016	372.72
16	128	512	700	701	256.74
32	128	256	226	227	331.34
64	128	256	66	68	197.78

4.3   Architecture Exploration: Dimensioning the Application

We have shown that type precision has a considerable impact on the achievable throughput of generated designs. As type precision also impacts applicative performance metrics a developer can not always act on the type precision, that can be fixed by application specific needs.

In this section, we chose to target 32 bits fixed point GEMM implementation, though it is not comparable to SGEMM subroutine on 32 bits floating points because of the complexity of floating point operations (even with dedicated DSPs), to demonstrate the ability of our methodology to explore multiple parameter sets with no changes to the original `Chisel` description.

Figures 3a and b respectively compare generated designs throughput and efficiency for various sizes of input matrices, and various I/O bandwidths. Efficiency e is defined as $\frac{\rho}{f \times \Delta_c} \times \frac{1}{\|\%resource\|} = \frac{2 \times n^3}{f \times \Delta_c \times \|\%resource\|}$, $i.e.$ $\frac{performance}{resource}$ ratio[1], unified with respect to computational complexity specified in Sect. 3. Using a n^3 factor allows to compare solution of different dimensions, since computing GEMM in $\mathcal{M}_n$ space is equivalent to 8 computations in $\mathcal{M}_{\frac{n}{2}}$. We can observe that for 32 bits implementations, the most efficient version (Fig. 3b) is to operate on matrix kernels of size 256×256, using 2×128 bits/cycle I/O, with an achieved throughput of 224 GOP/s - among the 80 architectures generated. For this design, clock frequency reach 331.4 MHz, the theoretical optimal bit rate is thus 2.8 GB/s. On the other hand, Fig. 3a shows that the most performant design is to operate on kernels of size 128×128, with 2×128 bits/cycle I/O, achieving a throughput of 226 GOP/s.

By generating and comparing those GEMM architectures, we showed that our generation flow allows to determine which architecture is the most performant or the most efficient, with respect to constraints one might have on integration.

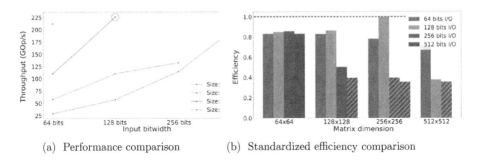

(a) Performance comparison   (b) Standardized efficiency comparison

Fig. 3. Metric comparison on 32 bits GEMM versions

4.4 Existing Solutions

GEMM implementations have been widely used to compare platform performances, as well as implementation choices. We propose to compare our implementations to GEMM instances on various platforms.

---

[1] Resource metric is defined as the maximum usage percentage for the 4 considered resources: *LUTs*, *Flip Flops*, *BRAMs* and *DSPs*.

fBLAS [4] implements both SGEMM and DGEMM variants, using HLS on two Intel Altera FPGAs. It is important to note that Intel Altera FPGAs embed dedicated floating point DSP, while Xilinx FPGAs does not include any floating point dedicated units.

Garg et al. [6] propose hybrid CPU-GPU SGEMM and DGEMM implementations based on Intel Ivy Bridge and AMD Richland platforms.

Our custom solutions present the most performant designs we generated for precision on 16, 32 and 64 bits. As VC709 target does not include floating point units, SGEMM and DGEMM will be compared respectively to fixed point solutions on 32 and 64 bits. We also choose to study results on 16 bits fixed point, since applicative accuracy needs might be compatible with lower precision type.

For each solution in Table 3, we can observe different implementations - variation of platform, target and type precision - and the associated achieved performances, given as implementation throughput. We can see that both our 32 and 64 bits custom versions are comparable in term of performance with the hybrid solution of [6], and with the fBLAS solution on Intel Altera Arria 10, if a fixed point solution is acceptable for a given application needs. Stratix 10 board being way wider than a VC709, we can not compare solutions fairly.

Table 3. Throughput for GEMM implementations on different platforms

Solution	Platform	Target	Precision	Throughput
Custom[a]	FPGA	VC709	16 bits	700 GOps
			32 bits	226 GOps
			64 bits	68 GOps
fBLAS [4]	FPGA	Arria 10	32 bits	200 GFlops
			64 bits	25 GFlops
		Stratix 10	32 bits	750 GFlops
			64 bits	75 GFlops
Hybrid [6]	CPU-only	Ivy Bridge	32 bits	170 GFlops
		Richland	32 bits	80 GFlops
			64 bits	40 GFlops
	GPU-only	Ivy Bridge	32 bits	140 GFlops
		Richland	32 bits	274 GFlops
			64 bits	27.3 GFlops
	CPU + GPU	Ivy Bridge	32 bits	235 GFlops
		Richland	32 bits	274 GFlops
			64 bits	57.4 GFlops

[a]Fixed point precision is used instead of floating point, as stated earlier.

4.5 Analysis and Contribution

With those experiments, we show that with a tool flow based on `Chisel` and a particular methodology, we are able to easily define a generic GEMM accelerator kernel, which presents multiple advantages when compared to HLS generated or RTL written ones.

We demonstrate that using `Chisel` allows a high controlability on generated hardware, and that, with a sufficient knowledge on hardware development, one can easily describe a precise architecture, with no worry on which inferences the tool flow could make when generating the circuit.

We also show that using generic architectures can be useful when it comes to evaluation of parameters influences, and that using higher level of abstractions, hardware developers can easily compare architectural trade-offs for a given application, in order to take the best of the available resources.

5 Conclusion

In this paper, we introduce a design methodology associated to a toolflow that can be used to implement computation kernels on FPGAs with higher abstraction level.

We demonstrate the functionality of this new tool through a use case on GEMM algorithm, which is highly representative for all algebra computations. We show that we can define generic architecture descriptions with parametrization, thanks to `Chisel`, allowing architecture generation and comparison.

Generated GEMM implementations performances are comparable to designs generated with HLS methodology, as well as CPU and/or GPU solutions proposed in the literature.

We now aim at reusing developed GEMM kernels to implement efficient, configurable and highly generic CNNs using the presented framework.

We also want to implement other computation kernels to study influence of applications and target environments on resource usage and achieved performances.

References

1. Alon, E., Asanović, K., Bachrach, J., Nikolić, B.: Invited: Open-Source EDA Tools and IP, A View from the Trenches, p. 3 (2019)
2. Bachrach, J., et al.: Chisel: constructing hardware in a Scala embedded language. In: Proceedings of the 49th Annual Design Automation Conference on - DAC 2012, San Francisco, California, p. 1216. ACM Press (2012)
3. Caulfield, A.M., et al.: A Cloud-Scale Acceleration Architecture, p. 13 (2016)
4. De Matteis, T., de Fine Licht, J., Hoefler, T.: FBLAS: streaming linear algebra on FPGA. arXiv:1907.07929 [cs], August 2019
5. Dongarra, J.J., Du Croz, J., Hammarling, S., Duff, I.S.: A set of level 3 basic linear algebra subprograms. ACM Trans. Math. Softw. **16**(1), 1–17 (1990)

6. Garg, R., Hendren, L.: A portable and high-performance general matrix-multiply (GEMM) library for GPUs and single-chip CPU/GPU systems. In: 2014 22nd Euromicro International Conference on Parallel, Distributed, and Network-Based Processing, Torino, Italy, pp. 672–680. IEEE, February 2014

7. Ouyang, J., Lin, S., Qi, W., Wang, Y., Yu, B., Jiang, S.: SDA: software-defined accelerator for large-scale DNN systems. In: 2014 IEEE Hot Chips 26 Symposium (HCS), Cupertino, CA, USA, pp. 1–23. IEEE, August 2014

8. Koenig, J., Biancolin, D., Bachrach, J., Asanovic, K.: A hardware accelerator for computing an exact dot product. In: 2017 IEEE 24th Symposium on Computer Arithmetic (ARITH), London, United Kingdom, pp. 114–121. IEEE, July 2017

9. Pedram, A., Gerstlauer, A., van de Geijn, R.A.: A high-performance, low-power linear algebra core. In: ASAP 2011–22nd IEEE International Conference on Application-Specific Systems, Architectures and Processors, Santa Monica, CA, USA, pp. 35–42. IEEE, September 2011

10. Underwood, K.D., Hemmert, K.S.: Chapter 31 - The implications of floating point for FPGAs. In: Hauck, S., Dehon, A. (eds.) Reconfigurable Computing, pp. 671–695. Systems on Silicon, Morgan Kaufmann, Burlington (2008)

11. Zhao, Z., Hoe, J.C.: Using Vivado-HLS for structural design: a NoC case study. arXiv:1710.10290 [cs], October 2017

Cycle-Accurate Debugging of Embedded Designs Using Recurrent Neural Networks

Habib ul Hasan Khan[(⊠)], Ariel Podlubne, Gökhan Akgün, and Diana Göhringer

Technische Universitaet Dresden (TUD), Dresden, Germany
{habib.khan,ariel.podlubne,goekhan.akguen,
diana.goehringer}@tu-dresden.de

Abstract. This research work presents a methodology for debugging embedded designs by using recurrent neural networks. In this methodology, a cycle-accurate lossless debugging system with unlimited trace window is used for debugging. The lossless trace resembles a time data series. A recurrent neural network trained either through a golden reference or from the actual time series can be used to predict the incoming debugging data. A bug can be easily isolated based upon the discrepancy between the received and the predicted time series. This allows to draw conclusions to speed up the debugging process.

Keywords: Cycle-accurate · Device start and stop · Recurrent Neural Network

1 Introduction

Hardware designs are increasing in size and complexity with every passing day. Hence, effective techniques for post-silicon validation are required to ensure the correctness of the design functionality [1]. Hardware-based prototyping techniques result in a speed-up as compared to traditional simulation-based verification. However, the inherent invisibility of the hardware increased the debugging complexity when a problem is encountered. The visibility can be increased by the inclusion of scan or trace-based techniques. Still, the manual analysis of the massive amount of trace data is not time-efficient. During the post-silicon debugging process, the following two scenarios are of utmost concern:

- Diagnostic of the design to verify how closely it resembles with any available Golden Reference (GR).
- Design debugging when a reference behavior for the Design Under Test (DUT) is not available.

This research work presents an intrusive debugging technique which permits cycle-accurate lossless debugging by managing the clock of the DUT. Our proposed solution depends heavily on the Recurrent Neural Network (RNN) based machine learning technique for trace diagnostics as well as for bug identification even in the absence of a GR.

© Springer Nature Switzerland AG 2020
F. Rincón et al. (Eds.): ARC 2020, LNCS 12083, pp. 73–83, 2020.
https://doi.org/10.1007/978-3-030-44534-8_6

The main contributions of this paper are:

- Propose an RNN-based debugging methodology for identification of intermittent errors or outliers (or anomalies) in the post-silicon validation cycle when the GR is available.
- Show that the presented debugging methodology for identification of intermittent errors still works in the absence of the GR.

The rest of the paper is organized as follows. Section 2 presents related work. Section 3 discusses the proposed debugging methodology. In Sect. 4, the use case will be explained. Section 5 discusses the results. The paper is concluded in Sect. 6.

2 Related Work

Predictive analysis techniques can be integrated with post-silicon validation for anomaly detection. Machine learning can be utilized for detection of anomalies. i.e. any deviation from normal behavior. However, training data is needed for learning the correct behavior. Similarly, data prediction can also be utilized for design validation. The test data retrieved from the DUT is used as input to a machine learning algorithm which can then be employed to make predictions about the bugs occurring on new designs [2]. In [3], the authors proposed to increase the observability of the internal signals at the post silicon level through a learning algorithm. In [4], the author suggested to use data mining for pattern extraction. They further proposed to use the methodology for functional verification by using the data mining techniques. In [5], the authors suggested to utilize machine learning for automating the diagnosis of trace dump and bug localization.

In [6], the authors proposed that the time series data can be predicted by using an RNN. Cycle-accurate lossless trace dump resembles time series data. In [7], a methodology is presented which generates continuous stream of lossless trace data by automatically stopping the clock based upon trace buffer occupancy. Similar techniques can be utilized to generate lossless time series debugging trace. Hence, in this research work, an RNN based machine learning framework is presented which can be used for bug identification during the debugging process even in the absence of GR. To the best of our knowledge, it is the first approach in which an RNN has been employed for lossless cycle-accurate trace-dumps which can be extremely helpful for debug data prediction.

3 Cycle-Accurate Debugging by RNN

3.1 Design Methodology

In Integrated Logic Analyzer (ILA) based debugging methodologies, data is limited to the capacity of the trace buffers. Once they are full, data is transmitted to the terminal for analysis. However, data transfer rate limitation of the communication channel results in data loss. This loss forbids the use of trace data as a time series. Hence, a debugging system providing lossless trace data is needed because time series data prediction requires consecutive, evenly spaced observation samples.

In our proposed debugging methodology, it is suggested to stop the clock for the DUT when the trace buffers are full. The DUT is clocked again when data has been transmitted and the trace buffers are ready to receive the debugging data. This results in a cycle-accurate lossless debugging trace as shown in Fig. 1. In order to keep the resource utilization for the debugging system low, we utilize only 4 KB trace buffers. Hence, we monitor 16 signals simultaneously (with 32 bits each) resulting in 512 bits. However, all the signals required to be monitored are routed through the access network ensuring full visibility. Consequently, a synchronized output for all the available nodes connected to the access network can be observed through the selection register. This can be accomplished by running the test from time T0 (the starting time of the debugging session) when the signal set is changed. This technique ensures a completely synchronized state of all the monitored signals. A controlling processor is utilized to transmit the data from onboard trace buffers to the terminal through Ethernet. The lossless debugging data saved in the logged file on the terminal (PC) resembles a time data series which can be used to predict future samples by using RNN.

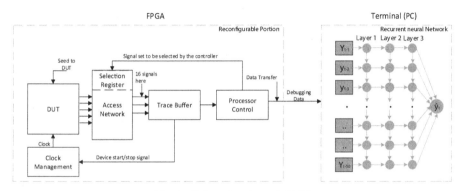

Fig. 1. Debugging through RNN

The authors in [8] compared the effect of different factors like seasonality, trend, randomness etc. on the accuracy of the time series prediction and pointed out that randomness has the biggest negative impact on prediction. They also highlighted that the accuracy decreased with an increase in forecasting horizon. Keeping in view the above two factors, we laid the following conditions upon the trace data to be debugable.

- The data should not be random. This can be ensured by checking the randomness using the Wald-Wolfowitz run tests [9] or any identical tests.
- Trace data should be covariance stationary. This implies that the time series data does not hold any hidden relationships between different time points and the behavior is stable. A statistical test such as Augmented Dickey-Fuller test (ADF) can be employed to get a good insight into the behavior of the data.
- The forecasting horizon should be minimum. The prediction of future samples can be performed with the following two options:

  – Train on $\{y_t, y_{t-1}, y_{t-2} \ldots\}$ to predict $\{y_{t+i}, \ for \ 1 \geq i \geq s \ holds \ for \ small \ s\}$. which means that using the previous samples to predict s number of samples.

– Train to predict $\{y_{t+1}\}$, *iterate to get* $\{y_{t+i}, \ for \ any \ i\}$.
  which means to use previous samples to predict one future sample.

We will follow the second option for this research work since extrapolating too far in the future is not recommended. Furthermore, training and testing is performed on (80%, 20%) basis respectively. In order to identify any overfitting, 5% of the training data, not seen by the RNN, is reserved for validation.

Our time-series prediction algorithm was implemented on the terminal (PC) by using RNN. RNNs are best suited for time series data prediction because of their ability to remember their inputs by making use of their memory. We used the sliding window method by using the data from previous 50 time steps to predict the value at the next time step hence requiring the width of first hidden layer to be 50. Using the previous samples, the trained RNN makes prediction for t + 1 sample. Hence, the RNN can be represented by the Eq. 3.1.

$$\hat{y}_t = \alpha_0 + \sum_{j=1}^{3} \alpha_j g \left(\beta_{0j} + \sum_{i=1}^{50} \beta_{ij} y_{t-i} \right) \tag{3.1}$$

Here y_{t-i} are the time lagged inputs and $\hat{y}_t$ is the predicted output. α_j and β_{ij} are the connection weights. α_0 and β_{0j} are the bias terms. g(x) is the activation function.

The error e_t between received y_t and predicted $\hat{y}_t$ at time t is:

$$e_t = y_t - \hat{y}_t \tag{3.2}$$

As the RNN is highly trained and cross-validated, assuming $e_t \approx 0$, the received input sample should be:

$$y_t \approx \hat{y}_t \tag{3.3}$$

which states that the predicted value is similar to the received sample and hence can be used to verify the received one. Similarly, the continuous stream of previous input samples can be used to predict the forthcoming sample iteratively.

However, when $e_t \napprox 0$, it indicates that the received and the predicted values do not coincide with one another highlighting the presence of a bug in either the trace data or the trained model itself. As the RNN is highly trained and the trace data observes the three conditions mentioned earlier, it can be assumed that the predicted value is correct thus highlighting the need to debug the identified bug at the indicated location. However, after analyzing the identified bug, if the trace data is found to be error-free; it points towards a discrepancy in the trained model. Hence the newly received error-free trace data can be used for further training of the RNN and subsequently the improved RNN can then be employed for debugging.

3.2   RNN Implementation

The proposed RNN comprises of 1-dimensional input layer, three hidden layers of sizes 50, 100, 50 and eventually a 1-dimensional output layer. The last layer is the dense layer because it is a feedforward case. The proposed neural network is based upon the Keras library [10] using tensor flow as the back-end. Mean squared error model was used to find the error during the forward propagation. The partial derivative of the error, adjusted through the back propagation process, was used by the Adam optimizer [11]. During our experimentation, we tried with different initial learning rates such as 0.001 and 0.0001. However, due to highly varying training dataset, we finally settled for 0.0001 which gave a good approximation of the function. Exponential decay rates for the estimates of first and second moments i.e. (mean and variance) were chosen to be 0.9 and 0.999, respectively [12].

In order to cater for exploding gradient problem, we used *Tanh* as the squashing function. We used LSTM so that it can memorize its past states as well. LSTM also gets rid of the vanishing gradient problem.

The RNN processes the trace data for training. The RNN can be trained based upon a GR for the specific DUT. However, in the absence of a GR, the neural network can be trained by the received trace acquired from the debugging system. It can use a portion of the data for training and validation. In this research work, we used 5% of the training data for validation to identify any overfitting. Once the data has been segregated into the training and validation datasets, the datasets are divided into batches i.e. the number of samples required by the network to perform a parameters update. We used a batch size of 64 for the current research work [13].

Moreover, sometimes, the loss function does not converge to a minimum defined value. In such cases, RNN should be trained using different optimizers and hyper parameters to find an optimized solution which results in a converging loss function.

4 Obstacle Avoidance as Use Case

The platform used is a 4 wheeled skid steer robot model simulated in Gazebo. Each wheel can be controlled independently resulting in a highly controllable platform. Incremental encoders attached to each motor and eight ultrasonic sensors for closed loop operation result in precise localization and environment sensing. Based upon the vehicle information, the control module calculates the control signal needed to maintain safe distance from the upcoming obstacle. The control signal is then sent to the actuation mechanism to divert the vehicle in order to avoid the obstacle. We used the robot for generating the time-series data and used its orientation as an input for our RNN.

The block diagram of the technique (Fig. 2) shows that the data from the ultrasonic sensors and encoders is sent to the controller to perceive the environment and compute corresponding control signals to avoid the obstacle. Subsequently, the linear and rotational velocity from the controller are transformed to right and left wheel velocity by using odometry model of the robot. Obstacle Avoidance (OA) algorithm uses this information along with data from the sensors to localize the robot. If the ultrasonic sensors do not sense any obstacle, the robot continues to move in its designated path. However, when an obstacle is sensed and the threshold distance between the robot and obstacle is reached, the robot stops at fixed distance from the obstacle. Then, it calculates the width of the obstacle through triangulation. It then follows the shorter path until it reaches the destination.

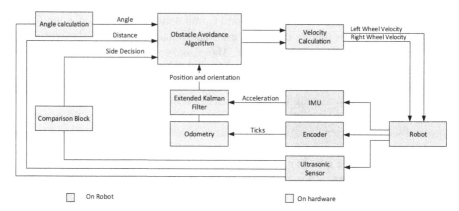

Fig. 2. Incorporation of Extended Kalman Filter with obstacle avoidance

Encoder and IMU sensors are utilized to determine the robot's position and orientation. However, such sensors may not give the exact position and orientation due to sensor errors. Hence, Extended Kalman Filter (EKF) is used to perform sensor data fusion in order to reduce the effect of such errors and better estimation of the optimal position and orientation of the robot. Integration between EKF and the OA algorithm is implemented as shown in Fig. 2. The data from an accelerometer, magnetometer and gyroscope is fused using EKF to have an optimal estimation of the position and orientation of the robot. Then, these estimated values are used to avoid the obstacle.

5   Results

The result section has been divided into three subsections. In the first subsection, the resource utilization for the proposed debugging system having unlimited trace window is presented. Then, the results of debugging using the proposed methodology is presented. Subsequently, the training requirements are discussed. The proposed methodology has been implemented on Digilent Zedboard having an XC7Z020-484 FPGA. Xilinx Vivado 2017.1 was used for designing the hardware. The RNN was implemented on the terminal (PC) having an Intel Core i7-6700 CPU running at 3.4 GHz and having 16 GB of RAM.

5.1   Resource Utilization

Resource utilization of the presented debugging methodology is shown in Fig. 3. It was noticed that the resource utilization is growing with an increase in debug window, as more BRAM blocks are required for trace buffers. Hence, the debugging system is synthesized with trace window of 64 samples. 16 signals are monitored with data width of 32 bits each. The resource utilization is compared with a similar research [7]. It is evident that the resources have been reduced to almost 2% of the available ones.

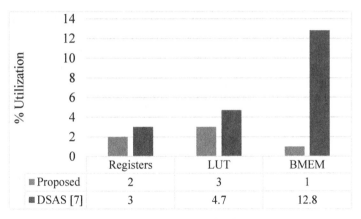

	Registers	LUT	BMEM
■ Proposed	2	3	1
■ DSAS [7]	3	4.7	12.8

Fig. 3. Resource utilization

5.2 Debugging Through RNNs

The OA algorithm was implemented in hardware. The controller, EKF, odometry calculation, comparison module etc. are some of the hardware implemented modules.

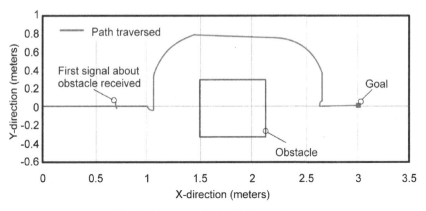

Fig. 4. Movement in the X, Y coordinates

As shown in Fig. 4, the robot continued to move in its designated path. However, when the ultrasonic sensors detected an obstacle, the robot stopped and then calculated the width of the obstacle through triangulation. It then decided to avoid the obstacle by following the shorter side. The robot then rotated 90° to avoid the obstacle and continued the process until it reached the other side of the obstacle. Then it followed its original path. The orientation of the robot is shown in Fig. 5. The time series data of the orientation is utilized to demonstrate the usage of the proposed RNN for debugging.

The lossless trace data logged by the proposed debugging system resembles a time data series. Hence, the RNN can be used to ease the debugging process. If a GR is available, the debug trace from the GR is used for training. Subsequently, the DUT trace data can be predicted using the trained RNN which can be used for bug identification. This methodology is explained in Sect. 5.2.1. However, in the absence of GR, the portion of the debug trace data generated by the DUT and known to be error free can be used for training the RNN. Then this trained RNN is used for predicting the upcoming debug data. This methodology will be presented in Sect. 5.2.2.

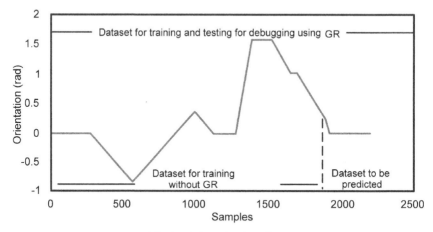

Fig. 5. Orientation in radians

5.2.1 Debugging Using GR

In the first experiment, we have a verified OA system which is used as a GR. We first programmed the robot to avoid the obstacle from the same start point and end goal as shown in Fig. 4. We collected the orientation data samples as shown in Fig. 5. After data collection, we checked the randomness using the Wald-Wolfowitz run test. Then, we performed ADF test to check for stationarity of the trace data. Once, the trace data qualified for use with RNN, we performed normalization during the data preparation phase. The data was then used to train the RNN. Subsequently, the trained RNN was used to predict the time data series generated by the DUT. The predicted data is de-normalized so that it can be compared with the debug trace data. Figure 6 shows the actual vs the predicted time series data. The red line shows the actual time series data and the green line in the figure shows the predicted data. As can be seen, the predicted data closely resembles the actual data. Hence, it can be assumed that the DUT resembles closely with the GR and is free from either functional or intermittent errors.

5.2.2 Debugging Without GR

The received lossless time series trace data can be used for RNN training if the GR is not available. However, the trace data used for training should be error free which can be ascertained through hardware checkers as suggested by Bertacco [14]. Moreover, the conditions stated in Sect. 3 should be fulfilled. For the current experiment, we used

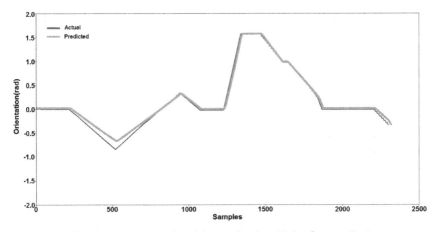

Fig. 6. Actual vs predicted time series data (Color figure online)

about 1800 samples for training as illustrated in Fig. 5. Then, we utilized the trained RNN for prediction. This predicted data is compared with the received trace data for bug identification as shown in Fig. 7. This eliminates the requirement of GR. The error generally resembles rarely occurring behavior i.e. intermittent or outlier. When an error occurs during the test phase, the RNN is not trained for this bug. Hence, it fails to predict the bug which can be easily isolated during the debugging process.

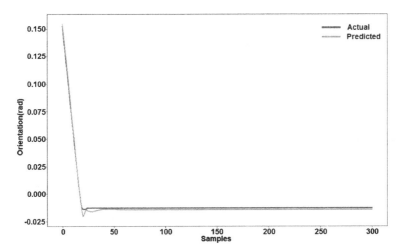

Fig. 7. Debugging without GR

In order to test the effectiveness of the proposed approach, a bug was introduced into the test data as shown in Fig. 8. As the RNN was trained based upon error free received data, it predicted well during the test phase. However, as it was not trained for the rarely occurring induced error, it failed to predict the data during the occurrence of error. This phenomenon is shown in Fig. 8 by a possible error. Whenever an intermittent error or bug, resembling an outlier behavior, is encountered during the test phase, a similar behavior is expected. Consequently, this phenomenon can be utilized in bug identification.

5.3 Training Dataset Requirement

The most important condition for training an RNN is the provision of the training data. The error in a DUT is considered to be random i.e. it can occur at any time. Hence, a large training dataset may not be available. This scenario is quite reasonable; because if training with small dataset can be performed, training with larger datasets will be definitely more accurate (assuming similar variance in both datasets).

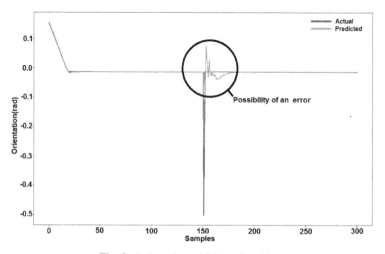

Fig. 8. Debugging with introduced bug

6 Conclusions

This research work presents a cycle accurate debugging technique using RNN. Our proposed solution depends heavily on machine learning techniques for trace diagnostics as well as for the bug identification. Results have shown that localizing potential bugs in the system can be done with or without the presence of a GR. This will help in problem identification and hence will increase time-efficiency.

The proposed methodology can be iterated to localize the bug. Once a bug has been identified in one of the debugged nodes, the nodes in its vicinity can be probed further to localize the bug.

Acknowledgements. This research has received funding under the grant number 100369691 by the German Federal State of Saxony.

References

1. Huang, C., Yin, Y., Hsu, C., Huang, T.B., Chang, T.: SoC HW/SW verification and validation. In: 16th Asia and South Pacific Design Automation Conference (ASP-DAC 2011), pp. 297–300, January 2011
2. Fania, M., Peiravi, P., Chandramouly, A., Yalla, C.: White paper: predictive analytics and interactive queries on big data. Intel (2013)
3. Jindal, A., Kumar, B., Jindal, N., Fujita, M., Singh, V.: Silicon debug with maximally expanded internal observability using nearest neighbor algorithm. In: 2018 IEEE Computer Society Annual Symposium on VLSI (ISVLSI), pp. 46–51, July 2018
4. Wang, L.: Experience of data analytics in EDA and test principles, promises, and challenges. IEEE Trans. Comput. Aided Des. Integr. Circuits Syst. **36**(6), 885–898 (2017)
5. Mandouh, E., Wassal, A.G.: Application of machine learning techniques in post-silicon debugging and bug localization. J. Electron. Test. **34**(2), 163–181 (2018)
6. Groß, W., Lange, S., Bödecker, J., Blum, M.: Predicting time series with space-time convolutional and recurrent neural networks. In: ESANN (2017)
7. Khan, H.H., Göhringer, D.: FPGA debugging by a device start and stop approach. In: 2016 International Conference on ReConFigurable Computing and FPGAs (ReConFig), pp. 1–6, November 2016
8. Petropoulos, F., Makridakis, S., Assimakopoulos, V., Nikolopoulos, K.: 'Horses for Courses' in demand forecasting. Eur. J. Oper. Res. **237**(1), 152–163 (2014)
9. Friedman, J.H., Rafsky, L.C.: Multivariate generalizations of the Wald-Wolfowitz and Smirnov two-sample tests. Ann. Stat. **7**(4), 697–717 (1979)
10. Chollet, F.: Deep Learning with Python, 1st edn. Manning Publications Co., Greenwich (2017)
11. Kingma, D.P., Ba, J.: Adam: a method for stochastic optimization. arXiv preprint arXiv:1412.6980
12. Bianchi, F.M., Maiorino, E., Kampffmeyer, M.C., Rizzi, A., Jenssen, R.: Properties and training in recurrent neural networks. In: Recurrent Neural Networks for Short-Term Load Forecasting. SCS, pp. 9–21. Springer, Cham (2017). https://doi.org/10.1007/978-3-319-70338-1_2
13. Masters, D., Luschi, C.: Revisiting small batch training for deep neural networks. arXiv preprint arXiv:1804.07612
14. Bertacco, V., Bonkowski, W.: ItHELPS: iterative high-accuracy error localization in post-silicon. In: 33rd IEEE International Conference on Computer Design (ICCD), pp. 196–199, October 2015

Soft-Error Analysis of Self-reconfiguration Controllers for Safety Critical Dynamically Reconfigurable FPGAs

Ludovica Bozzoli$^{(\boxtimes)}$ (iD) and Luca Sterpone (iD)

Politecnico Di Torino, Turin, Italy
{ludovica.bozzoli,luca.sterpone}@polito.it

Abstract. Reconfigurable SRAM-based Field Programmable Gate Arrays are increasingly deployed in the aerospace applications, due to their enhanced flexibility, high performance and run-time reconfiguration capabilities. The possibility to adapt on-the-fly the circuit functionality is made possible by the Internal Configuration Access Port (ICAP) that can be managed from the application through a dedicated controller. This feature enables the deployment of new optimized reconfigurable architectures for computationally intensive and fault-tolerant applications. In this context, a promising architecture is the Dynamically Reconfigurable Processing Module (DRPM), an FPGA-based modular system where the content of each reconfigurable module can be rewritten, overwritten or erased to perform performance optimization and functional modification at run-time. However, when these systems are adopted in avionic and space applications, SRAM configuration sensitivity to radiation induced soft-errors should be addressed. In this work, we evaluate the soft-error sensitivity of upsets in the configuration memory of two implementations of the ICAP controller within a DRPM system. We performed a radiation test campaign and a selective fault injection of upsets on the ICAP controller configuration memory to mimic the radiation profiles. The comparative analysis showed meaningful guidelines on the implementations of self-reconfigurable systems for the aerospace domain: the controller with distributed memory results the 28% more tolerant to low radiation environment compared to the integrated memory version, which in return results the 25% more robust considering radiation particles with higher energies.

Keywords: SRAM-based FPGA · Reconfigurability · DRPM · Radiation effects · SEUs · MBUs · Testing · Aerospace

1 Introduction

Commercial-of-the-shelf (COTS) reconfigurable SRAM-based FPGAs are increasingly adopted in aerospace applications such as cube-sat and mini-sat, due to their low cost, high computational performance and run-time upgradability [1–3]. The possibility to modify the functionality of the system after deployment, provides several opportunities for the development of optimized computing architectures exploiting run-time reconfiguration. This feature is possible in modern FPGA device since they embed on their fabric

© Springer Nature Switzerland AG 2020
F. Rincón et al. (Eds.): ARC 2020, LNCS 12083, pp. 84–96, 2020.
https://doi.org/10.1007/978-3-030-44534-8_7

the Internal Configuration Access Port (ICAP [4]), which enables access and update of configuration memory portions of hardware data-path according to the computational needs [1–3].

One of the most appealing reconfigurable architectures in this context is the Dynamically Reconfigurable Processing Module (DRPM), a modular system where the content of each reconfigurable module can be rewritten, overwritten or erased to perform computational modification on-the-fly [5, 6]. Such optimizations are highly appealing for computationally intensive algorithms that must full-fil power constraints and high reliability level such as the systems used for satellites applications [1, 7]. In fact, these applications typically require complex real-time operations to be executed with restrict power and space budgets and to be highly dependable.

However, when SRAM-based FPGAs are deployed in radiation environments, such as the high altitude of flight routes or the more critical satellite orbits, the configuration memory sensitivity to radiation effects should be evaluated and characterized [8, 9].

Typically, commercially available SRAM-based FPGAs are radiation tolerant in terms of total ionizing dose (TID) and Single Event Latch-up (SEL), while presenting a considerable sensitivity to the other Single Event Effects (SEEs). In fact, the configuration memory sensitivity to soft-errors, such as Single Event Upsets and Multiple Bits Upsets (SEUs and MBUs) is particularly critical. These are transient effects consisting on a change in the state of a memory cell caused by a particle crossing the device, producing a bit-flip in the configuration memory. Considering that the content of the configuration memory directly defines the behavior of the programmable logic, it is crucial to evaluate and quantify the application and device sensitivity to these effects before their deployment [10]. In particular, in case of DRPMs and for dynamically reconfigurable systems in general, the ICAP controller represents a key component and a possible point of failure, considering that it manages all the optimization procedures and it is implemented in the programmable logic [11].

For these reasons, in this work we evaluate the reliability of two different implementations of ICAP Controller for the DRPM system. Starting from experimental data from radiation test obtained in [12] for the 7 Family Xilinx SRAM-based FPGA, we were able to perform a detailed fault injection on the ICAP Controller that realistically mimics the radiation profiles for both Avionic and Space environments. We performed two separated analysis, the first to evaluate the effect of the single bit upsets of a low radiation scenario, while the second is focused on the multiple bit upsets which are more likely to happen in a high radiation environment, such as the one of space applications. This comparative analysis allows us to identify which implementation is more suitable for the target scenarios.

The rest of the paper is organized as follows: in Sect. 2 we provide a summary about the main scientific background and related works on reconfigurable architectures for the aerospace domain. Section 3 details the evaluation framework used to characterize the ICAP controller dependability, while the experimental results obtained by radiation test experiments and fault injection are presented in Sect. 4. Section 5 provides the conclusion and the future directions of this work.

2   Background and Related Works

The development of SRAM-based dynamically reconfigurable systems is enabled by the presence of an interface that allows the communication between the logic programmed on the FPGA and the configuration memory. This component is the ICAP and can be managed through a dedicated controller. This feature allows the development of flexible and upgradable architectures, such as the Dynamically Reconfigurable Processing Module (DRPM). These architectures are highly suitable for optimized and computationally intensive applications such as the ones required in avionics and space missions. Anyway, when SRAM-based FPGAs are deployed in these environments, their sensitivity to radiation effects should be considered and characterized, to ensure the application doesn't fail during its mission.

2.1   Internal Configuration Access Port and Internal Configuration Controller

The Internal Configuration Access Port (ICAP), is a primitive embedded in the recent Xilinx FPGA families. The ICAP enables the access to the configuration memory to read or write configuration data at run-time from the application programmed in the resource layer [4]. This procedure is performed through the circuitry shown in Fig. 1: The ICAP is controlled by the on-chip microprocessor or by custom logic on the FPGA through a dedicated controller; the building components of the controller are a Finite State Machine (FSM) and a dedicated memory module, containing Read and Write FIFO and Control Registers. The FSM manages the ICAP signals and Read/Write FIFOs to stream data from/to the ICAP. The data to exchange with configuration memory typically are stored in a large external memory: according to the required operation, the microprocessor sets the control registers and loads/stores the proper commands from/to Read/Write FIFOs [13].

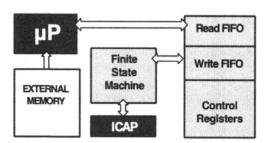

Fig. 1. Simplified block diagram of the ICAP controller for the management of the ICAP primitive in Xilinx FPGAs.

In its IP catalogue, Xilinx provides an optimized and customizable ICAP Controller with an AXI Interface [14], to facilitate the communication and the synchronization with the microprocessor. Although some works exist in literature suggesting optimized and reliable versions for ICAP controller [11, 15, 16], we analyzed the ICAP Controller provided by the vendor, considering that our test analysis can be applied also to previously developed reliable methods for the ICAP controller.

At the design stage, several parameters of the Controller can be customized. Among the possible settings, it is possible to implement the memory dedicated to Read and Write FIFO using Block RAM [17] or as a Distributed RAM by using the programmable resources inside the FPGA [18]. In general, Distributed RAMs are more efficient from the timing point of view when the memory size is restricted, while BRAM results preferable for bigger memories implementation.

2.2 Dynamically Reconfigurable Processing Module

The possibility to access the configuration memory at run-time allows the development of flexible and upgradable architectures, such as the Dynamically Reconfigurable Processing Module (DRPM) [5, 6].

In details, the DRPM is a hybrid architecture that exploits reconfigurability to perform several optimizations in terms of area, power, reliability and delay.

A simplified overview of the DRPM system is shown in Fig. 2. In the DRPM architecture there are three main regions: Hardwired, Static, and Dynamic. The Hardwired Components are the on-chip microprocessor and the ICAP, which communicate between each other through the ICAP Controller. The ICAP Controller is statically programmed in the FPGA programmable logic, as well as the Bus Macro, which is the communication interface connecting all the components. The Dynamic part of the system consists of several reconfigurable cores, where dedicated functions can be allocated or deallocated at run-time, by accessing the configuration memory settings.

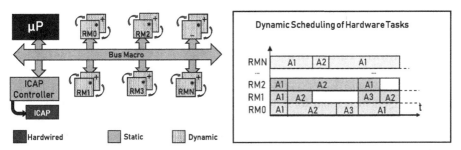

Fig. 2. Simplified block diagram of the DRPM architecture (left), and an example of dynamic scheduling of hardware tasks in Reconfigurable Modules (right).

The dynamic scheduling of hardware components can be driven by one or more optimization goals, such as performance, area efficiency, power saving and reliability [2, 5, 19]. In fact, this procedure can be used to time-multiplex the area and virtually increase the area physically available. Additionally, it is possible to scale power consumption with the current payload by erasing unused functionalities and eventually reprogramming them only when needed. Finally, the refresh of the configuration data allows to avoid or recover application failures related to transient faults in the configuration memory.

Although such architectures result highly suitable for avionics and space applications, when such systems are deployed in radiation environments, the SRAM configuration memory sensitivity to radiation effect should be taken into account [20].

2.3   SRAM-Based FPGAs Radiation Sensitivity and Evaluation Methodologies

The SRAM based FPGA configuration memory radiation sensitivity is a well-known problem. This criticality is related to the SRAM cells intrinsic susceptibility to radiation induced transient effects such as Single and Multiple Event Upsets (SEUs and MBUs) [1, 9]. An SEU is a change the state of a memory cell caused by one single ionizing particle crossing the device silicon. Although these effects can be recovered by refreshing the correct value inside the memory cell, if not recovered in time they can lead to errors in the application since configuration data directly control application functionality. Thus, it is fundamental to ensure through testing that such devices do not fail while deployed.

Three main approaches exist to perform this evaluation: accelerated radiation ground testing [9, 11], fault-injection campaigns [21, 22], and analytical methods and tools [23, 24].

Radiation testing mimics the radiation environment and provides realistic experimental data on the failure probability for a given radiation dose. On the other side, radiation tests imply high costs both in terms of experimental setup and beam time availability.

The fault-injection approach is a valid alternative, especially for the SEE evaluation on the FPGA. In fact, SEE tests are event-based tests where the number of detected events define the error rate for the application. Considering that in FPGA, these events coincide with bit-flips in configuration memory, it is easy to emulate such effects by loading in the configuration memory corrupted configuration data. For this reason, FPGA Fault Injection results a valid solution to estimate the SEUs or MBUs in the application, especially if it can be performed according to experimental data.

3   Evaluation Framework

The goal of this evaluation is to perform a reliability comparison among the ICAP Fabric and BRAM implementations for different levels of radiation in the DRPM context. The main difference among Fabric and BRAM implementation resides on the amount and the function of the logic programmed inside the FPGA. In BRAM Implementation a minor amount of programmable resources is used: considering the same placement area, the design is less congested with respect to Fabric Implementation. The other difference is that in BRAM Implementation most of the routing resources coincides with the Data, Address and Control Lines of the hardwired BRAM, while in the Fabric Implementation the memory cells and their control signals are distributed in the logic.

These different implementation characteristics can have different sensitivity to faults and different failure modes with respect to SEUs and MBUs.

For these reasons, we divide our evaluation in two parts: the first consisted of a classical fault injection of single bitflips, to mimic environment with low radiation dose; the second part of the analysis aims to characterize the failure probability in case of higher energy radiation producing MBUs. In order to properly mimic the two environments, we started from experimental data obtained through Ultra High Energy Ions, relative to the same target device [12].

3.1 DRPM Setup

To evaluate the ICAP controller sensitivity to bit upsets in the DRPM context, we developed an ad-hoc DRPM system. The system consists of the on-chip ZYNQ processing system [25] that runs the computation routine and schedules the modules configuration. The processor communicates with the ICAP Controller for both BRAM and Fabric implementation through the AXI bus macro and in case of error detection triggers a system reboot sending signals to a dedicated System Reset Core. Reconfigurable Modules are connected to the AXI bus macro through Partial Reconfiguration Decoupler [26] interfaces to make faster and safer the signal exchange at the modules boundaries. For this test, the reconfigurable modules can be programmed as Floating-Point Multiplication or Addition Accelerators.

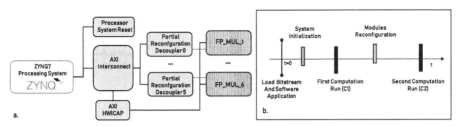

Fig. 3. The implemented DRPM architecture (a) and a simplified representation of the Software Application routine (b).

In order to properly evaluate and classify the faults effect on different computation tasks, the execution routine has been kept streamlined. The software application is loaded and initialized at the start-up. The first computation run is performed and test operands are sent to each module, which is configured for the multiplication. After this, the content of all the modules is refreshed by rewriting the partial configuration data. This procedure is the one managed by the ICAP Controller that acquires partial bitstreams from the external memory and loads them in the right portion of the configuration memory. At this point, a second run of computation is performed.

In the meanwhile, the software program checks for errors in the execution: it compares the results of the multiplications with the expected golden values for the computational section of the code, while for initialization and reconfiguration producers it checks all the functions return signatures. In case of errors in computation, it sends on the output a signal notification. In case of wrong return values from functions involved in the Initialization or Reconfiguration procedures, after the signal notification is done, it performs a safe reboot of the whole system. The Block Diagram of the implemented architecture and a simplification of the Software Application routine are reported respectively in Fig. 3a and b.

3.2 Fault Injection Platform

The Fault Injection Manager to perform the Injection Campaigns has been developed using the Python environment. The main routine of the Manager integrates the PyXEL tool, developed for the detailed manipulation of the Xilinx bitstreams and described in [27].

The Fault Injection Manager takes as inputs the golden bitstream of the Architecture under test (i.e., with the BRAM or Fabric Implementation of the ICAP Controller) and the settings for the campaign. These settings define the configuration memory target area, the bitflip cluster size (1 for the SEUs Injection Campaign; 2, 3, 4, 5, or 6 for the MBUs) and the number of injections to be performed.

According to these settings the main routine of injector identifies the specific coordinates in the configuration memory matrix of bits to flip and sends this information to the PyXEL tool. PyXEL produces a collection of corrupted bitstreams, according to the locations and the cardinality specified in the previous step. At the same time the main routine produces for all the faulty configuration bitstreams a TCL script to automatically program the FPGA (Fig. 4).

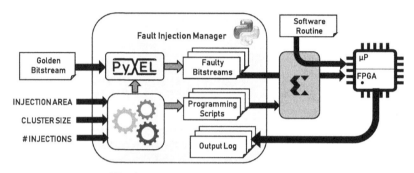

Fig. 4. Fault injection platform overview.

Once all the files required for the injection are produced, the Fault Injection Manager enters in *Fault-Injection* mode: it iterates on all the available programming scripts launching them in the Xilinx Software Command Line Tool; each programming script automatically loads one faulty bitstream in the FPGA configuration memory and the Software Application executable in the microprocessor instruction memory. Once the programming phase is concluded, the Fault Manager captures the system output log through the serial interface. When the application execution terminates, the log is saved, and a new TCL script is executed to run the next injection.

4   Experimental Results

The analysis has been performed on the PYNQ-Z2 Xilinx Board that is based on a Xilinx ZYNQ SoC embedding a 650 MHz dual-core Cortex-A9 processor, a Xilinx ZYNQ 7020 FPGA.

Two different implementations of the DRPM architecture have been realized: the first version uses Block RAM for the implementation of the Read and Write FIFOs and it will be referred as *BRAM Implementation*; the second version implements Read and Write FIFOs using Distributed RAM and it will be referred as *Fabric Implementation*.

In Table 1 the ZYNQ 7020 resources availability and their utilization for the two ICAP Controller implementations are reported.

Table 1. Resources available on ZYNQ 7020 and the utilization for BRAM and Fabric Implementations

	Available	BRAM Implementation	Fabric Implementation
Slice as LUTs	13,300	354	772
Slice registers	106,400	1,008	1,047
Block RAM18	280	2	0
Routing segments	–	568,378	1,977,640
Configuration frames	10.008	280	280

For both the implementations two different analysis have been performed: the first one oriented to the ICAP controller sensitivity to Single Bit Upsets, while the second consider the effect of Multiple Bit Upsets related to the same event. For both SEUs and MBUs analysis 2,500 injections have been performed in random locations. To perform a legitimate comparison, the two ICAP Controllers designs were placed in the same area and the injections have been performed on the same sub-portion of the configuration memory, using the same locations.

4.1 SEUs Injection Campaign Results – Avionic Environment

The first analysis we performed was focused on the avionic scenario, which presents a moderate radiation dose with respect to the space environment.

The goal of such analysis was to characterize the effect on the DRPM application of Single Bit Upsets on the configuration memory portion configuring the ICAP Controller. For the two implementations, 2,500 faulty bitstreams with one bit flipped in the HWICAP area have been loaded inside the FPGA executing the same computation routine.

Firstly, we classified the erroneous behaviors as *Critical* and *Detectable*. We marked as Critical the errors that cause the full hang of the application, making impossible to regain the control for a safe reboot. On the other hand, we marked as Detectable the errors that can cause misbehaviors in the execution but are detected by the application. These faults bring the system in an erroneous behavior but with a known state to perform a safe reboot. We also classified the results according to the stages they are affecting: Initialization (INIT), Reconfiguration (RCNFG), Computation Run before Reconfiguration (C1) and Computation Run after Reconfiguration (C2). Please note that we classified as fault in C2 the faults affecting only the computation after the reconfiguration.

In the graphs described in Fig. 5, we reported the results obtained. Figure 5a reports the total failure rate obtained by SEU fault injection on the whole area used by the ICAP controllers of the two applications. Figure 5b and c reports the percentage distribution of such errors in different computational stages.

As it possible to see, the Total Error Rate for the Fabric Implementation is slightly higher than the BRAM one. Anyway, if we look at the criticality of those errors, the Fabric Implementation presents a lower rate of Critical Errors.

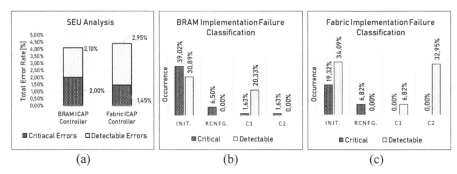

Fig. 5. SEUs injection results for BRAM and Fabric HWICAP Implementation (a). Error classification for the ICAP using BRAM implementation (b) and Fabric implementation (c).

If we look at the stage classification, we see that the two implementations again show a different behavior: even if for both of them the majority of the faults causes errors in the initialization stage, the ones in Fabric Implementation show a lower criticality; additionally, the Fabric Implementation doesn't show any critical fault in the Computation Runs and the majority of the Detectable errors are affecting only C2.

4.2 MBUs Injection Campaign Results – Space Environment

When environments with a higher radiation dose are considered, a single heavy ionizing particle with higher energy can flip more than one bit in the same area of the configuration memory. In this analysis we perform a fault injection campaign considering this effect. We injected in the ICAP Controller configuration memory portion clusters of bitflips, according to the results of the radiation test discussed in [12].

The type of clusters identified in [12] consists in maximum 6 bit-flips that may involve up to two neighborhood frames and span over 4 bits rows. For each size, 500 faulty bitstreams have been produced. The shape of the injected clusters was randomly chosen among the one identified in [12] for each cluster size. Thus, a total of 2,500 injections have been performed on the two Implementations. The same classification of Critical and Detectable errors for the total failure rate has been performed. The results relative to the overall error probability and to the critical failures are provided in Fig. 6. From the left graph, it is possible to see that the overall failure rate dramatically increases with the size of the clusters and this increment results sharper for the Fabric Implementation.

Considering Critical Failures, we can observe a similar trend but with a lower probability. This means that the error probability increases with the size of the clusters, but the main component of such growth are errors that still can be detected and managed by the application.

We complete our analysis on the overall failure probability by classifying errors according to the stage they are affecting. In the graph of Fig. 7, the distribution of the errors within the different stages is provided for the BRAM and Fabric Implementations and for each cluster size.

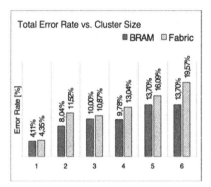
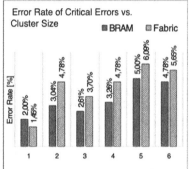

Fig. 6. Error rate for BRAM and fabric implementations with respect to MUB clusters: total errors (left) and critical errors (right).

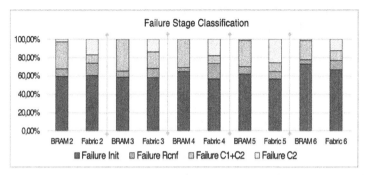

Fig. 7. Failure distribution within the application stages with respect to the cluster size for BRAM and Fabric Implementation.

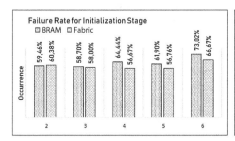
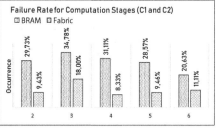

Fig. 8. Details of the failure occurrence in initialization (left) and computation (right) with respect to the cluster size for BRAM and Fabric Implementations.

The higher percentage of failures happens in the Initialization Stage, and this ratio is somehow constant for both implementations. The failures in the Reconfiguration Stage represent a higher portion in the Fabric Implementation, while the failures of both C1 and C2 result heavier for the BRAM Implementation, following the same behavior found with the SEUs analysis. Details of the percentage of failures in Initialization and Computation Stages are reported in Fig. 8, respectively left and right.

4.3 Discussion

After this study is possible to make some assumptions about the motivation of the different reliability profiles in the two ICAP solutions and which one is preferable according to the application.

At first, the higher congestion of the Fabric Implementation can explain why MBUs has a stronger effect: the density of the configuration bits allows single particle flipping multiple bits to affect more than one resource configuration. Additionally, the routing segments in the BRAM version represent a more critical point of failure with respect to the Distributed Fabric RAM, since a single fault in Data, Control or Address lines can heavily corrupt the Block RAM behavior. This explain the higher ratio of less critical and detectable errors in the Distributed version of the Controller: more sensitive bits exist but at the same time their failure has a lower impact in the overall circuit.

Table 2. Applicability of HWICAP implementations in different radiation environment

	Low radiation profile	High radiation profile
Computation-oriented application	Fabric	Fabric
Reconfiguration-oriented application	Fabric	BRAM
Availability-oriented application	Fabric	BRAM
Reliability-oriented application	BRAM	BRAM

Finally, considering the failure characteristics of the two implementations with respect to different radiation and for different stages of the application, it is possible to draw some conclusions. Beside Reliability-oriented systems, for low dose rates where the major concern are SEUs, the Fabric Implementation results more robust: it presents a general error rate comparable with the BRAM one, but the criticality is definitely lower, especially in the Computation Stage. In high radiation environment as well, if the main goal of the application is the computation, the Fabric Implementation remains preferable. For all the missions deployed in high radiation environments that require high dependability, high availability or massive usage of reconfiguration, the BRAM implementation should be preferred. In general, although BRAMs supports Error Correction Cores for SEU recovery and MBU detection, for mission critical systems some hardening techniques should be introduced. Table 2 summarizes this general indication about which implementation would be preferable according to the specific goal of the reconfigurable application and the radiation level of the environment in which it should be deployed.

5   Conclusions and Future Works

In conclusion, a comparative analysis on two different DRPM self-reconfiguration controllers has been performed in order to obtain an overall error rate estimation and identify their possible adoption in avionic or aerospace domains. To obtain this result, two different fault injection campaigns based on experimental radiation testing have been performed. The results of such analysis have shown that in general the controller implemented with distributed memory has a higher tolerance in low radiation environment. Anyway, in presence of radiation particles with higher energies, the controller that uses integrated memories is preferable. The observed sensitivity and failure mode variation in the two implementations is manly related to different resource density and employment.

In the future, we plan the perform a similar injection campaign on the overall DRPM reconfigurable system and to complete this analysis with experimental data through radiation testing.

References

1. Wirthlin, M.: High-reliability FPGA-based systems: space, high-energy physics, and beyond. Proc. IEEE **103**(3), 379–389 (2015)
2. Caffrey, M.: A space-based reconfigurable radio. In: Plaks, T.P., Athanas, P.M. (eds.) Proceedings of International Conference on Engineering of Reconfigurable Systems Algorithms, pp. 49–53. CSREA Press, Irvine, June 2002
3. Ferguson, R., Tate, R.: Use of field programmable gate array technology in future space avionics. In: Proceedings of 24th Digital Avionics Systems Conference (DASC 2005), vol. 2, p. 11, October/November 2005
4. 7 Series FPGAs Configuration User Guide UG470 (v1.13.1), 20 August 2018
5. Sterpone, L., Porrmann, M., Hagemeyer, J.: A novel fault tolerant and runtime reconfigurable platform for satellite payload processing. IEEE Trans. Comput. **62**(8), 1508–1525 (2013)
6. Koester, M., Luk, W., Hagemeyer, J., Porrman, M., Rueckert, U.: Design optimization for tiled partially reconfigurable systems. IEEE Trans. Very Large Scale Integr. Syst. **19**(6), 1048–1061 (2011)
7. Quinn, H., et al.: The Cibola flight experiment. ACM Trans. Reconfig. Technol. Syst. **8**, 1–22 (2014)
8. Dodd, P.E., Massengill, L.W.: Basic mechanisms and modeling of single-event upset in digital microelectronics. IEEE Trans. Nucl. Sci. **50**(3), 583–602 (2003)
9. Katz, R., et al.: Radiation effects on current field programmable technologies. IEEE Trans. Nuclear Sci. **44**(6), 1945–1956 (1997)
10. Quinn, H.: Challenges in testing complex systems. IEEE Trans. Nucl. Sci. **61**(2), 766–786 (2014)
11. Heiner, J., Collins, N., Wirthlin, M.: Fault tolerant ICAP controller for high-reliable internal scrubbing. In: 2008 IEEE Aerospace Conference, Big Sky, MT, pp. 1–10 (2008)
12. Du, B., et al.: Ultrahigh energy heavy ion test beam on Xilinx Kintex-7 SRAM-based FPGA. IEEE Trans. Nucl. Sci. **66**(7), 1813–1819 (2019)
13. AXI HWICAP v3.0 LogiCORE IP Product Guide Vivado Design Suite PG134, 5 October 2016
14. AXI Reference Guide, UG761 (v13.1), 7 March 2011
15. Ebrahim, A., Benkrid, K., Iturbe, X., Hong, C.: A novel high-performance fault-tolerant ICAP controller. In: 2012 NASA/ESA Conference on Adaptive Hardware and Systems (AHS), Erlangen, pp. 259–263 (2012)

16. Guohua, W., Dongming, L., Fengzhou, W., Adetomi, A., Arslan, T.: A tiny and multifunctional ICAP controller for dynamic partial reconfiguration system. In: 2017 NASA/ESA Conference on Adaptive Hardware and Systems (AHS), Pasadena, CA, pp. 71–76 (2017)
17. 7 Series FPGAs Memory Resources User Guide UG473 (v1.14), 3 July 2019
18. 7 Series FPGAs Configurable Logic Block User Guide UG474 (v1.8), 27 September 2016
19. Carmichael, C., Caffrey, M., Salazar, A.: Correcting single-event upsets through Virtex partial configuration. Xilinx Corporation, Technical report, XAPP216 (v1.0), 1 June 2000
20. Ceschia, M.: Identification and classification of single-event upsets in the configuration memory of SRAM-based FPGAs. IEEE Trans. Nucl. Sci. **50**(6), 2088–2094 (2003)
21. Azambuja, J.R., et al.: Evaluating neutron induced SEE in SRAM-based FPGA protected by hardware- and software-based fault tolerant techniques. IEEE Trans. Nucl. Sci. **60**(6), 4243–4250 (2013)
22. Entrena, L., Garcia-Valderas, M., Fernandez-Cardenal, R., Lindoso, A., Portela, M., Lopez-Ongil, C.: Soft error sensitivity evaluation of microprocessors by multilevel emulation-based fault injection. IEEE Trans. Comput. **61**(3), 313–322 (2012)
23. Desogus, M., Sterpone, L., Codinachs, D.M.: Validation of a tool for estimating the effects of soft-errors on modern SRAM-based FPGAs. In: 2014 IEEE 20th International On-Line Testing Symposium (IOLTS), Platja d'Aro, Girona, pp. 111–115 (2014)
24. Sterpone, L., et al.: A novel error rate estimation approach for UltraScale+ SRAM-based FPGAs. In: 2018 NASA/ESA Conference on Adaptive Hardware and Systems (AHS), Edinburgh, pp. 120–126 (2018)
25. Processing System 7 v5.5 LogiCORE IP Product Guide Vivado Design Suite PG082, 10 May 2017
26. Partial Reconfiguration Decoupler v1.0 LogiCORE IP Product Guide Vivado Design Suite PG227, 6 April 2016
27. Bozzoli, L., De Sio, C., Sterpone, L., Bernardeschi, C.: PyXEL: an integrated environment for the analysis of fault effects in SRAM-based FPGA routing. In: 2018 International Symposium on Rapid System Prototyping (RSP), Torino, Italy, pp. 70–75 (2018)

SysIDLib: A High-Level Synthesis FPGA Library for Online System Identification

Gökhan Akgün[1(✉)], Habib ul Hasan Khan[1], Marawan Hebaish[3],
Mahmoud Elshimy[3], Mohamed A. Abd El Ghany[3], and Diana Göhringer[1,2]

[1] Adaptive Dynamic Systems, Technische Universität Dresden, Dresden, Germany
{goekhan.akguen,habib.khan,diana.goehringer}@tu-dresden.de
[2] Centre for Tactile Internet with Human-in-the-Loop (CeTi),
Technische Universität Dresden, Dresden, Germany
[3] Electronics Department, German University in Cairo, New Cairo, Egypt
{marawan.hebaish,mahmoud.el-shimy,mohamed.abdel-ghany}@guc.edu.eg

Abstract. Model accuracy is the most important step towards efficient control design. Various system identification techniques exist which are used to estimate model parameters. However, these techniques have their merits and demerits which need to be considered before selecting a particular system identification technique. In this paper, various system identification techniques as the Kalman filter (EKF), recursive least square (RLS) and least mean square (LMS) filters are used to estimate the parameters of linear (DC motor) and nonlinear systems (inverted pendulum and adaptive polynomial models). FPGAs are widely used for rapid prototyping, real-time and high computationally demanding applications. Therefore, a real-time FPGA-in the loop architecture has been used for evaluating each identification algorithm of the SysIDLib library. The identification algorithms are evaluated regarding the convergence rate, accuracy and resource utilization performed on a system-onchip (SoC). The results have shown that the RLS algorithm estimated approximately the parameter values of a nonlinear system. However, it requires up to 17% less lookup-tables, 5.5% less flip-flops and 14% less DSPs compared to EKF with accurate results on the programmable logic (PL).

Keywords: Online system identification · Extended Kalman filter · Fixed-point format · High-level synthesis · Embedded control systems

1 Introduction

Real applications need to be expressed through mathematical equations in numerical tools to predict and analyze the system behavior. According to the analysis, a suitable controller can be developed based on the existing model within the simulation. This model can also be deployed for monitoring and diagnosis instances [1]. In case of a sensor malfunction, the faulty operation can be captured and the system can accomplish its operation in a safety mode [2]. Such an observer reconstructs mainly the remaining internal states of the system that

© Springer Nature Switzerland AG 2020
F. Rincón et al. (Eds.): ARC 2020, LNCS 12083, pp. 97–107, 2020.
https://doi.org/10.1007/978-3-030-44534-8_8

saves the deployment of further sensors in real applications. To achieve reliability, the model needs to be parameterized accurately. An inaccurate parameterized model can lead to non-deterministic effects as an oscillation occurs while the transient behavior [3]. Various experiments have to be performed in order to characterize the model. According to the type of the existing information, either a theoretical or an experimental model can be created. In the case of theoretical modeling, the system is associated with physical differential equations where the parameters often exist. The modeling of a real system becomes significantly complicated with the lack of information. Therefore, the input and output signals are measured and analyzed in case of experimental modeling. System identification algorithms are mainly deployed to estimate these unknown model parameters. The physical behavior is characterized using prior knowledge of the designer [3]. The algorithms compare mainly the output signals of the system and minimize the occurring error to determine each parameter value. Depending on the linear or nonlinear characteristic of the system, different identification algorithm can be deployed.

In this research work, we present various system identification techniques for linear and nonlinear systems. Table 1 shows a summary of the performed identification techniques with different applications. A discrete transfer function can be described as an adaptive filter. Thus, the LMS and RLS algorithms are applied to estimate the filter parameters. EKF is deployed when the system is represented in a state-space model. Besides, it is also performed to estimate the internal states of the system as an observer. Therefore, it can be further used for the diagnosis and monitoring purposes. To exploit the parallelism of field programmable gate arrays (FPGAs), the components of the SysIDLib are implemented using a high-level synthesis (HLS) tool and tested in a real-time FPGA-in the loop (FIL) simulation environment. This work compares all aspects of the identification techniques concerning the convergence rate, accuracy and resource utilization on Xilinx FPGAs. Particular attention is paid to the EKF algorithm in this work. The EKF implementation has been extended to an register transfer level (RTL) description language implementation to compare the merits and demerits of both implementations. For instance, the RTL implementation uses a fixed-point representation for identification. The accuracy and the resulting resource utilization are compared with the results from the HLS implementation.

Table 1. Overview about the deployed identification algorithms regarding the considered applications

Considered systems	Use case	SysIDLib component
Nonlinear systems	Inverted Pendulum	EKF
Linear systems	Lin. Inv. Pendulum, DC Motor	EKF, RLS, LMS
Nonlinear polynomial model	Volterra Series, Bilinear Filter	RLS, LMS

The rest of this paper is organized as follows. In Sect. 2, the related work is discussed and compared. Section 3 presents the hardware architecture of the SysIDLib library. In Sect. 4, the achieved results are compared regarding the accuracy, convergence rate and resource utilization. Finally, Sect. 5 contains the conclusion and outlook.

2   Related Work

Due to changing operating conditions, the system parameters vary within a process. Structural damage occurs abrupt and leads thus to the invalidity of existing parameters [4]. The parameters of a photovoltaic application need to be estimated again depending on actual temperature conditions [1]. In the case of an adaptive controller, the system parameters are continuously identified to adjust the control parameters at run-time [5]. The identification becomes even more complicated with regard to nonlinear system characteristics. This type of system can be linearized around a certain operating point. The parameters can be identified with linear parameter estimation techniques but the identified parameters have validity in this certain range [6]. A reliable result is achieved using nonlinear system identification techniques for such systems. However, different methodologies have been proposed to improve the demerits [7]. The parameters of nonlinear Volterra polynomials can be identified using the LMS algorithm [6,8]. This algorithm is associated with its slow convergence rate [7]. A faster estimation can be achieved using the RLS algorithm depending on the design requirements [3]. The RLS and LMS algorithms can also be performed to identify the parameters of linear systems [5,9–11]. In addition to these algorithms, EKF estimates the parameters accurately and has a fast convergence rate [1,3,4,12]. Furthermore, it can also be used for estimating the internal states of a system because not all variables can be directly acquired from sensor data [12]. EKF can also be performed for diagnosis and monitoring purposes [1,4]. The aforementioned identification techniques have computational complexity. For instance, the update of the covariance matrix requires a long computational time in the RLS algorithm. Therefore, multi-stage matrix multiplication and a trace technique are proposed in [10] to enhance the overall performance. The first approach reduces the computational time whereby the tracing technique diminishes the matrix computation. In [1], a convergence criterion is proposed for terminating the identification process in EKF. Another improvement can be achieved by exploiting the parallelism of FPGAs [1,5,9–12]. The algorithms can be implemented using RTL description languages [5,10] or HLS tools [11,12]. For instance, an application-specific instruction-set processor has been designed for the RLS algorithm in [9]. Moreover, a software-based solution [12] can be executed on SoCs. The pure hardware implementation entails using a fixed or floating-point format representation [5]. The fixed-point format represents a limited range of data, which may have difficulty to represent small or large values [5]. Contrary, high accuracy can be achieved using the floating-point representation. A disadvantageous of this representation is mostly high resource utilization [2].

3   The SysIDLib Components

3.1   LMS and RLS Algorithm

The LMS algorithm is considered to be a stochastic gradient algorithm which is the most used adaptive filtering algorithm due to its low computation complexity [13]. It updates the filter weights in each iteration to minimize the error ϵ_k based on the equations in [3]. RLS is a recursive method of the least squares algorithm which aims to minimize the sum of the error ϵ_k based on the equations in [3]. In the RLS algorithm, the update of the covariance matrix consists of matrix multiplications which can lead to a long computational time at run-time.

3.2   Extended Kalman Filter

Kalman filter (KF) is originally used to estimate the states of linear systems. It consists of a prediction and correction step. In the prediction step, KF estimates the internal states of the system $\hat{x}_k$ based on previous estimated states $\hat{x}_{k-1}$ and the previous control signal u_{k-1}. The dimension of the estimated states $\hat{x}_k$ needs to be extended for the system identification according to the use case. Besides, the extension of the state vector $\hat{x}_k$ entails to a nonlinear characteristic in the system dynamic $f(\hat{x}_{k-1}, u)$. Therefore, EKF updates the state vector $\hat{x}_{k+1}$ based on the equations in [3] for the DC motor and based on the Eq. (1) for the inverted pendulum. The parameter x_1 is the cart position, x_2 is the cart velocity, x_3 is the angular position of the pendulum and x_4 is the angular velocity of the pendulum. Furthermore, the parameter M describes the mass of the cart, m is the mass of the pendulum, d is the friction coefficient, l is the length of the pendulum and g is the gravitational constant.

$$\hat{x}_{k+1} = \underbrace{\begin{bmatrix} x_1 \\ x_2 \\ x_3 \\ x_4 \\ m \\ M \\ d \end{bmatrix}}_{\hat{x}_k} + \underbrace{\begin{bmatrix} x_2 \\ \frac{-d \cdot x_2 + m \cdot g \cdot x_3 + u}{M} \\ x_4 \\ \frac{-d \cdot x_2 + (m+M) \cdot g \cdot x_3 - u}{l \cdot M} \\ 0 \\ 0 \\ 0 \end{bmatrix}}_{f(\hat{x}_{k-1}, u)} \cdot T_S \tag{1}$$

The main difference is that the DC motor employs the discrete transfer function and the inverted pendulum uses the state-space model for the system identification. A more detail description regarding the use cases can be found in prior works [2,3,13].

3.3   Hardware Design of the SysIDLib Components

Each identification technique is written as a C-Code in Vivado HLS which generates an RTL description language. It provides directives to enhance latency,

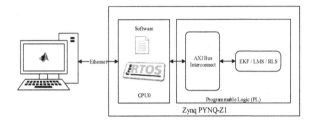

Fig. 1. System overview of the FIL architecture

resource utilization and throughput. However, the optimization has a trade-off between hardware resources and performance. The proposed algorithms have multiple matrices and vector operations. This leads to intensive computing within several loops and influences the latency. To meet the design and real-time requirements, the algorithms exploit the parallelism of FPGAs. Therefore, all loops have been optimized with UNROLL and PIPELINE directives. UNROLL directive splits the loops and thus executes the operations in parallel. Hence, the loop iterations are reduced and the data access and throughput are increased. However, it requires more hardware logic because of multiple copies of the loop in the RTL level. EKF and the RLS algorithm have computationally demanding matrix multiplications whereby all loops have been fully unrolled. PIPELINE directive allows concurrent operations in loops. Thus, a new input can be processed every clock cycle that also improves the latency of the algorithms. All mathematical operations are computed using the math library provided by Vivado HLS. The algorithms have floating-point operations in the IEEE-754 format to generate accurate results. Due to the low I/O operations, all ports are implemented as the AXI4-Lite interface. Figure 1 gives an overview about the deployed FIL architecture. The reference systems have been performed as models with a sampling time of 10 ms and random input signals in MATLAB 2018b. A Xilinx PYNQ-Z1 has been deployed for the identification algorithms. FreeRTOS is running on an ARM Cortex-A9 processor in the processing system (PS) to guarantee the real-time capability. A TCP/IP-application connects the reference models with the FPGA. The SysIDLib components are executed as accelerators on the PL and connected through the AXI4-Lite interface to the PS.

4   Evaluation

4.1   Analysis of the Accuracy and Performance Using the SysIDLib Library

EKF and the RLS algorithm have been performed to identify the parameters of the inverted pendulum. The results are shown in Fig. 2. EKF estimates exactly the values of the reference system within 80 s. The linearization of the inverted pendulum on the upright position ($\theta = \pi$) enables to use linear identification techniques. The RLS algorithm estimates the weight parameters W_k within

750 s but it has a significant difference in estimating the model parameters as compared to EKF (Fig. 2). The RLS algorithm has achieved an accuracy of 94.86% for the parameters a_3 and b_2. The reason is the linearization of the use case among a certain operating point which restricts the identification. The same algorithm has been performed on the DC motor (Fig. 3). The identified parameters have shown a deviation of 0.15% and identified the parameters within 30 s. The LMS algorithm has the highest error of 0.62% and estimates the values within 280 s. EKF has generated the most accurate results within 7 s. Compared to the inverted pendulum, the RLS algorithm has estimated more accurately the values of the DC motor. However, it is able to identify systems with nonlinear characteristics. The parameters of the Volterra series have been identified using the RLS and LMS algorithm as shown in Fig. 4. The RLS algorithm identifies the parameters accurately up to an error of 0.075%. The LMS algorithm estimates also the parameters accurately but the deviation to the reference parameter is slightly higher with 0.91%. It has been performed for 140 s to identify the system parameters whereby the RLS algorithm has been estimated the parameters within 50 s. The convergence rate depends on the total number of weight parameters. The RLS algorithm has also identified the parameters of the bilinear filter. The results show the highest deviation with 3% and 6% on the parameters $c_{0,1}$ and $c_{1,1}$ in Fig. 5. These coefficients describe the correlation between the input and output signals. However, the parameters have been identified within 0.3 s because of the recursive filter structure. The experiments have shown a worst-case scenario with the initial conditions in all cases. However, a faster convergence and more accuracy would have been achieved when the initial conditions are set to approximate parameter values.

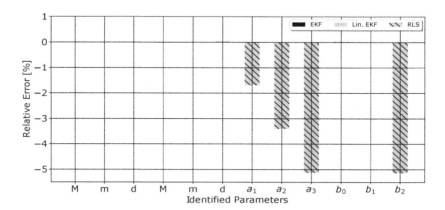

Fig. 2. The accuracy results of the RLS algorithm and EKF on the inverted pendulum

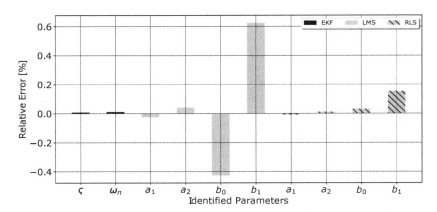

Fig. 3. The accuracy results of the RLS, LMS algorithm and EKF on the DC motor

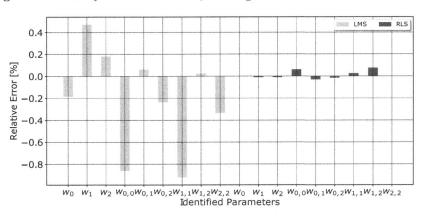

Fig. 4. The accuracy results of the RLS and LMS algorithm on the non-recursive adaptive filter (Volterra Series)

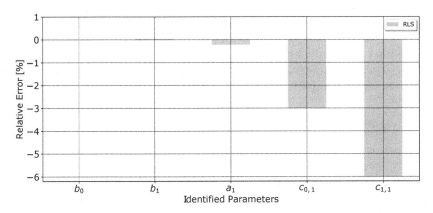

Fig. 5. The accuracy results of the RLS algorithm on the recursive adaptive filter (Bilinear Filter)

Table 2. Resource utilization of the identification algorithms generated by Vivado HLS for Zynq PYNQ-Z1

Component	LUT	FF	DSP48E	BRAM18K	Use case
Maximum of PYNQ-Z1	53200	106400	220	280	–
EKF	14769	12444	48	26	Inverted Pendulum
EKF	10061	9376	41	28	Lin. Inv. Pendulum
RLS	5899	6594	18	14	Inverted Pendulum
EKF	11493	8929	20	10	DC Motor
RLS	5334	5017	20	10	DC Motor
LMS	1462	1686	19	6	DC Motor
RLS	7097	6698	20	14	Volterra Series
LMS	3785	4125	48	4	Volterra Series
RLS	5568	5586	20	10	Bilinear Filter

4.2   Analysis of the Device Utilization Using the SysIDLib Library

Table 2 summarizes for each identification technique the required resources on the Xilinx PYNQ-Z1 board implemented with Vivado HLS. EKF requires the most resources in all scenarios. The linearization of the inverted pendulum has brought the advantage that the approach saves 8.84% lookup tables, 2.88% flip-flops and 3.18% DSPs as compared to the nonlinear system. Because of the reduced complexity, the RLS algorithm has saved more resources for this system. Therefore, it is a trade-off between the accuracy and computational complexity resulting in more resource utilization. In the event of the DC motor, the LMS algorithm has the lowest resource utilization. It estimates the parameters with vector multiplications and additions. The RLS algorithm has matrix operations which result comparatively in higher resource utilization on the PL. The same behavior exists on the Volterra series. The weight parameters of the bilinear filter are less than from the Volterra series in this work. However, the RLS algorithm requires the same amount of resources in both scenarios. This is related to the recursive filter structure of the bilinear filter. The Volterra series considers only the input signals. Therefore, the filter structure has also an effect to the overall resource utilization (Table 2).

4.3   Parameter Estimation of the Inverted Pendulum Using EKF

EKF is performed to estimate the parameters of the inverted pendulum. The results are shown in Fig. 6. It can be seen that the final parameters are identified within 80 s. The design requires 29.31% lookup tables and 12.42% flip-flops on the PL. Vivado HLS shows a latency of 2137 clock cycles for an operating frequency of 100 MHz. Our implementation requires approximately the same amount of hardware resources as presented in a recent related work [14]. Besides the efficiency in the area, we have reduced the latency to 62.48% compared

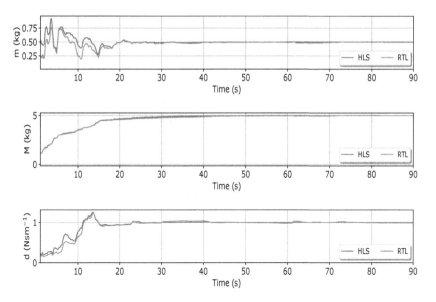

Fig. 6. Parameter estimation on the inverted pendulum using EKF

to the prior work. Furthermore, the execution time is 21.97 μs which means a speedup of 20 compared to [14]. However, more efficiency can be achieved using an RTL description language. Therefore, we have implemented EKF as a proof-of-concept in a fixed-point format. This approach saves 6.88% more lookup tables and 4.93% more flip-flops compared to the HLS implementation. The sampling time is measured as 2.7 μs. However, the results have shown a slight deviation during the convergence to the real system parameters (Fig. 6). This effect is caused due to the representation in a fixed-point format. The HLS implementation is realized in a single-precision floating-point format.

5   Conclusion

In this work, the SysIDLib library has been proposed with various system identification techniques for linear and nonlinear characterized systems (inverted pendulum, a DC motor and polynomial models). These algorithms are performed in a real-time FIL simulation. The most accurate results are generated with EKF in all use cases. However, its trade-off is the higher resource utilization as compared to the remaining identification techniques. However, it has the main advantage that EKF can still be used for diagnosis and monitoring purposes. The RLS and LMS algorithm have been performed to identify nonlinear adaptive filter structures. Both techniques have estimated accurately the parameter values. Due to the recursive filter structure, the RLS algorithm has identified the parameters with a faster convergence rate. Moreover, EKF has been compared for different type of implementations in this work. Although the RTL implementation has a slight difference in the transient behavior, it can estimate all final values in the fixed-point format. This leads to more saving of the hardware resources. However, reliable results have been generated with the SysIDLib library for different type of use cases. Due to its generality, it can be easily adapted to other system applications. The deployed real-time FIL architecture can also identify real system parameters with the proposed SysIDLib library.

Acknowledgment. The work described in this paper has been funded by the German Research Foundation (DFG, Deutsche Forschungsgemeinschaft) as part of Germany's Excellence Strategy – EXC 2050/1 – Project ID 390696704 – Cluster of Excellence "Centre for Tactile Internet with Human-in-the-Loop" (CeTI) of Technische Universität Dresden.

References

1. Ricco, M., et al.: FPGA-based implementation of dual Kalman filter for PV MPPT applications. IEEE Trans. Industr. Inf. **13**(1), 176–185 (2017)
2. Akgün, G., et al.: Dynamic tunable and reconfigurable hardware controller with EKF-based state reconstruction through FPGA-in the loop. In: 2018 International Conference on ReConFigurable Computing and FPGAs (ReConFig), pp. 1–8 (2018)
3. Akgün, G., et al.: System identification using LMS, RLS, EKF and neural network. In: 2019 IEEE International Conference of Vehicular Electronics and Safety (ICVES), pp. 1–6 (2019)
4. Yang, J.N., et al.: An adaptive extended Kalman filter for structural damage identifications II: unknown inputs. Struct. Control Health Monit. **14**(3), 497–521 (2007)
5. Salcic, Z., et al.: A floating-point FPGA-based self-tuning regulator. IEEE Trans. Ind. Electron. **53**(2), 693–704 (2006)
6. Ronquillo-Lomeli, G., et al.: Nonlinear identification of inverted pendulum system using Volterra polynomials. Mech. Based Des. Struct. Mach. **44**(1–2), 5–15 (2016)
7. Kapgate, S.N., et al.: Adaptive Volterra modeling for nonlinear systems based on LMS variants. In: 2018 5th International Conference on Signal Processing and Integrated Networks (SPIN), pp. 258–263 (2018)
8. Subudhi, U., et al.: Harmonics and decaying DC estimation using Volterra LMS/F algorithm. IEEE Trans. Ind. Appl. **54**(2), 1108–1118 (2018)
9. Morales-Velazquez, L., et al.: Special purpose processor for parameter identification of CNC second order servo systems on a low-cost FPGA platform. Mechatronics **20**(2), 265–272 (2010)
10. Ananthan, T., et al.: An FPGA-based parallel architecture for on-line parameter estimation using the RLS identification algorithm. Microprocess. Microsyst. **38**(5), 496–508 (2014)
11. Navarro, D., et al.: High-level synthesis for accelerating the FPGA implementation of computationally demanding control algorithms for power converters. IEEE Trans. Industr. Inf. **9**(3), 1371–1379 (2013)
12. Morello, R., et al.: Hardware-in-the-loop simulation of FPGA-based state estimators for electric vehicle batteries. In 2016 IEEE 25th International Symposium on Industrial Electronics (ISIE), pp. 280–285 (2016)

13. Haykin, S.S.: Adaptive Filter Theory, vol. 4. Prentice Hall, Upper Saddle River (2002)
14. Mie, S., et al.: Real-time UAV attitude heading reference system using extended Kalman filter for programmable SoC. In: 2017 IEEE 11th International Symposium on Embedded Multicore/Many-core Systems-on-Chip (MCSoC), pp. 136–142, September 2017

Optimal and Greedy Heuristic Approaches for Scheduling and Mapping of Hardware Tasks to Reconfigurable Computing Devices

Zakarya Guettatfi[1,2]([✉]), Paul Kaufmann[3], and Marco Platzner[1]

[1] Paderborn University, Paderborn, Germany
zakarya@mail.uni-paderborn.de, platzner@upb.de
[2] Center for Development of Advanced Technology, Algiers, Algeria
zguettatfi@cdta.dz
[3] University of Mainz, Mainz, Germany
paul.kaufmann@uni-mainz.de

Abstract. Executing real-time tasks on dynamically reconfigurable FPGAs requires us to solve the challenges of scheduling and placement. In the past, many approaches have been presented to address these challenges. Still, most of them rely on idealized assumptions about the reconfigurability of FPGAs and the capabilities of commercial tool flows. In our work, we aim at solving these problems leveraging a practically useful 2D slot-based FPGA area model. We present optimal approaches for reconfigurable slot creation, hardware task assignment, and placement creation. We quantitatively compare optimal and heuristics algorithms through simulation experiments and show that the heuristics are rather close to the optimal techniques in terms of solution quality, in particular for reconfigurable slot creation and hardware task assignment. Further, we also derive an indication for the amount of fragmentation of the FPGA surface that is inherent to our 2D area model.

1 Introduction

The FPGA utilization can be maximized if the hardware tasks can be arranged such that there is no simultaneous temporal and geometrical overlap between them. The resulting scheduling and floorplanning problems for two-dimensional resources are NP-hard [7,11]. There is substantial earlier work that deals with the interdependent problems of task scheduling and placement on FPGAs. These works differ in the characteristics of the task sets, i.e., whether tasks have deadlines or not, the optimization goals, whether they deal with off-line or on-line problems, and, most importantly, the area model for the FPGA surface. Many of the presented techniques use an area model with free placement where tasks can be placed rather flexibly on the FPGA fabric. While this model has received a lot of attention in the past, aspects such as reconfiguration schemes of commercial FPGAs, capabilities of commercial tool flows, and the infrastructure needed to

F. Rincón et al. (Eds.): ARC 2020, LNCS 12083, pp. 108–117, 2020.
https://doi.org/10.1007/978-3-030-44534-8_9

connect hardware tasks to the CPU, memory, and I/O, constitute major hurdles for practical realization. In VLSI design, there are works on optimal bin packing and metaheuristics for floorplanning. Still, only a few of these consider problem characteristics important for our work, such as preplaced modules [7,11] and "soft modules" that are specified only by their area instead of a geometric layout.

In previous work [4], we have introduced a tool flow for task scheduling and floorplanning based on a special 2D slot-based reconfiguration model, where reconfigurable slots comprise several micro slots. Micro slots constitute rectangular reconfigurable regions with a complete set of resource types and their creation and partial reconfiguration is supported by commercial tool flows. Under this area model, we have proposed heuristics for scheduling and placement.

In this paper, we present novel *optimal slot creation and task assignment as well as layout generation methods* for the 2D slot model. Based on the insight that slot-based reconfigurable task scheduling becomes a problem similar to mono and multi-processor scheduling, and that slot placement becomes very similar to the VLSI's floorplanning problem, we adopt corresponding approaches and develop optimal slot creation and task assignment (SCTA) as well as layout generation (LG) algorithms. We compare these optimal techniques with our previous heuristics.

The remainder of the paper is organized as follows: In Sect. 2, we discuss related work about task scheduling and placement on FPGAs. In Sect. 3 we summarize our previous special 2D slot-based reconfiguration model and the proposed heuristics for slot creation and task assignment as well as for layout generation. The mathematical modeling for the novel optimal and heuristic approaches is then presented in Sect. 4. In Sect. 5 experimental results are detailed. Finally, Sect. 6 is devoted to the conclusions.

2   Related Work

The majority of related projects described hardware tasks as rectangular-shaped regions of reconfigurable logic and used an area model that can be categorized into 1D vs. 2D and free placement vs. slot-based placement. In the 1D area model, tasks can be allocated along one dimension only. This approach simplifies the placement problem and matches the partial reconfiguration abilities of earlier Xilinx devices. In the 2D area model, the rectangular tasks have to be allocated on the rectangular-shaped device. A free placement would allow allocating such a task on any feasible position on the device. In contrast, the slot-based model foresees a pre-partitioning of the device into rectangular regions that can accommodate tasks. The slot-based models allow for an easier, practical realization. In the following, we present selected related work in some of the areas related to task scheduling and placement.

In [8], the authors formulate an online real-time scheduling problem and present two heuristics for placing aperiodic hardware tasks. These heuristics are denoted as the horizon and stuffing techniques, considering both 1D and 2D area models Improved placement strategies that lead to reduced fragmentation and lower total execution times were presented in, e.g., [12]. Along the same line, [2] showed a level look-ahead approach with a non-preemptive EDF that delays the allocation of hardware tasks to reduce the fragmentation. In [3], the authors investigated two preemptive scheduling algorithms for periodic real-time tasks: EDF Next Fit (EDF-NF) and Merge-Server Distributed Load (MSDL). In [5] proposed the Finishing-Aware EDF (FAEDF) algorithm, which is EDF augmented with a look-ahead capability to locate future releases of adjacent areas. Another line of research dealt with the task placement or area allocation problem, respectively, and focused on online placement of relocatable, rectangular-shaped tasks that can be placed anywhere on the 2D surface of an FPGA device. The first work establishing the problem of online placement in the 2D area model was [1], where the authors proposed a fast online placement algorithm based on handling empty spaces. Later, [10] presented another placement method that relies on a partitioning of the reconfigurable resource and uses a hash matrix data structure to maintain the free space. While the works mentioned above consider homogeneous FPGA architectures, there are also algorithms for 2D placement on heterogeneous devices, e.g., [6]. The challenge of hardware task placement can also be seen from the perspective of d-dimensional orthogonal bin packing [7] and floorplanning, which is the first stage in physical VLSI design in the Electronic Design Automation (EDA) [11].

3   The Area Model

This section describes the area model used by the slot creation and task assignment (SCTA) as well as layout generation (LG) algorithms. The area model and the heuristics are results of our previous work, presented in [4], but require a summary for the introduction and comparison to optimal SCTA and LG algorithms.

The area model of this paper bases on two ideas: First, an FPGA is subdivided into rectangular reconfigurable regions, so-called **micro-slots**. The partition is done in such a way that all micro-slots have the same type and amount of resources. This simplifies the mapping of hardware tasks to hardware. Additionally, the borders of the micro-slots follow the boundaries of the partially reconfigurable frames imposed by a vendor's partial reconfiguration tool flow. This makes the area model practically useful. Second, a task executed on an FPGA is mapped to one or multiple micro-slots. Micro-slots allocated to serve a task are forming a so-called **slot**, which has to be a consolidated and a rectangular region on an FPGA. The size of a micro-slot is selected sufficiently large to be able to serve a small task. At the same time, the micro-slot size is chosen as small as possible to minimize fragmentation. Figure 1 shows for the Xilinx Zynq 7020, 7030, and 7045 devices the subdivision of their area. Each micro-slot contains 600 slices, providing in total 2400 LUTs, 4800 registers, 180 kB RAM, and 20 DSP blocks.

Once the area model is defined, the algorithmic challenges of hardware task scheduling and slot allocation can be presented in detail. Assuming a list of

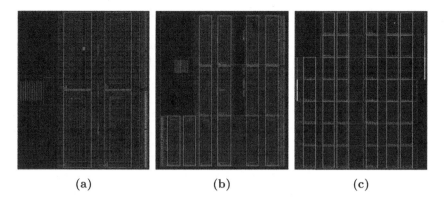

Fig. 1. Partitioning into micro slots: The Xilinx Zynq 7010 (a), the Xilinx Zynq 7020 (b) and the Xilinx Zynq 7045 (c) devices.

periodic and independent hardware tasks is given as $\Gamma = \{\tau_1, \tau_2, \ldots, \tau_n\}$, where for each task τ_i the amount of required micro slots k_i, execution time c_i, and period p_i are given as $\tau_i = (k_i, c_i, p_i)$. To justify hardware task reconfiguration, the total amount of required resources $\sum_i k_i$ should be larger than the number of micro slots available on the FPGA. The first question is: Given that every hardware task can be hypothetically instantiated and released at any point in time, is there a schedule guaranteeing all tasks meeting their deadlines and, at the same time, respecting the upper bound of available micro slots? The second question is: Given a valid schedule of hardware tasks, can the hardware tasks be mapped to slots, i.e., non-overlapping rectangular regions of micro slots?

The procedure of hardware task assignment and layout generation starts with a set of periodic real-time tasks that have been synthesized to an FPGA device family such as the Xilinx Zynq. The procedure runs in two phases, with the first one creating the reconfigurable slots in a way that each task with all its instances is accommodated in exactly one such slot and all tasks assigned to one slot are schedulable. The result is a list of reconfigurable slots, characterized only by their sizes. In a second phase, a feasible layout is generated for a given FPGA device, i.e., a layout that provides slots with widths and heights. Heuristic algorithms for both phases are presented in the following sections.

4   Optimal Techniques for Slot and Layout Creation

In this section, we detail the mathematical modeling of the two problems (i) reconfigurable slot creation and task assignment and (ii) layout generation in the form of Quadratic Constraint Programs (QCP). The QCPs can then be solved to optimality.

4.1   Optimal Slot Creation and Task Assignment Approach

We start the formalization of the QCP with $n \cdot m$ binary decision variables x_{ij} that indicate, whether the i'th task is mapped into the j'th slot S_j with n as the number of tasks and m as the number of slots:

$$x_{ij} = \begin{cases} 1 & \text{if } \tau_i \in S_j, \\ 0 & \text{otherwise.} \end{cases} \tag{1}$$

As a first constraint, we have to enforce that a task is mapped to exactly one slot:

$$\forall i \in \{1, ..., m\} : \qquad \sum_{j=1}^{m} x_{ij} = 1. \tag{2}$$

For the next modeling steps, we need an upper bound for the number of required slots. We can determine such a bound based on the time utilization factors of the tasks, defined as defined as $u_i = \frac{c_i}{p_i}$, in the following way:

$$m = \left\lceil \sum_{i}^{n} u_i \right\rceil + 1. \tag{3}$$

Let A_j be the area of the largest task assigned to the slot S_j. Then the following constraints on the areas of the reconfigurable slots must hold:

$$\forall j \in \{1, ..., m\}, \quad \forall i \in \{1, ..., n\} : \qquad A_j \geq x_{i,j} \cdot k_i. \tag{4}$$

The objective is to minimize the total area required to map all reconfigurable slots. Therefore, the cost function of our QCP accumulates the total slot area, and the objective is to minimize this expression:

$$\min \sum_{j=1}^{m} A_j. \tag{5}$$

4.2   Optimal Layout Generation Approach

The intuitive challenge of packing boxes into a container is computationally surprisingly complex. The search space becomes even larger when allowing boxes to be "soft", i.e., be configured only by the area and an interval for the aspect ratio. While in Sect. 2, we have given an overview of related work on two-dimensional box packing, our method presented here is inspired by an approach developed for arranging modules on a chip die [9]. There, the authors have formalized the task of placing blocks within a rectangular chip area as a mixed ILP [9]. We have adopted this model with a few modifications. In particular, we have introduced soft blocks and preplaced blocks to the model. Soft blocks are only specified by their area requirement, which is exactly what we find when trying to place the reconfigurable slots. Preplaced blocks are important, since we can use them to mask FPGA regions that do not contain any micro slots, e.g., regions that contain the processing system of an FPGA. The resulting model can, again, be cast as a QCP in the following way:

The geometrical position of a slot S_i is specified by its lower-left corner (x_i, y_i) and the width and height (w_i, h_i). Slots may not overlap and may not be placed outside the chip area with width W and height H. The first constraint can be enforced by introducing two binary variables p_{ij} and q_{ij} for each slot, ensuring that exactly one of the following inequalities is sharp, i.e., holds:

$$
\begin{aligned}
x_i + w_i &\leq x_j + W(p_{ij} + q_{ij}), & \text{slot i to the left of slot j} \\
x_i - w_j &\geq x_j - W(1 - p_{ij} + q_{ij}), & \text{slot i to the right of slot j} \\
y_i + h_i &\leq y_j + H(1 + p_{ij} - q_{ij}), & \text{slot i below slot j} \\
y_i - h_j &\geq x_j - H(2 - p_{ij} - q_{ij}), & \text{slot i above slot j}
\end{aligned}
\tag{6}
$$

Placing boxes outside the area of an FPGA is avoided by:

$$
\begin{aligned}
x_i + w_i &\leq W, \\
y_i + h_i &\leq H.
\end{aligned}
\tag{7}
$$

The objective of the QCP is to minimize the area xy of the rectangle enclosing all slots. However, to avoid a quadratic objective function, we minimize the rectangle's perimeter $2x + 2y$, which implicitly minimizes the area. The previously defined constraints are therefore sharpened to:

$$
\begin{aligned}
x_i + w_i &\leq x, \\
y_i + h_i &\leq y.
\end{aligned}
\tag{8}
$$

For slots specified only by their area A_i, a quadratic constraint ensures that the width w_i and height h_i of a slot are sufficiently large:

$$
w_i \cdot h_i \geq A_i \qquad \forall i \in \{1, ..., n\}
\tag{9}
$$

5   Evaluation

When comparing the optimal approaches presented in the previous section with the heuristics developped in [4], two main questions arise: By what margin are the heuristics behind the optimal approaches, and what are the computation times of the optimal algorithms? To answer these questions, we have designed two experiments. In the first experiment, the slot and layout creation algorithms are compared using task sets with increasing computational and resource requirements regarding generated slot and floorplan sizes as well as the computational times. In the second experiment, the algorithms are tested on how many of the task sets with FPGA time area product utilization factors between 0.1 and 1.0 can be successfully placed.

All optimal algorithms and the heuristic layout generator have been developed in C++ and use the Gurobi solver v.8.1.1. The slot generation and task assignment heuristic has been developed in Python.

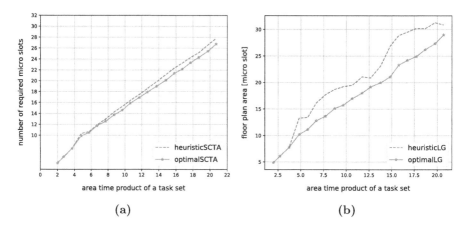

Fig. 2. Simulation results: (a) required number of micro slots and (b) the area of the floorplan depending on the application load of task sets given by the optimal and heuristic solutions. Each line point is an overage over 50 task sets.

5.1   Comparing Slot Set and Layout Sizes

To test the algorithms, we have generated 1000 task sets with the cumulated task set computation times in the range of 1 to 30 time units, resource requirements in the range of 1 to 6 micro slots, and time utilization factors in the range 0.10 to 0.50. Figure 2a shows for the optimal and heuristic SCTA algorithms the number of computed micro slots depending on the application load of a task set. The application load of a task set Γ is defined as $\sum_{\tau_i \in \Gamma} \frac{c_i}{p_i} \cdot k_i$, which represents the area-time product consumed by all tasks. The first observation is that the heuristic approach is very close to the optimal algorithm on average. Only for task sets with an accumulated application load beyond 7, a small difference starts to appear.

The computation times of optimal and heuristic SCTA algorithms differ, however, significantly. While the heuristic finishes within a few milliseconds, the QCP solver of the optimal approach often needs days on a large multi-core machine with a lot of main memory to be able to compute a result. This may be acceptable if the slot configuration is calculated once, at the design time of a system. Increasing the sizes of task sets further above 30 time units would render the optimal approach rather impractical.

The discrepancies between the optimal and heuristic LG algorithms are more prominent in Fig. 2b. Starting with an application load of 7, slots can be placed more compact by the optimal algorithm. The difference grows up to 5 slots for a time area utilization factor of 15 to 17.5. The results indicate that the naïve greedy (construction) heuristic approach we borrowed from strip-based bin packing has a lot of potential for improvement. We envision replacing the algorithm by a more computationally complex improvement heuristic, such as Simulated Annealing and Genetic Algorithms, to achieve better asymptotical results.

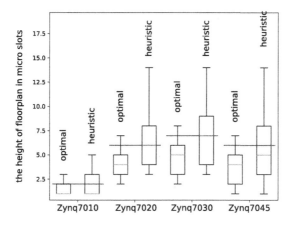

Fig. 3. Simulation results: Heights of the layout (floor plan) for different Zynq devices computed by optimal and heuristic approaches.

The computation time difference is significant but not as dramatic as for the SCTA algorithms. The heuristic LG approach can compute results within a few milliseconds, while the optimal algorithm takes up to a quarter of an hour on a large multi-core machine for a single slot set.

5.2   The Maximum Utilization Experiments

The goal of this experiment is to figure out to what extent the area utilization factor of an FPGA can be increased before the LG algorithms stop producing valid layouts. We would also like to understand better how pronounced the gap between the LG algorithms shown in Fig. 2b actually is. To this end, we have created slot sets with area utilization factors ranging from 0.1 to 1.0 with a step size of 0.1. Each slot set contains a series of slot areas randomly generated with respect to the area utilization. As target FPGAs, we have selected the Xilinx Zynq 7010, 7020, 7030, and 7045 devices. By fixing the FPGA's widths, we let the LG algorithms minimize the height of the surrounding box around the placed slots. Figure 3 shows boxplots for the achieved layout heights. The red lines in the figure indicate the maximal capacity, i.e., the height of the corresponding Zynq device. Hence, slot sets with a layout height below the red line can be executed on the according FPGA.

The first observation is that the optimal LG approach is very successful in mapping 75%, 87.5%, 87.5%, and 87.5% of the task sets to the target FPGAs. This indicates that the fragmentation inherent to the area model, which we accept in favor of efficient algorithmic task scheduling and slot mapping, lies around 25% for smaller task sets and reduces when FPGAs became larger. The heuristic LG lags behind, as already seen in the previous experiment. Only 50% to 62.5% of the task sets can be mapped. Compared to the optimal LG approach, 25%, 37.5%, 37.5%, and 25% fewer tasks can be mapped to the chosen FPGAs.

6   Conclusion

In this paper, we have presented the mathematical modeling of reconfigurable slot creation, including task assignment, and layout generation as QCPs. This allows us to solve these problems to optimality, where in previous work, we had developed and presented heuristics. We then have quantitatively compared the optimal approaches with the heuristics using a library of different randomly generated real-time task sets. We could show that the heuristics generally compute very good results. The results produced by the heuristic for reconfigurable slot creation, including task assignment, are very close to optimal; the results for the heuristic layout creation lag a bit behind. A further result is that the slot-based area model chosen in our approach adds roughly 25% fragmentation, which, however, reduces with larger task sets. The drawback of the optimal slot creation, task assignment, and layout generation approaches is their exhaustive computation times. The heuristic methods compute their outputs within a few milliseconds. While the optimal approaches are highly useful to evaluate the performance of our heuristics, applying them for larger tasks set is impractical. In future work, we aim at improving the heuristic for layout generation by taking inspiration from known floorplanning techniques in the electronic design automation domain.

Acknowledgment. This work has been partially supported by the German Research Foundation (DFG) within the Collaborative Research Centre 901 "On-The-Fly Computing" under the project number 160364472.

References

1. Bazargan, K., Kastner, R., Sarrafzadeh, M.: Fast template placement for reconfigurable computing systems. IEEE Des. Test Comput. **17**(1), 68–83 (2000)
2. Cui, J., Gu, Z., Liu, W., Deng, Q.: An efficient algorithm for online soft real-time task placement on reconfigurable hardware devices. In: 10th IEEE International Symposium on Object and Component-Oriented Real-Time Distributed Computing, ISORC 2007, pp. 321–328. IEEE (2007)
3. Danne, K., Platzner, M.: Periodic real-time scheduling for FPGA computers. In: Third International Workshop on Intelligent Solutions in Embedded Systems, pp. 117–127. IEEE (2005)
4. Guettatfi, Z., Platzner, M., Kermia, O., Khouas, A.: An approach for mapping periodic real-time tasks to reconfigurable hardware. In: 2019 IEEE International Parallel and Distributed Processing Symposium Workshops (IPDPSW), pp. 99–106, May 2019
5. Iturbe, X., Benkrid, K., Hong, C., Ebrahim, A., Arslan, T., Martinez, I.: Runtime scheduling, allocation, and execution of real-time hardware tasks onto Xilinx FPGAs subject to fault occurrence. Int. J. Reconfigurable Comput. **2013** (2013). 32 pages
6. Koester, M., Porrmann, M., Kalte, H.: Task placement for heterogeneous reconfigurable architectures. In: International Conference on Field-Programmable Technology, pp. 43–50. IEEE (2005)
7. Scheithauer, G.: Introduction to Cutting and Packing Optimization. ISORMS, vol. 263. Springer, Cham (2018). https://doi.org/10.1007/978-3-319-64403-5

8. Steiger, C., Walder, H., Platzner, M.: Heuristics for online scheduling real-time tasks to partially reconfigurable devices. In: Y. K. Cheung, P., Constantinides, G.A. (eds.) FPL 2003. LNCS, vol. 2778, pp. 575–584. Springer, Heidelberg (2003). https://doi.org/10.1007/978-3-540-45234-8_56

9. Sutanthavibul, S., Shragowitz, E., Rosen, J.B.: An analytical approach to floorplan design and optimization. IEEE Trans. Comput. Aided Des. Integr. Circuits Syst. **10**(6), 761–769 (1991)

10. Walder, H., Steiger, C., Platzner, M.: Fast online task placement on FPGAs: free space partitioning and 2D-hashing. In: Proceedings International Parallel and Distributed Processing Symposium, IEEE (2003). 8 pp.

11. Wang, L.T., Chang, Y.W., Cheng, K.T.T.: Electronic Design Automation: Synthesis, Verification, and Test. Morgan Kaufmann Publishers Inc., San Francisco (2009)

12. Zhou, X.G., Wang, Y., Huang, X.Z., Peng, C.L.: On-line scheduling of real-time tasks for reconfigurable computing system. In: IEEE International Conference on Field Programmable Technology, FPT 2006, pp. 57–64. IEEE (2006)

Design Space Exploration and Estimation Techniques

Accuracy, Training Time and Hardware Efficiency Trade-Offs for Quantized Neural Networks on FPGAs

Pascal Bacchus, Robert Stewart[(✉)], and Ekaterina Komendantskaya

Mathematical and Computer Sciences, Heriot-Watt University, Edinburgh, UK
{R.Stewart,E.Komendantskaya}@hw.ac.uk

Abstract. Neural networks have proven a successful AI approach in many application areas. Some neural network deployments require low inference latency and lower power requirements to be useful e.g. autonomous vehicles and smart drones. Whilst FPGAs meet these requirements, hardware needs of neural networks to execute often exceed FPGA resources.

Emerging industry led frameworks aim to solve this problem by compressing the topology and precision of neural networks, eliminating computations that require memory for execution. Compressing neural networks inevitably comes at the cost of reduced inference accuracy.

This paper uses Xilinx's FINN framework to systematically evaluate the trade-off between precision, inference accuracy, training time and hardware resources of 64 quantized neural networks that perform MNIST character recognition.

We identify sweet spots around 3 bit precision in the quantization design space after training with 40 epochs, minimising both hardware resources and accuracy loss. With enough training, using 2 bit weights achieves almost the same inference accuracy as 3–8 bit weights.

Keywords: Deep learning · Neural networks · Quantization · FPGA

1 Introduction

Neural networks have proved successful for many domains including image recognition, autonomous systems and language processing. GPUs are often used to train and test neural networks, since GPUs offer highest peak performance compared with CPUs and FPGAs. Due to their specialised support for floating-point arithmetic operations, GPUs can deliver the highest arithmetic performance for 32 bit floating point neural network inference. However, the use of GPUs operating at 200+ W is becoming prohibitively expensive for energy use, e.g. the carbon footprint of state-of-the-art AI algorithms performed by GPUs is about five times the lifetime emissions of an average car [16].

Supported by EPSRC grant EP/N028201/1.

F. Rincón et al. (Eds.): ARC 2020, LNCS 12083, pp. 121–135, 2020.
https://doi.org/10.1007/978-3-030-44534-8_10

Compared with GPUs and CPUs, peak performance of FPGAs becomes competitive for fixed-point representations [24], which are used in quantized neural networks. Special purpose FPGA based accelerators significantly increase inference speed which is useful in domains like stock market trading and autonomous vehicles, and reduce energy requirements useful for remote computer vision on smart sensors and drones where access to power is scarce.

Models trained on a GPU have a memory footprint that is too large for FPGAs. This prohibits the use of FPGA accelerators for executing full precision neural networks because they have limited hardware resources for storage and computation. Worse still, neural networks for these domains have grown from single hidden layer topologies with several hundred weights, to deep models with more than one hundred hidden layers with millions of weights, meaning their memory resource requirements is increasing with state-of-the-art models. Quantized fixed point representation can significantly reduce power and resource costs, e.g. [4] reports $\times 0.164$ area and $\times 0.136$ power costs with a 16-bit multiplier compared with a 32-bit multiplier for neural networks.

Neural network performance is often measured by its inference accuracy on unseen inputs. Other performance metrics become important when resource constrained accelerators are to be used:

- **Throughput** How many achievable inferences per unit of time.
- **Latency** The time to infer.
- **Energy** The energy consumed by the processor.
- **Compression ratio** A ratio between an original model size before and after compression algorithms are applied.
- **Training time** The time needed to obtain a neural network with acceptable inference accuracy.
- **Robustness** The robustness of the network when confronted with adversarial perturbated inputs.

Two motivations for compressing neural networks is speed and energy efficiency:

1. **Speed.** Many neural network layers are bandwidth bound. This introduces latency that dominates execution time because most time is spent to bring data to processors rather than performing computation. Effective pruning algorithms remove weights and layers entirely without adversely affecting accuracy, reducing memory access and thus reducing latency.
2. **Energy Efficiency.** It costs orders-of-magnitude more energy to access off-chip DDR memory compared to on-chip memory e.g. SRAM, BRAM and cache memory. Fitting weights into on-chip memories reduces frequency of energy inefficient off-chip memory accesses.

Neural network compression methods reduce both the memory size and computation time. The result of compression is neural networks with smaller spacial complexity, and low precision arithmetic operations that are cheaper to compute.

Several industry led neural network compression tools have recently emerged. Google's Tensorflow Lite is a framework that uses quantization-aware training [1] to quantize full precision models into 8 bit versions. Intel's Distiller [29] is a Python framework for compressing neural networks specified in PyTorch, with support for pruning and quantization.

There are several neural network frameworks for FPGAs. FPGAConvNet [23] supports convolutional neural networks (CNNs) but does not support quantization. Caffeinated FPGA [7] is an extension of the Caffe framework for compiling convolutional neural networks (CNNs) to FPGAs and supports binarization but not quantization. ReBNet [10] is a more general framework, supporting neural network types other than just CNNs, but is restricted to binarized networks and is not actively maintained.

Xilinx's FINN is another general framework for neural networks of various types to FPGAs. FINN initially supported binarized neural networks [22], then was extended for quantized networks [3] and Long-Short Term Memory Neural Networks (LSTM) [20].

Neural network throughput improvements can be achieved by reducing FPGA resource use e.g. [28]. Our paper relies on this assumption about throughput speedups, and instead focuses on the trade-off between accuracy and FPGA resource requirements. Rather than pruning, it explores the design space granted by FINN's ability to independently quantize weights and activation functions of multilayer perceptron (MLP) neural networks, with arbitrary bit-width values between 1 and 8.

The most closely related work to our systematic evaluation in Sect. 3 is [21], which evaluates the trade-offs between accuracy, throughput and hardware efficiency for 1, 2, 4, 8, 16 bit quantized and 32 bit full precision neural networks with FINN. Our paper extends this work in two ways. (1) Measuring impact of *training time* on the accuracy of quantized neural networks with 10, 20, 30, 50 and 100 epochs. (2) A more fine grained evaluation for 1..8 bit precision varying activation function precision and weight precision independently of each other, i.e. measuring training time, accuracy and hardware efficiency trade-offs across 64 quantized neural networks.

Contributions. The paper makes the following contributions:

- Evaluation of the inference accuracy for 64 quantized neural networks with 1–8 bit weights and activation function precision (Sect. 3.3).
- Evaluation of the effect that increased training time has on the accuracy of these quantized neural networks (Sect. 3.4).
- Evaluating the cost of LUTs, FFs and BRAMs for these quantized neural networks (Sect. 3.4).
- A relative performance comparison across different quantized neural networks showing the trade-off between required hardware resources and accuracy (Sect. 3.5).

2   Background: FINN

2.1   FINN Workflow

This section describes the workflow of the FINN framework. Our experiments in Sect. 3 assess very low precision neural networks, i.e. reducing precision from 32 bits to 1–8 bits to fit within the resource constraints of FPGAs. As such, quantization aware training is used.

Each experiment uses the following process:

1. **Prepare.** Import training and testing data as numpy arrays and the Theano [2] model described in Sect. 3.1.
2. **Train.** Set the precision for both parameters, chose the training time and training parameters. Once training is complete, we obtain a list of numpy arrays that correspond to the quantized trained weights. At this point we obtain the accuracy performance.
3. **Hardware Generation.** Numpy arrays are converted from floating point values into binary values and packed into binary files, and FINN compiles the quantized neural network to synthesisable C++.
4. **Synthesize Hardware.** Use HLS synthesis to obtain an estimation of the resources required.

2.2   Quantization

Quantization. Quantization [12] shifts values from 32 bit floating point continuous values to reduced bit discrete values. In a neural network, weights between neurons and activation functions can be quantized.

Binarization. Binarization [6] is a special case of quantization that represents weights and/or activation function outputs with a single bit. These methods replace arithmetic operation with bit-wise operations, reducing the energy consumption and memory requirements.

Quantized neural networks can significantly outperform binarized neural networks and can compete with the accuracy of full precision models [12].

Another neural network compression approach is weight reduction. Weight reduction keeps a high bit precision for preserved weights while removing unimportant parameters in the network, examples are *pruning* [11] and *weight sharing* [5]. Pruning keeps only the most useful connections between nodes. Weight sharing packs groups of weights together given they have similar values. A complete study of approximating neural network approaches is in [25].

2.3   Quantization for Training in FINN

FINN trains a neural network at the Python level with Theano, before generating synthesisable C++ for hardware. The weights and activation functions during training in Python operate on floating point values but Python functions simulate quantization to limit weights and activation function outputs to discrete values permitted by the chosen quantization configuration. When generating hardware, the arithmetic precision of weights and activation functions in the C++ match the quantized bit widths simulated during training.

Weight Binarization for Training. Binarization transforms every weight into either a 1 or −1 value. Binarization is shown in Eq. 1, which corresponds to the FINN implementation in Fig. 1. The output of the approximate sigmoid function **hard_sigmoid** is rounded to the nearest integer to shift the range of values before binarization. This function is monotonic in the interval $[0; 1]$, thus preserving the order of its domain. The value is rounded to either 0 or 1 and then it set to either −1 or 1.

$$BinariseWeight(x) = \begin{cases} 1 & \text{if } \|(hard\_sigmoid(x))\| > 0.5 \\ -1 & \text{otherwise} \end{cases} \tag{1}$$

```
1   class QuantizationBinary(object):
2       def __init__(self, scale=1.0):
3           self.scale = scale      <------------┤  The choice is either -1
4           self.min = -scale                    │  or 1 for binarization
5           self.max = scale
6
7       def quantizeWeights(self, X):
8           Xa = hard_sigmoid(X / self.scale)  <----┤  The range is converted to
9           Xb = Theano.round(Xa)                   │  [0;1] and then to -1 or 1
10          return Theano.switch(Xb,self.scale,-self.scale)
```

Fig. 1. Weight binarization in FINN for training

Weight Quantization for Training. FINN discretises the range of full precision values by rounding to a close neighbour using fixed point quantization. The *min* and *max* values for the quantization range are related to the quantization precision n, and they are defined by:

$$max = 2 - \frac{1}{2^{n-2}} \qquad\qquad min = -2 + \frac{1}{2^{n-2}}$$

The quantization formula for $x \in [min; max]$ is shown in Eq. 2.

$$QuantiseWeights(x) = \frac{\lfloor x2^n + 2^{n-1} - 1 \rfloor}{2^{n-2}} - 2 + \frac{1}{2^{n-2}} \tag{2}$$

Table 1 shows examples of quantized values with $min = -2$ and $max = 2$ with $2^n - 1$ values in this interval. The values are all strictly positive but the quantization range is symmetric. The step between each quantized value is $\frac{1}{2^{n-2}}$. When n increases, the number of quantized values increase and we can obtain values close to the upper and lower bound of the interval.

Table 1. Example of quantized weights

Value	Precision (bits)							
	1	2	3	4	5	6	7	8
0.136	1	0	0	0.25	0.125	0.125	0.125	0.140625
0.357	1	0	0.5	0.25	0.375	0.375	0.34375	0.359375
0.639	1	1	0.5	0.75	0.625	0.625	0.625	0.640625
1.135	1	1	1	1.25	1.125	1.125	1.125	1.140625
2	1	1	1.5	1.75	1.875	1.9375	1.96875	1.984375

Activation Function Quantization for Training. The quantization of activation functions works similarly to weight quantization. Figure 2 shows the Python used to simulate a binarized *tanh* function. The *round3* function used on line 5 is from [6], which approximates standard activation functions for deep learning algorithms. All quantized functions are strictly increasing and differentiable.

```
1  def hard_sigmoid(x):
2      return Theano.clip((x+1.)/2.,0,1)
3
4  def binary_tanh_unit(x):
5      return 2.*round3(hard_sigmoid(x))-1
```

> returns the result of the binarized tanh function

Fig. 2. Activation function binarization in FINN for training

For the quantized hyperbolic tangent function $tanh(x) = \frac{e^x - e^{-x}}{e^x + e^{-x}}$, the range of values in Table 1 is optimal because it has two asymptotes that goes towards -1 and 1, e.g. $tanh(2) = 0.964$. The saturation plateau of the activation function is almost attained. Figure 3 shows the shape of *tanh* for different quantization precisions.

3   Evaluation

For 64 neural network quantization weight and activation function configurations, the evaluation in this section measures:

1. *Absolute* accuracy and hardware resource costs of the 64 quantized neural networks (Sects. 3.3 and 3.4).
2. *Relative* performance comparison of accuracy and hardware resource costs of these neural networks (Sect. 3.5).

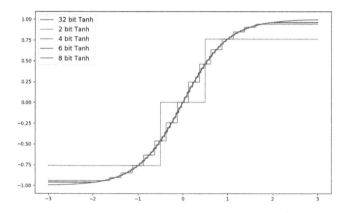

Fig. 3. Hyperbolic tangent with different quantization configuration

3.1 Neural Network Topology

Figure 4 shows the multilayer perceptron model used in the experiments. It is presented as Python code with Theano and Lasagne [8] libraries, to illustrate how quantized neural networks are constructed programmatically as input to the FINN framework. The input layer consists of 784 neurons that represent the 784 pixels from MNIST dataset [14] (28×28 grayscale images). The output layer has 10 neurons, one for each of the 10 possible classifications for recognised digits.

Between the input and output layers are three fully connected hidden layers that have all 1024 neurons, each using the same activation function, the hyperbolic tangent. The weight quantization is specified on line 10 and the activation function on line 16. The activation function quantization is defined in its constructor, elsewhere. Dropout layers (lines 6 and 22) are only used for training as a means of regularisation, and are not included in the generated hardware. This layer randomly removes some connections between two layers at each training batch to avoid overfitting and obtain a model that can generalize on new data.

Batch normalisation is used on the trained model, in the hidden layers (line 18) and as the last layer (line 31). Trained parameters from the `BatchNormaLayer` layers are included in synthesisable C++ for deployment to an FPGA. Batch normalisation is a stochastic operation that generally improves the speed and performance of a network. Lasagne's normalization is based on the following:

$$y = \frac{x - \mu}{\sqrt{\sigma^2 + \epsilon}} * \gamma + \beta$$

where μ is the current batch input x, σ is the variance of the current batch input x, ϵ is a small variable to avoid numerical discontinuity, γ is the average statistic computed during training time and β is the average statistic computed during training time. On line 31, *alpha* is the exponential moving average factor which is calculated during training time but also initiated by the user. These values are used during testing, and are also included as constants in the C++ to deploy the quantized neural network to an FPGA.

```
1   mlp = InputLayer(shape=(None,   1,   28,   28),        ┌─────────────────────────┐
2           input_var=input)   ◄ ─ ─ ─ ─ ─ ─ ─ ─ ─ ─ ─     │ Input size fits a       │
3                                                           │ 28*28 pixels image      │
4                                                           └─────────────────────────┘
5                                                           ┌──────────────────────────────────┐
6   mlp = DropoutLayer(mlp,p=dropout_in)   ◄ ─ ─ ─ ─        │ Reduce overfitting during training │
7                                                           │ with dropout regularization        │
8   for k in range(n_hidden_layers):                        └──────────────────────────────────┘
9       mlp = qn.DenseLayer(mlp,                            ┌──────────────────────────────────┐
10          quantization=weight_quant,   ◄ ─ ─ ─ ─          │ Enhanced DenseLayer function from │
11          W_LR_scale=W_LR_scale,                          │ Lasagne that uses quantized weight │
12          nonlinearity=identity                           └──────────────────────────────────┘
13          num_units=1024)
14                                                          ┌──────────────────────────────────┐
15      mlp = NonlinearityLayer(mlp,   ◄ ─ ─ ─ ─ ┤         │ Quantized activation function     │
16      nonlinearity=activation_function)                   │ a custom hyperbolic tangent       │
17                                                          └──────────────────────────────────┘
18      mlp = BatchNormLayer(mlp,                           ┌──────────────────────────┐
19          epsilon=epsilon,   ◄ ─ ─ ─ ─ ─ ─ ─ ─            │ Improves speed and stability │
20          alpha=alpha)                                    │ with normalized inputs       │
21                                                          └──────────────────────────┘
22      mlp = DropoutLayer(mlp,   ◄ ─ ─ ─ ─ ─ ─ ─ ─        ┌────────────────────────────────────┐
23              p=dropout_hidden)                           │ Regularization of the hidden layers │
24                                                          └────────────────────────────────────┘
25  mlp = qn.DenseLayer(mlp,
26          quantization=weight_quant,
27          W_LR_scale,   ◄ ─ ─ ─ ─ ─ ─ ─ ─ ─ ─ ─ ─ ─ ┤   ┌──────────────┐
28          nonlinearity=identity,                          │ Output layer │
29          num_units=num_outputs)                          └──────────────┘
30
31  mlp = BatchNormLayer(mlp,epsilon,alpha)
```

Fig. 4. Quantized neural network model expressed in Python

3.2   Measurements Platform

The training is done using 50000 images from the MNIST dataset. A validation dataset of 10000 images is then used to minimise overfitting. Finally, accuracy is measured over a testing dataset. FINN's backend converts the model (specifically, numpy arrays) to a binary weight file and a synthesisable C++ implementation for hardware.

Our experiments target the mid-range Xilinx Zynq Z7020 device with 53k LUTs, 106k FFs and 4.9 Mb BRAM. Of the 64 quantized neural networks, only four actually fit on this FPGA, validating the need for aggressive compression approaches such as quantization, on relatively small FPGA devices.

The software and library versions used in the experiments are Vivado 2018.3, Python 2.7.15 with Numpy 1.15, Scipy 0.19.1, Theano 0.9.0, and Lasagne 0.2.

3.3   Absolute Accuracy Performance

Each of the 64 neural networks is labelled with a quantized weight W-X and quantized activation function A-Y with $X, Y \in [1; 8]$. Accuracy is measured after 10, 20, 30, 50 and 100 epochs.

Figure 5 plots the inference error rate for each of the 64 quantized neural networks after training with 10, 20, 30, 50 and 100 epochs. Using 1–3 bits weights has a noticeable effect on accuracy, i.e. between 3.9%–4.7% dropping down to

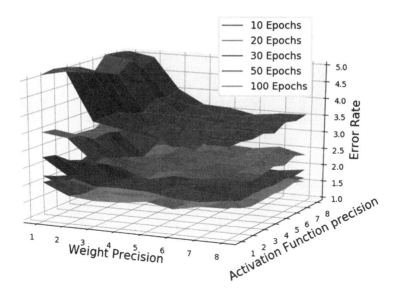

Fig. 5. Accuracy of QNNs with increasing training

below 3.7% using 4 bits or more. Training further with 40–100 epochs shifts the noticeable accuracy boundary to just 1 bit weight, meaning that with enough training, 2 bit weights achieves almost the same inference accuracy as 3–8 bit weights. The quantization of activation functions has a steady impact on accuracy, i.e. higher precision activation functions result in better accuracy, however, this is not as dramatic as the impact that quantized weight precision has on accuracy. With increased training time, the accuracy performance flattens, where absolute difference in accuracy between the best and worst quantization configuration greatly diminishes. Also, we observe a major gap between 1 and 2 bit weights versus 3–8 bit weights, especially for 10 and 20 epochs. Training beyond 40 epochs allows weights to be quantized from 3 to 2 bits without noticeable accuracy loss.

3.4 Absolute Resource Utilisation Performance

This section evaluates the trade-off between quantized precision and hardware resource use. The X axis is the number of bits for weights, the Y axis is the number of bits for the activation functions. The colour in the heat maps represents the relative measurement of the respective performance metric compared to the other 63 models.

Figure 6a shows that both weight precision and activation function precision contribute evenly to LUTs costs. Figure 6b shows that the precision of activation functions determines FF costs. While FFs and LUTs can store small amounts of data, BRAMs have greater storage capacity and are used by hardware synthesis

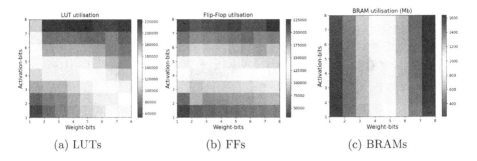

(a) LUTs   (b) FFs   (c) BRAMs

Fig. 6. Hardware resources required for 64 quantized neural networks

tools for larger data structures such as arrays. Figure 6c shows that BRAM consumption is determined exclusively by weight precision.

3.5   Relative Quantization Performance

Sections 3.3 and 3.4 present *absolute* performance values. This section evaluates the *relative* performance trade-offs between inference accuracy, BRAM, FFs and LUTs by comparing selected quantized configurations from the 64 networks.

Table 2. Relative performance for radar plots in Fig. 7

Metric	Relative performance	
	Worst	Best
Classification error rate	2.07%	1.52%
BRAM	1643	224
Flip Flops	226282	31954
Look Up Tables	223910	53336

Table 2 gives the best and worst relative performance numbers for the 64 quantized neural networks. The three radar plots in Fig. 7 represents different quantized neural network configurations, comparing accuracy and resource use (LUTs, FFs and BRAMs) performance relative to the best and values in Table 2. Each metric defines one branch in a radar chart. The three precision variations in Fig. 7 are:

1. Weight oriented distribution (Fig. 7a) increases the weight precision and keeps the activation function constant at 4 bits, i.e. W1-A4, W3-A4, W6-A4 and W8-A4.
2. Activation oriented distribution (Fig. 7b) increases the activation function precision and keeps the weight precision constant at 4 bits, i.e. W4-A1, W4-A3, W4-A6 and W4-A8.

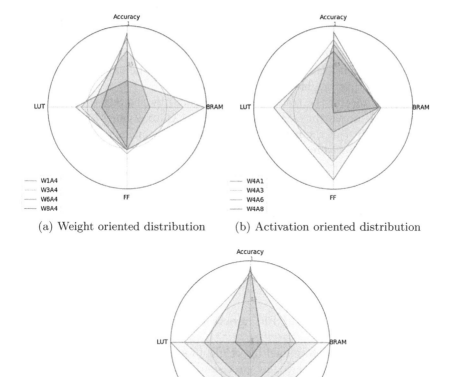

(a) Weight oriented distribution   (b) Activation oriented distribution

(c) Linear distribution

Fig. 7. Radar charts for different quantization configurations

3. Linear distribution (Fig. 7c) increases both the weight and activation function precision across the diagonal from the heat maps in Fig. 6, i.e. W1-A1, W2-A2, W4-A4 and W7-A7.

The radar plots compare the relative performance of these quantization configurations. Their scores are normalised between scores of 0 and 1. The model with the highest accuracy is plotted outermost in the radar plot in the *Accuracy* dimension whereas the models with lowest accuracy is plotted at the centre point. Likewise, the neural network using the fewest BRAMs is plotted outermost for the BRAM dimension, and the same for LUTs and FFs.

When activation functions are set to 3 bits, increasing weights from W1 to W3 causes the greatest relative accuracy score improvement (Fig. 7a). When weights are fixed at 4 bits, all accuracy scores are in the top half, with increases of activation function precision costing significantly more LUT and FF resources, with BRAM costs largely the same (Fig. 7b). Scaling both precision linearly has an equal impact on FF, LUT and BRAM scores, yet their accuracy score are all in the top quartile when weights are 2–8 bits (Fig. 7c). In summary, if top-half relative accuracy performance is the goal, the most important constraint is 2+ bits for representing weights.

The importance of the trade-offs is highlighted by the fact that most of the neural networks do not fit on the target device (Xilinx Zynq Z7020). It has 280 BRAMs and only 7 of the networks meet this constraint, and 106400 FFs with 22 of the networks within this constraint.

3.6   Discussion

These experiments confirm observations in previous work [20] that beyond 3 bits there is no significant improvement to accuracy performance given sufficient training, but does have the undesirable effect of increasing the required hardware resources. The sweet spot in the quantization design space for the purpose of MNIST character recognition is about 3 bit weights and 3 bit activation functions. These experiments show:

- The amount of LUT and FF resources is mostly affected by activation functions.
- BRAM memory is determined by weight precision.
- Accuracy is highest with higher precision, i.e. least aggressive quantization. The biggest improvement step in accuracy is switching from 1 to 2 bits weight precision.
- With enough training beyond 50 epochs, 2 bit weights achieves almost the same inference accuracy as 3–8 bit weights.

Our experiment use the quantization scheme implemented in Xilinx's FINN framework. Developing compression algorithms for embedded devices is a research area of its own, e.g. a dynamic precision data quantization algorithm in [18], performed layer-by-layer from a corresponding floating point CNN, with the goal of improving bandwidth and resource utilisation. Other compression approaches are focused on specific goals e.g. reducing power consumption, or target specific hardware e.g. GPUs or FPGAs, or target specific domains or even specific application algorithms.

Target Specific. Recent work explores the performance trade-offs between reduced precision of neural networks and their speed on GPUs, e.g. performance aware pruning can lead to ×3−10 speedups [19]. Multi-precision FPGA hardware for neural networks significantly reduces model sizes, which in [28] enables an ImageNet network to fit entirely on-chip for the first time, significantly speeding up throughput. Another recent study [20] measures the hardware cost, power consumption, and throughput for a High Level Synthesis extension of FINN that supports Long Short-Term memory (LSTM) models on FPGAs. [26] proposes a design flow for constructing low precision, low powered FPGA-based neural networks with a hybrid quantization scheme. [15] shows that resource-aware model analysis, data quantization and efficient use of hardware techniques can be combined to jointly map binarized neural networks to FPGAs with dramatically reduced resource requirements whilst maintaining acceptable accuracy.

Domain Specific. The FPGA-based processor architecture in [27] achieves a clock frequency of 100 MHz and supports acceleration of quantized CNNs for image processing. Refined still further, some quantization methods target specific algorithms, e.g. a resource-aware weight quantization framework for performing object detection on FPGAs [9]. Similarly, [17] shows that 3-bit weight quantization is required to fit an MNIST character recognition network entirely on-chip for the Xilinx XC7Z045 device, keeping power consumption to less than 5 W.

4 Conclusion

This paper evaluates the trade-off between inference accuracy, quantized precision, hardware resources and training time of a neural network performing character recognition. It identifies sweet spots around 3 bit precision in the quantization design space after training with 40 epochs, to minimise both hardware resources and accuracy loss.

Whilst this paper exhaustively measures resource use and accuracy design space between 1 and 8 bits for MNIST character recognition, to assess the reproducibility of these results at scale, the experiments should be repeated: (i) on state-of-the-art networks comprising tens/hundreds of deep hidden layers, (ii) on hardware-friendly activation functions such as ReLU and its variants, (iii) with inference latency as an additional trade-off, and (iv) on networks with tens/hundreds of output classes.

These results are timely, with technology for compressing neural networks evolving rapidly. FINN recently added support for PyTorch models and uses a new framework called Brevitas[1] for quantization-aware training. Intel's Open-Vino toolkit [13] supports neural network quantization for computer vision applications, and targets CPUs, GPUs and FPGAs. Future work will compare this paper's results with the same experimental setup using Distiller, OpenVino and Brevitas across multiple neural network models on resource constrained FPGAs and embedded GPUs. We also plan to evaluate performance trade-offs with multi-precision neural networks, and explore how multi-precision quantization (e.g. [28]) can maximise compression whilst minimising accuracy loss and preserving robustness of neural networks to adversarial attacks.

References

1. Abadi, M., et al.: TensorFlow: large-scale machine learning on heterogeneous systems (2015). https://www.tensorflow.org/lite, software available from tensorflow.org

---

[1] https://xilinx.github.io/brevitas/.

2. Al-Rfou, R., et al.: Theano: a Python framework for fast computation of mathematical expressions. CoRR abs/1605.02688 (2016). http://arxiv.org/abs/1605.02688

3. Blott, M., et al.: FINN-R: an end-to-end deep-learning framework for fast exploration of quantized neural networks. Trans. Reconfigurable Technol. Syst. **11**(3), 16:1–16:23 (2018)

4. Chen, T., et al.: DianNao: a small-footprint high-throughput accelerator for ubiquitous machine-learning. In: ASPLOS 2014, Salt Lake City, UT, USA, 1–5 March 2014, pp. 269–284. ACM (2014)

5. Cheng, Y., Yu, F.X., Feris, R.S., Kumar, S., Choudhary, A.N., Chang, S.: Fast neural networks with circulant projections. CoRR abs/1502.03436 (2015)

6. Courbariaux, M., Bengio, Y.: BinaryNet: training deep neural networks with weights and activations constrained to +1 or −1. CoRR abs/1602.02830 (2016)

7. DiCecco, R., Lacey, G., Vasiljevic, J., Chow, P., Taylor, G.W., Areibi, S.: Caffeinated FPGAs: FPGA framework for convolutional neural networks. In: FPT 2016, Xi'an, China, 7–9 December 2016, pp. 265–268. IEEE (2016)

8. Dieleman, S., et al.: Lasagne: first release, August 2015. https://doi.org/10.5281/zenodo.27878

9. Ding, C., Wang, S., Liu, N., Xu, K., Wang, Y., Liang, Y.: REQ-YOLO: a resource-aware, efficient quantization framework for object detection on FPGAs. In: FPGA 2019, Seaside, CA, USA, 24–26 February 2019, pp. 33–42. ACM (2019)

10. Ghasemzadeh, M., Samragh, M., Koushanfar, F.: ResBinNet: residual binary neural network. CoRR abs/1711.01243 (2017)

11. Han, S., Pool, J., Tran, J., Dally, W.J.: Learning both weights and connections for efficient neural network. In: Advances in Neural Information Processing Systems 28: Annual Conference on Neural Information Processing Systems 2015, Montreal, Quebec, Canada, 7–12 December 2015, pp. 1135–1143 (2015)

12. Hubara, I., Courbariaux, M., Soudry, D., El-Yaniv, R., Bengio, Y.: Quantized neural networks: training neural networks with low precision weights and activations. J. Mach. Learn. Res. **18**, 187:1–187:30 (2017)

13. Intel: Intel OpenVino Toolkit. https://software.intel.com/en-us/openvino-toolkit

14. LeCun, Y., Cortes, C.: The MNIST database of handwritten digits (1998)

15. Liang, S., Yin, S., Liu, L., Luk, W., Wei, S.: FP-BNN: binarized neural network on FPGA. Neurocomputing **275**, 1072–1086 (2018)

16. Lu, D.: Creating an AI can be five times worse for the planet than a car, June 2019. https://www.newscientist.com/article/2205779-creating-an-ai-can-be-five-times-worse-for-the-planet-than-a-car/, new Scientist

17. Park, J., Sung, W.: FPGA based implementation of deep neural networks using on-chip memory only. In: ICASSP 2016, Shanghai, China, 20–25 March 2016, pp. 1011–1015. IEEE (2016)

18. Qiu, J., et al.: Going deeper with embedded FPGA platform for convolutional neural network. In: Proceedings of the 2016 ACM/SIGDA International Symposium on Field-Programmable Gate Arrays, Monterey, CA, USA, 21–23 February 2016, pp. 26–35. ACM (2016)

19. Radu, V., et al.: Performance aware convolutional neural network channel pruning for embedded GPUs. In: IISWC 2019. IEEE, October 2019

20. Rybalkin, V., Pappalardo, A., Ghaffar, M.M., Gambardella, G., Wehn, N., Blott, M.: FINN-L: library extensions and design trade-off analysis for variable precision LSTM networks on FPGAs. In: FPL 2018, Dublin, Ireland, 27–31 August 2018, pp. 89–96. IEEE Computer Society (2018)

21. Su, J., et al.: Accuracy to throughput trade-offs for reduced precision neural networks on reconfigurable logic. In: Voros, N., Huebner, M., Keramidas, G., Goehringer, D., Antonopoulos, C., Diniz, P.C. (eds.) ARC 2018. LNCS, vol. 10824, pp. 29–42. Springer, Cham (2018). https://doi.org/10.1007/978-3-319-78890-6_3

22. Umuroglu, Y., et al.: FINN: a framework for fast, scalable binarized neural network inference. In: FPGA 2017, Monterey, CA, USA, 22–24 February 2017, pp. 65–74. ACM (2017)

23. Venieris, S.I., Bouganis, C.: fpgaConvNet: mapping regular and irregular convolutional neural networks on FPGAs. IEEE Trans. Neural Netw. Learn. Syst. **30**(2), 326–342 (2019)

24. Véstias, M.P., Neto, H.C.: Trends of CPU, GPU and FPGA for high-performance computing. In: FPL 2014, Munich, Germany, 2–4 September 2014, pp. 1–6. IEEE (2014)

25. Wang, E., et al.: Deep neural network approximation for custom hardware: where we've been, where we're going. ACM Comput. Surv. **52**(2), 40:1–40:39 (2019)

26. Wang, J., Lou, Q., Zhang, X., Zhu, C., Lin, Y., Chen, D.: Design flow of accelerating hybrid extremely low bit-width neural network in embedded FPGA. In: FPL 2018, Dublin, Ireland, 27–31 August, pp. 163–169. IEEE Computer Society (2018)

27. Zhang, Q., Cao, J., Zhang, Y., Zhang, S., Zhang, Q., Yu, D.: FPGA implementation of quantized convolutional neural networks. In: ICCT 2019, Xi'an, China, 16–19 October, pp. 1605–1610. IEEE (2019)

28. Zhao, Y., et al.: Automatic generation of multi-precision multi-arithmetic CNN accelerators for FPGAs. In: ICFPT 2019, Tianjin, China, 9–13 December 2019, pp. 45–53. IEEE (2019)

29. Zmora, N., Jacob, G., Zlotnik, L., Elharar, B., Novik, G.: Neural network distiller (2018). https://doi.org/10.5281/zenodo.1297430

Accelerating a Classic 3D Video Game on Heterogeneous Reconfigurable MPSoCs

Leonardo Suriano$^{(\boxtimes)}$ ⓘ, David Lima, and Eduardo de la Torre ⓘ

Universidad Politécnica de Madrid, Madrid, Spain
{leonardo.suriano,eduardo.delatorre}@upm.es,
david.lima.astor@alumnos.upm.es

Abstract. Heterogeneous Reconfigurable MPSoCs, coupling microprocessors with Programmable Logic, are becoming extremely important
in High-Performance Embedded Computing domain where energy consumption is a key factor to be considered by every designer. However,
efficient hardware/software co-design still requires experience and a big
effort: finding an optimal solution and an acceptable trade-off between
performance and energy may require several tests and it is strongly
platform-dependent. To this respect, a Dataflow-based method is used in
this work for exploring different hardware/software configurations (number of hardware accelerators and FPGA frequency). As a use case, the
acceleration of a well-known 3D video game (DOOM) is presented. The
method offers rapid trade-off analysis in terms of non-functional parameters such as computing performance or power/energy measurements.

Extensive experimental results show that is possible to speed up the
game and, at the same time, reduce the energy consumption of the whole
platform. A custom Linux-based Operating System for Zynq Ultrascale+
was created, including a GPU driver to support a graphical interface on
an HDMI screen and drivers to manage custom hardware accelerators on
the FPGA side.

The best solution to save up to 63% of energy corresponds to the
use of four parallel hardware accelerators, where a function speed up of
x3.6 and an application speed up of x2 (in line with Amdahl's law) is
obtained.

Additionally, a set of Pareto optimal solutions are reported in the
results section.

Keywords: Hardware acceleration · FPGA · Performance
measurement · Power measurement · Energy measurement · Design
space exploration · Pareto Front · MPSoC · Zynq Ultrascale+ · Linux ·
Driver · 3D video game · DOOM

1 Introduction

Nowadays, heterogeneous Multi-Processor Systems on Chip (MPSoCs) with
programmable hardware accelerators are becoming extremely important for

© Springer Nature Switzerland AG 2020
F. Rincón et al. (Eds.): ARC 2020, LNCS 12083, pp. 136–150, 2020.
https://doi.org/10.1007/978-3-030-44534-8_11

commercial uses and for research activities. The reason resides in the versatility that such devices can provide: high performance, high flexibility and low power consumption are key features that make them extremely attractive. Top-of-the-line products of Xilinx and Intel (e.g. Xilinx Zynq UltraScale+ MPSoC [45], Intel Stratix 10 [19]) clearly show the trend of Field Programmable Gate Array (FPGA) devices.

The heterogeneous nature of such MPSoCs is due to the coexistence of several general purpose Central Processing Units (CPUs) together with a Graphic Process Unit and an S-RAM-based FPGA on the same chip [43]. However, the increasing complexity of the devices is the major cause of the software productivity gap [8]: making efficient use of the available hardware is a challenge and is the central core problem addressed in this paper.

Generally, compute-intensive tasks may be offloaded to specialized hardware accelerators created ad-hoc; this strategy can bring benefits in terms of performance improvement and energy consumption reduction. In contrast, as mentioned above, the productivity and the Time-to-Market can be heavily affected: the knowledge of the designers should range from the hardware description languages to the low-level firmware implementation to drive the custom logic on the FPGA.

In this paper, an analysis is performed that, starting from a complex application such as a 3D video game, gives the possibility to explore many hardware/software alternatives by just describing an application using the Dataflow Model of Computation (MoC). A rapid prototyping method is used to test the impact of the new solutions on the real platform. Through in-situ measurement, it is shown that intuitive predictions not always fit with the reality because, perhaps, some important aspects might be not taken into account in early analysis (i.e. cache misses, Operating System (OS)'s context switches, et cetera).

Besides, this paper should be intended as an experiment for productivity evaluation: the same results were obtained in two different ways. From one side, a master student was guided to perform an analysis of the source code of the DOOM in order to execute it on Zynq Ultrascale+ (accelerating part of it through the use of hardware accelerators on the Programmable Logic (PL)). From the other side, the same analysis was performed using the tools first presented in [40] and extended and formalized in [38]. The analysis conducted by the student was completed in one month while, using **DAMHSE** (DAtaflow Method for Hardware/Software Exploration [38]), the same results are collected in one working day.

Summarizing, the contributions of this paper are:

* ⋆ the analysis of a complex application (such as a 3D video game) executing it on an MPSoC exploiting hardware acceleration[1];
* ⋆ the creation of a flexible hardware accelerator IP using High-Level Synthesis (HLS) techniques and optimization;
* ⋆ the creation of a custom Linux-based OS with (1) a graphic interface, (2) the Mali GPU driver, and (3) the low level Linux driver of SDSoC to manage

---

[1] https://bitbucket.org/d_lima/tfm_doom/.

the accelerator on the PL. The open-source available scripts[2] can, so, be used and improved by the community in other projects;

⋆ the use of **DAMHSE** [38] on a real use case to speed up the Design Space Exploration (DSE) process to meet a reasonable trade-off between function execution time and energy consumption; a demonstration is also available.

The rest of the paper is organized as follow: in Sect. 2 an overview of the State-of-the-Art is given while, in Sect. 3, a brief description of the tools used in this workflow is reported. In Sect. 4 the analysis-steps and the method adopted to speed up the process of rapid prototyping the application are depicted. Finally, in Sect. 5, the results are plotted and discussed. In the last Section, the conclusions are stated together with the main contribution of the work.

2   Background

Over the two last decades, to cope with the design complexity and the design productivity gap, many DSE methods were proposed [32]. In the literature, the DSE usually refers to the activity of exploring design alternatives prior to implementation [21]. Traditionally, during the exploration of the different options for an MPSoC, a designer is looking for an optimal (1) spatial building (i.e. mapping) and (2) temporal binding (i.e. scheduling). The former refers to the process of assigning the execution of a specific *task* to a specific *resource*. The latter defines the sequential order of execution of the couple *task-resource*.

Often, the parameters to be considered in order to achieve an optimal implementation are performance and energy consumption. The map-and-scheduling process is generally considered an NP-hard problem [36] (i.e. one of the mathematical millennium problem with no known solution). According to the design space search criterion [17,33], the DSE can be classified into three main categories: (1) exhaustive evaluation of every design point, (2) random search and (3) heuristic search mechanisms. In the first category, all the possible combinations of the input parameters are considered. In the random search, a subset of all the possible combinations of the problem space is considered: Monte Carlo approximations [6], Simulated Annealing [16,28], and Tabu Search [23,46] fall under this category. The last category, Heuristic search mechanisms, involve knowledge of the design space to speed up the convergence to the final solution. The exploration is so "guided" by using this knowledge of characteristics of design space. Markov Decision Process (MDP) [4,35], Genetic [22,27] and Evolutionary Algorithms [14,25] are examples of these techniques.

The exhaustive evaluation of every design point is discussed in [3,5,24]. When the design space is small, such techniques can be useful while their usage is prohibitive for large design due to "the latency involved in such unguided search processes" [33]. In the analysis proposed in this paper, a rapid prototyping of the application accelerated by dedicated hardware on the FPGA is conducted. Usually, the design of the application (with one or more accelerators on the PL

---

[2] https://bitbucket.org/d_lima/desktop_image_zcu102/.

side) can be time-consuming and can require a large effort and attention (checking memory management for the shared memory accesses, synchronizing threads with semaphores, building low level drivers for the hardware, et cetera.). Additionally, in such scenario, even a simple bug can become difficult to locate and correct. Moreover, a little modification of a parameter may require a manually arduous data re-distribution. These are the reasons that brought us to test the method proposed in [38] for this analysis.

Additionally, as claimed in the introduction, one of the secondary (but important) contributions of the proposed work is the creation of a custom ad-hoc Linux-based OS that must be able, among other, to

- ⋆ to handle all the possible hardware accelerators hosted in the PL;
- ⋆ to communicate through the Mali GPU with the HDMI interface and the screen;
- ⋆ to dynamically upload a new generated bitstream on the PL from the User-Space;
- ⋆ to have all the common features typically included in a classic Linux-based OS (such as a packet manager, a compiler, a linker and so on).

SDSoC is an Electronic Design Automation (EDA) tool developed by Xilinx [34] that gives the possibility to automatically create an OS with important limitations: it does not include any driver for the GPU and the HDMI interface; it also does not include the possibility of using any packet manager similar to apt or yum (i.e. it is not possible to install any program). Moreover, the OS automatically generated is a pre-compiled binary ready to be copied in an empty SD-card: this eliminates the possibility of manually include any libraries, programs and tools. With the scripts created in this work and free available on github, a researcher can have the possibility to work with an OS similar to the ones available for the Raspberry Pi platform which is used in many research areas: smart cities [30], Internet-of-Things [37], Wireless Sensor Network [18], network traffic analysis application and security [7,11] among others. Thus, the additional use of accelerators is enabled when using a Zynq Ultrascale+.

The aim of the OS is to provide an easy and transparent access to the hardware resources [13]. In this context, a developer does not need to be an expert of all the low-level hardware details and concepts and can focus his attention on the application implementation. In the work presented in [1], ReconOS is proposed: an operating system developed for reconfigurable computing. In ReconOS, the concept of *delegate threads* is introduced, where an hardware module is seen as a software thread by the system. In order to cope with hardware accelerators and reconfigurable platform, many other approaches can be found in literature: RTMS [9], SPREAD [42], FUSE [20] are some of them. However, the idea proposed in this paper is (1) to let SDSoC create the whole hardware structure and generate the bitstream, (2) to compile (or cross-compile) the source codes together with the generated hardware information against the additional libraries a user may need to use. After, the compiled executable can simply be copied on the custom OS proposed that includes all the features necessary for the project (as, for example, Python libraries, image processing libraries et cetera). The low-level drivers to exchange information with the PL are already included in the kernel source (all the patches are included and downloadable as previously mentioned) and enabled by the node xlnk of the Device Tree[3].

3   Tools

In this section, after a brief introduction of the chosen video game, the tools are presented. This will help to justify their use for the analysis proposed.

3.1   DOOM

The DOOM is a game released in 1993 that consolidated the first-person shooter genre. It is coded in C language, and it was mainly developed for DOS systems. But, following the release of the code in 1997, which is usually known as the Vanilla DOOM version, it has been ported to numerous platforms by users. The Chocolate-DOOM [10] is one of these source ports adapted by users and has been chosen mainly due to its similarity with the original release of the game.

Although the source code has been released, the graphics contents of the game, such as the different episodes and the sound content, are not free. Despite this, there is a shareware version which consists of a small enough content to carry out research projects and demos [15]. It should be mentioned that many open source DOOM version can be found but, to the best of our knowledge, none of them exploit hardware acceleration.

3.2   DataFlow Model of Computation

Traditionally, Dataflow Models of Computation (MoCs) are used to model stream processing algorithm in many areas: video and audio processing [29,41], computer vision algorithms [31], and telecommunications [12] are some examples of their utilization. The increasing popularity of Dataflow MoCs is due to their natural expressiveness of parallelism together with their advanced analyzability as explained by Arrestier et al. in [2]. In [12] the authors show how an application can be described through *actors* that communicate through *First-In First-Out queues (FIFOs)*. Basically, an actor *fires* (perform some processing) when enough data (namely *tokens*) are available on its input buffers. Then, after the whole processing of the actor, one (or more) data token(s) are produced so other actors of the graph may fire following the natural "Flow of Data". Making use of the enhanced version of the tools presented in [38], we use the Dataflow MoC to describe a piece of the DOOM code (as shown in Fig. 1) which was identified through a prior performance analysis (described in details in Sect. 4).

---

[3] The hack comes from the Xilinx's documentation: "SDSoC Environment Platform Development Guide UG1146 (v2017.4) January 26, 2018" and was adapted for our purpose. In the document, it is used with Petalinux. However, the use of Petalinux is avoided in this work.

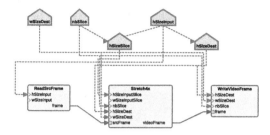

Fig. 1. Dataflow description of a piece of DOOM's code. (Color figure online)

3.3 SDSoC

SDSoC [34] is a complete design environment developed by Xilinx. It gives the possibility to automatically create (1) the whole hardware structure (hardware accelerators, DMAs, interconnections et cetera) and (2) the low level software library to actually use the generated hardware. Also, a lightweight Linux-based OS can be created with the limitation described in Sect. 2:

* no drivers for the GPU and for the HDMI interface are included;
* no packet manager is included: impossible to install any kind of additional software/library;
* a pre-compiled binary ready-to-use is generated: impossible to modify any of the feature already included on it.

These are the motivations that have pushed us to propose another OS version, fully compatible with the executable programs built by SDSoC, where all the abovementioned features are embedded. In this way, it is possible to compile the game and play it on the Zynq Ultrascale+.

4   Procedure Description

The first step of the analysis consists in executing the software version of the game [10] on the Zynq Ultrascale+ directly, being sure to compile the source code with the additional option -pg in the CFLAGS environment variable. This action will instrument the code so that gprof (an open source performance analysis tool for Unix applications) can report detailed information about the performance execution of every single function of the application. This includes, but is not limited to, the CPU-time occupation percentage of the functions themselves. From this preliminary analysis, it was noted that the function I_Stretch4x occupies the CPU 67% of the time, making itself the best candidate to be offloaded on the FPGA. The identified function was, so, isolated in order to be studied. Essentially, the I_Stretch4x operates between two buffers: an input frame buffer of 320 × 200 pixels and an output buffer of 1280 × 960 pixels. It is in charge of re-arrange the pixels in order to adapt the natural resolution of the game frame

(320×200) to higher resolution (1280×960) in order to be correctly visualized on the screen. An HLS version of the function is proposed (and available on the same git repository) where the C-code was reshaped and enriched with Vivado's pragmas [44].

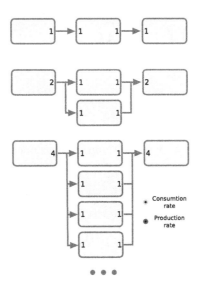

Fig. 2. Simplified schematic view of the different kind of scenarios obtained by changing the firing rules of Fig. 1

The algorithm of the isolated function was, afterwards, described with Dataflow MoC [38]. In that way, the firing rules of the actors can be easily changed by just modifying the values of the parameters in the blue boxes of the high level Dataflow description reported in Fig. 1. As explained in [38], the tool will generate automatically the code performing: (1) the split of the input buffer in many pieces as specified in the nbSlice box of the Fig. 1 and (2) replicating the function call according to the change of the firing rules. A **simplified schematic view** of what happen after the graph transformation of the tool proposed in [38] is given in Fig. 2: when the nbSlice is set up to 1 only one function replica is generated managing the whole buffer. When set up to 2 the ReadScrFrame actor will generate two output data tokens that will fire twice the actor Stretch4x, thus generating two function replicas and so on. With this algorithm description, the number of nbSlice coincides with the number of function replicas automatically generated (that are also the instances of hardware accelerators to be placed in the PL). It must be noted that the height of the input image must be multiple of nbSlice. If this condition is not respected, the buffer cannot be homogeneously divided among the accelerators. This means that 3, 6 and 7 are not acceptable value for nbSlice and are not considered. Moreover, if the number of accelerators exceeds 8, SDSoC is not able to complete the synthesis of the hardware on the FPGA because the number of the interrupt lines available between the Processing System (PS) and the Programmable Logic is not enough. The frequencies considered in this analysis are all the possibles synthesizable frequencies that SDSoC allows to choose (i.e. intermediate frequencies are not allowed). Furthermore, Vivado completes the map and routing with a maximum of two accelerators when the frequency is set up to 400 MHz.

The analysis is now straightforward: the automatically generated code can be copied directly on SDSoC and built. The executable and the bitstream are ready to be executed on the Zynq Ultrascale+ with the custom OS version. Besides, all the generated codes, in all the different scenarios, were automatically instrumented in order to measure:

1. the clock cycles needed to execute the function;
2. the function speed up achieved;
3. the game speed up was evaluated by using the Amdahl's law:

$$S_{latency}(s) = \frac{1}{(1-p) + \frac{p}{s}} \tag{1}$$

where:
- $\star$ $S_{latency}$ is the speedup of the execution of the whole task
- $\star$ s is the speedup of the part of the task that benefits from improved system resources;
- $\star$ p is the proportion of execution time that the part benefiting from improved resources originally occupied (i.e. 67% in our case);

4. the power consumption measurement was performed by using an INA226, included in the ZCU102 platform;
5. the energy consumption was calculated using the formula:

$$E = P \cdot \Delta t \tag{2}$$

where:

$$\Delta t = \frac{\Delta Cycles}{frequency} \tag{3}$$

The results are collected and reported in the following Section.

5   Results

All the results reported are collected on an average of one thousand measurements. In Fig. 3 the CPU clock cycles needed to execute the function in many conditions are reported. It is possible to note that, using more hardware accelerators in parallel, less clock cycles are needed to complete the execution of I_Stretch4x. Furthermore, increasing the clock frequency of the FPGA, the acceleration is even more evident. The speed up of the function was obtained by comparing the data in Fig. 3 with the number of clock cycles needed by the software version of the function (i.e. the original C code of the video game). The result is shown in Fig. 4.

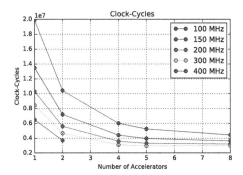

Fig. 3. Execution clock cycles of the Video Game's task as a function of Number of Hardware Accelerators used.

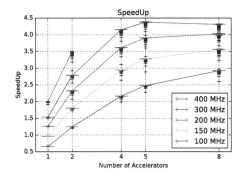

Fig. 4. Speed up of the Video Game's task as a function of Number of Hardware Accelerators used (the comparison is with the respect to the original sotware version).

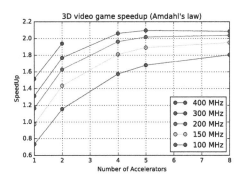

Fig. 5. Speed up of the whole video game (Amdahl's law)

Using the Eq. 1 of the Sect. 4, the theoretical speed up limit of the entire application was estimated and reported in Fig. 5.

From the Figs. 3, 4, and 5, it is clear that the performance of the system is limited. Through the instrumented version of the generated code [26,39], it was discovered that the *cache misses* of the application running on Linux increase with the velocity of the function and with the number of hardware accelerators used (Fig. 6). There is a logical dual reason that explains the phenomena: when data should be sent (/received) to (/from) the hardware, a parallel software thread is created for this purpose. When the CPU switches from one thread to the other, a context switch is needed. Besides, the more the number of accelerators, the more data-hungry the system is and the cache may be not so fast (or large enough) to host all the data at the same time.

Another interesting result can be noted by analyzing the power and energy measurement (respectively in Fig. 7 and Fig. 8). As the hardware logic increases, the power consumption of the FPGA increases as well. The same for the frequency: higher frequency corresponds to a higher power consumption. With the energy, the behavior is different because increasing the frequency and number of accelerators to complete the same task, a higher peak of power is needed but it is also true that the task is completed sooner. The consequence is that less energy is needed. However, because the speed up is limited by the cache misses (Fig. 6), the energy consumption is affected too.

Experimentally, it can be concluded that the best scenario for saving energy is in correspondence of the use of four hardware accelerators working at 200 MHz: comparing the energy consumption of this point with the worst case (i.e. one hardware accelerator working at 100 MHz in Fig. 8) gives $\frac{(0.0063-0.0023)J}{0.0063J} \approx$ 63.5% of energy saved together with a function speed up of x3.6 (Fig. 4). Nevertheless, the best scenario for the speed up (up to x4.3) is in correspondence of using five hardware accelerators working at 300 MHz.

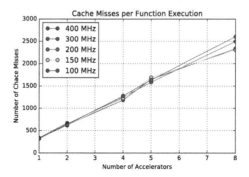

Fig. 6. Number of cache misses per function execution measured using PAPIFY [26].

However, there does not typically exist a feasible solution that minimizes all objective functions simultaneously (in this case speed up and energy at the same time). Therefore, attention is paid to Pareto optimal solutions reported in Fig. 9.

From the above experiments, it can be observed that maximum energy efficiency and performance can be obtained with a large number of accelerators, before the bus occupancy or the cache miss rate diminish the efficiency of the acceleration by entering into memory bounded mode. This analysis can be carried out with the methodology, the tools and the architecture proposed.

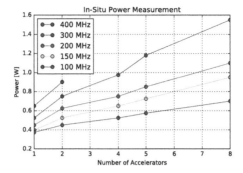

Fig. 7. Power measurements obtained by using an INA226

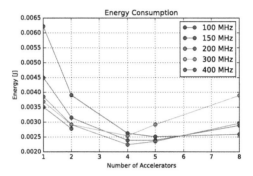

Fig. 8. Energy consumption in all the different cases.

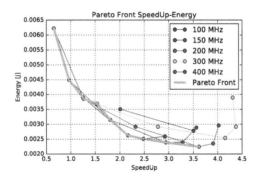

Fig. 9. Moving along the Pareto Front, an optimal design point is found. Solutions cannot be improved in any of the objectives without degrading at least one of the other objectives.

6   Conclusion

In this paper a new open-source version of a classic 3D video game enriched with hardware acceleration is proposed. A custom Linux-based OS is created to be able to execute the video game on the Zynq Ultrascale+ and show it on a screen together with all the kernel drivers necessary to handle the hardware IPs. The project follows the open source philosophy and all the scripts and patches are available on *github* in order to give the possibility to replicate the steps with the aim of further community improvement.

The software version of the game was first analyzed (with *gprof*) to locate the candidate function to be studied and moved into the FPGA. An HLS version of the mentioned function is presented. Besides, the split of the source (and destination) frame buffers of the function in smaller data-independent pieces enables the parallel data-computation on multiple accelerators.

Thanks to the instrumented version of the code, the speed up of the function was measured in different conditions and hardware/software configurations. Moreover, online Power Measurement were collected. From the extensive results analysis, it is possible to conclude that adding more parallel hardware tasks can bring benefits in terms of speed up as well as in terms of energy consumption. However, the increase in speedup is limited by the L1 cache used (in this case by the size and speed of the L1 cache of the system that causes cache misses). Consequently, improving the performance on the FPGA side is worthless: the speed up does not increase anymore (and can get worse) while the power and the energy used by the system increase almost linearly with the number of hardware accelerators instantiated. Finally, a set of Pareto optimal solution is proposed.

Acknowledgments. This work was supported by the Spanish Ministry (Ministerio de Economía y Competitividad) under projects PLATINO under Grant TEC2012-31145.

References

1. Agne, A., et al.: ReconOS: an operating system approach for reconfigurable computing. IEEE Micro **34**(1), 60–71 (2014)
2. Arrestier, F., Desnos, K., Pelcat, M., Heulot, J., Juarez, E., Menard, D.: Delays and states in dataflow models of computation. In: Proceedings of the 18th International Conference on Embedded Computer Systems: Architectures, Modeling, and Simulation, SAMOS 2018, pp. 47–54. ACM, New York (2018). https://doi.org/10.1145/3229631.3229645
3. Baghdadi, A., Zergainoh, N., Cesario, W., Roudier, T., Jerraya, A.A.: Design space exploration for hardware/software codesign of multiprocessor systems. In: Proceedings 11th International Workshop on Rapid System Prototyping, RSP 2000. Shortening the Path from Specification to Prototype (Cat. No. PR00668), pp. 8–13, June 2000. https://doi.org/10.1109/IWRSP.2000.854975
4. Beltrame, G., Fossati, L., Sciuto, D.: Decision-theoretic design space exploration of multiprocessor platforms. IEEE Trans. Comput. Aided Des. Integr. Circuits Syst. **29**(7), 1083–1095 (2010). https://doi.org/10.1109/TCAD.2010.2049053
5. Blythe, S.A., Walker, R.A.: Efficient optimal design space characterization methodologies. ACM Trans. Des. Autom. Electron. Syst. **5**(3), 322–336 (2000). https://doi.org/10.1145/348019.348058

6. Bruni, D., Bogliolo, A., Benini, L.: Statistical design space exploration for application-specific unit synthesis. In: Proceedings of the 38th Design Automation Conference (IEEE Cat. No. 01CH37232), pp. 641–646, June 2001. https://doi.org/10.1145/378239.379039

7. Caldas-Calle, L., Jara, J., Huerta, M., Gallegos, P.: QoS evaluation of VPN in a Raspberry Pi devices over wireless network. In: 2017 International Caribbean Conference on Devices, Circuits and Systems (ICCDCS), pp. 125–128, June 2017. https://doi.org/10.1109/ICCDCS.2017.7959718

8. Castrillon, J., Leupers, R.: Programming Heterogeneous MPSoCs: Tool Flows to Close the Software Productivity Gap. Technical report, Lehrstuhl für Software für Systeme auf Silizium (2013)

9. Charitopoulos, G., Koidis, I., Papadimitriou, K., Pnevmatikatos, D.: Hardware task scheduling for partially reconfigurable FPGAs. In: Sano, K., Soudris, D., Hübner, M., Diniz, P.C. (eds.) ARC 2015. LNCS, vol. 9040, pp. 487–498. Springer, Cham (2015). https://doi.org/10.1007/978-3-319-16214-0_45

10. Open-Source Community: Chocolate doom Wiki-pages (2019). https://www.chocolate-doom.org/wiki/index.php/Chocolate_Doom

11. Coşar, M., Karasartova, S.: A firewall application on SOHO networks with Raspberry Pi and snort. In: 2017 International Conference on Computer Science and Engineering (UBMK), pp. 1000–1003, October 2017. https://doi.org/10.1109/UBMK.2017.8093414

12. Desnos, K., Pelcat, M., Nezan, J.F., Bhattacharyya, S.S., Aridhi, S.: PiMM: parameterized and interfaced dataflow meta-model for MPSoCs runtime reconfiguration. In: 2013 International Conference on Embedded Computer Systems: Architectures, Modeling, and Simulation (SAMOS XIII), pp. 41–48. IEEE (2013)

13. Eckert, M., Meyer, D., Haase, J., Klauer, B.: Operating system concepts for reconfigurable computing: review and survey. Int. J. Reconfigurable Comput. **2016**, 1–11 (2016)

14. Erbas, C., Cerav-Erbas, S., Pimentel, A.D.: Multiobjective optimization and evolutionary algorithms for the application mapping problem in multiprocessor system-on-chip design. IEEE Trans. Evol. Comput. **10**(3), 358–374 (2006). https://doi.org/10.1109/TEVC.2005.860766

15. FANDOM: Doom Wiki (2019). https://doom.fandom.com/wiki/Shareware

16. Gajski, D.D., Vahid, F., Narayan, S.: SpecSyn: an environment supporting the specify-explore-refine paradigm for hardware/software system design. IEEE Trans. Very Large Scale Integr. (VLSI) Syst. **6**(1), 84–100 (1998). https://doi.org/10.1109/92.661251

17. Gries, M.: Methods for evaluating and covering the design space during early design development. Integr. VLSI J. **38**(2), 131–183 (2004)

18. Harish Kumar, B.: WSN based automatic irrigation and security system using Raspberry Pi board. In: 2017 International Conference on Current Trends in Computer, Electrical, Electronics and Communication (CTCEEC), pp. 1097–1103, September 2017. https://doi.org/10.1109/CTCEEC.2017.8455140

19. Intel: Stratix 10 GX/SX device overview (2018). https://www.altera.com/en_US/pdfs/literature/hb/stratix-10/s10-overview.pdf

20. Ismail, A., Shannon, L.: FUSE: front-end user framework for O/S abstraction of hardware accelerators. In: 2011 IEEE 19th Annual International Symposium on Field-Programmable Custom Computing Machines (FCCM), pp. 170–177. IEEE (2011)

21. Kang, E., Jackson, E., Schulte, W.: An approach for effective design space exploration. In: Calinescu, R., Jackson, E. (eds.) Monterey Workshop 2010. LNCS, vol. 6662, pp. 33–54. Springer, Heidelberg (2011). https://doi.org/10.1007/978-3-642-21292-5_3

22. Kang, S., Kumar, R.: Magellan: a search and machine learning-based framework for fast multi-core design space exploration and optimization. In: 2008 Design, Automation and Test in Europe, pp. 1432–1437, March 2008. https://doi.org/10.1109/DATE.2008.4484875

23. Kreutz, M., Marcon, C.A., Carro, L., Wagner, F., Susin, A.A.: Design space exploration comparing homogeneous and heterogeneous network-on-chip architectures. In: Proceedings of the 18th Annual Symposium on Integrated Circuits and System Design, SBCCI 2005, pp. 190–195. ACM, New York (2005). https://doi.org/10.1145/1081081.1081130

24. Lahiri, K., Raghunathan, A., Dey, S.: System-level performance analysis for designing on-chip communication architectures. IEEE Trans. Comput. Aided Des. Integr. Circuits Syst. **20**(6), 768–783 (2001). https://doi.org/10.1109/43.924830

25. Liu, J., Zhong, W., Jiao, L.: A multiagent evolutionary algorithm for combinatorial optimization problems. IEEE Trans. Syst. Man Cybern. Part B (Cybernetics) **40**, 229–240 (2010)

26. Madroñal, D., et al.: Automatic instrumentation of dataflow applications using PAPI. In: Proceedings of the 15th ACM International Conference on Computing Frontiers, pp. 232–235. ACM (2018)

27. Nag, K., Pal, T., Pal, N.R.: ASMiGA: an archive-based steady-state micro genetic algorithm. IEEE Trans. Cybern. **45**(1), 40–52 (2015). https://doi.org/10.1109/TCYB.2014.2317693

28. Orsila, H., Salminen, E., Hämäläinen, T.: Parameterizing simulated annealing for distributing Kahn process networks on multiprocessor SoCs. In: 2009 International Symposium on System-on-Chip, pp. 019–026, November 2009. https://doi.org/10.1109/SOCC.2009.5335683

29. Park, C., Chung, J., Ha, S.: Extended synchronous dataflow for efficient DSP system prototyping. IEEE, June 1999

30. Parthornratt, T., Burapanonte, N., Gunjarueg, W.: People identification and counting system using Raspberry Pi (AU-PICC: Raspberry Pi customer counter). In: 2016 International Conference on Electronics, Information, and Communications (ICEIC), pp. 1–5. IEEE (2016)

31. Pelcat, M., et al.: PREESM: a dataflow-based rapid prototyping framework for simplifying multicore DSP programming. In: 2014 6th European Embedded Design in Education and Research Conference (EDERC), pp. 36–40. IEEE (2014)

32. Pimentel, A.D.: Exploring exploration: a tutorial introduction to embedded systems design space exploration. IEEE Des. Test **34**(1), 77–90 (2017)

33. Qadri, M.Y., Qadri, N.N., McDonald-Maier, K.D.: Fuzzy logic based energy and throughput aware design space exploration for MPSoC. Microprocess. Microsyst. **40**, 113–123 (2016)

34. Sekar, C., et al.: Tutorial T7: designing with Xilinx SDSoC. In: 2017 30th International Conference on VLSI Design and 2017 16th International Conference on Embedded Systems (VLSID), pp. xl–xli. IEEE (2017)

35. Shani, G.: Task-based decomposition of factored POMDPs. IEEE Trans. Cybern. **44**(2), 208–216 (2014). https://doi.org/10.1109/TCYB.2013.2252009

36. Singh, A.K., Shafique, M., Kumar, A., Henkel, J.: Mapping on multi/many-core systems: survey of current and emerging trends. In: 2013 50th ACM/EDAC/IEEE Design Automation Conference (DAC), pp. 1–10. IEEE (2013)

37. Sogi, N.R., Chatterjee, P., Nethra, U., Suma, V.: SMARISA: a Raspberry Pi based smart ring for women safety using IoT. In: 2018 International Conference on Inventive Research in Computing Applications (ICIRCA), pp. 451–454, July 2018. https://doi.org/10.1109/ICIRCA.2018.8597424

38. Suriano, L., et al.: DAMHSE: programming heterogeneous MPSocS with hardware acceleration using dataflow-based design space exploration and automated rapid prototyping. Microprocess. Microsyst. **71**, 102882 (2019)

39. Suriano, L., Madroñal, D., Rodríguez, A., Juárez, E., Sanz, C., de la Torre, E.: A unified hardware/software monitoring method for reconfigurable computing architectures using PAPI. In: 2018 13th International Symposium on Reconfigurable Communication-Centric Systems-on-Chip (ReCoSoC), pp. 1–8. IEEE (2018)

40. Suriano, L., Rodriguez, A., Desnos, K., Pelcat, M., de la Torre, E.: Analysis of a heterogeneous multi-core, multi-hw-accelerator-based system designed using PREESM and SDSoC. In: 2017 12th International Symposium on Reconfigurable Communication-centric Systems-on-Chip (ReCoSoC), pp. 1–7. IEEE (2017)

41. Theelen, B.D., Geilen, M.C., Basten, T., Voeten, J.P., Gheorghita, S.V., Stuijk, S.: A scenario-aware data flow model for combined long-run average and worst-case performance analysis. In: Fourth ACM and IEEE International Conference on Formal Methods and Models for Co-Design, MEMOCODE 2006. Proceedings, pp. 185–194. IEEE (2006)

42. Wang, Y., et al.: SPREAD: a streaming-based partially reconfigurable architecture and programming model. IEEE Trans. Very Large Scale Integr. (VLSI) Syst. **21**(12), 2179–2192 (2013)

43. Wolf, W., Jerraya, A.A., Martin, G.: Multiprocessor system-on-chip (MPSoC) technology. IEEE Trans. Comput. Aided Des. Integr. Circuits Syst. **27**(10), 1701–1713 (2008)

44. Xilinx: Vivado design suite user guide - high level synthesis (2018)

45. Xilinx: Zynq UltraScale+ MPSoC design overview (2018). https://www.xilinx.com/support/documentation-navigation/design-hubs/dh0070-zynq-mpsoc-design-overview-hub.html

46. Xin, B., Chen, J., Zhang, J., Dou, L., Peng, Z.: Efficient decision makings for dynamic weapon-target assignment by virtual permutation and Tabu search heuristics. IEEE Trans. Syst. Man Cybern. Part C (Appl. Rev.) **40**(6), 649–662 (2010). https://doi.org/10.1109/TSMCC.2010.2049261

Cross-layer CNN Approximations
for Hardware Implementation

Karim M. A. Ali[1(✉)], Ihsen Alouani[2], Abdessamad Ait El Cadi[1],
Hamza Ouarnoughi[1], and Smail Niar[1]

[1] LAMIH, Université Polytechnique Hauts-de-France, Valenciennes, France
{karim.ali,abdessamad.aitelcadi,hamza.ouarnoughi,smail.niar}@uphf.fr
[2] IEMN, Université Polytechnique Hauts-de-France, Valenciennes, France
ihsen.alouani@uphf.fr

Abstract. Convolution Neural Networks (CNNs) are widely used for image classification and object detection applications. The deployment of these architectures in embedded applications is a great challenge. This challenge arises from CNNs' high computation complexity that is required to be implemented on platforms with limited hardware resources like FPGA. Since these applications are inherently error-resilient, approximate computing (AC) offers an interesting trade-off between resource utilization and accuracy. In this paper, we study the impact on CNN performances when several approximation techniques are applied simultaneously. We focus on two of the widely used approximation techniques, namely quantization and pruning. Our experimental results showed that for CNN networks of different parameter sizes and 3% loss in accuracy, we can obtain up to 27.9%–47.2% reduction in computation complexity in terms of FLOPs for CIFAR-10 and MNIST datasets.

Keywords: CNNs · FPGA · Approximate computing

1 Introduction

Artificial Intelligence (AI) has recently been used in several domains for different purposes. Computer vision is one of the domains where AI is widely applied, especially using Convolutional Neural Networks (CNN). Image classification, image segmentation, and object detection are among the functions where CNNs are able to obtain high accuracy. However, high CNNs efficiency is gleaned at the cost of high algorithm complexity.

When constrained-resource systems are used to support such algorithms, such as for edge processing and IoT, memory and processing-demands reduction techniques need to be used. In this case, FPGA-based architectures are among possible alternative to energy-hungry based GPUs systems. FPGA solutions provide, in general, a superior trade-off of performance and accuracy over GPU-based systems for CNNs. However, designers need to have tools to explore the impacts of

© Springer Nature Switzerland AG 2020
F. Rincón et al. (Eds.): ARC 2020, LNCS 12083, pp. 151–165, 2020.
https://doi.org/10.1007/978-3-030-44534-8_12

the different optimization techniques to reduce the high memory and processing needs of CNNs.

Optimizing the implementation of CNNs on FPGA is the focus of a large amount of research projects [1]. The problem is tackled at two levels. The first level concerns the CNN hardware implementation. The aim here is to tune the hardware architecture in order to improve the CNN performances of the inference phase. To apply such optimizations a strong background on the hardware platform is required. This is not always the case of AI and CNN experts. The second optimization level concerns the algorithmic aspect of the CNN. Its purpose is to reduce the CNN complexity while keeping an acceptable level of accuracy. Such a work requires a background of the CNN internal structure in order to decide which optimization can be applied. While different approximation techniques are used in the literature, the optimization of their use to reach efficient trade-offs is still an open research direction.

Approximation techniques for convolution neural networks can be classified into: (1) At the architectural-level: They are related to the convolution network architecture like pruning. (2) At the data-level: They are related to data like quantization. (3) At the computational-level: They are related to the computations like approximated multipliers or multiplier-less convolutions. These approximations are presented in literature independently from each other. In this paper, our objective aims to study the effect of applying two or more of them to the same neural network under a certain accuracy constraint. As an example, we presented the guidelines for how to apply both quantization and pruning approximations to convolution neural networks. We can summarize our contributions in this paper as following:

1. We proposed a reconfigurable hardware architecture for CNN inference.
2. We applied approximations to different size CNNs at two different levels: (i) at the data-level (quantization). (ii) at the architectural-level (pruning).
3. We studied the effect of applying cross-layer approximations on CNN network accuracy, hardware utilization, computation complexity, ...

The remainder of this paper is organized as follows. Section 2 presents a literature review of approximate computing techniques applied on CNNs and their hardware implementation. Section 3 presents our hardware architecture dedicated to CNN inference. Section 4 details the different approximate computing techniques proposed for CNN optimization. Section 5 discusses and compares the obtained results before and after applying our approaches. Section 6 concludes the paper by giving an overview and the future perspectives of the work.

2   Related Works

Motivated by the challenge of overcoming the implementation constraints of deep neural networks (DNNs), three main approximation levels have been studied in the literature.

The first is the data-oriented approximation by reducing precision of operands. Practically, the process aims at minimizing the error between the quantized and the raw data. The precision is correlated to the number of quantization levels and consequently to the number of bits required to represent the data. The simplest quantization approach consists of a linear mapping with uniform distance between each quantization level. It usually consists of converting values from floating point to an N-bit fixed point number. Authors in [12] reduce the weights bitwidth to 8 bits and the activation to 10. In [7], both weights and activation can reach 8-bits with fine-tuning. In [6], authors manage to reduce even more aggressively the data bitwidth. By introducing the concept of binary weights (-1 and 1), the multiply operation is reduced to addition and subtraction only. The same idea is extended in [5] by using binary parameters, thereby reducing the MAC operation to an XNOR. However, these two approaches have a dramatic accuracy loss of 19% and 29.8%, respectively [15].

While these works rely on linear quantization with uniformly spaced out values, the weights and activations distributions are not uniform [8,13]. For example, in [7,13], weights are quantized to powers of two. Consequently, the multiply operation is substituted by a bitshift operation. In [3], authors suggest weight sharing. The approach consists of assigning a single value to different weights in order to reduce the number of unique weights by filter.

Besides the approach of tuning the data precision, a plethora of works in literature has focused on reducing the network size and the number of performed operations. The second main approximation level is the network-oriented approximation by reducing the network size and optimizing the number of operations. This includes techniques such as compression, pruning and compact network architectures.

The sparsity of the rectified linear unit (ReLU) output activation is exploited in [4] to reduce memory access, particularly to costly off-chip memory access. The proposed reconfigurable hardware skips reading the weights and performing the MAC for zero-valued activation thereby reducing energy cost by 45%. Authors in [2] go even further and instead of just gating the read and MAC operation, they suggest to skip the cycle to increase the throughput by $1.37\times$.

Networks are usually over-parameterized and a large amount of redundancy exists within their weights. Network pruning techniques such those proposed in [10,17] aim at removing the redundancy. To maintain the primary accuracy level, aggressive network pruning techniques may require weights fine-tuning.

These techniques are particularly efficient in reducing CNNs size and complexity. However, since the used platforms are in a high abstraction level, they do not take into account FPGA intrinsic characteristics. To the best of our knowledge, this is the first study that explores **FPGA-dedicated** data-level and network-oriented approximations.

3   Hardware Architecture

Figure 1 shows our hardware platform for accelerating CNN inference. The system is partitioned on both Processing System (PS) and Programmable Logic (PL).

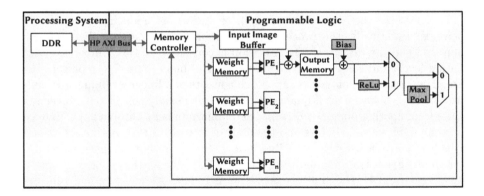

Fig. 1. Hardware architecture for CNN inference

On PL, N processing elements (PE) are synthesized where each PE calculates one output channel. At the level of processing element, the input image is convolved in parallel with kernel of size k × k. The weights are loaded from *Weight Memory* while the input feature map is loaded from *Input Image Buffer* and distributed over the processing elements. There is no need to resynthesize the hardware architecture to run different CNN architectures of convolution layers of kernel size (k × k) or less; thus, the synthesized hardware architecture is CNN independent. The output of convolution is then accumulated in *Output Memory* until the output feature map pixel is calculated for all the input channels. The output pixel is rectified if the activation function (ReLU) is enabled while max pooling is calculated if MAX poll is enabled as well. Finally, the output pixel is written back to the DDR memory through high-performance AXI bus.

In the DDR memory, weights for all convolution layers are stored sequentially such that during runtime weights corresponding to a certain convolution layer are copied to the weight memory of the processing elements. The input/output feature maps for each layer are stored such that the output of one layer will be considered as the input for the successive layer. During CNN network configuration, three memory pointers are defined for each convolution layer. These pointers correspond to the address for weights, input and output feature maps memories.

On the processing system (PS), the architecture of CNN is defined as well as it controls the data transfer for weight memory and image buffer. For each convolution layer, we define the following parameters: (1) The size of the input feature map (*Win, Hin*). (2) The number of input channels (*CHin*). (3) The number of output channels (*CHout*). (4) If some features are enabled or not for that convolution layer like: padding, stride, activation and pooling functions.

If the number of output channels of the convolution layer is larger than the number of synthesized PEs (N), then for the same PE, it will be responsible for executing the output channels of order m, m + N, m + 2N, ... where m is the order of the output channel. If the memory size for the weight memory is smaller than the total number of weights for a certain convolution layer, then the processing is done in folds where in each fold, the weights corresponding to a number of output channels are loaded to the weight memory.

4   CNN Approximations

4.1   Pruning

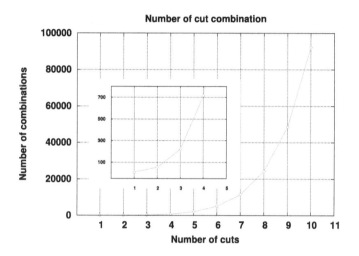

Fig. 2. Number of cut combinations increases exponentially

Pruning is used as an approximation technique to reduce the structure of the neural network. Using pruning decreases the computation complexity while having a small degradation in network accuracy. Several research works explored different granularity for pruning which could be classified into: fine-grained [9,10], intra-kernel, kernel [11] and filter pruning [14]. In our case, we applied filter pruning because our CNNs are executed over hardware architecture of N processing elements, where each processing element processes one output channel. In general, pruning decreases the computation complexity but two conditions should be satisfied: (1) The granularity of pruning should be at the filter level. (2) The number of pruned filters should be multiples of the number of the processing elements implemented over the hardware architecture.

Our pruning criterion is cutting the output channels of the convolution layer of the smallest absolute sum of weights. Filter pruning is applied at layer-level where the number of pruned channels could be from one or different convolution layers. For example, for a CNN of m convolution layers and maximum number of cuts $= n$; then, we will have $\sum_{i=1}^{n} C_{m-1}^{i+m-1}$ possible combinations to find the pruned combination that satisfy our accuracy constraint. Figure 2 shows that for a CNN of 10 convolution layers, the number of possible pruned combinations to be examined can grow exponentially. In practical, we are not able to test all possible pruning combinations to find the optimal one. Instead of that, we will apply greedy algorithm to converge rapidly to the solution.

The pruning algorithm is executed in four steps. In the first step, the absolute sum of weights for each convolution layer are sorted in ascending order. The second step is to prune each convolution layer independently by increasing the number of cuts till either we reach to the maximum predefined number of cuts or the accuracy loss is violated before that. After defining the maximum number of possible cuts that could be applied for each convolution layer independently, we can search in the new space for the cut combination that maximize our objective while the accuracy loss condition is still satisfied. In the third step, we formulate two matrices as depicted in Fig. 3. The first matrix is denoted as *Accuracy Loss Matrix* (A_{ij}) while the other one is denoted as *Decision Matrix* (X_{ij}) where i refers to the index of the convolution layer while j refers to the number of pruned output channels per convolution layer such that j is a multiple of the number of processing elements in the hardware architecture (N). (i.e. j = N, 2N, 3N, ...). For example, if we did 4N pruned channels to the fifth convolution layer then $X_{5,4} = 1$.

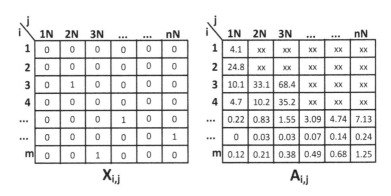

Fig. 3. Example for *Decision Matrix* (X_{ij}) and *Accuracy Loss Matrix* (A_{ij}). N denotes the number of processing elements while xx denotes that this cut is skipped because at that moment all the output channels of this layer will be removed.

Our objective is to minimize the number of network parameters while subjected to a constraint that the total accuracy loss is less than a certain threshold $(Acc_{threshold})$. Assume a CNN network of m convolution layers. i is the index of the convolution layer with I_i input channels, O_i output channels and kernel of size $k_i * k_i$. The total number of parameters for that convolution network can be calculated from the following equation.

$$Num.\ of\ parameters = \sum_{i=1}^{m} O_i\ [k_i^2 * I_i + 1] \tag{1}$$

Let P_i denotes the number of pruned output channels at convolution layer i. Then the total number of parameters after pruning can be calculated by the following equation.

$$Num. \ of \ parameters \ after \ pruning = \sum_{i=1}^{m}(O_i - P_i)[k_i^2(I_i - P_{i-1}) + 1] \quad (2)$$

where $P_0 = 0$

We can formulate our problem as an optimization problem as following: Assume X_{ij} is the decision matrix and (A_{ij}) is the accuracy loss matrix for a network of (m) convolution layers (i.e. i = 1 to m) and maximum number of pruned channels $(n \times N)$ executed on hardware architecture of (N) processing elements (i.e. j = 1 to n).

Our objective function is to minimize the number of the network parameters:

$$\sum_{i=1}^{m}[O_i - \sum_{j=1}^{n}X_{i,j} \times N \times j] \ [k_i^2(I_i - \sum_{j=1}^{n}X_{i-1,j} \times N \times j) + 1] \quad (3)$$

and subjected to the following constraints:

$$\sum_{j=1}^{n}X_{ij} \leq 1 \ \forall \ i \quad (4)$$

$$\sum_{i=1}^{m}\sum_{j=1}^{n}X_{ij} * A_{ij} < Acc_{threshold} \quad (5)$$

$$\sum_{j=1}^{n}X_{0,j} * N * j = 0 \quad (6)$$

Equation (3) represents the objective function which is induced by substituting P_i in Eq. (2) by $\sum_{j=1}^{n}X_{i,j} \times N \times j$. While P_0 in Eq. (2) is formulated as a constraint as stated in Eq. (6). For each row in the decision matrix (X_{ij}) either we did pruning or not; therefore, the summation along the same row is either 0 or 1 which is formulated as a constraint as mentioned in Eq. (4). Equation (5) formulates that the estimated accuracy loss should be less than or equal to a certain threshold $Acc_{threshold}$ given by the designer.

For cross layer pruning, the metric we use for the accuracy loss is the sum of the independent accuracy losses calculated from $A_{i,j}$ matrix.

Let a_k and a_k^* be the measured accuracy and the estimated accuracy respectively for a given run k. The relative error is thereby given by the following Equation:

$$RE = \frac{a_k^* - a_k}{a_k} \quad (7)$$

Figure 4 shows that RE follows a normal distribution with a mean value of -0.1 and a standard deviation of 0.21. Moreover, we calculated the correlation between the measured and the estimated accuracy. This correlation is higher than 98%, thereby insuring the coherence of our estimated accuracy. Hence, we assume that our metric of summing independent accuracy losses can be used in the exploration phase. Nevertheless, the final results are validated based on real measured accuracy.

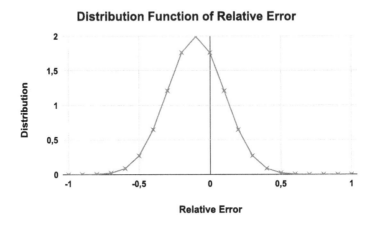

Fig. 4. Probability distribution function of the relative error.

In the fourth step, we run CPLEX optimizer to find the optimal pruning combination that respect the constraints and minimize the total number of parameters. The output of CPLEX is the pruning configuration and the estimated accuracy loss ($Acc_{estimated}$) due to that pruning. To validate our result, we test experimentally the pruning configuration by classifying the test dataset to obtain the real accuracy loss (Acc_{test}). If the obtained accuracy loss (Acc_{test}) is less than the defined accuracy threshold ($Acc_{threshold}$) then the pruning configuration is valid. Otherwise, the value for $Acc_{threshold}$ in Eq. (5) is updated with the obtained value by CPLEX ($Acc_{estimated}$) during that round as indicated in Eq. (8). After that, we rerun CPLEX for a second round to find the new optimal configuration. We keep iterating until the accuracy constraint is satisfied experimentally.

$$\sum_{i=1}^{m}\sum_{j=1}^{n} X_{ij} * A_{ij} \leq Acc_{estimated} \tag{8}$$

4.2 Quantization

Weights and activations for CNN are usually presented in floating-point. Applying approximations by representing them in fixed-point is an inevitable step to realize CNN over reconfigurable architectures to reduce both hardware and execution time. Fixed-point numbers are represented in Q-format where the number of integer and fractional bits are defined. For example, Q3.5 has 3 bits for integer including the sign bit and 5 bits for the fractional number. It is important to choose the appropriate number of bits to avoid a significant degradation in the inference accuracy.

In our approach weight quantization is applied in 2 steps. Firstly, the integer number of bits is determined by scanning the weights for the maximum absolute value in addition to one bit for signed numbers as indicated in the following equation: Num of I bits $= Max(log_2 \lceil\mid w \mid\rceil + 1)$ where w $\in$ weights.

Secondly, for the fractional number of bits, we examined the inference accuracy for a range of bits that extends from 0 to N-bits. Algorithm 1 explains how the number of fractional bits is chosen. For each weight, we quantize it at different number of bits dedicated for the fractional part (F). We calculated the ceiling and floor quantized values then the value of the minimum error difference is selected.

Input: Weights, maximum number of fractional bits (N)
Result: Number of fractional bits (F)
for $F \leftarrow 0$ **to** N **do**
 for $w \in weights$ **do**
  $w_1 = w * 2^F$
  $w_{ceil} = \lceil w_1 \rceil / 2^F$
  $w_{floor} = \lfloor w_1 \rfloor / 2^F$
  if $\mid w_{ceil} - w_1 \mid\leq\mid w_{floor} - w_1 \mid$ **then**
   $w_{quantized} = w_{ceil}$
  else
   $w_{quantized} = w_{floor}$
  end
 end
 for $i \leftarrow 0$ **to** $testimages$ **do**
  if $detected\ class == truth\ class$ **then**
   correct++
  else
   false++
  end
 end
end

Algorithm 1: Choosing the number of fractional bits for weight representation

Order of Applying Approximations. Sorting the weights of the output channels for each convolution layer is considered as a step for applying pruning. The output channels are sorted according to the absolute sum of their weights. Consequently, quantization should be firstly applied so that the quantized weights are sorted during pruning to allow correct results.

Table 1. CNN properties

	CNN 1	CNN 2	CNN 3
Total num. of parameters	4, 389, 418	14, 488, 650	27, 187, 210
Num. of conv. layers	9	14	17
Accuracy for CIFAR-10	85.49	85.92	86.84
Accuracy for MNIST	99.02	99.09	99.1
Conv. (# CHin, # CHout, output image)	L1 (3, 32, 32 × 32)	L1 (3, 64, 32 × 32)	L1 (3, 128, 32 × 32)
	L2 (32, 32, 30 × 30)	L2 (64, 64, 32 × 32)	L2, L3, L4 (128, 128, 32 × 32)
	L3 (32, 64, 30 × 30)	L3 (64, 128, 32 × 32)	L5, L6, L7 (128, 128, 30 × 30)
	L4 (64, 64, 28 × 28)	L4 (128, 128, 32 × 32)	L8 (128, 256, 30 × 30)
	L5 (64, 256, 14 × 14)	L5 (128, 128, 30 × 30)	L9 (256, 256, 30 × 30)
	L6 (256, 256, 12 × 12)	L6 (128, 128, 30 × 30)	L10 (256, 256, 28 × 28)
	L7 (256, 512, 6 × 6)	L7 (128, 256, 30 × 30)	L11 (256, 512, 14 × 14)
	L8 (512, 512, 6 × 6)	L8 (256, 256, 30 × 30)	L12 (512, 512, 14 × 14)
	L9 (512, 10, 1 × 1)	L9 (256, 256, 28 × 28)	L13 (512, 1024, 14 × 14)
		L10 (256, 512, 14 × 14)	L14 (1024, 1024, 12 × 12)
		L11 (512, 512, 12 × 12)	L15 (1024, 512, 6 × 6)
		L12 (512, 768, 6 × 6)	L16 (512, 512, 6 × 6)
		L13 (768, 768, 6 × 6)	L17 (512, 10, 1 × 1)
		L14 (768, 10, 1 × 1)	

5   Experimental Results

By comparing the distribution of weights and operations for different CNN models in the literature; we can easily conclude the following: (1) Fully connected layers has the large portion of the network's weights. (2) The convolution layers contribute to the large portion of operations. For example in VGG-16, the weights for the fully connected layers represent 90% of the total weight while the convolution layers contribute to 92% of the computation complexity.

During our experiments, we focused on studying the effect of approximations (quantization and pruning) on convolution layers. For that reason, we designed three convolution neural networks which are similar to the conventional networks like Alexnet or VGG but without having fully connected layers.

We trained three convolution networks CNN1, CNN2 and CNN3 on two datasets CIFAR-10 and MNIST. The training was held on a machine equipped by NVIDIA Quadro P5000 GPU card. Table 1 listed the properties of the three networks. For each CNN, we listed the total number of parameters, the number of convolution layers, the structure of the network and its accuracy to classify CIFAR-10 and MNIST datasets. Without using fully connected layers, we relied on max-pooling and non-padded convolutions to reduce the size of the input image.

The hardware architecture presented in Sect. 3 was synthesized by Vivado Design Suite 2015.2 on Xilinx Zynq 706 evaluation board [16]. As listed in

Table 2. Resource utilization for CNN hardware architecture at different cores number

Number of PE	Precision	SLICE	FF	LUT	BRAM (18K)	DSP
16	Floating point	22154	68912	67070	218	768
16	Fixed point	4071	9456	12327	186	173
32	Fixed point	5604	8465	16021	326	317
64	Fixed point	8699	10725	24829	614	605

Table 2, when the hardware architecture was synthesized for 16 processing elements at floating point precision, 85% of DSP was consumed (Max. DSP = 900) with 15% FF and 30% LUT utilization.

Firstly, we applied quantization to reduce the DSP utilization. For the integer part of the weights, we examined the weight parameters for the maximum and minimum values. After that, we could deduce the required number of bits to represent the integer part. For example, the minimum and maximum weight values while training CNN1 on CIFAR-10 were -1.22545 and 1.11254 respectively. Therefore, two bits were enough to represent the integer part including the sign bit.

For the fractional part of the weights, we could choose the correct number of bits by running Algorithm 1. Figure 5 depicted the accuracy while classifying CIFAR-10 and MNIST datasets. It showed the classification accuracy of the three networks CNN1, CNN2 and CNN3 by quantizing the weights at different fractional bit width extending from 0 to 16 bits. From the figure, we could deduce that 6 bits for the weight fractional part were enough to keep the same classification accuracy as it was while representing the weights in floating-point.

By synthesizing the hardware architecture for 16 processing elements with fixed-point representation, we were able to reduce the DSP utilization by 78%, FF by 86%, LUT by 81% and BRAM by 15%. This reduction in hardware resources gave us the possibility to duplicate the number of realized processing elements as listed in Table 2.

Secondly, we applied pruning to reduce the computation complexity. Channel pruning is applied at multiples of the number of processing elements otherwise some processors will be idle while the other will be utilized. To apply convolution layer pruning for an architecture containing 16 PEs means to prune the output channels in multiples of 16. For example, a pruning setup for CNN1 like following $(0, 5, 10, 1, 2, 0, 0, 0, 0)$ means to prune 80 (5×16), 160 (10×16), 16 (1×16), 32 (2×16) output channels from convolution layers L8, L7, L6, and L5 respectively.

During our experiments, we searched for the pruning setup that had an accuracy loss less than 3%. Choosing that value was arbitrary and could vary from one application to another. As a first step, the accuracy loss matrix (A_{ij}) was calculated for each convolution network. To achieve that step, we tested the maximum possible pruning that could be done for each convolution layer separately without exceeding 3% in accuracy loss. After that, by using CPLEX tool,

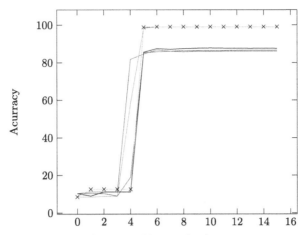

Number of fractional bits in fixed-point representation

Fig. 5. Fixed-point inference accuracy for CNN1-Cifar10 ____, CNN2-Cifar10 ____, CNN3-Cifar10 ____, CNN1-MNIST ____, CNN1-MNIST ―×― and CNN1-MNIST ____.

the three CNN networks were modelled by using Eqs. 3, 4, 5 and 6 to find the optimal pruning setup.

For CIFAR-10 dataset in Table 3, points #1, #3 and #7 represent CNN1, CNN2 and CNN3 before pruning at floating point precision. While points #2, #4 and #8 represent the pruning setup for them with accuracy loss of 2.89%, 2.6% and 2.9% and percentage decrease in computation complexity of 23.4%, 19.5% and 27.9% respectively. For the same CNN, the optimal pruning setup found by CPLEX can change by varying the number of synthesized processing elements (PEs) in the hardware architecture. For example for CNN3, points #8, #10, and #11 represent the pruning setup when it is executed on hardware architecture of 16, 32 and 64 processing elements respectively. We can notice that CNN3 achieves 27.9%, 25.6% and 21.8% decrease in computation complexity respectively. The reason behind is that each hardware architecture has a different multiple of pruned channels (i.e. multiples of 16 for 16-PEs, multiples of 32 for 32-PEs and multiples of 64 for 64-PEs). Therefore, fine pruning can be achieved on architectures of fewer PEs. For example, with PE = 16, one cut will remove only 16 channels, while with PE = 64, one cut will remove 64 channels at once which could violate our accuracy loss constraint.

The pruning step changes when floating-point weights are quantized. For instance, the pruning setup for CNN3 at point #8 did not achieve the same accuracy loss when its weights were quantized to Q2.5 at point #16. Therefore, we should take into consideration the impact of quantization. To achieve accuracy loss less than a certain objective; in our case, we fixed accuracy loss to $\leq 3\%$; while combining quantization and pruning. Firstly, the convolution network is quantized then the pruning search process is run to find the optimal pruning setup. For example, the weights of CNN3 were quantized to

Table 3. Pruning setup for CNN1, CNN2 and CNN3 trained for CIFAR-10 and MNIST dataset

Point	Architecture	Pruning setup (L17, L16, L15, ... L3, L2, L1)	Num of param.	Acc. loss (%)	FLOP	Dec. ↓ (%)
Image classification CIFAR-10 dataset						
1	CNN1-16PE-FP	No pruning	4389418	0	2.97E+08	0
2	CNN1-16PE-FP	(0, 5, 10, 1, 2, 0, 0, 0, 0)	2847466	2.89	2.27E+08	23.4
3	CNN2-16PE-FP	No pruning	14488650	0	2.68E+09	0
4	CNN2-16PE-FP	(0, 3, 22, 15, 9, 0, 1, 0, 0, 0, 0, 0, 0, 0)	7486282	2.6	2.158E+09	19.5
5	CNN2-16PE-6Bit	(0, 3, 22, 15, 7, 0, 0, 0, 0, 0, 0, 0, 0, 0)	7712122	3	2.246E+09	16.2
6	CNN2-16PE-5Bit	(0, 3, 10, 10, 7, 0, 0, 0, 0, 0, 0, 0, 0, 0)	10152330	2.7	2.364E+09	11.8
7	CNN3-16PE-FP	No pruning	27187210	0	5.346E+09	0
8	CNN3-16PE-FP	(0, 3, 7, 19, 20, 4, 1, 1, 3, 0, 0, 0, 0, 0, 0, 0, 1)	16873418	2.9	3.853E+09	27.9
9	CNN3-16PE-FP	(0, 3, 5, 20, 20, 1, 7, 0, 1, 3, 0, 0, 0, 0, 0, 0, 0)	17028202	4.2	3.861E+09	27.8
10	CNN3-32PE-FP	(0, 1, 3, 9, 10, 2, 0, 0, 1, 0, 0, 0, 0, 0, 0, 0, 1)	17524234	1.7	3.978E+09	25.6
11	CNN3-64PE-FP	(0, 1, 1, 4, 5, 1, 0, 0, 0, 0, 0, 0, 0, 0, 0, 0, 0)	18259594	2.4	4.183E+09	21.8
12	CNN3-16PE-6Bit	No pruning	27187210	0.22	5.346E+09	0
13	CNN3-16PE-6Bit	(0, 3, 3, 20, 21, 1, 7, 0, 1, 2, 0, 0, 0, 0, 0, 0, 1)	17225930	3	3.872E+09	27.6
14	CNN3-16PE-5Bit	No pruning	27187210	2.17	5.346E+09	0
15	CNN3-16PE-5Bit	(0, 1, 3, 19, 22, 1, 7, 0, 1, 2, 0, 0, 0, 0, 0, 0, 1)	17353258	2.9	3.865E+09	27.7
16	CNN3-16PE-5Bit	(0, 3, 7, 19, 20, 4, 1, 1, 3, 0, 0, 0, 0, 0, 0, 0, 1)	16873418	7.5	3.853E+09	27.9
17	CNN3-32PE-5Bit	(0, 0, 1, 9, 11, 0, 3, 0, 0, 1, 0, 0, 0, 0, 0, 0, 1)	18080106	1.9	3.981E+09	25.5
18	CNN3-64PE-5Bit	(0, 1, 0, 4, 5, 0, 1, 0, 0, 0, 0, 0, 0, 0, 0, 0)	19218122	2.7	4.256E+09	20.3
Digit recognition MNIST dataset						
19	CNN1-16PE-FP	No pruning	4388842	0	2.97E+08	0
20	CNN1-16PE-6Bit	(0, 19, 8, 5, 0, 0, 3, 0, 0)	1923290	2.85	1.566E+08	47.23
21	CNN1-16PE-5Bit	(0, 15, 5, 5, 0, 0, 3, 0, 0)	2343882	2.85	1.71E+08	42.2
22	CNN2-16PE-FP	No pruning	14487498	0	2.67E+09	0
23	CNN2-16PE-6-bit	(0, 26, 36, 15, 15, 0, 1, 1, 0, 0, 0, 0, 0)	4307498	3	1.94E+09	27.7
24	CNN2-16PE-5-bit	(0, 25, 10, 10, 15, 0, 0, 0, 0, 0, 0, 1, 1, 1)	7432362	2.7	2.116E+09	21
25	CNN3-16PE-FP	No pruning	27184906	0	5.343E+09	0
26	CNN3-16PE-6-bit	(0, 3, 20, 30, 35, 0, 0, 0, 2, 1, 1, 0, 0, 0, 0, 0, 5)	11753034	2.9	3.302E+09	38.2
27	CNN3-16PE-5-bit	(0, 4, 23, 36, 35, 0, 5, 0, 0, 0, 1, 1, 0, 1, 0, 0, 5)	10341322	3	3.216E+09	39.8

Q2.5 (5-bit) and Q2.6 (6-bit) with accuracy loss of 0.22% and 2.17% at points #12 and #14 respectively. Then pruning is applied to the quantized networks to achieve total loss of 3% and 2.9% with decrease in FLOP by 27.6% and 27.7% at points #13 and #15.

Regarding computation complexity, pruned floating-point networks (point #8) are less in FLOP than pruned quantized one (points #13 and #15) by 0.5% and 0.31% respectively. In contrast, regarding hardware utilization, quantized implementations are smaller than floating-point one in average by 80% for LUT, FF and DSP. Therefore, both quantization and pruning can be combined for better results.

For digit recognition MNIST dataset, pruned networks with weight quantization at Q2.5 and Q2.6 achieved reduction in computation complexity up to 42.2% and 47.23% for CNN1, up to 21% and 27.7% for CNN2 and up to 39.8% and 38.2% for CNN3 respectively.

6   Conclusion

Using approximation techniques to reduce CNN complexity is inevitable to implement these networks on embedded platforms such as FPGAs. While different approximation techniques are presented in the literature independently, we aimed in this paper to study the effect of applying more than one approximation to the same neural network. We presented a through FPGA-oriented exploration of both quantization and pruning to reduce the hardware cost and computation complexity with controlled loss in CNN accuracy. We succeeded to reduce hardware resources by 80%, computation complexity by 30% with accuracy loss less than 3%. As a future work, we will develop a tool for estimating the effect of different approximation techniques when applied to a certain CNN in terms of frame rate, accuracy and hardware cost. The tool will generate automatically the corresponding CNN structure with the hardware architecture required to achieve those objectives.

References

1. Abdelouahab, K., Pelcat, M., Sérot, J., Berry, F.: Accelerating CNN inference on FPGAs: a survey. CoRR abs/1806.01683 (2018). http://arxiv.org/abs/1806.01683
2. Albericio, J., Judd, P., Hetherington, T., Aamodt, T., Jerger, N.E., Moshovos, A.: Cnvlutin: ineffectual-neuron-free deep neural network computing. In: 2016 ACM/IEEE 43rd Annual International Symposium on Computer Architecture (ISCA), pp. 1–13, June 2016
3. Chen, W., Wilson, J.T., Tyree, S., Weinberger, K.Q., Chen, Y.: Compressing neural networks with the hashing trick. In: Proceedings of the 32nd International Conference on International Conference on Machine Learning - Volume 37, ICML2015, pp. 2285–2294. JMLR.org (2015)
4. Chen, Y., Krishna, T., Emer, J.S., Sze, V.: Eyeriss: an energy-efficient reconfigurable accelerator for deep convolutional neural networks. IEEE J. Solid-State Circuits **52**(1), 127–138 (2017)
5. Courbariaux, M., Bengio, Y.: BinaryNet: training deep neural networks with weights and activations constrained to +1 or −1. CoRR abs/1602.02830 (2016)

6. Courbariaux, M., Bengio, Y., David, J.P.: BinaryConnect: training deep neural networks with binary weights during propagations. In: Cortes, C., Lawrence, N.D., Lee, D.D., Sugiyama, M., Garnett, R. (eds.) Advances in Neural Information Processing Systems 28, pp. 3123–3131. Curran Associates Inc., Red Hook (2015)
7. Gysel, P., Motamedi, M., Ghiasi, S.: Hardware-oriented approximation of convolutional neural networks. CoRR abs/1604.03168 (2016). http://arxiv.org/abs/1604.03168
8. Han, S., Mao, H., Dally, W.J.: Deep compression: compressing deep neural network with pruning, trained quantization and Huffman coding. In: ICLR (2016)
9. Han, S., Mao, H., Dally, W.J.: Deep compression: compressing deep neural network with pruning, trained quantization and Huffman coding. In: 4th International Conference on Learning Representations, ICLR 2016, San Juan, Puerto Rico, 2–4 May 2016, Conference Track Proceedings (2016)
10. Han, S., Pool, J., Tran, J., Dally, W.J.: Learning both weights and connections for efficient neural networks. In: Proceedings of the 28th International Conference on Neural Information Processing Systems - Volume 1, NIPS 2015, pp. 1135–1143. MIT Press, Cambridge (2015)
11. He, Y., Zhang, X., Sun, J.: Channel pruning for accelerating very deep neural networks. http://arxiv.org/abs/1707.06168 (2017)
12. Ma, Y., Suda, N., Cao, Y., Seo, J., Vrudhula, S.: Scalable and modularized RTL compilation of convolutional neural networks onto FPGA. In: 2016 26th International Conference on Field Programmable Logic and Applications (FPL), pp. 1–8, August 2016
13. Miyashita, D., Lee, E.H., Murmann, B.: Convolutional neural networks using logarithmic data representation. CoRR abs/1603.01025 (2016)
14. Molchanov, P., Tyree, S., Karras, T., Aila, T., Kautz, J.: Pruning convolutional neural networks for resource efficient transfer learning. arXiv:1611.06440 (2016)
15. Rastegari, M., Ordonez, V., Redmon, J., Farhadi, A.: XNOR-Net: ImageNet classification using binary convolutional neural networks. CoRR abs/1603.05279 (2016)
16. Xilinx: ZC706 Evaluation Board for the Zynq-7000 XC7Z045 All Programmable SoC User Guide, July 2013
17. Yang, T., Chen, Y., Sze, V.: Designing energy-efficient convolutional neural networks using energy-aware pruning. In: 2017 IEEE Conference on Computer Vision and Pattern Recognition (CVPR), pp. 6071–6079, July 2017

Technique for Vendor and Device Agnostic Hardware Area-Time Estimation

Deshya Wijesundera[✉], Kushagra Shah, Kisaru Liyanage, Alok Prakash,
Thambipillai Srikanthan, and Thilina Perera

Nanyang Technological University, 50 Nanyang Avenue, Singapore 639798, Singapore
{deshya.w,alok,astsrikan}@ntu.edu.sg, kushagrashah298@gmail.com,
kisarur@gmail.com, pere0004@e.ntu.edu.sg

Abstract. This work proposes a novel technique for hardware area-time estimation of applications on FPGA. The application C code is first converted to the target independent LLVM IR prior to wrapping the basic blocks as functions using a LLVM transformation pass. The LegUp tool's 'LLVM IR functions to RTL modules' conversion is carried out to facilitate RTL synthesis using the Altera Quartus tools. In order to support FPGAs other than Altera, the soft IP cores generated by LegUp were replaced as generic RTL components. Further, additional modules have been incorporated to support floating point operations. This approach, has made it possible to support FPGAs from other vendors with high area-time estimation accuracy. The proposed technique relies on the free versions of the vendor tools and LegUp. Moreover, the approach does not necessitate time consuming post synthesis steps such as Place & Route and Bit Stream Generation in order to obtain reasonably accurate area estimation measures.

Keywords: Generic · Hardware estimation · FPGA

1 Introduction

The complexity of designing embedded systems continue to escalate with the increasing complexity in applications and stringent design requirements. The time-to-market (TTM) pressure has reached a level where a delay of a single quarter to reach the market, results in a loss of $1/3$ of the expected revenue [9]. At the same time, the non-recurring engineering (NRE) cost is rising exponentially with shrinking process technology [15]. Hence, meeting the myriad of conflicting design requirements in terms of performance, area and power limitations combined with the TTM pressure and NRE cost make customized solutions the only viable option in the domain of embedded systems design [17]. As such, embedded systems designed on Application-Specific Integrated Circuits (ASIC) and platform Field Programmable Gate Arrays (FPGA) are fast becoming the main competitors at the forefront of hardware (HW) customization.

ASICs provide the optimal configuration based on the requirements for performance, area or power for a given application but incur long TTM and

© Springer Nature Switzerland AG 2020
F. Rincón et al. (Eds.): ARC 2020, LNCS 12083, pp. 166–177, 2020.
https://doi.org/10.1007/978-3-030-44534-8_13

high NRE cost. In contrast, FPGAs provide configurability and flexibility with shorter TTM and low NRE cost, even though the performance is comparatively low. For example, FPGAs typically reach the production stage within 3–5 months, whereas ASICs require 12–18 months for the same [1]. Further, modern FPGAs constituting reconfigurable logic, processors, memory subsystems, etc. have become the ideal platform to perform acceleration for critical parts of an application along with support for realizing an entire System-on-Chip. Thus, owing to the shorter development cycles, re-usability and heterogeneity of FPGAs, they are considered as an attractive alternative over ASICs for customized HW designs. This is exemplified by the 7.23 billion USD FPGA market expected in 2022, with a Compound Annual Growth Rate (CAGR) of 7.41% from 2016 [7].

However, the design of FPGA-based Configurable SoC is a challenging task due to the conflicting design constraints of performance, power, area and cost. Further, the flexibility of heterogeneity introduces the cost of added complexity. As such, the productivity of electronic design automation (EDA) tools is of paramount importance in meeting the aforementioned criteria. However, the productivity of EDA tools utilized in the development of embedded systems has significantly lagged behind the improvements achieved in HW process technologies, which is referred to as the *design productivity gap* [6]. The widening of this design productivity gap with improvement in HW process technologies, has created a major challenge for modern embedded systems designers.

Another important factor to note is the selection of the most suitable FPGA device for application requirements from the different FPGA vendors and device families. This decision is based on the HW area consumption and performance of the application on each FPGA device. HW area consumption and performance depend on the architecture of the FPGA device. The architectural features of a FPGA differs across vendors and devices. As such, existing techniques for HW area-time estimation are limited to a single FPGA device or a few devices from a single vendor, even though it is an area of research that has been extensively studied [18]. Extending such techniques to support different devices requires modelling of the architecture of each FPGA device, entailing detailed analysis of the architectural features of the device. However, in order to make optimal use of HW area-time estimation by providing the user the option to select between devices, it is important to support different devices.

This paper proposes a technique that leverages on existing open source tools and subsequently uses vendor synthesis tools to perform HW area-time estimation across different FPGA vendors and devices, without the need for detailed architectural analysis and modelling. The main contributions of this paper are,

- A technique to encapsulate basic blocks within a wrapper to obtain area consumption of basic blocks using existing free versions of vendor tools
- A technique to generate RTL code for synthesis on different vendor tools
- A unified methodology that can be applied for hardware area-time estimation across different FPGA vendors and device families

2 Hardware Area-Time Estimation

FPGA compilation flow typically constitutes time-consuming logic synthesis, design placement and routing. The need to evaluate HW designs at early stages in the design cycle in order to trade-off between design options has resulted in research efforts for HW performance estimation. Existing work in HW performance estimation for FPGAs can be broadly categorized as high-level estimation, high-level synthesis (HLS) based estimation and RTL/logic-level estimation [4]. Some of the work combines two or all of these strategies [18].

High Level Estimation. In high level estimation, HW area and time are estimated prior to scheduling. Typically, this category of approaches rely on probabilistic models and integer linear programming (ILP) models. Most of the early research efforts in HW performance estimation rely on high level estimation [18]. HW performance estimation for efficient design space exploration by obtaining the lower bound execution time of a DFG, subject to area constraints is discussed in [12]. A parametric area estimation methodology modeling low-level metrics as a function of high-level variables using high-level and low-level parameters derived through high-level model tuning (with synthesized RTL) and low-level model tuning (with the circuit netlist) using 20 SystemC designs is proposed in [3]. Todman et al. presented a high-level design exploration framework, featuring a HW performance estimator using area-time constraints and a C application as input [14]. Meeuws et al. uses a statistical model in estimating HW resources introducing 92 software (SW) complexity metrics and several SW measurement techniques as indicators of different aspects of SW descriptions [10].

High Level Synthesis (HLS) Based Estimation. The advent of HLS tools which could translate algorithmic descriptions in high level languages to RTL has led to the development of interest on HLS based estimation. HLS tools typically perform scheduling and resource binding based on the IR of the application. The RTL generated by the tools consist a data path and a control path. An estimation technique based on execution traces generated from simulation of Matlab programs to estimate area and performance of a FPGA implementation, incorporating a greedy scheduling and binding algorithm has been proposed [4]. A methodology to estimate delays and resources on FPGA for applications written in Java is proposed [4]. Bilavarn et al. performs area, performance and power estimation by transforming C functions to Hierarchical Control Data Flow Graphs (HCDFGs) [2]. Lieu et al. rely on the Trimaran compiler infrastructure in the area-time estimation framework proposed in [4].

RTL/Logic-Level Estimation. The input RTL description or the netlist of the circuit is used for estimation at RTL/logic-level. The techniques proposed in [13] use a commercial HDL parser [11] in resource estimation. An area-time estimation technique using an input netlist is proposed in [19]. The authors in this work, decompose the netlist into LUTs and allocate the LUTs with the most common inputs to the same configurable logic block (CLB). In estimating the routing resources, the work also predicts the placement and shape of CLBs. Both CLB delays and wire delays are used in calculating the path delays.

HW area consumption and performance is dependent on the architecture of the FPGA device. The architectural features of a FPGA device differs across vendors and also FPGA device families. As such existing techniques for HW area-time estimation are limited to a single FPGA device or a few devices from a single vendor. Extending such techniques to support different devices require individual modelling of each of the devices which is cumbersome and time consuming. Also, due to this factor scaling such techniques to support new devices will require modeling of each of those devices as well. However, making optimal use of HW area-time estimation by providing the user with the option to select between devices, requires support for different devices.

3 Methodology

In this section, we present the proposed FPGA vendor and device agnostic technique for HW area-time estimation, in detail. The technique also provides the user with the opportunity to select the granularity (i.e. function, basic block or application level) of obtaining HW area-time information. Figure 1 shows the proposed methodology constituting of 5 key stages. Initially, the application C code is converted to LLVM Intermediate Representation (IR) using the LLVM profiler [8]. Next, if the user requires information at basic block level, then the process moves to the second stage which is further explained in Sect. 3.2. If the estimation is required only at function or application level, the process moves to stage 3 which converts the LLVM IR/modified LLVM IR (from stage 2) to RTL. Finally, the code is synthesized on the free version of the vendor tool, and the area-time information is extracted.

3.1   C to LLVM IR Conversion

Here, the application C code is converted to LLVM IR (using LLVM profiler), which is later used to obtain the RTL code for area-time estimation. LLVM IR is a low-level intermediate representation used by the LLVM compiler framework.

3.2   Basic Block Wrapper

In the proposed technique, we use an RTL code to obtain the HW estimation using the synthesis flow of vendor tools. The RTL code is obtained by converting the LLVM IR using 'LLVM IR functions to RTL modules' conversion of LegUp [16]. In the LegUp LLVM IR to RTL conversion process, functions in the LLVM IR (functions in C code map to functions in LLVM IR) are converted to modules in the Verilog RTL description. As such, it is possible to obtain area

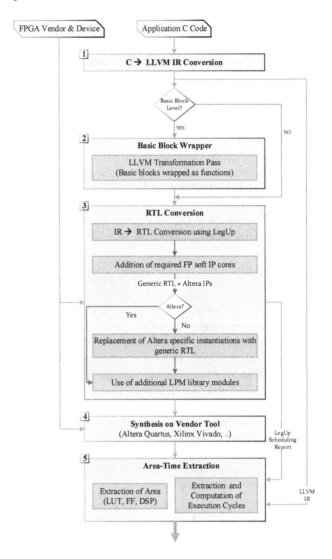

Fig. 1. Proposed methodology

estimation at function level granularity by synthesizing this RTL code (as functions are mapped into RTL modules by LegUp). However, the synthesis flow does not provide area estimation of basic blocks of the C code. Thus, we wrap basic blocks as functions which in turn map to RTL modules.

Since the RTL code is obtained by converting the LLVM IR using LegUp, it is necessary to provide a modified version of the LLVM IR such that LegUp can generate the RTL at the required granularity. To this end, we have developed a LLVM Transformation Pass to wrap basic blocks inside functions. The pseudo code of the LLVM Transformation Pass is shown in Algorithm 1. The inputs to the pass consist of the LLVM IR and the list of basic blocks which need to be

---

Algorithm 1: Pseudocode of LLVM Transformation Pass

    Input   : LLVM IR, List of basic blocks to be wrapped and their respective functions

    Output: Modified version of LLVM IR

1 GV: List of global variables

2 **for** *Each Basic Block j* **do**

3 | Create a new function j'

4 | Add terminator instruction to function j'

5 | **for** *Each Instruction i in Basic Block j* **do**

6 | | **if** *i == terminator instruction of j* **then**

7 | | | Continue

8 | | **else**

9 | | | Move i to new function j' before terminator instruction

10 | | **end**

11 | | **for** *Each source operand n in i* **do**

12 | | | **if** $n \in k,\ k \neq j'$ **then**

13 | | | | **if** $n \notin GV$ **then**

14 | | | | | Create new global variable n_gv

15 | | | | | Add store instruction to j

16 | | | | | Add load instruction to j'

17 | | | | **end**

18 | | | **end**

19 | | **end**

20 | **end**

21 | **for** *Each destination operand m in j'* **do**

22 | | **if** $m \in j'',\ j'' \neq j'$ **then**

23 | | | Create new global variable m_gv

24 | | | Add store instruction to j'

25 | | | Add load instruction to j

26 | | **end**

27 | **end**

28 | Add call instruction to j

29 **end**

---

wrapped as functions. The basic steps of wrapping a basic block inside a function are given below.

1. Create a new function
2. Move all instructions except terminator instructions to the new function
3. Resolve all data dependencies using global variables

Initially, for each basic block j, a new function $j\prime$ is created. Next, the pass moves all the instructions (in sequence) in the basic block j except the terminator instruction to the new function $j\prime$. Thereafter, a *call* instruction is added to the basic block j to invoke the new function $j\prime$. In the next stage, the pass resolves data dependencies. Here, we define data dependencies as cases where a variable modified inside one basic block is used by another basic block. To resolve data dependencies, all the operands created or used outside the new function $j\prime$ is converted to global variables. The *store* instruction represents preserving data on created global variables and *load* instruction represents retrieving the stored data to where it is needed. For source operands, *store* instructions are added inside the basic block j while *load* instructions are added in the new function $j\prime$. For destination operands, *store* instructions are added inside the new function $j\prime$, while *load* instructions are added to the other basic blocks j that use the destination operand.

3.3   RTL Conversion

In this stage, we convert the LLVM IR (for function level) or modified LLVM IR (for basic block level) to RTL code using the 'LLVM IR functions to RTL modules' conversion of LegUp. It should be noted that the application level performance can be obtained in both cases. However, we observe that the RTL code generated by LegUp is not generic as it contains code specific to Altera FPGAs (this is because LegUp offers full support only for the Altera FPGA devices). Hence, the generated RTL code cannot be synthesized on other FPGA vendor tools to obtain HW area-time estimates. Therefore, it is necessary to modify the generated RTL code to accommodate different FPGA vendors. It was observed that (i) integer divide and block RAM (instantiated as *lpm_divide* and *altsyncram*) modules use Altera soft IP cores and (ii) floating point operations use soft IP cores that use Altera specific *LPM simulation* library for integer arithmetic operations. The Altera soft IP cores were made compatible for other FPGA vendor tools by adding the extra library modules that the Altera FPGA tools use. Each of the listed soft IP cores mentioned the need for certain LPM library modules in their source code. But a lesser number of modules were actually used in the source code. It was observed that the addition of only four LPM library modules (*lpm add sub, lpm compare, lpm mult, lpm mux*) satisfies the requirements of all sixteen floating-point operations. Other than this, *lpm divide* and *altsyncram* library modules were added for the integer divide and block RAM instantiations in the RTL code. Moreover, the Altera soft IP cores need to be generated using the *MegaWizard Plug-In Manager* and added to the synthesis project. The exact algorithm of modifying the RTL code to make it synthesizable on Altera as well as other FPGA vendor tools is mentioned in Algorithm 2.

Initially, the FPGA vendor is identified because different approaches are followed for Altera and other FPGA vendor tools. For the Altera FPGA tools, the LegUp generated RTL code is scanned for any occurrences of floating-point operations. Then, the required Altera soft IP cores for floating-point operations are added by modifying the Quartus project files. For the other FPGA tools (we consider the Xilinx FPGA tools in this case without any loss of generality), first the Altera specific *integer divide* and *block RAM* instantiations are replaced with generic RTL code. Then, the LegUp generated RTL code is scanned for any occurrences of floating-point operations. Next, the required Altera soft IP cores for floating-point operations are added. Finally, the additional LPM library modules are added to support the synthesis on any FPGA vendor tool.

Algorithm 2: Pseudocode of RTL Modification

    Input   : LegUp generated RTL code, FPGA vendor for synthesis
    Output   : Modified version of RTL code
    Resources: FP soft IP cores, LPM library modules, Generic 'integer divide'
                  and 'block RAM', Makefile for LegUp, TCL script template for
                  Xilinx ISE

  1 **if** $FPGA\ vendor == Altera$ **then**
  2   Use Makefile to generate Altera Quartus project
  3   **for** $Each\ FP\ operation\ type\ f$ **do**
  4   Find 'n' = number of occurrences of FPop f in the RTL code
  5   **if** $n \neq zero$ **then**
  6   Add FPop f source code to the Altera Quartus project
  7   [Done by modifying the Quartus .qsf file]
  8   **end**
  9   **end**
10 **else**
11   Create new TCL script using the TCL script template
12   Replace 'integer divide' with generic module instantiation
13   Replace 'block RAM' with generic module instantiation
14   **for** $Each\ FP\ operation\ type\ f$ **do**
15   Find 'n' = number of occurrences of FPop f in the RTL code
16   **if** $n \neq zero$ **then**
17   Add new lines to TCL script to include FPop f
18   **end**
19   **end**
20   Add the LPM library modules to the RTL code
21   Run TCL script to generate Xilinx ISE project
22   Delete TCL script
23 **end**

3.4 Synthesis on FPGA Tools

Typically, synthesis tools provide area estimates of the RTL code. Therefore, after generating the generic RTL code suitable for synthesis on the given FPGA vendor tool, we infer the synthesis tool (non-commercial version) of the relevant FPGA vendor. The synthesis report generated by the tool is used to extract the area estimates in the subsequent stage.

3.5 Area-Time Extraction

The HW area is obtained in terms of look-up-table (LUT), digital signal processing (DSP) block, register (REG) and block RAM (BRAM) resources on the FPGA. This data is extracted from the synthesis report of the vendor tool. However, the process of wrapping basic blocks in the LLVM IR into functions in the LLVM IR in Sect. 3.2 introduces an overhead due to the additional *load* and *store* instructions. We account for this overhead by deducting the area required for these instructions (we have experimentally obtained the area consumption of *load* and *store* instructions) from the actual extracted area estimates for each basic block. However, estimation at function level does not cause this overhead. The execution time of basic blocks as well as functions is directly extracted from the LegUp scheduling report.

4   Results and Discussion

All experiments were carried out on a virtual machine running Ubuntu on an Intel Xeon CPU host at 3.5 GHz with 8 GB RAM. Initially, we modify the LegUp generated RTL code to incorporate the *block RAM* and *integer divide* generic codes. Thereafter, the floating-point soft IP cores are added. Additional library modules are also added for the case of non-Altera devices. Thus, it is necessary to ensure that the functionality of the application remains unaltered. The functional correctness in terms of output values is verified using micro-benchmarks. Further, timing-synchronisation is maintained to ensure functional correctness of the complete application.

Table 1. Verification results for floating point operations

FP operation	Latency	Expected op	Altera op	Xilinx op	Error in %
Adder (1)	14	18.01	18.0100	18.0100	0.000001271
Adder (2)	14	18.90	18.8999	18.8999	0.000002018
Adder (3)	14	36.91	36.9099	36.9099	0.000004134
fptosi32	6	18	18	18	0
fptosi64	6	18	18	18	0
sitofp32	6	18.00	18.00	18.00	0
sitofp64	6	18.00	18.00	18.00	0
Extend	6	18.01	18.0100	18.0100	0.000001271
Truncate	6	18.01	18.0100	18.0100	0.000001271

We used custom floating-point test files to validate the techniques specifically targeting applications involving floating-point operations. We ran comprehensive tests for each floating-point operation in different scenarios. We obtained the results for multiple Altera and Xilinx FPGA families to ensure generality of results. Table 1 shows the results for a floating-point test file run on Altera Cyclone V and Xilinx Kintex 7 device families. The latency and output of some floating-point operations is shown for the aforementioned Altera and Xilinx FPGAs. The accuracy of the output shown in Table 1 is calculated using the expected output of the floating-point operations as the base. It can be clearly identified from Table 1 that the results for floating-point operations are very accurate and identical for Altera and non-Altera FPGA devices.

Table 2. Area-time estimation values for ADPCM

Basic Block	Xilinx Kintex 7					Altera Cyclone V				
	LUT	REG	DSP	BRAM	Time	LUT	REG	DSP	BRAM	Time
1	0	0	0	1	3600	29	18	0	0	3600
2	0	0	0	1	3450	12	9	0	0	3450
3	69	161	0	0	3300	77	107	0	0	3300
4	5	67	0	0	4400	41	56	0	0	3300
5	12	134	0	0	3000	82	112	0	0	3000
6	82	384	6	0	3000	233	318	4	0	4000
7	0	0	0	1	2268	0	0	0	1	2268
8	10	134	0	0	1944	82	112	0	0	1944
9	144	402	4	0	1944	238	304	0	0	1944
10	70	12	6	0	3240	116	86	4	0	3240

Table 3. Area-time estimation values for DFSIN

Basic Block	Xilinx Kintex 7					Altera Cyclone V				
	LUT	REG	DSP	BRAM	Time	LUT	REG	DSP	BRAM	Time
1	10	20	0	0	11080	49	30	0	0	11080
2	8	16	0	0	13296	29	24	0	0	11080
3	10	20	0	0	10080	41	30	0	0	8400
4	240	897	0	0	5540	896	949	0	0	5540
5	460	160	0	0	4180	173	208	0	0	4180
6	76	176	0	0	4180	84	200	0	0	4180
7	0	0	0	0	3344	0	0	0	0	5016
8	759	860	0	0	5016	444	908	0	0	3344
9	1052	1200	0	0	2508	133	1224	0	0	2508
10	0	0	0	2	4180	0	0	0	2	4180

For a wholistic verification, we used applications from the popular CHStone [5] benchmark suite to validate the proposed techniques. In this section, we only present the results obtained for the Xilinx Kintex 7 and Altera Cyclone V FPGA devices. However, we have tested this technique for 5 device families commonly used in FPGA-based applications, Altera Cyclone V, Cyclone II and Arria II and also Xilinx Kintex 7 and Artix 7. Even though, we have used the full benchmark suite for experimentation, we select 2 applications for analysis of results. Further, since an application contains a large number of basic blocks, for ease of representation we depict the results for the 10 most frequently executed blocks in each application. It is important to note that the proposed technique can be used either for all the basic blocks in the application or for any given subset of basic blocks. Tables 2 and 3 show the area-time estimation values obtained from the proposed approach for ADPCM and DFSIN applications respectively. The results are presented for Xilinx Kintex 7 and Altera Cyclone V FPGA devices. The area is shown in terms of LUT, REG, DSP and BRAM resources. The time value indicates the number of clock cycles the basic block requires to execute on HW.

As can be clearly identified from Tables 2 and 3, the area and time for the applications differ across the selected FPGA devices. The reason for the difference in the resource consumption is due to the size and architectural differences of the FPGA resources. Further, it can be observed that there are changes in the type of resources utilized across devices. For example, basic blocks 1 and 2 in ADPCM only use BRAM in the Xilinx Kintex 7 device, while in the case of Altera it uses only LUT and REG resources. It is also interesting to note that basic block 9 in ADPCM utilizes DSP blocks in the Xilinx Kintex 7 while it does not use DSP blocks in Altera Cyclone V. Thus, the differences in resource consumption on different vendors and devices can be observed.

5   Conclusion

This paper, proposed a technique for HW area-time estimation of applications on FPGAs that can be applied across different FPGA vendors and device families.

References

1. FPGA Market by Type, Verticals, Architecture, Technology Node, and Geography - Forecast to 2022 (2016). https://bit.ly/2u0Tq5r
2. Bilavarn, S., et al.: Design space pruning through early Estimations of area/delay tradeoffs for FPGA Implementations. In: TCAD 2006 (2006)
3. Brandolese, C., et al.: An area estimation methodology for FPGA based designs at systemc-level. In: DAC 2004 (2004)
4. Chuong, M.: Rapid area-time estimation technique for porting C-based applications onto FPGA platforms. Scalable Comput. Pract. Exp. **8**(4), 359–371 (2008)
5. Hara, Y., et al.: CHStone: a benchmark program suite for practical C-based high-level synthesis. In: ISCAS 2008 (2008)
6. International Technology Roadmap for Semiconductors (2011). https://bit.ly/2t9LRJj
7. Joshi, A.: Embedded systems: technologies and markets - IFT016E (2014). https://bit.ly/37DRvT5
8. LLVM: The LLVM Compiler Infrastructure. http://llvm.org/
9. Mark, H.: "Time = Money: Faster Time to Market with Formal Verification", Mentor Graphics (2013). https://bit.ly/3404j3o
10. Meeuws, R., et al.: Quipu: a statistical model for predicting hardware resources. ACM Trans. Reconfigurable Technol. Syst. **6**(1), 25 (2013)
11. Quinton, B., et al.: News (2016). http://www.verific.com/
12. Rim, M., et al.: Estimating performance characteristics of loop transformations. In: ISCAS 1994

13. Schumacher, P., et al.: Fast and accurate resource estimation of RTL-based designs targeting FPGAS. In: FPL 2008
14. Todman, T., et al.: Reconfigurable design automation by high-level exploration. In: ASAP 2012
15. Tong, V.: Opportunities and challenges: 28nm and 2.5/3-D IC design and manufacturing (2012). https://bit.ly/33VR3g5
16. University of Toronto: LegUp High-Level Synthesis. http://legup.eecg.utoronto.ca
17. Wijesundera, D., et al.: Framework for rapid performance estimation of embedded soft core processors. TRETS **11**(2), 1–21 (2018)
18. Wijesundera, D., et al.: Wibheda+: framework for data dependency-aware multi-constrained hardware-software partitioning in FPGA-based SoCs for IoT applications. In: HEART 2018
19. Xu, M., et al.: Area and timing estimation for lookup table based FPGAs. In: EDTC 1996

Resource Efficient Dynamic Voltage and Frequency Scaling on Xilinx FPGAs

Gökhan Akgün[1(✉)], Lester Kalms[1], and Diana Göhringer[1,2]

[1] Adaptive Dynamic Systems, Technische Universität Dresden, Dresden, Germany
{goekhan.akguen,lester.kalms,diana.goehringer}@tu-dresden.de
[2] Centre for Tactile Internet with Human-in-the-loop (CeTi),
Technische Universität Dresden, Dresden, Germany

Abstract. As FPGA devices become increasingly ubiquitous, the need for energy-conscious implementations for battery-powered devices arises. These new energy constraints have to be met in addition to the well-known area, latency and throughput requirements. Furthermore, the power dissipation of such systems is usually considered as a hardware problem. However, it can be solved effectively through hardware and software implementations of power-saving techniques. One generic energy-saving technique that does not require retroactive alteration of an HW/SW-design is dynamic voltage and frequency scaling (DVFS) which adjusts the power consumption and performance of an embedded device at run-time based on its workload and operating conditions. This work investigates the power monitoring and scaling capabilities of Xilinx Zynq-7000 SoCs and UltraScale+ MPSoCs. A real-time operating system (RTOS) manages the resources of an application, the voltage/frequency scaling and the power monitoring with its preemptive scheduling policies. Furthermore, the frequency is scaled without using additional hardware resources on the programmable logic from the processing system. The methodology can easily be used for changing the processor frequency at run-time. As a case study, we apply our technique to find energy-optimal voltage and frequency pairs for an image processing application designed using the open-source high-level synthesis library HiFlipVX. The proposed frequency scaling architecture requires up to 20% less flip-flops and look-up tables as compared to the same design with clocking wizard on the programmable logic.

Keywords: Dynamic voltage and frequency scaling · Image processing application HiFlipVX · Frequency scaling without MMCM

1 Introduction

A major objective of running an application on battery-operated embedded devices is the total power dissipation. This key requirement has an impact on the development of applications and the management of available resources. Applying power-saving techniques can further improve the amount of power

© Springer Nature Switzerland AG 2020
F. Rincón et al. (Eds.): ARC 2020, LNCS 12083, pp. 178–192, 2020.
https://doi.org/10.1007/978-3-030-44534-8_14

consumption on Field Programmable Gate Arrays (FPGAs). One such popular power capping technique is dynamic voltage and frequency scaling (DVFS) that adjusts dynamically the voltage and frequency to reduce the static and dynamic power based on the workload, fabrications and operating conditions [1,2]. Performance, reliability and real-time requirements can be met through this optimization technique. Depending on the embedded architecture, the power consumption can be adjusted through on-board voltage regulators. To monitor the overall power consumption of the system, an I2C based Power Management Bus (PMBus) communication protocol has to be used to retrieve the voltage and current values from on-board voltage regulators. However, the monitoring exhibits a latency which affects safety-critical applications running on processors. Baremetal systems are unable to handle such applications whereby a real-time operating system (RTOS) guarantees a proper execution of such applications through their built-in preemptive scheduling policies. Besides, several works have been published for power monitoring and saving on Xilinx FPGAs. A clocking wizard is mainly deployed for the frequency scaling on the programmable logic (PL). In this work, we show the possibility to scale the frequency at run-time without using additional hardware resources on the PL from the processing system (PS). The proposed methodology can easily be used for changing the processor frequency according to the existing workload. As an use case, we have implemented the Canny edge detector, which detects features in images [3]. Features are points of interest that can be corners, edges or blobs. Feature detection is part of many larger algorithms, such as object detection [4]. For our implementation, we used HiFlipVX, an open-source high-level synthesis (HLS) FPGA library for image processing [5]. Based on the OpenVX standard and HiFlipVX, we have added the missing functions needed for the Canny edge detector, namely the Non-Max Suppression and Threshold.

The paper is organized as follows: Sect. 2 introduces the related work in the area of power-saving techniques on FPGAs and operating systems (OSs), and our use case. Section 3 describes the proposed methodologies and the contributions of this work. Section 4 presents the use case whereby its results are shown in Sect. 5. The paper is concluded in Sect. 6.

2   Related Work

In this section, we overview the state-of-the-art in power-saving techniques on FPGAs and OSs, and our use case.

2.1   Power-Saving Techniques on Xilinx FPGAs

Several new multi-processor system-on-chip technologies have been released in the last years which broadens the power reduction capabilities. An adaptive DVFS framework is presented in [6] which has exploited a deep learning application based on FINN binarized neural network on the Xilinx Zynq UltraScale+ MPSoC ZCU102. The experiments have shown a manual voltage scaling from the nominal voltage (850 mV) to 550 mV on this board. The framework has identified a maximum operating frequency for each adjusted voltage level. Hence, the performance and energy efficiency of the running application has been enhanced by up to approximately 80% in this work. For instance, a power-aware implementation is proposed in [7] for the Xilinx Zynq-7000 SoC ZC702 board. The experiments have shown that the voltage was scaled from the nominal voltage (1 V) to 750 mV. It has led to a power reduction of 49% on the PL. The voltage scaling has been handled by a written software code from the ARM processor. A similar DVS approach is presented for image processing applications in [8]. In this work, selected portions of the application have been running through Xilinx SDSoC on the PL. The voltage has been also scaled through a written software code from the ARM processor. The experiments show an overall power reduction of 37%. The nominal voltage of the UltraScale+ technology is 850 mV. Hence, we compare the power-saving capabilities of Xilinx Zynq-7000 and UltraScale+ FPGA using an image processing application in this research work. Xilinx FPGAs retrieve the overall power consumption from on-board voltage regulators through a communication protocol known as PMBus based on I2C which operates usually on a frequency of 400 kHz [9,10]. The communication leads to an additional latency in running applications [11]. However, the latency can be shortened when the required power domains are only monitored at run-time which is also concerned in this work. In [12], the voltage V_{CCINT} has been scaled below 400 mV so that the PL lost its configuration. This has saved the power consumption on the PL while the hardware modules are idle for a certain period. Therefore, we adjust the voltage until 550 mV in this work.

2.2 Power-Saving with Operating Systems

The effects of DVFS regarding operating systems have been widely investigated in the literature. Most of the works are proposing an energy-aware scheduler. A multi-core supported low-power scheduler is proposed for Linux OS in [13]. It exploits the slack time of a running task to scale the frequency at run-time and is implemented based on the earliest deadline first policy. The scheduler enables to meet the soft or hard real-time requirements of the safety-critical application. The results have shown that the system achieved an overall energy reduction of approximately 27% for an H.264 decoder. It alternates the frequency from 666 MHz to 333 MHz [11]. A similar approach based on a hypervisor architecture is presented in [14]. In this work, the scheduling policy deals with the power awareness of the system and partitioned the tasks regarding real-time requirements. In the same way, as proposed in [11], the frequency is alternated only from 400 MHz to 33 MHz and vice versa on the ARM processor of the Xilinx Zynq-7000 SoC ZC702. The experiments have shown an overall power reduction of approximately 33%. Nevertheless, the operating frequency can only be adjusted at run-time for certain frequency values with the Linux kernel driver *cpufreq* on the ARM processor in [11,13,14]. In this case, the frequency values are handwritten in the kernel configuration. The methodologies enable to adjust only the clocking behavior of the processors in the PS. Therefore, we propose a flexible frequency scaling approach for RTOSs, as well as for bare-metal applications. The main benefit of the proposed technique is that it can adapt the performance of the running application regarding the system requirements at run-time without having any restrictions on the frequency values. Furthermore, the clocking primitive is adjusted without using any additional hardware resources in the PL.

2.3 Feature Detection Application

Several papers have implemented the Canny edge detector for FPGAs. Lee et al. have implemented an efficient Canny edge detector for advanced mobile vision applications [15]. They have made several optimizations to reduce the resource utilization without seriously impacting the detection performance. They compare also themselves with other implementations to underpin their work. In comparison, we can also achieve a very low resource consumption, as our evaluation shows, although it contains the AXI4-Stream wrapper. However, the resource consumption of the flip-flops would become higher if the frequency of the HLS core is increased. For energy efficiency, we use DVFS techniques or sacrifice some of the resources for vectorization. Maheshwari et al. show an implementation of a scalable real-time Canny edge detector integrated into an HDMI stream [16]. They also use HLS, but utilize much more resources.

3 Proposed Methodology

The power consumption of an FPGA architecture consists of a static and dynamic part described as

$$P_{Total} = \underbrace{I_{Leakage} \cdot V_{DD}}_{P_{Static}} + \underbrace{\alpha \cdot C_L \cdot V_{DD}^2 \cdot f_{System}}_{P_{Dynamic}} \qquad (1)$$

which describes the relation between the switching activity α, total switched capacitance C_L, leakage current $I_{Leakage}$, supply voltage V_{DD} and operating frequency f_{System} [17]. Equation (1) shows how the operating frequency influences linearly the dynamic power in which the supply voltage has a quadratic behavior, respectively, and effects linearly the static power at the same time. The following subsections describe the details of the implemented DVFS and power monitoring on the Xilinx Zynq-7000 and UltraScale+ platforms.

3.1 Platform Description of Xilinx Zynq-7000 SoCs and UltraScale+ MPSoCs

Xilinx Zynq-7000 SoC ZC702 (XC7Z020). The platform consists of a dual-core ARM Cortex-A9 processor and an FPGA [9]. It is equipped with three digital power controllers (UCD9248) by Texas Instruments (TI) [18]. These controllers provide ten power rails to supply the PS, PL and other parts of the evaluation board. The power controllers are wired with the PMBus which is connected to a 1-to-8 channel I2C bus switch (PCA9548) [9]. Using the PMBus commands [18], it is possible to read the voltage and current on each power rail. In this research work, we investigate only the characteristics of the PS internal logic supply voltage (V_{CCPINT}) and the PL internal supply voltage (V_{CCINT}). The nominal voltage is 1 V for the PS and PL [19].

Xilinx Zynq UltraScale+ MPSoC ZCU102 (XCZU9EG). This platform consists of a quad-core ARM Cortex-A53 processor and a dual-core ARM Cortex-R5 real-time processing unit. It is equipped with three different voltage regulators (MAX20751EKX, MAX15301, MAX15303) by Maxim Integrated [20]. The controllers have in total 25 power rails to supply the evaluation board. Furthermore, the device has multiple power domains (full power, low power, battery power, PL power) [21] to turn off independently each rail at run-time. The three power controller are tied to the PMBus which is connected to a 4-channel I2C multiplexer (PCA9544A) [22]. A second power monitor circuit (INA226) by TI [23] enables to report separately the sensed parameters from the PMBus. INA226 is also connected to the same I2C multiplexer. The PMBus commands [10] are used to read the sensed data from the voltage regulators by Maxim Integrated. Only the characteristics of the PS full-power domain supply voltage ($V_{\text{CC\_PSINTFP}}$), the low-power domain supply voltage ($V_{\text{CC\_PSINTLP}}$) and the PL internal supply voltage (V_{CCINT}) are considered in this work. Besides, the board has a nominal voltage of 850 mV for the PS and PL.

3.2 Voltage Scaling on Xilinx Zynq-7000 and UltraScale+

Xilinx provides already a driver for the Xilinx Zynq-7000 SoC ZC702 to retrieve the voltage and current data [24]. This driver has been extended in [25] for Xilinx Zynq UltraScale+ MPSoC ZCU102. Once the system setup is correctly initialized and the sensed data are read, the voltage parameters can be adjusted at run-time. Algorithm 1 describes the voltage scaling with the PMBus commands on both platforms. The steps have to be followed as the board has off-the-shelf protection mechanisms [10]. The mechanism has protection limits to prevent that an overcurrent, overvoltage and undervoltage fault occur on the technology. Without a proper setup of the PMBus commands, the fault management is active and turns off immediately the board. Thus, the appropriate commands have to be adapted to the redefined setpoints while scaling the voltage as shown in Algorithm 1 (lines 4–12 and 15–23). Based on previous research works, we have limited the voltage scaling between 1 V and 550 mV to prevent a faulty operation on both Xilinx FPGAs. The proposed approach enables to adjust all voltage values from the regulators.

3.3 Frequency Scaling on Xilinx Zynq-7000 and UltraScale+

As discussed in the related work (Sect. 2), researchers have used a Linux kernel driver *cpufreq* for frequency scaling on the PS. Furthermore, the frequency

---

Data: Voltage scaling of the power rails:
$V_{CC\_PSINTFP}$, $V_{CC\_PSINTLP}$ and V_{CCINT}
Result: Scaling the voltage to the setpoint

1 nominal voltage = 0.85V;
2 **if** *setpoint $\leq$ 1.00V and setpoint $\geq$ 0.55V* **then**
3   **if** *setpoint$\leq$nominal voltage* **then**
4   Modify the following PMBus commands:
5   POWER_GOOD_OFF = 85% of the setpoint
6   POWER_GOOD_ON = 90% of the setpoint
7   VOUT_UV_FAULT_LIMIT = 85% of the setpoint
8   VOUT_MARGIN_LOW = 95% of the setpoint
9   DVS with VOUT_COMMAND to the setpoint
10   VOUT_MARGIN_HIGH = 105% of the setpoint
11   VOUT_MAX = 110% of the setpoint
12   VOUT_OV_FAULT_LIMIT = 115% of the setpoint
13   **end**
14   **if** *setpoint>nominal voltage* **then**
15   Modify the following PMBus commands:
16   VOUT_MARGIN_HIGH = 105% of the setpoint
17   VOUT_MAX = 110% of the setpoint
18   VOUT_OV_FAULT_LIMIT = 115% of the setpoint
19   DVS with VOUT_COMMAND to the setpoint
20   POWER_GOOD_OFF = 85% of the setpoint
21   POWER_GOOD_ON = 90% of the setpoint
22   VOUT_UV_FAULT_LIMIT = 85% of the setpoint
23   VOUT_MARGIN_LOW = 95% of the setpoint
24   **end**
25 **end**

Algorithm 1: DVS on Zynq-7000 SoCs and UltraScale+ MPSoCs

values are defined while setting up the kernel of the OS. Hence, DFS can only be applied in a certain frequency range. Therefore, we propose a methodology to scale flexible the frequency values from real-time or standalone applications. The Zynq-7000 platform has three main clock domains: ARM PLL, DDR PLL and IO PLL [26]. The processor clock is connected to the ARM PLL which is set to 1333.333 MHz in this research work. The clock frequency of the CPUs can be defined through appropriate divisors. To set the clock source of the CPUs, for instance, to 133.333 MHz, the divisor has to be declared as 10. The adjustment is easily done by changing register values. Algorithm 2 presents the registers which have to be modified on the Zynq-7000 System-on-Chips (SoCs). The same algorithm allows the adjustment of the frequency on the Zynq UltraScale+ family by means of adapting the appropriate registers based on [27] as shown in Algorithm 2. It is also possible to change the PL fabric clock at run-time. The proposed approach avoids the need for a Mixed-Mode Clock Manager (MMCM) primitive for frequency scaling on the PL.

Result: Frequency scaling from CPU

```
 1 if DFS on Zynq-7000 then
 2 │   Unlock the SLCR register with 0xDF0D;
 3 │   if DFS on CPU then
 4 │   │   Adapt the divisor on SLCR_ARM_CLK_CTR_ADDR;
 5 │   end
 6 │   if DFS on PL then
 7 │   │   Adapt the two divisors on FPGAx_CLK_CTRL;
 8 │   end
 9 │   Lock the SLCR register with 0x767B;
10 end
11 if DFS on Zynq UltraScale+ then
12 │   if DFS on ACPU then
13 │   │   Adapt the feedback divisor portion on ACPU_CTRL;
14 │   end
15 │   if DFS on CPU_R5 then
16 │   │   Adapt the 6-bit divider on CPU_R5_CTRL;
17 │   end
18 │   if DFS on PL then
19 │   │   Adapt the two 6-bit divider on PLx_REF_CTRL;
20 │   end
21 end
```

Algorithm 2: DFS on Zynq-7000 SoCs and UltraScale+ MPSoCs

3.4 Power-Aware Real-Time Architecture

A bare-metal system cannot execute simultaneously multiple applications. Considering the power monitoring, it would block the execution flow because of the latency through the communication protocol. The latency increases with the amount of retrieved data from the voltage regulator. Therefore, a scheduler is required that deals with different processes. For instance, FreeRTOS has a preemptive scheduler. The power monitoring requires 5 ms for reading of one value from the voltage regulator. While waiting for an event, the power monitoring task can be suspended for a defined period. At the same time, the scheduler can execute other tasks in the ready list. Based on [28], the scheduling policy of FreeRTOS can be extended to Rate-Monotonic Scheduling (RMS), Deadline-Monotonic Scheduling (DMS) and Earliest Deadline First (EDF). These algorithms allow performing tasks within a defined deadline period. It distributes efficiently the available workload on the processor which is eligible for low-power applications. In the case of a bare-metal application, Core 0 can execute the power monitoring whereby Core 1 runs the remaining application. An interrupt can synchronize both software routines. This leads to increased power consumption due to the multi-processing system. Depending on the design requirements, one of the aforementioned methodologies can be used. Nevertheless, the required data should only be read from the voltage regulators because of the communication latency.

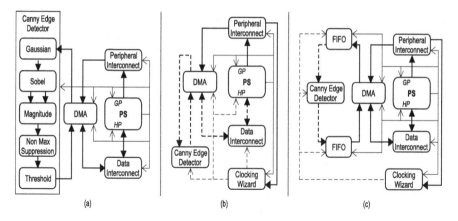

Fig. 1. The three different hardware designs of the system. In (a), the architecture shows the proposed frequency scaling approach. In (b), the clocking wizard changes the frequency of the application. In (c), FIFOs decouple the application frequency. Bus signals are thicker than clock signals. The second clock domain is represented by dashed lines. GP = General-Purpose port, HP = High-Performance port, PS = Processing System.

4   Description of the Use Case

4.1   Hardware Architecture

The Vivado 2018.2 toolchain has been used for the hardware implementation. The architecture is the same for both platforms: Zynq-7000 SoC ZC702 and UltraScale+ MPSoC ZCU102. Figure 1 shows the three different hardware architectures of this work. It illustrates buses and data signals with thicker lines and clock signals with thinner lines. The second clock domain is represented by dashed lines. The PS can control the DMA and clocking primitive using the Peripheral Interconnect via the General-Purpose (GP) port. The DMA reads/writes data from/to the external memory via the High-Performance (HP) port. Both GP and HP ports have their own clock. The AXI4-Stream Protocol is used to connect the Canny edge detector with the DMA or the FIFOs.

The first design (a) is the simplest one and is used to evaluate DVS and the proposed frequency scaling from the software side. Changing the frequency changes the frequency of the entire design. This design has the lowest resource utilization, which demonstrates the benefit of our proposed method of changing frequencies directly from the ARM processor. A standard way of changing the frequency is by adding a clocking wizard as shown in the other two designs. The disadvantage is that it increases the utilized resources of the design. In the second design (b), the clocking wizard can change the frequency of the application and the complete data buses to the memory. Separating the control and data buses from each other is advantageous since control and data buses do not need the same performance. With our proposed approach, we can also omit the clocking wizard and use the different clocks from the PS to scale the frequency of multiple clock domains from the ARM processor. The third design (c) shows that the application frequency can also be decoupled using FIFOs. For a single application, it increases the resources, but it does not affect the rest of the system. The main advantage comes to bear when different applications with different clock domains have to be connected to the same DMA. This can be the case if resources have to be saved or if not enough HP ports are available.

4.2 Application Description

The implemented application in this design is the Canny edge detector. The implementation is based on the HiFlipVX library. Additionally, we have implemented the last two functions using the OpenVX standard and the HiFlipVX approach, since they were missing. They will also be added to the open-source library. The algorithm is illustrated on the left of Fig. 1. First, a 3×3 Gaussian standard kernel smooths the input image. Then the 3×3 Sobel operator is used to compute the first-order derivatives in x and y-direction. Afterwards, the gradient magnitude is computed for each pixel. Pixels, which are not maximum in a 3×3 window are suppressed using the Non-Max Suppression function. The last function marks a pixel as edge if its value meets the hysteresis threshold.

All functions are implemented using Vivado HLS. The data type of the input and output pixels are 8-bit. The functions are fully pipelined and get one input pixel per clock cycle. Each function passes its results to the next function using one element FIFOs. Therefore, all functions run in parallel. The performance of all functions can be increased using vectorization, where data pixels are processed in a SIMD manner. The vector sizes can be one, two, four or eight. Vectorization can also be used to reduce the total energy consumption, as shown in the evaluation. The application uses the AXI4-Stream protocol to receive and send data.

4.3 Software Architecture

Besides the presented application running on an ARM processor, we have implemented the DVFS routine with the monitoring of a co-processor. Accordingly to an interrupt signal, the co-processor runs the power control and monitoring unit while the application runs in parallel. In the beginning, the application executes its dedicated tasks in the nominal operation mode. For instance, the Canny edge detector starts its execution to generate correct reference values for comparison. This comparison allows validating the correctness of the resulting values while adjusting the power dissipation. The Zynq-7000/UltraScale+ can lose its configuration on the PL when the V_{CCINT} is scaled below $750\,mV/680\,mV$ (V_{DRINT}) [19,29]. Therefore, it is important to have reference values to detect a faulty operation. The power-aware architecture enables directly to capture and adjust the faulty operation with a correct voltage or frequency scaling from the co-processor. Once the power-saving capabilities of the whole system are identified, the application has to be integrated with the DVFS routine in the RTOS.

Based on the proposed scheduling policy, the scheduler will handle these multiple routines within a certain time.

5 Evaluation

As presented in Sect. 4, we have performed DVFS on the Canny edge detector based on two different case studies. The first case study demonstrates the effects of the vectorization while scaling the voltage on the PL. The second case study compares the different hardware designs shown in Fig. 1 while scaling the frequency and voltage on the PL. The required hardware resources for both case studies are summarized in Table 1 for the two FPGA technologies. The proposed methodology with the frequency scaling architecture requires up to approximately 20% less flip-flops and look-up tables. The first case study reduces energy consumption through voltage scaling as shown in Fig. 2. The parallelization enables to enhance the performance and reduce energy consumption. At the same time, the increasing vectorization leads to a higher resource utilization whereby the power consumption increases slightly. The measurements are performed on both hardware platforms. The Zynq-7000 returns incorrect values while the voltage is 700 mV or less. Because it is scaled below the V_{DRINT} and lost its configuration. However, a vectorization of 8 gives also incorrect values for 750 mV. Although the Zynq UltraScale+ is scaled below the V_{DRINT}, it loses

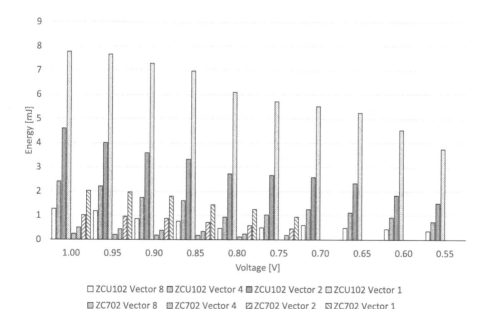

Fig. 2. The experimental results of DVS on an accelerated Canny edge detector with different vectorizations running in the PL of Xilinx Zynq-7000 SoC ZC702 and Ultra-Scale+ MPSoC ZCU102

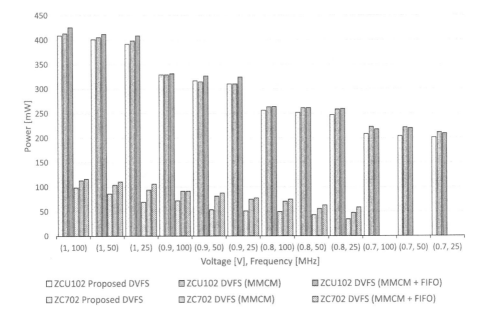

Fig. 3. The experimental results of DVFS regarding the power consumption on an accelerated Canny edge detector with different hardware characteristics running in the PL of Xilinx Zynq-7000 SoC ZC702 and UltraScale+ MPSoC ZCU102

its configuration below 550 mV. The experiments have shown a correct operation between the voltage range of 1 V to 550 mV. The V_{DRINT} can be taken as a reference value but the results of the running application should be continuously validated through the routine in the co-processor. The software architecture is able to detect faulty behavior as described in Sect. 4.3. The execution time of the application needs 21 ms for 1080p images and a frequency of 100 MHz for no vectorization. It scales the execution time to 2.6 ms with vectorization 8 (Table 1). Besides the efficiency in the parallelization of an application, the frequency scaling has also an impact on the overall power consumption as shown in Fig. 3. The application is executed for different frequencies (100 MHz, 50 MHz and 25 MHz) on various voltage levels. This experiment is performed on the highest vectorization level of the application with respect to the increasing resource utilization. In the power-saving, the voltage scaling has a dominant behavior because of its quadratic influence in the dynamic power and linear factor in the static power (shown in Eq. (1)). The frequency scaling affects directly the dynamic power. Therefore, the overall power consumption has been reduced up to 50% with the DVFS technique on both Zynq platforms.

An increasing frequency leads to a higher performance whereby the required energy consumption is reduced as shown in Fig. 4. The execution time is measured as 2.62 ms, 5.24 ms and 10.49 ms for a frequency of 100 MHz, 50 MHz and 25 MHz respectively. A further enhancement is achieved through the voltage scaling from 1 V to 700 mV in the experiments.

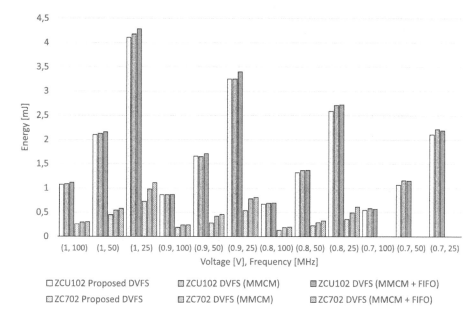

Fig. 4. The experimental results of DVFS regarding the energy consumption on an accelerated Canny edge detector with different hardware characteristics running in the PL of Xilinx Zynq-7000 SoC ZC702 and UltraScale+ MPSoC ZCU102

Besides the advantages of both techniques, our proposed methodology of the frequency scaling enables to achieve similar or better results than the convenient frequency scaling with the reconfigurable clocking source. Furthermore, it requires up to 20% less flip-flops and look-up tables as compared to the same design with clocking wizard on the programmable logic. Additional, our methodology has the advantage that it can be applied to any Zynq platforms as proven with the set of experiments.

The toolchain can generate a bitstream with an operating frequency of 333 MHz for the PL on the UltraScale+ platform. As compared to the Zynq-7000 platform with a frequency of 150 MHz, the UltraScale+ board allows enhancing more the performance of the system. This would result in a higher energy-efficiency with scaling the voltage on the PL. However, the increasing frequency results in higher resource utilization. The ZCU102 (ZC702) board consumes 25.3 (25.4)% more flip-flops and 3.4 (7.8)% more look-up tables for our proposed design using a vectorization of 8. We have chosen 100 MHz as a reference frequency, to have a comparable frequency for all designs and configurations.

Table 1. Resource consumption and latency in clock cycles of the implemented hardware of the Canny Edge Detector (CED) for different vector sizes and for the complete hardware designs of the ZCU102 and ZC702.

Design	FF	LUT	BRAM	DSP	Latency
Available (zc702)	106400	53200	140	220	
zc702 CED (Vector 1)	922	737	3	1	2076607
zc702 CED (Vector 2)	1329	1010	3	2	1038847
zc702 CED (Vector 4)	2062	1562	3	4	519967
zc702 CED (Vector 8)	3649	2739	6	8	260527
zc702 (Proposed DVFS)	9248	6767	15	8	
zc702 (MMCM)	11613	8361	18	8	
zc702 (MMCM + FIFO)	11695	8461	17.50	8	
Available (zcu102)	548160	274080	912	2520	
zcu102 CED (Vector 1)	754	717	3	1	2076606
zcu102 CED (Vector 2)	1021	1016	3	2	1038846
zcu102 CED (Vector 4)	1587	1471	3	4	519966
zcu102 CED (Vector 8)	2484	2717	6	8	260526
zcu102 (Proposed DVFS)	10430	8805	15	8	
zcu102 (MMCM)	12607	10348	18	8	
zcu102 (MMCM + FIFO)	12689	10432	17.50	8	

6   Conclusion

In this work, we have shown the possibility to scale the frequency at run-time without using additional hardware resources on the PL from the PS. The proposed architecture requires up to 20% less flip-flops and look-up tables. It can easily be used for changing the processor frequency according to the existing workload. Furthermore, the proposed frequency scaling can be deployed on each Xilinx SoC. As a case study, we apply our technique to find energy-optimal voltage and frequency pairs for an image processing application designed using the open-source high-level synthesis library HiFlipVX. The DVFS routine has been performed on a co-processor. The approach enables to identify faulty operation during the voltage and frequency scaling. Once the voltage and frequency pairs are known, an RTOS manages the application with the power monitoring and controlling unit. In doing so, we have proposed different types of scheduling policies to handle various tasks. The energy consumption has been reduced to 46% (41%) with the voltage scaling from 1 V to 700 mV on the ZCU102 (ZC702) board. The work presented here can be extended to the frequency scaling in the PS. Because it allows reducing the power consumption of the ARM processors. Furthermore, Xilinx Ultrascale+ FPGAs allow to turn off parts of the PS in order to reduce the power consumption which can also be investigated in the future.

Acknowledgment. The work described in this paper has been supported in part by the German Federal Ministry of Education and Research BMBF (grant nr. 16KIS0663 SysKit_HW) and funded by the German Research Foundation (DFG, Deutsche Forschungsgemeinschaft) as part of Germany's Excellence Strategy – EXC 2050/1 – Project ID 390696704 – Cluster of Excellence "Centre for Tactile Internet with Human-in-the-Loop" (CeTI) of Technische Universität Dresden.

References

1. Nunez-Yanez, J., Beldachi, A.: Run-time power and performance scaling with CPU-FPGA hybrids. In: 2014 NASA/ESA Conference on Adaptive Hardware and Systems (AHS), pp. 55–60, July 2014
2. Kuon, I., Rose, J.: Measuring the gap between FPGAs and ASICs. IEEE Trans. Comput. Aided Des. Integr. Circuits Syst. **26**(2), 203–215 (2007)
3. Canny, A.: Computational approach to edge detection. IEEE Trans. Pattern Anal. Mach. Intell. **8**(6), 679–698 (1986)
4. Cho, H., Sung, M., Jun, B.: Canny text detector: fast and robust scene text localization algorithm. In: 2016 IEEE Conference on Computer Vision and Pattern Recognition (CVPR), pp. 3566–3573, June 2016
5. Kalms, L., Podlubne, A., Göhringer, D.: HiFlipVX: an open source high-level synthesis FPGA library for image processing. In: Hochberger, C., Nelson, B., Koch, A., Woods, R., Diniz, P. (eds.) ARC 2019. LNCS, vol. 11444, pp. 149–164. Springer, Cham (2019). https://doi.org/10.1007/978-3-030-17227-5_12
6. Nunez-Yanez, J.: Energy proportional neural network inference with adaptive voltage and frequency scaling. IEEE Trans. Comput. **68**(5), 1 (2018)
7. Beldachi, A.F., Nunez-Yanez, J.L.: Accurate power control and monitoring in ZYNQ boards. In: 2014 24th International Conference on Field Programmable Logic and Applications (FPL), pp. 1–4, September 2014
8. Podlubne, A., et al.: Low power image processing applications on FPGAs using dynamic voltage scaling and partial reconfiguration. In: 2018 Conference on Design and Architectures for Signal and Image Processing (DASIP), pp. 64–69, October 2018
9. Xilinx: ZC702 Board User Guide. UG850, pp. 1–78 (2019)
10. Maxim Integrated: InTune Automatically Compensated Digital PoL Controller with Driver and PMBus Telemetry. MAX15301, pp. 1–30 (2013)
11. Railis, K., Tsoutsouras, V., Xydis, S., Soudris, D.: Energy profile analysis of Zynq-7000 programmable SoC for embedded medical processing: study on ECG arrhythmia detection. In: 2016 26th International Workshop on Power and Timing Modeling, Optimization and Simulation (PATMOS), pp. 275–282, September 2016
12. Hosseinabady, M., Nunez-Yanez, J.L.: Run-time power gating in hybrid ARM-FPGA devices. In: 2014 24th International Conference on Field Programmable Logic and Applications (FPL), pp. 1–6, September 2014
13. Li, S., Broekaert, F.: Low-power scheduling with DVFS for common RTOS on multicore platforms. SIGBED Rev. **11**(1), 32–37 (2014)
14. Poggi, T., et al.: A hypervisor architecture for low-power real-time embedded systems. In: 2018 21st Euromicro Conference on Digital System Design (DSD), pp. 252–259, August 2018
15. Lee, J., Tang, H., Park, J.: Energy efficient canny edge detector for advanced mobile vision applications. IEEE Trans. Circuits Syst. Video Technol. **28**(4), 1037–1046 (2018)

16. Maheshwari, B.C., Burns, J., Blott, M., Gambardella, G.: Implementation of a scalable real time canny edge detector on programmable SOC. In: 2017 International Conference on Electrical and Computing Technologies and Applications (ICECTA), pp. 1–5, November 2017
17. Najam, Z., Qadri, M.Y., Najam, S.: Real-time implementation of DVFS enhanced LEON3 MPSoC on FPGA. In: 2016 6th International Conference on Intelligent and Advanced Systems (ICIAS), pp. 1–6, August 2016
18. Texas Instruments: UCD92xx Digital PWM System Controller PMBus Command Reference. SLUU337, pp. 1–50 (2018)
19. Xilinx: Zynq-7000 SoC: DC and AC Switching Characteristics. DS187, pp. 1–72 (2018)
20. Xilinx: ZCU102 Evaluation Board User Guide. UG1182, pp. 1–122 (2019)
21. Xilinx: Zynq UltraScale+ MPSoC Software Developer Guide. UG1137, pp. 1–611 (2018)
22. Texas Instruments: Low Voltage 4-Channel I2C and SMBus Multiplexer With Interrupt Logic. PCA9544A, pp. 1–34 (2014)
23. Texas Instruments: INA226 High-Side or Low-Side Measurement, Bi-Directional Current and Power Monitor with I2C Compatible Interface. INA226, pp. 1–39 (2015)
24. Zynq-7000 AP SoC Low Power Techniques Part 3 - Measuring ZC702 Power with a Standalone Application Tech Tip. https://xilinx-wiki.atlassian.net. Accessed 09 March 2020
25. Ali, M., Amini Rad, P., Göhringer, D.: RISC-V based MPSoC design exploration for FPGAs: area, power and performance. In: Rincn, F. et al. (eds.) ARC 2020. LNCS, vol. 12083, pp. 193–207. Springer, Cham (2020)
26. Xilinx: Zynq-7000 SoC Technical Reference Manual. UG585, pp. 1–1843 (2018)
27. Xilinx: Zynq Migration Guide. UG1213, pp. 1–156 (2016)
28. Kase, R.: Efficient scheduling library for FreeRTOS. In: KTH, School of Information and Communication Technology (ICT), pp. 1–55 (2016)
29. Xilinx: Zynq UltraScale+ MPSoC Data Sheet: DC and AC Switching Characteristics. DS925, pp. 1–108 (2019)

RISC-V Based MPSoC Design Exploration for FPGAs: Area, Power and Performance

Muhammad Ali$^{(\boxtimes)}$, Pedram Amini Rad, and Diana Göhringer

Technische Universität Dresden, Dresden, Germany
{muhammad.ali,pedram.amini_rad,diana.goehringer}@tu-dresden.de

Abstract. Modern image processing applications, like object detection or image segmentation, require high computation and have high memory requirements. For ASIC-/FPGA-based architectures, hardware accelerators are a promising solution, but they lack flexibility and programmability. To fulfill flexibility, computational and memory intensive characteristics of these applications in embedded systems, we propose a modular and flexible RISC-V based MPSoC architecture on Xilinx Zynq Ultrascale+ MPSoC. The proposed architecture can be ported to other Xilinx FPGAs. Two neural networks (Lenet-5 and Cifar-10 example) were used as test applications to evaluate the proposed MPSoC architectures. To increase the performance and efficiency, different optimization techniques were adapted on the MPSoC and results were evaluated. 16-bit fixed-point parameters were used to have a compression of 50% in data size and algorithms were parallelized and mapped on the proposed MPSoC to achieve higher performance. A 4x parallelization of a NN algorithm on the proposed MPSoC resulted in 3.96x speed up and consumed 3.61x less energy as compared to a single soft-core processor setup.

Keywords: MPSoC · NoC · RISC-V · FPGA · SoC · Power estimation

1 Introduction

Multiprocessor System-on-Chip (MPSoC) is a System-on-Chip (SoC) that contains multiple-processors. MPSoCs are becoming a standard to be used in embedded systems to overcome high performance and low power constraints [1]. MPSoCs are composed of processing elements (PEs), memory systems, bus management, and network interconnection. Based on the PEs, MPSoCs can be categorized either as homogeneous or heterogeneous. PEs in MPSoCs can be, e.g. general-purpose processors, application-specific processors (ASIPs) or hardware accelerators. Another way to classify MPSoCs is based on the memory system used. It can be shared or distributed. In a shared memory system, the PEs of the MPSoC share a common memory region among each other and a scheduling technique is needed to avoid conflicts while accessing the memory. In a distributed memory system, the PEs of the MPSoC are connected over a network and have dedicated memories. The PEs communicate over the network to exchange data based on the application requirements.

© Springer Nature Switzerland AG 2020
F. Rincón et al. (Eds.): ARC 2020, LNCS 12083, pp. 193–207, 2020.
https://doi.org/10.1007/978-3-030-44534-8_15

Many object detection and image processing applications have huge memory and computational costs. These key constraints can be overcome, if the hardware architecture is flexible and can be adapted to different application needs making the architecture robust. In recent years, the performance of artificial intelligence applications from video and image classification to natural language processing has been dramatically improved due to advances in the field of deep learning. Among deep learning algorithms, convolutional neural networks (CNNs) are widely used because they show remarkable performance in solving complex machine learning problems. With more advancements and research in this domain, CNNs are becoming more computational and memory intensive. Though it improves the accuracy of the CNN architectures, it also makes it very challenging to develop FPGA/ASIC based designs for embedded system applications. For CNNs, GPUs outperform any other platform due to the high level of parallelism and higher operational frequency [2]. They also consume more power as compared to FPGAs [2]. This makes GPUs not a feasible platform for low power designs. On the other hand, FPGAs consume very less power as compared with GPUs but optimizations and parallelization for CNN design needs to be implemented. For inference of CNNs on FPGAs, hardware accelerators are the most efficient solution as they are low power and achieves a high performance [3]. However, hardware accelerator's lack of programmability and data movement in between CNN layers is a bottleneck [3]. CNNs consist of pipelined layers which are: convolutional (conv), pooling, activation and fully connected (FC) layers. The main bottleneck of CNN layers is convolutional layers and FC layers. Convolutional layers are involved in more than 90% of the computation in CNN [4]. While fully connected layers have most parameters [5].

For fast prototyping and adaptions to different applications and their requirements, field-programmable gate array (FPGA) platforms make the best use. FPGA platforms not only allow the designer to prototype faster but also provides high programmability and low risks [6]. Modern FPGA platforms also provide a lot of pre- and post- design estimations for the area, power and performance of hardware designs. Power and energy estimations are very important for FPGA users since, e.g. battery life, packaging and cooling costs highly depend on it.

To overcome these computational and memory intensive constraints, and have more flexibility and programmability in the system, we propose a flexible MPSoC for Xilinx FPGA platforms. The proposed MPSoC is based on homogeneous softcore processing elements but it can be extended to a heterogeneous platform. The FPGA platform allows adapting our MPSoC architectures depending on the application and optimization requirements. Our proposed architecture is a distributed system, with PEs having dedicated memory and communication as well as data transfer is over a network-on-chip (NoC). The proposed MPSoC is extendable and more PEs can be added depending on the computational requirements. Two CNN applications were used as a test case since CNNs have high memory requirements and are computationally intensive. For best results, parameter and variable optimizations were used and MPSoC parallelization was exploited. For accurate power monitoring of the MPSoC architectures, a power monitoring library, available at [7], is developed for Xilinx Zynq Ultrascale+ MPSoC ZCU102. This allows to monitor power in runtime and to compute precise energy estimation for our proposed MPSoC architectures.

The rest of this paper is organized as follows: Sect. 2 provides related work. Section 3 presents the design concept and implementation. Section 4 shows our experimental results. Section 5 provides a conclusion based on the evaluation.

2   Related Work

There are many different platforms available for the execution of object detection algorithms like CNNs, e.g. GPUs, ASICs, CPUs, and FPGA implementations. All of them have different tradeoffs based on area, power, and performance [8]. FPGAs provide fast prototyping and operate on lower frequencies as compared with GPUs and CPUs [2]. This makes FPGA design low power [9] and feasible for embedded system applications.

NoC based architectures for neural network (NN) applications are gaining attention. Usually, the processing element (PE) is some kind of accelerator with an interface controller for communication with other PEs. In [10], a simulation-based reconfigurable NN architecture using a NoC is presented. For PEs of the NoC, a "neuron unit" is developed, which can be adapted based on the application. They also allow multiple logic units to be implemented at one PE and perform dynamic reconfiguration on the proposed architecture based on application demands. A theoretical analysis of determining an optimum interconnect architecture of a NoC for NN is presented in [11]. Different NoC interconnect architectures are evaluated based on performance and cost for NN application. Bui et al. in [12] proposed a NoC based implementation for NN on FPGAs. Their work is based on MNIST data set for training and testing. The PEs of the proposed work consists of parallel neurons which are connected to the router. A PE controller is also developed to control the data flow from the PE. In [13], a survey on CNNs with reconfigurable architectures on edge computing is presented. This work discusses different CNNs, optimizations to overcome CNN constraints as well as different types of architecture topologies.

In our work, we propose a RISC-V based MPSoC for NN. A lot of work is already done in developing MPSoCs using RISC-V [14]. RISC-V is an open-source instruction set architecture (ISA), which allows industry and researchers to develop processors based on their application requirements. The work of [15] proposes a modular memory system for RISC-V based MPSoC with a shared memory system between the cores. "RI5CY" [16] cores are used in this bus-based MPSoC. The proposed MPSoC is extendable, which means more cores can be added on the shared bus. In [17], a framework is presented which allows developing a RISC-V based NoC. This work is more focused on the NoC and its network interface (NI). This work is further extended in [18], where a framework is presented for developing a hardware emulation for large NoC architectures with RISC-V as PE. In a recent work [19], an ultra-low power tightly coupled cluster of RISC-V processors is presented named as "PULP-NN". This work makes a comparison between the number of cores added to the system and their performance. This work also suggests that adding SIMD (single instruction multiple data) extensions and bit manipulation extensions will heavily increase the performance as compared to a RISC-V (RV32IMC) implementation.

For accurate power estimation, a lot of work has been done for Xilinx Zynq FPGAs. In [20], the technology of Xilinx Zynq devices is presented and how it can be used to control and monitor power at run-time. The work shows that both hardware and software techniques can be used to control power. It also presents the impact of power control techniques and selection, on monitoring speeds, accuracy, power consumption and area overhead. In [21], an adaptive dynamic voltage and frequency scaling framework is presented which exploits a deep learning application on Xilinx Ultrascale+ MPSoC ZCU102. This work uses *maxpowertool* provided by Maxim Integrated [22]. Our work extends this concept by providing a software solution to measure and control the power of the Xilinx ZCU102 board. With our proposed MPSoC, we overcome CNN's computational and memory intensive constraints by having a flexible system and we provide a run-time power and energy estimation library.

3 Concept and Implementation

In this work, an MPSoC architecture with a distributed memory system was developed. The MPSoC architecture also allows adding tightly coupled hardware accelerators with the PEs or loosely coupled accelerators as a PE themselves. The implementation of the proposed work is divided into four subsections; first, a brief overview of the test applications and their constraints are presented, then the RISC-V architecture used as a PE is described, followed by the NoC architecture used to develop the MPSoC and finally, an overview of the overall MPSoC architecture is described along with the HW/SW co-design of the system.

3.1 Test Applications

In the scope of this paper, we take advantage of two CNN applications: Lenet-5 [23] and an example case for Cifar-10 [24], to evaluate our proposed platform. Lenet-5 uses a lightweight architecture to train and predict the MNIST data set. MNIST is used for digit recognition and is comprised of 10,000 samples of size 28×28 images. Lenet-5 consists of 7 layers, including 2 convolutional layers (conv), 2 max-pooling layers (max), and 3 fully connected layers (FC). The size of each conv layer filter is 5×5. The Cifar-10 example used, carries out a lightweight object detection process on the Cifar-10 dataset. The Cifar-10 dataset consists of 60,000 color images of size 32×32. There are 10 classes of images, with 6,000 images per class. The architecture of Cifar-10 consisted of 8 layers, which are 4 conv layers, 2 max layers, and 2 FC layers. The size of each convolution filter is 3×3 and a zero-padding method is also deployed. Memory requirements are calculated for each layer and FC layers were most memory intensive. For Lenet-5 and Cifar-10, memory required for FC layers (16-bit fixed-point parameters) is 85.45 KB and 2379.29 KB, respectively. The Cifar-10 example was used to provide a proof of concept that the proposed MPSoC architectures are flexible to be adapted for different algorithms.

3.2 RISC-V as Processing Element (PE)

The PE of an MPSoC is one key component that determines the performance of the system along with the memory system and communication infrastructure. The overall architecture of the proposed PE is shown in Fig. 1. A RISC-V based "RI5CY" [16] soft-core is used as the main core of the PE with two tightly coupled memories (TCM), one for instructions (I-TCM) and other for data (D-TCM). An AXI-crossbar is used to connect the RI5CY core and other peripherals. An external memory is designed using Xilinx dual-ported BRAM with the AXI interface and is connected to the RI5CY core. This is called the BOOT memory and it is a read-only memory. An additional shared memory can also be added, if more cores are needed. AXI-crossbar is used to develop a bus-topology system and it allows to add more peripherals to the architecture. Some key peripherals used are Platform-Level Interrupt Controller (PLIC), AXI-stream FIFOs and a tightly coupled accelerator. PLIC is added to connect the global interrupts of the system. A priority threshold is developed in it, which defines the priority of different tasks from different peripherals. AXI-stream FIFOs are used as a network interface (NI) between the PE and the router of the NoC. AXI-stream FIFOs are memory-mapped peripherals to the system. RI5CY core is a master of this bus-based system.

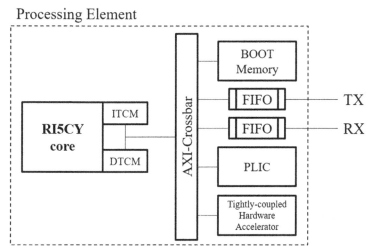

Fig. 1. Architecture of proposed PE with RI5CY core and peripherals. ((Platform-Level Interrupt Controller (PLIC), Instruction Tightly Coupled Memory (ITCM), Data Tightly Coupled Memory (DTCM), AXI-stream FIFO (FIFO))

In the proposed PE structure, RI5CY core has two tightly coupled memories; ITCM and DTCM as well as one BOOT memory on AXI-crossbar. All three implemented memories of the PE can be adapted depending on the application requirements. BOOT memory is used to program the RI5CY core of the processing system. To program the PEs, a cross compiler is used. A bare-metal application method is used for programming the PEs. Using the RI5CY GNU toolchain [25], a co-efficient file (binary file) is generated from source file (.C), linker script, startup file (.S) and some additional header files. The linker script defines the memory regions of the PE and needs to be adapted if any memory adjustments are made based on the application requirements. After generating the binary file, it is added to the BOOT memory (Xilinx BRAM blocks). On the startup, the binary file is loaded to the ITCM and DTCM of the RI5CY core depending on the initialization program and the application of the PE starts to execute.

3.3 Network-on-Chip (NoC)

In-order to develop the MPSoC, a router architecture similar to [26] was used. A two-dimensional (2D)-mesh topology is used for routers to form a NoC. Routers are address-able by 3-bit X- and Y-coordinates. This permits to have a maximum of an 8×8 mesh size of the NoC and is extendable by increasing the address bits. X- and Y-coordinates are embedded in the header flit of the data package which allows the NoC to transmit data to the destination router. The router has four inputs and outputs (I/O) labeled as directions (North, South, East, and West) and a local I/O which is used to add a PE to the NoC. Different routing algorithms can be implemented in the routers. For this work, the XY-routing algorithm is used, since it is deterministic and the shortest path is calculated using only the destination addresses. All I/Os of the router have an AXI-stream interface. The local I/O port of the NoC is connected to the FIFOs (TX/RX) of the PE. The stream-ing interface of the router also allows adding loosely coupled hardware accelerators with the streaming interface.

3.4 Hardware/Software Co-design

A hardware/software co-design methodology is realized to develop the MPSoC for a specific NN. To explain the process of MPSoC design, an abstract model as shown in Fig. 2 is used. Different partitions show different MPSoC architectures for different NNs and different parallelization levels used in each system. Figure 2 presents a 5×2 NoC which has 8 RISC-V PEs, ARM Cortex-A53 with a DMA controller (ARM+DMA) and a loosely coupled hardware accelerator.

Hardware design is implemented using the Xilinx Vivado 2017.4 tool. ARM+DMA is used on each MPSoC design. This is used to send input images to the MPSoC and to send parameters to the PEs allowing to update parameters of the NN at runtime if needed. ARM is also used to run the power monitoring library in parallel and estimate energy consumption. This is described later in detail. In Fig. 2, for Lenet-5 (2x-parallelization), a 2×2 NoC is implemented with 2 PEs and ARM+DMA. For Lenet-5 (4x-parallelization), a 3×2 topology is used with 4 PEs and ARM+DMA. For Cifar-10 (2x parallelization), a 5×2 NoC is implemented using 10 routers, 8 PEs, and ARM+DMA. For the Lenet-5 proposed MPSoCs, the complete inference was executed on PEs and ARM+DMA was not used for processing. But for Cifar-10, FC1 and FC2 were executed on the ARM for additional computational power. Once a specific architecture is implemented, the PEs are programmed depending on how the application is mapped on the MPSoC.

For programming the MPSoC, each PE is programmed based on the application mapped for it. This depends on the parallelization and parameters used. The linker script is adjusted depending on the memory sizes used for the PEs and the co-efficient file is generated using the RISC-V GNU toolchain.

3.5 Software Optimizations

Before programming the PEs, some software optimizations and verifications are per-formed to achieve better performance. First, the NN applications were quantized and the parameters were converted to the fixed-point. This helps to reduce parameter size and to reduce the memory requirements. Secondly, the benchmarks were parallelized since there can be multiple PEs. This resulted in a better performance, which is demonstrated later.

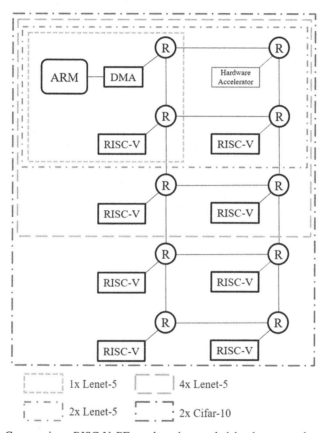

Fig. 2. MPSoCs overview: RISC-V PEs, a loosely coupled hardware accelerator and ARM Cortex-A53 with Direct Memory Access Controller (DMA). The dotted area presents the MPSoC model opted for a NN and parallelization used in the architecture.

Parameter Optimization

Fixed point optimized parameters are used for the proposed MPSoC. For fixed-point conversion, we take advantage of two-stage quantization. First, dynamic fixed-point parameters are generated using the Ristretto tool on Caffe [27]. The generated parameters of each layer are represented by $X_{i,n}$ in (1), where "i", and "n" are layer number and number of fraction bits, respectively. 16-bit fixed-point parameters are then generated and converted to $X'_{i,n}$ through (1).

$$X'_{i,n} = X_{i,n} \times 10^n \tag{1}$$

$$Y'_{i,n} = Round\left(Y_{i,n}/10^n\right) \tag{2}$$

After the convolution and FC layers are carried out, outputs of their layer, as represented by Y_n, are divided by the factor 10^n and then rounded in (2), to avoid overflow in the next layers. Finding the suitable quantized model is performed through a heuristic procedure in which some combination of fraction bit number "n" for each layer is selected and then accuracy is tested to achieve the highest accuracy. For Lenet-5, we chose $n = 3$ for each layer. In Cifar-10, $n = 4$ and $n = 3$ are selected for FC and conv layers, respectively.

The accuracy was verified by implementing a C++ code for the inference of both NN. The accuracy analysis of the network is shown in Table 1. The table shows the accuracy of the CNNs based on the different data types for parameters from the Ristretto tool [27]. 16-bit fixed-point parameters were generated using the Caffe tool and its accuracy was computed and compared with the findings from the Ristretto tool [27] (in Table 1). It was 97.3% for Lenet-5 and 72.12% for Cifar-10. For Cifar-10 some layers had n = 4 which resulted in the loss of information when optimizing thus resulted in a decrease in the accuracy. These models were then translated to be compatible with the proposed MPSoC. With quantized parameters at 16-bit, 50% compression is achieved in parameter memory usage. This also prevents the use of a floating-point unit (FPU) on the RI5CY core used in the PEs and saves more resources on the FPGA.

Table 1. Accuracy analysis of quantized CNN models

CNN	Floating point (32-bit) [27]	Dynamic fixed point [27]	Fixed-point implementation (16-bit)
Lenet-5	99.15%	98.81%	97.3%
Cifar-10	81.69%	81.44%	72.12%

Also, the output variables were optimized to maintain a 16-bit fixed-point data type to minimize memory requirements. For this, an intermediate output variable (Z) of 32-bit, with a smaller length is used for intermediate operations and rounded off and stored in a 16-bit output variable before exiting the final loop. This increased computation but resulted in up to 46.8% compression in memory usage for output variables.

Application Parallelization Method

Both CNN's used for evaluation were parallelized and mapped on respective MPSoC architectures. Parallelization and mapping of a NN was based on data independent operations and the size of parameters of each layer. For convolution layers, the parallelization is based on the number of output feature maps (OFM) and for fully connected layers it is based on the filter size. For parallelization, after each layer, the outputs are needed to be transmitted to the next layer PEs. For data transmission over the NoC, a message passing interface (MPI) library was implemented for uniform programming. For each parallelization of the NN, first, a functional verification was done in Eclipse IDE before mapping the parallelized NN on the proposed MPSoC. Since Lenet-5 is a small CNN as compared to Cifar-10, after parallelization, all layers fit in one PE. That is, if Lenet-5 is parallelized by 2x or 4x, it is possible to be mapped to 2 PEs or 4 PEs, respectively. For the 2x parallelization of Lenet-5, the BOOT memory and DTCM sizes of both PEs is increased to 128 KB since the parameters of FC 1 are too big to fit in a normal 64 KB space. A single core design is also developed for Lenet-5 with no parallelization. For Cifar-10, conv1 is mapped on 2 PEs, conv2 and max1 are mapped on other 2 PEs, conv3 on separate 2 PEs and, conv4 and max2 on additional 2 PEs (total 8 PEs). FC1 and FC2 were mapped on the ARM processor. PEs used for conv2/max1 and conv4/max2 have memory size of 128 KB, while all other PEs have regular 64 KB size of memories. Since in Cifar-10, layers were implemented to independent PEs, this allows forming a pipeline in executing an inference for multiple images.

Message Passage Interface

A message passage interface (MPI) [28] library was implemented for data transmission over the NoC. Different functions were implemented based on the open MPI standard and added to the source files. The functions implemented for the MPSoC are: platform initialization, send, receive and synchronization. Platform initialization is used to initialize the NI. Send and receive MPI functions are memory-mapped operations to the FIFOs for sending and receiving data over the NoC. Since the header packet (first data packet) has 6-bits which describe the destination (3-bits for X- and 3-bits for Y- coordinates), packeting and de-packeting of the header packet with data flits is implemented in send and receive MPI functions. In case the transmission data is bigger than the FIFO depth, the data is transmitted in the form of chunks. A synchronization function is used to synchronize the PEs before data transmission.

A data transfer schedule was developed for data transmission after the execution of each layer in the application. This was developed to avoid any deadlocks in the NoC and to ensure the correct transfer of data among PEs. For this, a round-robin schedule is implemented between respective PEs. Synchronization MPI was used to ensure whether the PEs are ready for receiving a new transmission to avoid deadlocks in NoC.

3.6 Power Estimation in Xilinx Zynq Ultrascale+ MPSoC ZCU102 (XCZU9EG)

Xilinx Zynq Ultrascale+ MPSoC ZCU102 consists of a quad-core ARM Cortex-A53 processor and a dual-core ARM Cortex-R5 real-time processing unit. It is equipped with three different voltage regulators (MAX20751EKX, MAX15301, MAX15303) by

Maxim Integrated [29]. The controllers have in total 25 power rails to supply the evaluation board. Furthermore, the device has multiple power domains (full power, low power, battery power, PL power) [30] to turn off each rail at run-time. The power controllers are tied to the PMBus which is connected to a 4-channel I2C multiplexer (PCA9544A) [31]. A second power monitor circuit (INA226) by TI [32] allows monitoring parameters from the PMBus. INA226 is also connected to the I2C multiplexer. In this research work, a C++ library is implemented to access data directly from the on board voltage regulators. This allows to monitor the power consumption of the FPGA at run-time. The sensor data is retrieved using PMBus commands in [33]. The data received is used to estimate the power and energy needed for an application execution.

Table 2. Resource utilization of PE, router, proposed MPSoCs and MicroBlaze used for the application.

	LUT	FF	BRAM	DSP
RI5CY core with I/DTCM	7322	1451	32	6
AXI-Crossbar	216	66	0	0
BOOT Memory	46	8	14.5	0
PLIC	48	2	0	0
AXI-FIFO TX/RX	518	289	2	0
Router	319	41	0	0
Lenet-5(1x)	12381	4161	81	6
Lenet-5 (2x)	20678	5971	160	12
Lenet-5 (4x)	38984	10149	226.5	24
Cifar-10 (2x)	74090	17959	512	48
MB (Area opt)	5505	5921	68	0
MB (area opt + multiplier)	5999	6196	68	3
MB (performance opt)	6536	6639	69	3

4   Evaluation

4.1   Resource Utilization

The proposed MPSoC architectures have been implemented on Xilinx Zynq Ultrascale+ MPSoC ZCU102 FPGA. Resource utilization is calculated using Xilinx Vivado 2017.4. For a system with all three memories: I-TCM, D-TCM and BOOT memory of the size 64 KB, resource utilization is presented in Table 2. Also, resource utilization of a single router used and the proposed MPSoCs for NNs are mentioned in the table. From Table 2, we can see that Lenet-5 2x-MPSoC utilizes an average of 1.76x more resources than 1x-MPSoC. Lenet-5 4x-MPSoC on average utilizes 3.09x more resources than 1x-MPSoC. If 4x and 2x-MPSoC are compared, 4x-MPSoC consumes on average 1.74x more resources as compared with 2x-MPSoC. Resource utilization of Cifar-10 2x-MPSoC is also shown in the table. Resource utilization of MicroBlaze (MB) [34] is also mentioned in the table with different optimizations used in each test. MicroBlaze is a soft-core processor from Xilinx. Overall MicroBlaze utilizes slightly fewer resources as compared with Lenet-5 1x-MPSoC. For most performance efficient comparison, Lenet-5 4x MPSoC utilized on average 4.67x more resource as compared to a single MicroBlaze with full performance optimizations.

4.2 Energy Estimation

An energy estimation library was developed for our proposed architecture, which allows reading voltage regulators of the Xilinx ZCU102 board via the I2C bus at runtime. These regulators estimate power consumption (voltage, current, and power) of different FPGA board regions. With the help of (3), energy of the proposed MPSoCs was estimated. Power "P" is calculated in "mW" through the library running on the ARM Cortex-A53 in parallel and time "t" is the execution time of an MPSoC to complete an application.

$$E = P \times t \tag{3}$$

According to Fig. 4, for Lenet-5, 4x-MPSoC utilized 1.82x and 3.61x times less energy as compared with 2x-MPSoC and 1x-MPSoC, respectively. However, compared to ARM it consumes 2.53x more energy. All proposed MPSoCs consumed less energy as compared with all three MicroBlaze setups. This is because MicroBlaze takes a lot of execution time. The results were similar for Cifar-10 MPSoC. 2x-MPSoC consumed 2.02x more energy as compared with ARM.

4.3 Performance

Performance evaluation was performed based on the overall execution time of inference. Execution time was also compared with the performance of a Xilinx MicroBlaze using different core optimizations and ARM Cortex-A53. MicroBlaze and our proposed MPSoCs were set at 100 MHz frequency to be comparable. The proposed MPSoC for different parallelization performed better as compared to a single MicroBlaze setup. 4x-MPSoC was 29x, 2x-MPSoC was 14x and 1x-MPSoC was 7x faster as compared with the performance-optimized MicroBlaze with all other optimizations enabled. A single ARM processor outperforms all MPSoC implementations. This is because ARM is not a soft-core processor and it uses enhanced branch prediction techniques to achieve high performance for applications with nested loops. According to Fig. 4, 2x and 4x-MPSoC executed Lenet-5, 1.9x and 3.96x times faster as compared with 1x-MPSoC, respectively. 4x-MPSoC was 1.9x times faster as compared with 2x-MPSoC execution time. The performance of a hardware accelerator [35] is also shown in Fig. 4 and it is the fastest as compared with the rest. A hardware specific implementation will always be faster as compared to a processor. For Cifar-10, 2x-MPSoC results were quite similar. 2x-MPSoC was much slower as compared with ARM.

The proposed MPSoCs performed better as compared with MicroBlaze with different optimizations but resulted in more area utilization. MicroBlaze provides a lot of configuration options which results in different optimizations. MicroBlaze design is optimized for FPGA implementation and can operate on higher frequency as compared with RI5CY (100 MHz). RI5CY implements hardware loops to increase the efficiency of loop operations. RI5CY also supports non-standard extensions for multiply-accumulate and half-word multiplications to improve efficiency. Although MicroBlaze is very easy to use soft-processor for FPGAs, RI5CY being open source, provides a platform for mico-architecture research for academics and industry (Fig. 3).

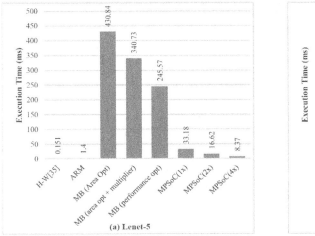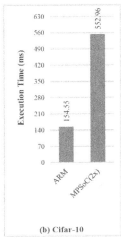

Fig. 3. Performance evaluation of MPSoCs for Lenet-5 (a) and Cifar-10 (b).

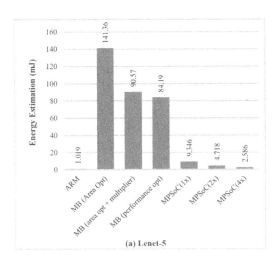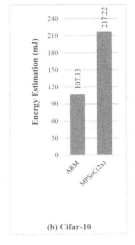

Fig. 4. Energy estimation of MPSoCs for Lenet-5 (a) and Cifar-10 (b).

5 Conclusion and Future Work

In this work, a RISC-V based MPSoC with a distributed memory system and a flexible architecture is proposed to tackle memory and computational requirements of object detection algorithms. The proposed architecture allows to take care of the computational complexity of convolutional layers of a NN by exploiting parallelism on the MPSoC. Xilinx Zynq Ultrascale+ MPSoC ZCU102 is used as a development platform for fast adaptions to proposed MPSoC architectures. From performance and resource utilization evaluation we can see that a 4x-parallelization in MPSoC outperforms 1x- and 2x-parallelization MPSoC designs by 3.9x and 1.9x times. The 4x-MPSoC was also 29x faster as compared to Xilinx MicroBlaze running at the same clock frequency. The 4x-MPSoC utilizes more resources (on average 3.09x, 1.74x and 4.67x) as compared with 1x, 2x-MPSoC and Microblaze, but it utilizes 3.61x, 1.82x and 32x times less energy to execute the same application. For accurate energy estimation, a power monitoring library is developed to control the voltage regulators of the FPGA at runtime. The proposed MPSoC is extendable and can be developed for larger algorithms.

For future work, custom RISC-V PEs should be developed for executing respective CNN layers [36]. Custom PEs with distributed and shared memory system and loosely coupled accelerators will increase complexity in architecture but will achieve a higher performance.

Acknowledgments. This work has been funded partially by the German Federal Ministry of Education and Research BMBF as part of the PARIS project under grant agreement number 16ES0657 and partially by COllective Research NETworking (CORNET) project AITIA: Embedded AI Techniques for Industrial Applications. CORNET-AITIA is funded by the BMWi (Federal Ministry for Economic Affairs and Energy) under the IGF-project number: 249 EBG.

References

1. Dorta, T., Jimenez, J., Martın, J.L., Bidarte, U., Astarloa, A.: Overview of FPGA-based multiprocessor systems. In: International Conference on Reconfigurable Computing and FPGAs, pp. 273–278, December 2009
2. Thomas, D.B., Howes, L., Luk, W.: A comparison of CPUs, GPUs, FPGAs, and massively parallel processor arrays for random number generation. In: Proceedings of the ACM/SIGDA International Symposium on Field Programmable Gate Arrays, FPGA 2009, pp. 63–72. ACM, New York (2009)
3. Abdelouahab, K., Pelcat, M., Serot, J., Berry, F.: Accelerating CNN inference on FPGAs: a survey. CoRR abs/1806.01683 (2018). http://arxiv.org/abs/1806.01683
4. Ma, Y., Cao, Y., Vrudhula, S., Seo, J.: Optimizing the convolution operation to accelerate deep neural networks on FPGA. IEEE Trans. Very Large Scale Integr. VLSI Syst. **26**(7), 1354–1367 (2018). https://doi.org/10.1109/TVLSI.2018.2815603
5. Rastegari, M., Ordonez, V., Redmon, J., Farhadi, A.: XNOR-Net: ImageNet classification using binary convolutional neural networks. CoRR abs/1603.05279 (2016). http://arxiv.org/abs/1603.05279
6. Zhang, W.-T., et al.: Design of heterogeneous MPSoC on FPGA. In: 7th International Conference on ASIC, pp. 102–105, October 2007

7. Ali, M., Amini Rad, P., Göhringer, D.: Power_Monitoring_Xilinx_ZCU102, February 2020. https://github.com/TUD-ADS/Power_Monitoring_Xilinx_ZCU102

8. Nurvitadhi, E., Sheffield, D., Jaewoong, S., Mishra, A., Venkatesh, G., Marr, D.: Accelerating binarized neural networks: comparison of FPGA, CPU, GPU, and ASIC. In: International Conference on Field-Programmable Technology (FPT), pp. 77–84, December 2016

9. Feng, G., Hu, Z., Chen, S., Wu, F.: Energy-efficient and high-throughput FPGA-based accelerator for convolutional neural networks. In: 13th IEEE International Conference on Solid-State and Integrated Circuit Technology (ICSICT), pp 624–626, October 2016

10. Theocharides, T., Link, G., Vijaykrishnan, N., Invin, M.J., Srikantam, V.: A generic reconfigurable neural network architecture as a network on chip. In: Proceedings of IEEE International SOC Conference, pp. 191–194, September 2004

11. Vainbrand, D., Ginosar, R.: Network-on-chip architectures for neural networks. In: Fourth ACM/IEEE International Symposium on Networks-on-Chip, pp. 135–144, May 2010

12. Thanh Bui, T.T., Phillips, B.: A scalable network-on-chip based neural network implementation on FPGAs. In: IEEE-RIVF International Conference on Computing and Communication Technologies (RIVF), pp. 1–6, March 2019

13. Vestias, M.P.: A survey of convolutional neural networks on edge with reconfigurable computing. Algorithms **12**(8), 154 (2019)

14. RISC-V. https://riscv.org/. Accessed 17 Feb 2020

15. Kamaleldin, A., Ali, M., Amini Rad, P., Gottschalk, M., Göhringer, D.: Modular memory system for RISC-V based MPSoCs on Xilinx FPGAs. In: IEEE 13th International Symposium on Embedded Multicore/Many-core Systems-on-Chip (MCSoC), pp. 68–73, October 2019

16. Davide Schiavone, P., et al.: Slow and steady wins the race? A comparison of ultra-low-power RISC-V cores for Internet-of-Things applications. In: 27th International Symposium on Power and Timing Modeling, Optimization and Simulation (PATMOS), pp. 1–8, September 2017

17. Elmohr, M.A., et al.: RVNoC: a framework for generating RISC-V NoC-based MPSoC. In: 2018 26th Euromicro International Conference on Parallel, Distributed and Network-based Processing (PDP), pp. 617–621, March 2018

18. Khamis, M., El-Ashry, S., Shalaby, A., AbdElsalam, M., El-Kharashi, M.W.: A configurable RISC-V for NoC-based MPSoCs: a framework for hardware emulation. In: 11th International Workshop on Network on Chip Architectures (NoCArc), pp. 1–6, October 2018

19. Garofalo, A., Rusci, M., Conti, F., Rossi, D., Benini, L.: PULP-NN: accelerating quantized neural networks on parallel ultra-low-power RISC-V processors. CoRR abs/1908.11263 (2019). http://arxiv.org/abs/1908.11263

20. Beldachi, A.F., Nunez-Yanez, J.L.: Accurate power control and monitoring in ZYNQ boards. In: 24th International Conference on Field Programmable Logic and Applications (FPL), pp. 1–4, September 2014

21. Nunez-Yanez, J.: Energy proportional neural network inference with adaptive voltage and frequency scaling. IEEE Trans. Comput. **68**(5), 676–687 (2019)

22. Maxim Integrated. https://www.maximintegrated.com/en/products/power. Accessed 17 Feb 2020

23. Lecun, Y., Bottou, L., Bengio, Y., Haffner, P.: Gradient-based learning applied to document recognition. Proc. IEEE **86**(11), 2278–2324 (1998)

24. Keras: CIFAR-10 CNN. https://keras.io/examples/cifar10_cnn/. Accessed 17 Feb 2020

25. Pulp-platform. https://github.com/pulp-platform/ri5cy_gnu_toolchain. Accessed 17 Feb 2020

26. Rettkowski, J., Göhringer, D.: ASIR: application-specific instruction-set router for NoC-based MPSoCs. Computers **7**(3), 38 (2018)

27. Gysel, P., Pimentel, J., Motamedi, M., Ghiasi, S.: Ristretto: a framework for empirical study of resource-efficient inference in convolutional neural networks. IEEE Trans. Neural Netw. Learn. Syst. **29**(11), 5784–5789 (2018)

28. Open MPI: Open MPI: Open Source High Performance Computing. https://www.open-mpi.org/. Accessed 17 Feb 2020
29. Xilinx: ZCU102 Evaluation Board User Guide. https://www.xilinx.com/support/documentation/boards_and_kits/zcu102/ug1182-zcu102-eval-bd.pdf. Accessed 17 Feb 2020
30. Xilinx: Zynq UltraScale+ MPSoC Software Developer Guide. https://www.xilinx.com/support/documentation/user_guides/ug1137-zynq-ultrascale-mpsoc-swdev.pdf. Accessed 17 Feb 2020
31. Texas Instruments: PCA9544A Low Voltage 4-Channel I2C and SMBus Multiplexer With Interrupt Logic. http://www.ti.com/lit/ds/symlink/pca9544a.pdf. Accessed 17 Feb 2020
32. Texas Instruments: INA226 high-side or low-side measurement, bidirectional current and power monitor with I2C compatible interface. http://www.ti.com/lit/ds/symlink/ina226.pdf. Accessed 17 Feb 2020
33. Maxim Integrated: InTune automatically compensated digital pol controller with driver and pmbus telemetry. https://datasheets.maximintegrated.com/en/ds/MAX15301.pdf. Accessed 17 Feb 2020
34. Xilinx: MicroBlaze Soft Processor Core. https://www.xilinx.com/products/design-tools/microblaze.html. Accessed 17 Feb 2020
35. Feng, G., Hu, Z., Chen, S., Wu, F.: Energy-efficient and high-throughput FPGA-based accelerator for convolutional neural networks. In: 13th IEEE International Conference on Solid-State and Integrated Circuit Technology (ICSICT), pp. 624–626, October 2016
36. Lou, W., Wang, C., Gong, L., Zhou, X.: RV-CNN: flexible and efficient instruction set for CNNs based on RISC-V processors. In: Yew, P.-C., Stenström, P., Wu, J., Gong, X., Li, T. (eds.) APPT 2019. LNCS, vol. 11719, pp. 3–14. Springer, Cham (2019). https://doi.org/10.1007/978-3-030-29611-7_1

High-Level Synthesis

A Modular Software Library for Effective High Level Synthesis of Convolutional Neural Networks

Hector Gerardo Munoz Hernandez$^{(\boxtimes)}$, Safdar Mahmood ,
Marcelo Brandalero , and Michael Hübner

Brandenburg University of Technology Cottbus - Senftenberg Computer
Engineering Group, Cottbus, Germany
{hector.munozhernandez,safdar.mahmood,marcelo.brandalero,
michael.huebner}@b-tu.de
https://www.b-tu.de/fg-technische-informatik

Abstract. Convolutional Neural Networks (CNNs) have applications
in many valuable domains such as object detection for autonomous cars
and security using facial recognition. This vast field of application usually
places strict non-functional requirements such as resource-efficient implementations on the hardware devices, while at the same time requiring
flexibility. In response, this work presents a C++-based software library
of reusable modules to build arbitrary CNNs that support High-Level-
Synthesis to be implemented as FPGA hardware accelerators for the
inference process. Our work demonstrates how parametrization and modularization of basic building blocks of a CNN enable easier customization
of the hardware to match the software model. This project also works
with low-precision parameters throughout the CNN to provide a more
resource-efficient implementation.

Keywords: High Level Synthesis · Modular approach · HW
acceleration · Convolutional Neural Networks · Inference acceleration ·
Library of components · Machine learning · C library · FPGA

1 Introduction

Nowadays, Convolutional Neural Networks (CNNs) are a very well known tool for
image processing and classification. Due to their convolutional and maxpooling
layers, CNNs exploit feature detection, which differentiates them from standard
Artificial Neural Networks (ANNs) [1].

CNNs have very high accuracy, but they use a lot of resources, requiring
up to 38GOP/s to classify a single frame [1]. This is why Graphical Processing
Units (GPUs) have been a prevalent option due to their high parallelism. There
is, however, an increasing interest in low-power, resource-efficient platforms, and
there is where Field Programmable Gate Arrays (FPGAs) come into play.

© Springer Nature Switzerland AG 2020
F. Rincón et al. (Eds.): ARC 2020, LNCS 12083, pp. 211–220, 2020.
https://doi.org/10.1007/978-3-030-44534-8_16

Being more energy efficient than the GPUs, FPGAs have other problems like small on-chip memory. Also, FPGAs have flexibility in terms of hardware dynamic adaptability. In other words, when the model is updated, the FPGA provides the opportunity to reprogram the FPGA, adjusting performance and energy efficiency to the new model as well. This is why there has been an increasing search for efficient CNNs implementations for FPGAs [1, 6, 8, 21, 24–26]. While some focus on automating the complete process of transforming a trained in software network into a hardware implementation [10, 21, 24, 26], others limit themselves to show different approaches to tackle specific problems in the implementation of CNNs in FPGAs [4, 6, 12, 25].

In this paper, we show an approach that combines some of the methods that proved to be effective. Our work currently presents the following contributions.

- A software library for Convolutional Neural Networks where each layer is processed independently, where the reduced precision makes it smaller and faster, with a small loss of accuracy.
- Evaluation of said network with two very well-known dataset MNIST and USPS in terms of utilization, implemented on a Xilinx Zynq Pynq-Z2 testing board.
- The code sources itself, as an open-source framework that is compatible with the HDF5 format for loading parameters such as weights, biases, and kernels.[1]

The main idea behind the third point is that anyone can contribute to the framework and also use it to accelerate their own previously trained CNNs and implement them on their test board. As the framework is compatible with HDF5 format, it can work out-of-the-box when the network was trained with some of the most popular open-source libraries for creating neural networks like Tensorflow, Caffe, among others.

The paper is organized as follows. Section 2 gives a little background knowledge for the Convolutional Neural networks. Section 3 exposes some related work information. Later in Sect. 4, the architecture of our approach is exposed. Section 5 presents the evaluation methodology so that the results can be shown and discussed. Finally, the conclusion of the work and the planned future work are in Sect. 6.

2   Background

The interest in Convolutional Neural Networks has grown a lot since their first application for image recognition in the recent ImageNet classification challenges in 1990 [16]. Previously, a work from Fukushima and Miyake [7] in 1982 concerning a new algorithm for pattern recognition called Neocognitron was presented, cited also by LeCun *et al.* [16], which contributed in forming the basis of Convolutional Neural Networks (CNN). Convolutional Neural Networks are a subclass of Deep Neural Networks mostly applied in the domain of visual image

---

[1] https://github.com/CEatBTU/Modular_CNN.git.

analysis [3] such as image classification, object detection, and in some rare cases natural language processing [18]. A typical CNN consists of several layers and nodes. A node is a computational unit that serves a specific purpose inside a layer. A layer is a mixture of nodes and computations. Each layer has a specific purpose, like to carry out a series of convolutions or reduce the number of inputs, for example. The input layer consists of a specific number of nodes equal to the size of an image passing through the network. In contrast, the final output layer contains nodes which equal the number of image categories that can be classified. In between these two layers, there are convolutional layers, maxpooling layers, activation layers, and fully connected layers that constituent a CNN.

The convolutional layers of CNNs use the concept of local receptive fields, shared weights, shared bias, and feature maps, whereas, shared weight and shared bias correspond to a specific filter alternatively known as a kernel or local receptive field that is applied to an input image to generate feature maps [20]. This layer is the most operation costly, as the number of MACs is the highest among the other layers.

An activation function decides whether a particular node should fire or not. In a convolution layer, there are several different types of activation functions such as *ReLU, Tanh, Sigmoid*, etc. [28], which can form an activation layer to provide the desired functionality in CNNs. An activation layer in CNNs is connected to the output nodes (or features maps) of a convolutional layer and generates an output that passes on to the max-pooling layer. The purpose of such an activation layer is to introduce non-linearity e.g., to clip off or modify the outputs of the convolution layer [20].

A Max-pooling layer performs a condensation operation on feature maps to eventually reduce its size to carry out further operations such as flattening and feeding to a fully connected layer, or passing it to another following convolution layer if it is present in a given architecture.

A fully connected layer, as the name suggests, connects all the flattened-out neurons from the previous layer to all the neurons present in the output layer [20]. This layer behaves like a network of fully connected multi-layer perceptrons, as shown in Fig. 1, which depicts the complete structure of a regular CNN. The fully connected layer network follows the usual traits of a regular artificial neural network with a possibility of more than one hidden layer, weighted interconnects, biases, and neuronal activation functions such as Sigmoid (σ)).

3   Related Work

Our work proposes an approach that employs the concept of modularization to accelerate CNNs on FPGA while exploiting the features of High-Level Synthesis. On the other hand, there have been numerous contributions in the area of CNN acceleration on FPGAs [5, 10, 19, 23, 25]. In a similar approach [11], a layer-based structured design of Convolutional Neural Networks has been presented, which also exploits the features of High-Level Synthesis such as loop optimizations for parallelism and pipelining. For experimental purposes, Huang *et al.* [11] uses

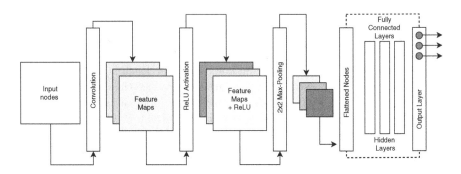

Fig. 1. Typical structure of a Convolutional Neural Network

23-layered SqueezeNet [13] for its design and implementation on a Xilinx VC709 FPGA Board. The proposed architecture in [11] organizes and distributes different layers in an FPGA and a corresponding processing system based on how compute-intensive a specific layer is. More compute-intensive layers are deployed on FPGA, while the rest of the relatively less time-consuming layers are cordoned off inside a CPU [11]. It is, however, not clear if specific layers can be synthesized as separate hardware IP blocks to be used as re-arrangeable modules for custom CNN implementations on FPGAs.

Hailesellasie *et al.* [9] presents a framework called Mulmapper, which automates the process of converting a Caffe-based [14] CNN model to a hardware IP targeted for Zynq-based FPGAs. Mulmapper [9] uses Vivado High-Level-Synthesis tool to generate a CNN processor. At the same time, it provides an optimum design space exploration for target device resources, data-width concerning quantization, and target core mode in which a Multiplier-Accumulator (MAC) can be implemented with or without a multiplier core. Another framework proposed by Leon *et al.* [17] provides an extension to Tensorflow framework for the automatic generation of CNN accelerators for target devices like FPGAs and ASICs. Although, the CNN inference generator creates an optimized HDL description for synthesis and implementation rather than exploiting High-Level-Synthesis (HLS).

There have been several implementations that adopt the traits of scalability and modularization. Ma *et al.* [27] proposes such an approach where High-Level Synthesis and RTL optimizations can be amalgamated to provide a more flexible solution. This approach also uses separate processing units or modules for different sort of computations such as Convolution module, Normalization module, Pooling Module, including a custom DMA Configuration Module which controls the data flow between each of these units with unique source and destination addresses [27]. Here the processing units or modules are not connected in a back-to-back fashion [27], like in our proposed model where the feature data can be transferred through a streaming bus without any additional control logic.

In 2017, Bacis *et al.* [2] presented a pipelined and scalable dataflow implementation of Convolutional Neural Networks on FPGA. In this work [2,19], an idea of a modular and scalable methodology was achieved by exploiting thee dataflow pattern of convolutions, based on the acceleration techniques of *Iterative Stencil Loops*. One of the main contributions of this paper is to provide each layer of the CNN with a highly or parallelized methodology. This work resulted in the comparison of two main CNNs datasets, namely USPS and CIFAR-10. The latter was compared with the latency of an accelerator proposed by a Microsoft team using the same dataset [22], claiming a 3.36x acceleration over it. Bacis *et al.* [2] used floating point for the parameters types through the iteration process, which can be highly costly for these types of implementations. Lastly, the code and sources of this experiment are not provided, which makes it difficult to reproduce or to compare with further implementations.

In summary, compared to previous works, this work is the first one in which some of the already proved-to-be-efficient techniques to accelerate CNNs in FPGAs come together. Some of the techniques are the streaming architecture [25], reduced data precision [4], modular approach [2], and exploiting parallelism of the FPGAs [1].

4   Design Proposal

A streaming approach was chosen to create the design. This means that the data gets streamed through the entire model, namely the images, kernels, weights, and biases. The advantage of streaming the data in the inference process is that each layer can be active the moment it receives the first value. In this way, the subsequent layer does not have to wait for previous layer to send the data.

Each layer was implemented independently so that high modularity and customization could be achieved. The block diagram is shown in Fig. 2 describes the architecture of a fundamental CNN architecture that consists of one Convolutional layer, a max-pooling layer, one fully connected layer, and an output layer. This architecture was chosen to appreciate the flow quickly.

The Direct Memory Access (DMA) is instructed by the Processing system to start the streaming of the input image into the first layer. The first layer is the **Convolutional + ReLu** layer, which also reads a *kernel stream* with all the kernels that the convolution will use. When working with streaming data, *Line Buffers* are a safe choice because they help to store the data temporarily so that it does not get lost due to the streaming nature of the design. We also used a *Window* with the kernel data loaded to slide it over the line buffer to do each convolution operation.

The second layer is the **max-pooling**, where every feature map is compressed and forwarded to the next layer. The *Line Buffer* and *Window* approach was also used here to isolate each section of the array from where we want to find the maximum value.

The **Fully connected layer** also receives a stream with the weights and the biases. *Line Buffers* were also used in this layer to store the values temporarily from the streams. For every output, the inputs are multiplied by their corresponding weights and added to the bias. The sum of this result gets then introduced into the sigmoid function.

The **output layer**, is where all the outputs from the previous layer are processed by the *softmax* function. After the output layer finishes, the stream gets back into the DDR3 memory in non-blocking mode so that writing and reading can be done in parallel. This way, the Processing System can choose the maximum value of the output stream, thus completing the classification process.

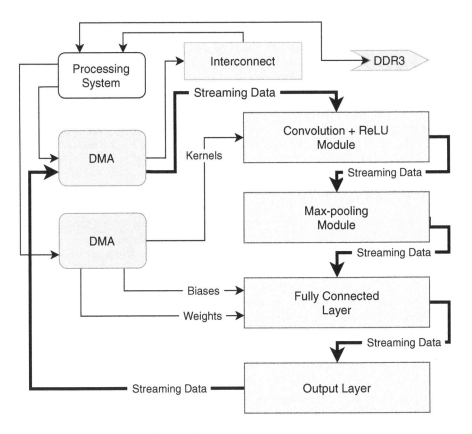

Fig. 2. Block diagram: approach

5 Evaluation

Vivado High-Level Synthesis (HLS) was used to create the RTL code for each layer. In this way, the user can use higher-level programming languages such as C++, as well as some directives that help the compiler to optimize the design according to the user's need to obtain later RTL code. This RTL code got incorporated into Vivado 2018.3 in the form of a block diagram to generate the bitstream. Later, Vivado SDK was used to test the design with a simple application that feeds the image of a handwritten digit and waits for the result of the

Output Layer to later classify the image. For all the tests, the selected operating frequency was of 100 MHz.

As one of the objectives of the current work is to provide an open-source framework to accelerate CNNs, the chosen platform to implement the design was the PYNQ-Z2 board (equipped with XC7Z020), due to its low cost and increasing popularity.

Table 1. Utilization of each layer

Layer	BRAM	DSP	FFs	LUT
Convolution	0	4	3,005	7,802
Maxpool	2	0	3,201	7,754
Fully Connected	5	11	3,193	4,020
Output	3	14	5,100	9,638
Total	10	29	14,499	29,214
Percentage of resources used	4%	13%	13%	55%

Table 1, displays how many Block RAMs, digital signal processing blocks, Flip Flops, and Look Up Tables each layer is using from the FPGA. The percentage shown at the bottom of the table represents the number of resources used out of the total amount of the specific available resources in this FPGA. For these results, the network is shown in Fig. 2 was translated into hardware. The parameters of the network are as follows: An image from the MNIST dataset (28 × 28 dimensions) is fed into the convolutional layer, which has 16 5 × 5 kernels resulting in an output of the same number of images of 28 × 28 dimensions. The max-pool layer has a window size of 2 × 2 and a stride also of 2. This means that the output would be the same 16 images but of 14 × 14 dimensions. The next layer is then the fully connected layer, which outputs 1,000 values. Another fully connected layer follows, converting the output to 10 values.

In another test, our model was compared to Bacis et al. [2]. They use a very similar approach, as already mentioned in the related work. On our work, however, the floating-point values were replaced by half-precision point values; this is because of a size of 16 bits in the parameters of the CNNs, which was proved to be very efficient [27]. The test case was conducted over the USPS dataset, which also classifies handwritten digits. The architecture of the said neural network is the following:

The dataset is composed of 16 × 16 images, which are fed into the first convolutional layer, which has six outputs. The second layer is a max-pool with a window size of 2 × 2 and a stride of 2. The third layer is a convolutional layer again but with six images as inputs and 16 outputs. These images are fed into a fully connected layer that has ten outputs.

As it is shown in Table 2, we achieved a much smaller implementation, using 14x less BRAMs blocks, 81.1x less DSP slices, 9.8x less Flip Flops, and around

7.7x less Look-Up Tables. The latency was also reported; this measurement also took into consideration the time it takes for the DMA communication to take place, which is configured with a 16-bit data width.

The trade-off comes in terms of latency, and this can be seen in Table 3. This means that our proposed implementation is ideal for a small or portable device, where the latency is not time-critical. This work provides an implementation approximately 8 times slower than the one in Bacis *et al.* [2]. However, being able to process 20,833 images per second, our implementation is still able to comply with a lot of applications where timing is highly regarded.

Table 2. Comparison of utilization USPS dataset

Design	BRAM	DSP	FFs	LUT
Bacis *et al.* [2]	98	1,541	249,559	154,410
This work	7	19	25,431	20,131

Table 3. Comparison of performance USPS dataset

Design	GFLOPS	Image Latency (ms)	Images/s
Bacis *et al.* [2]	5.2	.0058	172,414
This work	0.6	.048	20,833

6   Conclusion

In this work, an accelerator of CNNs was presented. The model has a streaming architecture, is modular, has a reduced data precision, and exploits the parallelism of the FPGAs. The complete dataflow starts from a couple of C++ scripts that can be configured to create a custom layer from the CNN, to create a hardware version of the CNN. RTL code gets generated with the help of Vivado HLs, and the resulting IP can be used in a block diagram to configure the Programmable Logic in a ZYNQ device. With this approach, we show an improvement in resource utilization concerning a similar approach. The model is going to be open-source for everyone to contribute and use.

6.1   Future Work

The tool flow showed throughout this paper is planned to be an automatized one, which means that we are planning to provide scripts to make more accessible the porting process from previously created CNNs on software to a hardware model ready to be implemented. Also, a PYNQ interface is planned, to facilitate even more the resulting applications of the tool, so that the users can accelerate their CNNs and test them in user-friendly interfaces like Jupyter Notebooks [15] for example.

References

1. Abdelouahab, K., Pelcat, M., Serot, J., Berry, F.: Accelerating CNN inference on FPGAs: a Survey (2018). arXiv: 1806.01683 [cs.DC]
2. Bacis, M., Natale, G., Del Sozzo, E., Santambrogio, M.D.: A pipelined and scalable dataflow implementation of convolutional neural networks on FPGA. In: 2017 IEEE International Parallel and Distributed Processing Symposium Workshops (IPDPSW), May 2017, pp. 90–97 (2017)
3. Bhandare, A., Bhide, M.V., Gokhale, P., Chandavarkar, R.: Applications of Convolutional Neural Networks (2016)
4. Courbariaux, M., Hubara, I., Soudry, D., El-Yaniv, R. Bengio, Y.: Binarized neural networks: training deep neural networks with weights and activations constrained to $+1$ or -1 (2016). arXiv: 1602.02830 [cs.LG]
5. Farabet, C., et al.: Hardware accelerated convolutional neural networks for synthetic vision systems. In: Proceedings of 2010 IEEE International Symposium on Circuits and Systems, May 2010, pp. 257–260 (2010)
6. Fu, C., Zhu, S., Su, H., Lee, C.-E., Zhao, J.: Towards fast and energy-efficient binarized neural network inference on FPGA (2018). arXiv: 1810.02068 [cs.LG]
7. Fukushima, K., Miyake, S.: Neocognitron: a new algorithm for pattern recognition tolerant of deformations and shifts in position. Pattern Recogn. **15**, 455–469 (1982)
8. Guan, Y., et al.: FP-DNN: an automated framework for mapping deep neural networks onto FPGAs with RTL-HLS hybrid templates. In: 2017 IEEE 25th Annual International Symposium on Field-Programmable Custom Computing Machines (FCCM), May 2017, pp. 152–159, IEEE Computer Society, Los Alamitos (2017). https://doi.ieeecomputersociety.org/10.1109/FCCM.2017.25
9. Hailesellasie, M., Hasan, S.R., Mohamed, O.A.: MulMapper: towards an automated FPGA-Based CNN processor generator based on a dynamic design space exploration. In: 2019 IEEE International Symposium on Circuits and Systems (ISCAS), May 2019, pp. 1–5 (2019)
10. Hao, Y.: A general neural network hardware architecture on FPGA (2017). arXiv: 1711.05860 [cs.CV]
11. Huang, C., Ni, S., Chen, G.: A layer-based structured design of CNN on FPGA. In: 2017 IEEE 12th International Conference on ASIC (ASICON), October 2017, pp. 1037–1040 (2017)
12. Hubara, I., Courbariaux, M., Soudry, D., El-Yaniv, R., Bengio, Y.: Quantized neural networks: training neural networks with low precision weights and activations (2016). arXiv: 1609.07061 [cs.NE]
13. Iandola, F.N., et al.: SqueezeNet: AlexNet-level accuracy with 50x fewer parameters and <0.5MB model size (2016). arXiv: 1602.07360 [cs.CV]
14. Jia, Y., et al.: Caffe: convolutional architecture for fast feature embedding. *arXiv preprint* arXiv:1408.5093 (2014)
15. Kluyver, T., et al.: Jupyter notebooks - a publishing format for reproducible computational workflows. In: Loizides, F., Scmidt, B. (eds.) Positioning and Power in Academic Publishing: Players, Agents and Agendas, pp. 87–90. IOS Press, Amsterdam (2016). https://eprints.soton.ac.uk/403913/
16. LeCun, Y., et al.: In: Touretzky, D.S. (ed.) Advances in Neural Information Processing Systems 2, pp. 396–404. Morgan-Kaufmann, Burlington (1990). http://papers.nips.cc/paper/293-handwritten-digit-recognition-with-a-back-propagation-network.pdf

17. Leon, V., et al.: A tensorflow extension framework for optimized generation of hardware CNN inference engines in technologies 2020, MDPI 2020. https://www.mdpi.com/2227-7080/8/1/6

18. Li, P., Li, J., Wang, G.: Application of convolutional neural network in natural language processing. In: 2018 15th International Computer Conference on Wavelet Active Media Technology and Information Processing (ICCWAMTIP), December 2018, pp. 120–122 (2018)

19. Natale, G., Bacis, M., Santambrogio, M.D.: On how to design dataflow FPGA-based accelerators for convolutional neural networks. In: 2017 IEEE Computer Society Annual Symposium on VLSI (ISVLSI), July 2017, pp. 639–644 (2017)

20. Nielsen, M.: Neural Network and Deep Learning. Determination Press. http://neuralnetworksanddeeplearning.com/

21. Noronha, D.H., Salehpour, B., Wilton, S.J.E.: LeFlow: enabling flexible FPGA high-level synthesis of tensorflow deep neural networks (2018). arXiv: 1807.05317 [cs.LG]

22. Ovtcharov, K., et al.: Accelerating deep convolutional neural networks using specialized hardware, February 2015. https://www.microsoft.com/en-us/research/publication/accelerating-deep-convolutional-neural-networks-using-specialized-hardware/

23. Solovyev, R.A., Kalinin, A.A., Kustov, A.G., Telpukhov, D.V., Ruhlov, V.S.: FPGA Implementation of Convolutional Neural Networks with Fixed-Point Calculations (2018). arXiv: 1808.09945 [cs.CV]

24. Umuroglu, Y., et al.: FINN. In: Proceedings of the 2017 ACM/SIGDA International Symposium on Field-Programmable Gate Arrays - FPGA 2017 (2017). http://dx.doi.org/10.1145/3020078.3021744

25. Venieris, S.I., Kouris, A., Bouganis, C.-S.: Toolflows for mapping convolutional neural networks on FPGAs: a survey and future directions (2018). arXiv: 1803.05900 [cs.CV]

26. Wang, E., Davis, J.J., Cheung, P.Y.K.: A PYNQ-based framework for rapid CNN prototyping. In: 2018 IEEE 26th Annual International Symposium on Field-Programmable Custom Computing Machines (FCCM), April 2018, p. 223 (2018)

27. Ma, Y., Suda, N., Cao, Y., Seo, J., Vrudhula, S.: Scalable and modularized RTL compilation of Convolutional Neural Networks onto FPGA. In: 2016 26th International Conference on Field Programmable Logic and Applications (FPL), August 2016, pp. 1–8 (2016)

28. Zaheer, R., Shaziya, H.: GPU-based empirical evaluation of activation functions in convolutional neural networks. In: 2018 2nd International Conference on Inventive Systems and Control (ICISC), January 2018, pp. 769–773 (2018)

HLS-Based Acceleration Framework for Deep Convolutional Neural Networks

Ashish Misra(iD) and Volodymyr Kindratenko(✉)(iD)

University of Illinois, Urbana, IL 61801, USA
{ashishm,kindrtnk}@illinois.edu

Abstract. Deep Neural Networks (DNNs) have been successfully applied in many fields. Considering performance, flexibility, and energy efficiency, Field Programmable Gate Array (FPGA) based accelerator for DNNs is a promising solution. The existing frameworks however lack the possibility of reusability and friendliness to design a new network with minimum efforts. Modern high-level synthesis (HLS) tools greatly reduce the turnaround time of designing and implementing complex FPGA-based accelerators. This paper presents a framework for hardware accelerator for DNNs using high level specification. A novel architecture is introduced that maximizes data reuse and external memory bandwidth. This framework allows to generate a scalable HLS code for a given pre-trained model that can be mapped to different FPGA platforms. Various HLS compiler optimizations have been applied to the code to produce efficient implementation and high resource utilization. The framework achieves a peak performance of 23 frames per second for SqueezeNet on Xilinx Alveo u250 board.

Keywords: Accelerator design · High level synthesis · FPGA

1 Introduction

Deep Neural Networks (DNNs) have made a profound impact on applications such as image classification [1, 2] and speech recognition [3, 4]. However, they demand extensive computations and impose extreme timing constraints because of their deep topological structures, complicated cross-layer connections, and massive amounts of data to process. As a result, it becomes challenging to achieve high performance and good energy efficiency when mapping DNNs onto generic computing systems. To mitigate this problem, many hardware (HW) accelerators for DNN inference have been explored. Among these designs, Field-Programmable Gate Array (FPGA) based accelerators have gained great popularity due to their reconfigurability, massive fine-grained parallelism, and performance per watt advantage.

The extreme scale integration of modern system on-chip (SoC) and burgeoning design complexity of emerging applications has made it imperative to design at a higher level of abstraction in order to achieve high productivity. To manage this issue, high-level synthesis (HLS) tools have emerged to allow application developers to describe the hardware accelerator using common software (SW) programming languages, such as C/C++, by automatically generating RTL from behavioral descriptions [5, 7].

© Springer Nature Switzerland AG 2020
F. Rincón et al. (Eds.): ARC 2020, LNCS 12083, pp. 221–231, 2020.
https://doi.org/10.1007/978-3-030-44534-8_17

A typical DNN architecture has multiple layers that extract features from the input data. Convolution is the most computationally expensive function which requires millions of floating-point operations (FLOPs) in these networks. Thus, it needs a good accelerator architecture which should balance maximum memory access and computation and software linkage to DNN frameworks. Currently, many open-source software frameworks have been released for DNN research but most of them suffer from scalability problems. Existing FPGA-based convolutional neural network (CNN) accelerator designs primarily focus on optimizing the computational resources without considering the impact of the external memory transfers or optimizing the external memory transfers through data reuse [5], or on optimizing only the convolution layers [8].

To address the above-mentioned problems, we present a systematic methodology for maximizing the throughput of an FPGA-based accelerator for an entire DNN model consisting of convolution, pooling and certain layers executed in software. In this paper, we describe a framework, which starts from a trained network (Caffe/TensorFlow) and generates a deployable accelerator for image classification. The entire compilation procedure is end-to-end and automated, which makes it possible for DNN researchers and users to use FPGA as a powerful device to perform model inference. In this paper, we introduce this novel architecture and provide the following contributions:

1. A configurable streaming framework for DNN accelerators that exploits operator level, loop level, input channel and output channel parallelism.
2. Automatically generated verification network in C++ that allows users to test the correctness of the design. The framework can be exploited either as individual kernels or as a set of layers scheduled on the hardware.
3. The framework allows to use certain layers as HW and certain layers as SW, providing the designer with a choice of possible configurations.

2   Related Work

The analysis of a good accelerator design in the context of DNNs should be based on three factors: (i) Number of frames per second (FPS) achieved at run-time; (ii) Flexibility of the design to handle many classes of DNNs; and (iii) Minimum loss of accuracy for classification of an image with dataset with hundreds of classes. We only focus on the related work that have demonstrated at least two of these requirements.

Shawahna et al. [9] present an extensive comparison of accelerator designs for FPGAs; but they do not consider first and third factor in their comparison. Guan et al. [8] present an extensive framework showing VGG-19, ResNet-152 and LSTM-LM; but they do not report latency or FPS obtained after deployment. Qiu et al. [10] report the comparison of latency for VGG16-SVD network for FPGA, CPU and GPU. The latency reported is 224.60 ms and total operations is 30.76 giga operations (GOPs), hence the overall performance is 136.97 GOPs/second (GOPS). The FPS reported is 4.45 for 16-bit quantized weights and 5.88 for 8-bit. While this work demonstrates the best possible frame rate for a large network, it still does not report the accuracy of the network after quantizing the weights. Also, the authors modified VGG-16 to VGG16-SVD, hence the actual 30.76 GOPs parameter have been downsized. Zhang et al. [11] also report 158.8 ms for VGG16-SVD network. This is a significant improvement as compared to previous results, but the authors also do not report the FPS. Suda et al. [12] also present the latency of VGG-16 as 651.2 ms. This work reports all three factors and can be used for comparison.

Using the fixed-point data types requires that trained weights must be quantized as reported by Song H. et al. [13]. This work however shows that with appropriate quantization of the weights, acceleration can be achieved at the expense of accuracy. Xilinx ml-suite [14] reports the best possible performance of 4127 images/sec on int8 data type with GoogleNet.

Other optimizations that can be applied include: (1) Algorithmic optimizations for convolution operations, for example, the core of computation engine can be designed using a Wallace tree [6] or a systolic array. Our work focuses on balanced tree for multiply and accumulate (MAC) int16 operations. (2) Dataflow optimizations for maximum memory bandwidth. The dataflow model requires that there is a non-stop dataflow from memory-in to memory-out with maximum data transfer in each cycle. The work in [6] introduces a roof-line model for analysis of the design for memory throughput. Authors in [15] show how efficiently streaming can be applied in the design.

3 Proposed Design

3.1 Architecture Design

Here we describe the proposed design that exploits the concurrency features intrinsic in convolution function. Figure 1 shows each unit and function in the proposed architecture. The design works on 128 input channels, 64 output channels and kernel size, w_{size}, either 3 or 1. The complete module as shown in Fig. 1 is instantiated four times, allowing to compute 256 output channels concurrently. The weight file obtained after quantization is stored as int16 and each weight is multiplied by 64. The value of 64 is chosen based on that no layer in SW shows underflow or overflow. No change is made to the input image. Multiplication is carried out in int16 but results are maintained as int for bias addition and finally divided by 64 to scale down the values to int16. Next, we describe the HW and SW units that are used to implement the network.

Funtion_0: The first layer of each network is different, for example, the kernel size can vary from 1 to 11, the number of input channels is usually 1 or 3 and the input dimension can be arbitrary high as 448. Hence this layer can be executed in the SW or HW framework, depending on its complexity. The first layer requires significant amount of MAC operations; hence it is better to design a new kernel customized for parameters.

HW_Interface_1: The proposed architecture has been built on the dataflow model (recognized by #pragma HLS Dataflow), which allows to concurrently access non-overlapping data stored in different memory banks. Hence input data and weight data for a layer have been placed in two DDR memory banks and concurrently accessed using AXI4 interface as shown in Fig. 1.

HW_Unit_1: The first two functions in the design are accessing data from each DDR bank and convert it to 128 input streams and 128 weight streams. The weight streamer saves the data in on-chip buffer (*wgt_buff[128][64][9]*) and then streams are created in a different loop structure. The aim of using the *wgt_buff* is to initialize the streams to zero if the number of input channels is less than 128. Since the size of the input data is larger than the weight data, more cycles can be spend checking the number of channels and creating a second loop structure in the *stream_weight()* function. Each of the streams is mapped to FIFO which can be mapped to either LUTs or BRAMs present on the chip.

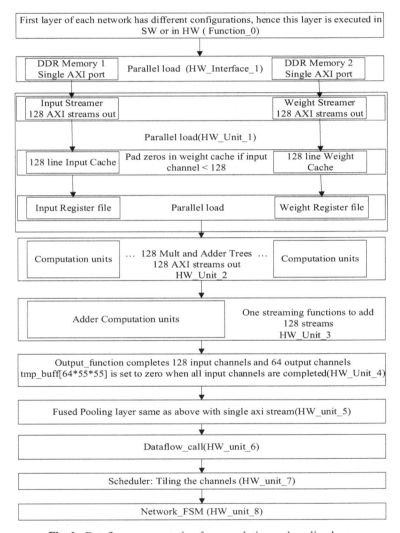

Fig. 1. Dataflow representation for convolution and pooling layer.

HW_Unit_2: This unit contains 128 identical convolutional functions, each with a different stream interface. This is because streams are static in high level synthesis flow. Hence 256 streams (one input and one weight) from HW_function_1 reach to 128 concurrent computation units.

There are primarily three objectives to be achieved in this unit. The line buffer receives the data from a stream which should not be stalled as shown in Algorithm 1. This is achieved by overlapping the computation and stream access (as multiplication and loading are parallel). The loading of *wgt_mac_0* for computation; streaming out the data; and loading new line in the line buffer is done by pipelining. The kernel weights should not be loaded again and again for the output channel. This is achieved by looping for 64 or less output channels.

Algorithm 1. Convolution

```
1)   Input: Two axi streams for each convo() function
2)   Given: osize, stride, padding, wsize, ochan, ichan .
3)   Output:  one output stream
4)     for yy  = 0 to osize:
5)       for ochan_no = 0 to ochan:
6)         load wgt_mac register
7)         for xx = 0 to osize:
8)           if wsize == 1:
9)             call convo_1d()
10)          else:
11)            load wgt_mac_0 from line buffer
12)            stream_convo_out_1_0 <<  call convo_2d()
13)          if  ochan_no == 0:
14)            load line buffer next line
15)   call rotate line buffer
```

Once the line buffer is loaded, instead of completing an input channel frame, first line of 64 output channels is computed and then the line buffer is updated. If there are more than 128 input channels, a temporary buffer is used to store the data and this data is accessed again for computing all the input channels.

The third objective in the computation algorithm is to achieve a pipelined MAC tree for sum of product operation. The HLS tool can produce a balanced tree if integer operations are performed, hence objective is achieved in the synthesis process. The delay of the tree is given as worst delay of an operator. Though the latency of the tree may be high, the initiation interval is one, which means next input can be taken after one cycle.

HW_Unit_3: This unit contains one streaming function to add data coming from 128 computation units and produces one output stream.

HW_Interface_2: The two DDR memories discussed in HW_Interface_1 were used for getting input data. Similarly, remaining two DDR memories are used for storing output and network parameters data. Temporary buffer can also be utilized if enough BRAMs are present in the chip and one DDR bank can be eliminated. Since this design computes 64 output channels and 128 input channels, this means if 1024 input channels are present, then intermediate tile data of size $64*i_{size}*i_{size}$ has to be stored in a DDR bank (*temp_buff*). This DDR bank should be accessed when adding the values to the next tile computed. All the parameters of the network such as weight offset and bias offset are precomputed and copied to DDR 4.

HW_Unit_4: This unit receives one stream from HW_Unit_3 and contains one function to read/write data from two DDR banks or temporary buffer (*para_buff*). The bias is added at this stage and data is stored back in one of the DDR banks or *para_buff*. Algorithm 2 demonstrates this process. This unit also checks whether pooling is required, if yes then stream data goes to a pooling function else the polling unit is bypassed.

Algorithm 2. DDR Access

```
 1)  Input: One axi stream. Given: osize, ochan,
               bias buffer, bb, ichan_en, aa, out_offset.
 2)  Output: Data written to DDR banks
               declare out_buff for burst use
 3)    for yy = 0 to osize:
 4)      for ochan_no = 0 to ochan:
 5)        for xx = 0 to osize:
 6)          datatype_inh sum = 0;
 7)          datatype_inh sum1 = 0;
 8)          datatype_inh dp_0;
 9)          stream_adder_out_0 >> dp_0;
10)          if bb > 0 :
11)            sum1 = dp_0 + para;
12)          else:
13)            sum1 = dp_0;
14)          para_buff[xx] = sum1;
15)          sum = sum1 + bias[ochan + aa*ochan_fac] ;
16)          if  sum > 0 :
17)            out_buff[xx] = sum >> 64;
18)          else:
19)            out_buff[xx] = 0;
20)          if bb == ichan_index-1:
21)            if (pool_on ==1):
22)              Stream_out_pool_fused << out_buff[xx];
23)            else:
24)              write_ddr3_with_burst();
25)              write_ddr4_with_zero();
26)              para_buff_with_zero();
27)          else:
28)            write_ddr4with data();
```

Algorithm 2 works in conjunction with Algorithm 3. It takes bias buffer which is pre-loaded, *bb* variable which is dependent on the number of input channels ($bb > 0$ if $i_{chan} > 128$), *aa* variable which is dependent on the number of output channels ($aa > 0$ if $o_{chan} > 64$), and i_{chan_en} variable that defines the number of iteration for all the input channels. The streams bring the data in, which is then summed up with temporary data from previous iteration, bias is added, relu activation is applied, last iteration is checked, data is written to DDR3 bank and *para_buff* is initialized to zero again.

HW_Unit_5: This unit contains three functions to complete pooling in a fused manner. First function receives one stream from previous unit and caches it in a small memory. Second function does the pooling operation and third function stores the data in the DDR. If a convolution unit with stride of 2 is required, this unit is enabled as well.

HW_Unit_6: This unit defines one function that calls all the above units in a dataflow model. Total of (128×4) 512 input streams, (128×4) 512 weight streams, 4 adder streams, 4 output streams, 12 pooling streams, are defined in this function. This function connects all the streams with one input function and one output function, 512 convolution functions 4 adder functions, 4 pooling functions. All the units are instantiated in this function.

HW_Unit_7: This unit, calls the HW_unit_6 in a sequential way for completing one layer. Since the architecture works on input and output of tile size 128×256, the scheduler calls HW_unit_6. Suppose the output channels are less than 256, then $o_{chan\_index}=1$, if $o_{chan} > 256$, then $o_{chan\_index} = o_{chan}/256$ (Algorithm 3).

If $i_{chan} < 128$, then $i_{chan\_index}=1$, else it is shifted by 7. The call function (line 8) takes weight offset ($aa * i_{chan} * out_{chan} * w_{size} * w_{size} + bb * 128 * w_{size} * w_{size} + wgt\_offset$) and output offset ($aa * out_{chan} * o_{size} * o_{size} + out_{offset}$) as arguments.

Algorithm 3. Scheduler (layer_128ic_256oc())

```
1)   Input: DDR pointers.
2)   Given: osize, stride, padding, wsize, ochan, out_offset, wgt_offset.
     Output:  one output streams
3)   Delare ochan_index, outchan, ichan_index
4)     if ochan <= 256:
5)        ochan_index = 1;
6)        out_chan = ochan;
7)     else:
8)        ochan_index = ochan >> 8;
9)        outchan = 256;
10)    if ichan <= 128:
11)      ichan_index = 1;
12)    else:
13)      ichan_index = ichan >> 7;
14)    if (ochan <= 256):
15)      ochan_fac = ochan >> 2;
16)    else:
17)      ochan_fac = 64;
18)    for aa = 0 to ochan_index:
19)      for bb = 0 to ichan_index:
20)         call hw_unit_6
```

HW_Unit_8: All the layers are completely scheduled by an FSM designed in HW. A python script generates this FSM along with weight offset, bias offset and output offset for each layer. The generated HW creates FIFO channels for each parameter in HW_unit_7. Such an FSM helps with DDR bank swapping and no host intervention is required (Algorithm 4).

Vivado HLS schedule reports the initiation interval for each function, which determines how well the dataflow is pipelined. The initiation intervals for each function reported are *convo* (1 cycle), *addstreams* (1 cycle), *stream_in* (1 cycles), *stream_out* (1 cycle), *stream_weight* (1 cycles) and *pooling* (1 cycle).

Algorithm 4. Layer Scheduler

```
1)  Input: Input data, complete weights,
2)  Given: externally generated FSM with weight and output offsets
3)  Output:  data for last layer
4)  Restart FSM,
5)  Load bias in bias buffer,
6)  Call HW_unit_6
7)  If last state is reached, go to 10
8)  Swap the DDR pointers
9)  Go to 6 for next layer,
10) For next image wait for signal to toggle and go to 4
```

From a given trained Caffe-based network, weight and network parameters are extracted to generate the complete network scheduler. A python program has been written to generate all the linear weights and output offset. The weights are then quantized using scripts and standard deviation process. This process is discussed in Algorithm 5.

Algorithm 5. Network Scheduler

```
1)  Input: Input data, complete weights,
2)  Given: extracted weight file, paramters and network from
          caffe model/tensorflow
3)  Perform offline quantization to generate new weight file.
4)  Output:  image class
5)  Load new image
6)  Multiply each weight each 64 and store in DDR banks as int16.
7)  Call layer scheduler, Copy the output for last layer
8)  Call the tensorflow function for last layer or output the results
9)  Go to 5 for a new image
```

Table 1 shows that 29% FF, 78% LUT, 52% DSP, 54% BRAM and 44% URAM are utilized in the design. The entire design is set to synthesize at 200 MHz, but the functions report a frequency of 300 MHz. There is still possibility that more computation can be done, however maintaining the LUTs resources utilization at this level becomes difficult.

3.2 Verification Setup and Executable Setup

Firstly, the implemented DNN is verified in Caffe/TensorFlow and tested for ten images from a trained data set (trained.caffemodel) and a DNN architecture file (deploy.prototxt). The complete network is then rebuild in C++ using a python script from the parameters extracted from deploy.prototxt file. The SW emulation of written HLS code is tested in this C++ network. Each layer testing can also be done using the C++ layer data. In this work, the reported results are on Vivado SDx with all layers in HW.

Table 1. Resource consumption of each function in Vivado HLS.

	FFs	LUTs	DSPs	BRAMs	URAM
Stream_in x1	14555	38191	128	0	0
Stream_wgt	13682	38191	38	0	512
Mac tree/Convo_0 x512	609/1571	105/1971	9/11	0/5	0
Stream_adder 0 x4	1610	5465	1	0	0
Stream_out x4	346	917	2	2	0
Stream_out_pool_fused x4	1231	2741	0	16	0
Layer_128ic_64oc	896837	1249546	5845	2648	512
Kernel_7_layer (first layer)	107284	91492	648	280	0
CNN (top)	1018689 (29%)	1350874 (78%)	6501 (52%)	2945 (54%)	704 (55%)
Total on Alveo u250	3456000	1728000	12288	5376(18 Kb)	1280

4 Results

The design has been implemented with Xilinx SDx 2019.1 on Xilinx Alveo u250 board. We present the results of SqueezeNet tested on Alveo u250. Table 3 shows the FPGA execution time for all layers executed in HW. The total number of MAC operations in SqueezeNet is 861.34 M [16] and the total convolution operations comprising of MACs result in 861.34 * 2=1722.68 M. The total comparators are 9.67 M and the additions in other layers are 226 K. This yields to total operations as 1732.546 MFLOPs. For calculating the GFLOPS, we first calculate the total number of operations in network and then divide this by the execution time 1732.546/0.043 = 40.291 GFLOPS.

Four processing units use 5845 DSP, out of which 5333 can be active at any time with kernel size 3 is running. Int16 takes one DSP slice hence the peak performance achieved is $5333 \times 200 \times 10^6 = 1066.6$ GFLOPS. Similarly, when kernel size 1, peak performance is $128 \times 4 \times 200 \times 10^6 = 102$ GFLOPS. The layer 1 has kernel size 7 and is designed separately for achieving better performance. The same dataflow model architecture has been used with a configuration of three input channels and 24 output channels. Similarly, when kernel size 7 is running, peak performance is $648 \times 200 \times 10^6 = 129$ GFLOPS.

The verification results from the execution on Vivado SDx [17] shows top-1 accuracy for the SqueezeNet reported in Caffe framework as 57.5%. Our framework shows an additional loss of 1.2% due to the quantization process applied and int16 used as the base data type.

Table 3. Comparison of HW and SW based on SqueezeNet

Platform	Type	Latency (sec)	FPS
Caffe CPU	Intel i7-6700 K	0.1701	5
FPGA	Alveo u250	0.043	23

5   Conclusion

In this work we have successfully tested SqueezeNet in our framework with a frequency of 200 MHz. We have achieved a frame rate of 23 frames/second. The accelerator and the verification setup have been generated using python scripts which allow user the configurability and scalability of input and output channels with kernel size of 3 or 1.

Acknowledgments. This work is funded by the National Science Foundation's Major Research Instrumentation program, grant #1725729. We thank Yuan Ma for his help in setting up the simulation using Caffe and Tanitpong Lawphongpanich for his contribution with TensorFlow testing.

References

1. Krizhevsky, A., Sutskever, I., Hinton, G.E.: ImageNet classification with deep convolutional neural networks. In: Advances in Neural Information Processing Systems, pp. 1097–1105 (2012)
2. Russakovsky, O., et al.: ImageNet large scale visual recognition challenge. Int. J. Comput. Vision **115**(3), 211–252 (2015)
3. Graves, A., Mohamed, A.-R., Hinton, G.: Speech recognition with deep recurrent neural networks. In: 2013 IEEE International Conference on Acoustics, Speech and Signal Processing (ICASSP), pp. 6645–6649. IEEE (2013)
4. Abdel-Hamid, O., Mohamed, A.-R., Jiang, H., Deng, L., Penn, G., Yu, D.: Convolutional neural networks for speech recognition. IEEE/ACM Trans. Audio Speech Lang. Process. **22**(10), 1533–1545 (2014)
5. Sankaradas, M., et al: A massively parallel coprocessor for convolutional neural networks. In: 20th IEEE International Conference on Application-Specific Systems, Architectures and Processors, ASAP 2009, pp. 53–60. IEEE (2009)
6. Zhang, C., Li, P., Sun, G., Guan, Y., Xiao, B., Cong, J.: Optimizing FPGA-based accelerator design for deep convolutional neural networks. In: Proceedings of the 2015 ACM/SIGDA International Symposium on Field-Programmable Gate Arrays, pp. 161–170. ACM (2015)
7. Ovtcharov, K., Ruwase, O., Kim, J.-Y., Fowers, J., Strauss, K., Chung, E.S.: Accelerating deep convolutional neural networks using specialized hardware. Microsoft Research Whitepaper **2**(11), 1–4 (2015)
8. Guan, Y., et al.: FP-DNN: an automated framework for mapping deep neural networks onto FPGAs with RTL-HLS hybrid templates. In: 2017 IEEE 25th Annual International Symposium on Field-Programmable Custom Computing Machines (FCCM), pp. 152–159. IEEE (2017)

9. Shawahna, A., Sait, S.M., El-Maleh, A.: FPGA-based accelerators of deep learning networks for learning and classification: a review. IEEE Access **7**, 7823–7859 (2018)
10. Qiu, J., et al.: Going deeper with embedded FPGA platform for convolutional neural network. In: Proceedings of the 2016 ACM/SIGDA International Symposium on Field-Programmable Gate Arrays, pp. 26–35. ACM (2016)
11. Zhang, J., Li, J.: Improving the performance of OpenCL-based FPGA accelerator for convolutional neural network. In: Proceedings of the 2017 ACM/SIGDA International Symposium on Field-Programmable Gate Arrays, pp. 25–34. ACM (2017)
12. Suda, N., et al: Throughput-optimized OpenCL-based FPGA accelerator for large-scale convolutional neural networks. In: Proceedings of the 2016 ACM/SIGDA International Symposium on Field-Programmable Gate Arrays, pp. 16–25. ACM (2016)
13. Han, S., Mao, H., Dally, W.J.: Deep compression: compressing deep neural networks with pruning, trained quantization and huffman coding. arXiv preprint arXiv:1510.00149 (2015)
14. https://www.xilinx.com/products/acceleration-solutions/xilinx-machine-learning-suite.html. Accessed 21 Aug 2019
15. Aydonat, U., O'Connell, S., Capalija, D., Ling, A.C., Chiu, G.R.: An OpenCL^{TM} deep learning accelerator on arria 10. In: Proceedings of the 2017 ACM/SIGDA International Symposium on Field-Programmable Gate Arrays, pp. 55–64. ACM (2017)
16. https://dgschwend.github.io/netscope/#/preset/squeezenet. Accessed 21 Aug 2019
17. https://www.xilinx.com/support/documentation/sw_manuals/xilinx2017_4/ug1027-sdsoc-user-guide.pdf. Accessed 21 Aug 2019

FPGA-Based Computational Fluid Dynamics Simulation Architecture via High-Level Synthesis Design Method

Changdao Du$^{(\boxtimes)}$, Iman Firmansyah, and Yoshiki Yamaguchi

University of Tsukuba, Tsukuba, Ibaraki 305-8577, Japan
duchangdao@hpcs.cs.tsukuba.ac.jp

Abstract. Today's High-Performance Computing (HPC) systems often use GPUs as dedicated hardware accelerators to meet the computation requirements of applications such as neural networks, genetic decoding, and hydrodynamic simulations. Meanwhile, FPGAs have also been considered as alternative suitable hardware accelerators due to their advancing computational capabilities and low power consumption. Moreover, the developments of High-Level Synthesis (HLS) allow users to generate FPGA designs directly from mainstream languages, e.g., C, C++, and OpenCL. However, writing efficient high-level programs with good performance is still a time-consuming task, and the lack of knowledge about FPGA architecture can lead to poor scalability and portability. In this paper, we propose an architecture design for Computational Fluid Dynamics (CFD) simulations based on the HLS method. Our design can adjust the performance by utilizing the parallelism inside both temporal and spatial domains of CFD simulations. We also discuss the data reuse buffer optimization choices while considering the potability of HLS codes. A performance model is introduced to guide the design space exploration under the constraints of available resources on FPGA. We evaluate our design via a Xilinx VCU1525 FPGA board and compare the results with other state-of-the-art studies. Experiment results show that VCU1525 can achieve 629.6 GFLOP/s in D2Q9 LBM-BGK model and the design and optimization methods can be used for developing various CFD applications.

Keywords: HPC · FPGA · HLS · CFD

1 Introduction

Recently, the heterogeneous High-Performance Computing (HPC) systems have received growing attention from both academic and industrial fields. In addition to standard CPUs, these computing systems use dedicated accelerators to improve the computing capabilities to meet the needs of high-performance applications. Among these hardware devices, GPUs have been proven to be the most popular accelerators in the last decade due to their parallel architecture and

© Springer Nature Switzerland AG 2020
F. Rincón et al. (Eds.): ARC 2020, LNCS 12083, pp. 232–246, 2020.
https://doi.org/10.1007/978-3-030-44534-8_18

high memory bandwidth [1,2]. However, not all applications can fully utilize the advantage of these features. The high memory bandwidth of GPUs is based on the wide memory bus which requires the coalesced memory access patterns. This often places restrictions on the data layout of applications. Meanwhile, branch instructions also have a significant impact on the performance of unified GPU cores.

On the other hand, many recent studies have shown that FPGAs can provide GPU-like computing capabilities and are superior in power efficiency, making FPGAs a strong competitor in the HPC field as hardware accelerators [3,4]. However, the traditional hardware-oriented FPGA development environment has discouraged mainstream users in the HPC field. To solve this problem, a bunch of research is devoted to improving the usability of FPGA development approach [5,6]. High-Level Synthesis (HLS) tools can generate hardware designs directly from popular high-level languages such as C, C++, and OpenCL that enables designers to focus on describing the behavior of architectural questions rather than specific hardware operations.

However, porting software-based code to HLS tools often fails to achieve the expected performance on FPGAs. This is mainly due to the following reasons. These high-level languages were originally designed for developing programs on CPUs, rather than describing the hardware structure. Using these software-based languages to develop hardware makes traditional software development techniques inapplicable. In addition, designing efficient FPGA structures requires the flexible use of special hardware components, e.g., shift-registers, FIFOs, and block memories, which were not initially supported by software-based languages. Finally, due to the flexibility of FPGAs, it allows developers to explore large design spaces with various choices of HLS optimizations strategies. Choosing the suitable combinations of these strategies remains a time-consuming task.

Computational Fluid Dynamics (CFD) predicts and analyzes fluid flows by numerically solving the conservation equations of fluid motion. CFD simulations have been widely adopted in many scientific and engineering fields. In this paper, we propose an HLS-based design for implementing CFD simulations on FPGA, and choose a typical CFD method, the Lattice Boltzmann Method (LBM), to illustrate our design. The main contributions of this work are as follows:

- Our proposed design can exploit parallelism of CFD simulations in both spatial and temporal domains. The exploration of design space can be characterized by two main design parameters s_{unroll} (spatial domain) and t_{unroll} (temporal domain). We can easily adjust these two parameters based on the target FPGA hardware resources to expand simulation performance.
- We present a FIFOs and registers based data reuse buffer structure with the consideration of portability between different HLS compilers.
- A performance model is devised to guide the design parameters tuning under the target FPGA resource constraints.
- We evaluate our framework on a VCU1525 FPGA board with the Xilinx HLS programming environment.

2   Background

2.1   Lattice Boltzmann Method

Lattice Boltzmann Method (LBM) is a typical CFD method which uses to simulate complex fluid flows [7]. The process of LBM is founded on solving the Boltzmann transport equation.

$$\frac{\partial f}{\partial t} + \vec{u} \cdot \nabla f = \Omega \tag{1}$$

where $f(\vec{x}, t)$ is the distribution function, which means the expected value of finding a particle in position $\vec{x}$ at time t. $\vec{u}$ represents the particle velocity and Ω is the collision operator. LBM simplifies Eq. 1 by restricting particles into a multi-dimensional lattice grid. The particle movement is discretized into two main stages, i.e., collision and propagation. Figure 1 shows a two-dimensional LBM model (D2Q9) which means the particles inside one lattice can move along 9 possible directions. These 9 velocity vectors are described as

$$\vec{e_i} = \begin{cases} (0,0) & i = 0 \\ (1,0), (-1,0), (0,1), (0,-1) & i = 1,2,3,4 \\ (1,1), (-1,1), (-1,-1), (1,-1) & i = 5,6,7,8 \end{cases} \tag{2}$$

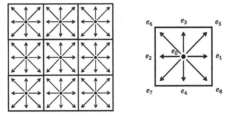

Fig. 1. An example for LBM grid.

The simulation process of LBM is defined as

$$f_i(\vec{x} + \vec{e}\,\Delta t, t + \Delta t) - f_i(\vec{x}, t) = \frac{f_i^{eq}(\vec{x}, t) - f_i(\vec{x}, t)}{\tau} \tag{3}$$

where the left hand of the equation represents the propagation stage and right is the collision stage. τ is the time relaxation factor calculated from the fluid viscosity. The collision model is govern by the equilibrium distribution function f_i^{eq}, which can be solved by

$$f_i^{eq}(\vec{x}, t) = \omega_i \rho + \rho s_i(\vec{u}(\vec{x}, t)) \tag{4}$$

where

$$s_i(\vec{u}) = \omega_i \left[3\frac{\vec{e} \cdot \vec{u}}{c} + \frac{9}{2}\frac{(\vec{e} \cdot \vec{u})^2}{c^2} - \frac{3}{2}\frac{\vec{u} \cdot \vec{u}}{c^2} \right] \tag{5}$$

$$\rho(\vec{x},t) = \sum_{i=0}^{8} f_i(\vec{x},t), \vec{u}(\vec{x},t) = \frac{1}{\rho}\sum_{i=0}^{8} cf_i\vec{e_i} \tag{6}$$

c is the lattice speed $\frac{\Delta x}{\Delta t}$, and the constant ω_i are 4/9 for rest particles ($i = 0$), 1/9 for $i = 1, 2, 3, 4$ and 1/36 for $i = 5, 6, 7, 8$. We can summarize the implementation algorithm of LBM as follows

---

Algorithm 1. Lattice Boltzmann Method

1: Initialization LBM distribution function f_i
2: **for** time $t = 0$; $t < T_{end}$; $t = t + \Delta t$ **do**
3:     **for** every lattice $\vec{x}$ in the simulation grid **do**
4:         Calculate density ρ and velocity vector $\vec{u}$ (Eq. 6)
5:         **for** every possible direction $\vec{e_i}$ **do**
6:             Calculate the equilibrium function f_i^{eq} (Eq. 4 and Eq. 5)
7:             Calculate the new distribution $f_i^{new} = \frac{1}{\tau}(f_i^{eq} - f_i) + f_i$ (Eq. 3)
8:             Update the particle $f_i(\vec{x} + \vec{e}\Delta t, t + \Delta t) = f_i^{new}$
9:         **end for**
10:    **end for**
11: **end for**

2.2   Related Works

Many studies have been focused on implementing LBM in various computing platforms. Works in [8–10] relied on CPUs to achieve high performance at that time. [8] first proposed a parallel LBM algorithm. Later studies [9] and [10] improved the algorithm mainly from the aspects of cache usage, loop rearrangement, and memory consumption.

Nevertheless, due to the high parallel architecture and float-point performance of GPUs, studies have found that GPU-based implementations are able to provide one order of magnitude better performance [11–13] than general CPUs. However, since LBM is heavily data intensive, their peak performance is often bounded by the external memory bandwidth. Although GPUs have relatively high bandwidth, the data movement in the collision and propagation stages causes a large amount of non-coalesced memory accesses, which hurts the bandwidth performance. [11] proposes a memory layout called Structure of Arrays (SOA) that store discrete velocity data into separate arrays based on the direction to increase data coalescence. [12] improves the previously mentioned strategies by utilizing the shared memory and they observed that performing non-coalesced read operations are faster than write operations. Other optimizations are described in [13]. The authors reduce the non-coalesced data accesses while improving data locality through tiling, and the branch optimizations are also discussed.

Currently, few researchers focused on implementing LBM directly on FPGA, especially using the HLS method. [14] builds a FPGA-based HPC platform called Maxwell and evaluated the performance of the platform with LBM simulation. They tend to use LBM as a performance benchmark, hence, did not discuss the optimization strategies in detail to efficiently utilize the characteristics of LBM. A comprehensive and recent study of LBM simulations is shown in [15]. The authors proposed an optimized implementation of FPGA-based LBM simulation. Their design takes advantage of both spatial and temporal parallelism inside LBM to exploit the FPGA pipeline architecture. The streaming computing they use also helps FPGA overcome the bandwidth bottleneck. However, Their development method was based on their domain-specific language which still used explicit pipeline delays and clock-cycles to synchronize the computing blocks. These low-level hardware description features prevent the way to generalize the design to other similar applications.

3   Implementation

In this section, we first introduce the optimization strategies for parallel processing LBM simulation. Then, we discuss the data reuse buffer design method. Finally, we present the simulation architecture overview.

3.1   Parallelization

Regardless of the type of computing platform, the key to achieving high performance in LBM simulation is to use the parallelism of LBM. Algorithm 1 consists of two main loops. The inner loop traverses all the lattices in the simulation area. In LBM, spatial parallelism can be exploited by unrolling this inner loop, i.e., processing multiple lattices in parallel at the same time step. The number of lattices processed in parallel is equal to the spatial unroll parameter.

Since there is no data dependency for parallel processing lattices at the same time step, the method based on spatial parallelism is an intuitive way to improve the LBM performance. However, this method requires parallel access to multiple data, and the target simulation area is often too large to fit in the high-speed on-chip memory. Therefore, the external memory bandwidth of the computing platform is evidently the performance bottleneck. The GPU-based implementations can achieve high performance through spatial parallelism due to their large number of unified thread processors and extremely high external memory bandwidth.

On the other hand, applying spatial parallelism method on FPGA can not fully utilize the features of FPGA architecture. Compared to GPUs, FPGAs typically have lower external memory bandwidth. Instead of the number of thread processors, the parallelism of FPGA usually comes from the complexity of the pipeline structure. These features however allow FPGAs to take advantage of another type of parallelism inside LBM, namely temporal parallelism. Temporal parallelism can scale performance with the same bandwidth requirement. The outer loop in Algorithm 1 traverses 0 to the end of LBM simulation time. Temporal parallelism can be exploited by unrolling the outer loop, i.e., computing multiple time steps simultaneously. However, to complete the propagation stage of LBM, a lattice needs data from its surrounding lattices, which can cause a data dependency or loop-carried dependency issue when computing lattices across different time steps. We can overcome this problem by utilizing FPGA on-chip memory resource. FPGAs have a large amount of on-chip memory resources that can be configured in various structures. This flexibility allows developers to construct application-specific buffer structures to avoid data dependencies. Figure 2 shows a detailed example to illustrate the idea.

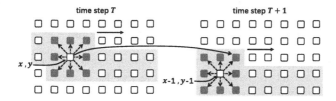

Fig. 2. Cyclic buffers for two sequential time steps

At time T, we need to access data from 8 neighbors of lattice (x, y) during the propagation stage. Therefore, we store these 9 lattices data (including lattice (x, y) itself) into an on-chip buffer. Since there exist strong opportunities for data reuse when performing LBM simulation in consecutive order, we can also store more relevant lattices data into this buffer to reduce redundant external memory accesses. For example, suppose we cache all lattices in the dark area (Fig. 2), and then propagating lattice $(x+1, y)$ only needs to load one new lattice $(x+2, y+1)$ from the external memory. After finishing the entire simulation of lattice (x, y) at time T, the result can be sent to a replicated buffer structure which is responsible for processing simulation at time $T+1$. As a result, simulations of lattice $(x+1, y)$ at time T and lattice $(x-1, y-1)$ at time $T+1$ are able to be computed in parallel.

This is a well-known buffer design (also known as *sliding window buffer*) and commonly used to construct a deep pipelined architecture on FPGAs. The reuse buffer design has a significant impact on the performance of the LBM simulation. We will describe the detailed design of our reuse buffer in the next part of this section.

3.2 Data Reuse Buffer Design Analysis

Previous studies have mainly discussed how to use similar data reuse buffer structure on FPGAs for exploiting temporal parallelism in stencil-like applications with HLS method [16,17]. They choose to abstract the aforementioned reuse buffer as a shift-register based behaviour, that is, every time it shifts the fresh data into the head of the shift-register and evicts the used data from the shift-register's tail, and the computing data are directly accessed from the middle points of shift-register.

However, their shift-register based structure can only work well with the Intel HLS environment. The reasons are as follows:

- The high-level shift-register behaviour description is generally synthesised to a register-transfer-level or low-level implementation through the shift-register IP core. Intel shift-register IP core [18] provide a support for accessing multiple data (called taps) at certain points of shift-registers, which other shift-register IPs (e.g., Xilinx [19]) often do not have.
- "stall-free" mechanism. The large arrays declared by high-level languages are often realized using the block-ram (BRAM) resources. Since BRAMs have limited memory ports, parallel accessing data from BRAMs may cause stall operations. Intel HLS compiler will automatically solve this problem by using techniques e.g., double pumping or memory replication.

These features of Intel HLS compiler allow users to use a more abstract description of memory structure without considering the detail architecture and topological properties, which increases the design productivity. However, these features also make their designs more dependent on a particular compiler. Furthermore, for applications with complex memory access patterns, the compiler will use redundant resources to make sure the "stall-free" memory accesses.

Another thing that deserves our attention is the support for exploiting spatial parallelism. LBM simulations are memory-bound applications, scaling up performance with spacial parallelism will increase bandwidth requirements. However, in the aspect of resource consumption, especially memory resources, employing spacial parallelism shows more optimization opportunities. Increasing the degree of temporal parallelism needs to add replicated reuse buffers and simulation computing blocks. For spatial parallelism, these components can consume fewer hardware resources due to reuse or sharing some resources.

Our proposed design explicitly describes the data reuse buffer structure by using memory resources e.g., FIFOs and registers with the consideration of portability. Moreover, our reuse buffer structure also can support scalable spacial parallelism with optimal buffer size and "stall-free" memory accesses. Figure 3 shows the basic design with spatial parallelism s_{unroll} equal to 1. For processing simulation on lattice M_1, the data movement is described as follows. the U_2 register reads 1 fresh lattice data from the external memory or previous data reuse buffer at each time step. Registers U_1 and U_0 reuse data in U_1 and U_2. Data of register M_2 are popped from $FIFO_{up}$. Registers M_1 and M_0 reuse data in M_2 and M_1 respectively. Register D_2 reads data from $FIFO_{down}$. D_1 and D_0 reuse data in D_2 and D_1. After the simulation processing, U_0 and M_0 are pushed into $FIFO_{up}$ and $FIFO_{down}$ respectively. Result of M_1 is sent to the next reuse buffer or the external memory.

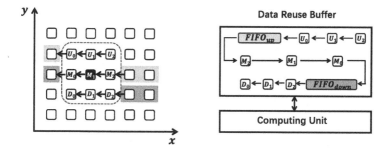

Fig. 3. Reuse buffer design with FIFOs and registers.

Figure 4 shows the extended reuse buffer design with spatial parallelism $s_{unroll} = 4$, i.e., 4 lattices belong to the same time step are simulated in parallel. To achieve memory accesses without the stall, we re-construct the basic reuse buffer to provide 4 times higher internal bandwidth. In this specific case, we build this data reuse buffer with 4 pair FIFOs and 18 register blocks. It works as follows:

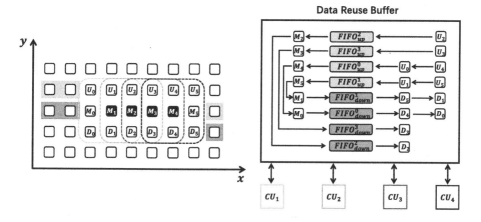

Fig. 4. Example of a scalable reuse buffer design with $s_{unroll} = 4$.

1. At each time step, the up floor registers U_2 to U_5 read 4 consecutive fresh lattices from the external memory or previous layer. U_0 reuses data in U_4, U_1 reuses data in U_5;
2. Registers M_2, M_3, M_4, M_5 are popped from $FIFO_{up}^2$, $FIFO_{up}^3$, $FIFO_{up}^0$, $FIFO_{up}^1$ respectively. M_0 and M_1 reuse data in M_4 and M_5;
3. Down floor registers D_2 to D_5 are popped from $FIFO_{down}^2$, $FIFO_{down}^3$, $FIFO_{down}^0$, $FIFO_{down}^1$. D_0 and D_1 reuse data in D_4 and D_5;
4. After finishing simulations, U_0, U_1, U_2, U_3 are pushed into $FIFO_{up}^0$ to $FIFO_{up}^3$ respectively. Similarly, M_0 to M_3 are pushed into $FIFO_{down}^0$ to $FIFO_{down}^3$.

5. Simulation results of lattices M_1 to M_4 are sent to the next layer or to the external memory.

This reuse buffer structure can be easily generalized to other values of spatial parallelism s_{unroll}. Registers are the key to make sure the memory accesses without stalls. The number of registers depends on the LBM simulation model window and the level of spatial parallelism. It can be defined as

$$n_{reg} = s_{unroll} \times N_{window} - (s_{unroll} - 1) \times O_{neighbor} \qquad (7)$$

where N_{window} represents the number of lattices in one simulation window, which is equal to 9 for D2Q9 LBM model. $O_{neighbor}$ denotes the number of lattices inside the overlap area of 2 consecutive simulation windows, in this case, equal to 6. FIFOs are main storage components which are responsible for moving data around registers. The number of FIFOs have linear relationship with the value of s_{unroll} and the "height" of simulation window. It is defined as

$$n_{FIFO} = s_{unroll} \times H_{window} \qquad (8)$$

where H_{window} is the measurement of target LBM window from base to top. In LBM D2Q9 model, the H_{window} is equal to 2.

The most benefits of employing this spatial parallelism method is the memory resources cost of the reuse buffer. In Fig. 3, we store $2M + 3$ lattices data into the basic reuse buffer structure to perform LBM simulation on 1 lattice at each time step. On the other side, Fig. 4 shows we can cache $2M + 6$ lattices into the extended buffer structure to simulate 4 lattices at each time step. In case we only exploit temporal parallelism, the total memory cost for parallel computing 1 lattice in 4 different time steps will be $4 \times (2M + 3)$. Therefore, for a specific LBM simulation and a certain FPGA, we need to scale up the degree of parallelism in both spacial and temporal domain to achieve the expected performance.

3.3 Simulation Architecture Design

Our simulation architecture is mainly composed of multiple Processing Elements (PEs), as shown in Fig. 5. One PE is responsible for processing the LBM simulation at one time step. LBM spatial parallelism is exploited inside the PE. All PEs use the replicated structure for a certain simulation. The inputs of a PE can come directly from the previous PE or external memory, and similarly, the outputs can go to the next PE or external memory. PEs are cascaded together to form a deep-pipeline architecture, which utilizes temporal parallelism of LBM.

The structure of a PE comprises two main parts-i.e., the aforementioned data reuse buffer and Computation Units (CUs). The number of CUs is equal to the degree of spatial parallelism s_{unroll}. A CU performs the collision and propagation operations on a lattice by accessing data from the reuse buffer. Our CU is implemented with the one-step algorithm that fuses the separate collision and propagation stages [20]. For the target lattice, collision can be computed by

---

Algorithm 2. Computing Unit with Pull Scheme

1: $e[9][2] \leftarrow \vec{e}, \; w[9] \leftarrow \omega_i$
2: **for** i in range $(0, 9)$ **do**
3:     $\rho+ = f[i]$
4: **end for**
5: $ux = (f[1] + f[5] + f[8] - (f[3] + f[6] + f[7]))/\rho$
6: $uy = (f[2] + f[5] + f[6] - (f[4] + f[7] + f[8]))/\rho$
7: **for** i in range $(0, 9)$ **do**
8:     $cu = e[i][0] \cdot ux + e[i][1] \cdot uy$
9:     $f_{eq} = w[i] \cdot \rho \cdot (1 + 3 \cdot cu + cu^2 - 1.5 \cdot (ux^2) + uy)^2$
10:    $f^{new} = f[i] \cdot (1 - \frac{1}{\tau}) + \frac{f_{eq}}{\tau}$
11: **end for**

---

directly using its neighboring lattice instead of its own particles (*pull scheme*), thereby avoiding extra propagation.

To implement the simulation architecture with HLS, PE can be defined as a function, and the link between PEs can be declared as the FIFO interface (Fig. 5). We use the Ping-Pong FIFO structure to connect PEs. The scheduling system is divided into two cases, namely even and odd. In an even case, each PE reads data from the "Ping" FIFO and produces results to the "Pong" FIFO. Similar to the even case, each PE reads data from the "Pong" FIFO and writes to the "Ping" FIFO in the odd case. The "Ping-Pong" FIFO connection enables our simulation architecture to run in full pipeline. Since "Ping-Pong" FIFO is a well-known technique, several HLS compilers have made special optimizations for implementing this structure. For example, in the Xilinx HLS environment, if users can follow the target program pattern and meet certain specific conditions, the compiler will automatically generate the corresponding "Ping-Pong" FIFO structure (e.g., *pragma* dataflow in Vivado HLS). However, as mentioned earlier, some compiler-relevant optimizations can improve productivity, but at the expense of portability.

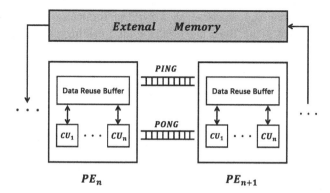

Fig. 5. Overview of the LBM simulation architecture.

3.4   Performance Model

To achieve the maximum performance of LBM simulation on a target FPGA board, we focus on adjusting two design parameters: s_{unroll} and t_{unroll} to represent the level of spatial and temporal parallelism respectively. We introduce this performance model to search an optimal combination of s_{unroll} and t_{unroll} that can make full use of the various resources on the FPGA board. For performing a D2Q9 LBM simulation on a $N \times M$ area with T_{step} time steps, the total number of lattices $S_{lattice}$ to be simulated is

$$S_{lattice} = T_{step} \cdot (N \times M) \tag{9}$$

Since our design scale performance with both types of parallelism, the total degree of simulation parallelism is calculated as:

$$p_{total} = s_{unroll} \times t_{unroll} \tag{10}$$

$$s_{unroll} = \frac{n_{CU}}{n_{PE}}, \; t_{unroll} = n_{PE} \tag{11}$$

where s_{unroll} is equal to the number of CUs inside one PE, and the LBM temporal parallelism is implemented by n_{PE} PEs. For a fully pipelined architecture, the peak performance of our design is:

$$P_{peak} = p_{total} \times f_{design} \tag{12}$$

where P_{peak} is the architecture peak throughput and f_{design} is the design running frequency. Then, the whole simulation time is:

$$t_{LBM} = \frac{S_{lattice}}{P_{peak}} + t_{init} \tag{13}$$

$$t_{init} = n_{PE} \times \left(\frac{C_{PE}}{f_{design}} \right) \tag{14}$$

where t_{init} means the pipeline structure initialization cost which can be measured with the time between the pipeline takes the first input and produces the first result. C_{PE} represents the total clock cycles for finishing one computation in one PE.

For a target FPGA board, the choices of these two parameters are limited by:

$$R_{design} + R_{platform} \leq R_{max} \tag{15}$$

$$R_{design} = n_{PE} \cdot \left(R_{buffer} + \frac{n_{CU}}{n_{PE}} \cdot R_{CU} \right) \tag{16}$$

$$f_{design} \times s_{unroll} \times W_{LBM} \leq \frac{B_{peak}}{2} \tag{17}$$

where R_{max} is the maximum value of different resources on an FPGA. R_{design} is the resource consumption of our architecture design. $R_{platform}$ means the computing platform resources consumed by, e.g., SDRAM controller and PCIe IP cores. Most of the resources in our design are consumed by the PEs. Inside one PE, the computing resources are used by the CUs and the memory resources are used by the data reuse buffer. The peak performance of the SDRAM bandwidth (B_{peak}) sets a limit on parameter s_{unroll}. W_{LBM} is the data-width of LBM lattice structure.

4 Results

4.1 Experimental Setup

We evaluate the LBM simulation results with Xilinx UltraScale VCU1525 board. However, we **do not** use the entire FPGA hardware resources to perform the experiment. The target FPGA chip uses Super Logic Regions (SLRs) to support the large resource capacity, e.g., 3 SLRs for the XCVU9P chip. We map our architecture design to 1 SLR which is connected with 2 DDR4 memory banks. Although we can span our design to other dies, the performance bottleneck will be mainly limited by the inter-SLR connections, which is out of the scope of this paper. Our HLS development environment is based on Xilinx SDAccel 2018.3. It allows FPGA kernel to be described as high-level languages e.g., C, C++, SystemC or OpenCL. For the experiments, we choose the D2Q9 LBM-BGK model and bounce-back boundary rule [7].

4.2 FPGA Performance

According to the performance model in Sect. 3.4, we mainly rely on two design parameters (s_{unroll} and t_{unroll}) to adjust the LBM simulation performance on FPGA. Since the LBM simulation is a memory-bound application. The spatial design parameter s_{unroll} is easily constrained by the external bandwidth. In this case, the 2 DDR4-2400 memory banks can provide 2×19.2 GB/s memory bandwidth. One lattice cell contains 9 particle vectors, i.e., takes 4×9 Bytes for single precision. Assuming our FPGA is running at 250 MHz, the maximum value of s_{unroll} is 2 without memory stalls ($2 \times 250 \times 36 = 18$ GB/s ≤ 19.2 GB/s).

The design parameter t_{unroll} is determined by the resource consumption of PEs. BRAMs are the key resource for implementing the reuse buffer. For the target simulation area (1024×2048), one reuse buffer costs 56 BRAMs, which limits the number of reuse buffers to $4320/(3 \times 56) = 25$. The cost of DSPs sets a limit on the number of CUs (n_{CU}). In this benchmark, one CU needs to consume 103 DSPs. Thus, the maximum n_{CU} is $6840/(3 \times 103) = 22$. If we allocate one CU (at least) and one reuse buffer to one PE, the maximum value of n_{PE} (t_{unroll}) is 22.

Table 1 shows the LBM simulation performance with different combinations of s_{unroll} and t_{unroll} under the constraint of the target FPGA hardware resources. We can achieve the top performance when p_{total} is equal to 20. In this benchmark, the p_{total} can be implemented with two configurations-i.e., 20 PEs,

Table 1. D2Q9 LBM simulation with 1 SLR of the VCU1525 FPGA

P_{total} ($s_{unroll} \times t_{unroll}$)	Performance (MLUP|GFLOP/s)	Frequency (Mhz)	BRAMs	DSPs	LUTs	FFs
(1×8)	2030|259.8	267	31%	36%	25%	13%
(1×16)	3911|500.6	264	63%	72%	53%	25%
(1×20)	4791|613.2	243	78%	90%	68%	31%
(1×22)	4024|515.1	Failed or very low	86%	99%	77%	35%
(2×8)	4071|521.0	268	33%	36%	25%	13%
(2×10)	4919|629.6	255	41%	88%	62%	32%

each PE has 1 CU or 10 PEs, each PE has 2 CUs. Both configurations provide almost the same performance (about 600 GFLOP/s). However, the configuration with spatial parallelism ($s_{unroll} = 2$) shows better results in terms of resource consumption, especially from the BRAMs usage (41% compare to 78%). As a result, this configuration is able to support a larger simulation area or more complex LBM models without considering tilling strategies.

Besides of hardware resources like BRAMs, DSPs, FFs, and LUTs, our design is also bounded by the routing resources inside FPGA. Unlike fixed architecture (e.g., CPUs or GPUs), the implementation of FPGA designs relies on the routing resources to connect hardware components. For congestion implementations, wires can be detoured, which will downscale the design frequency or even terminate the placement and routing (P&R) process. In our case, the theoretical peak performance is achieved by the configuration of (1×22). However, this configuration generates a large congestion area. As a consequence, the design frequency is either very low or failed at P&R stage. Compare with design (1×20), the design (1×22) uses more hardware resources but achieves sub-optimal performance. In fact, through some HLS optimization methods, the congestion area can be reduced. We leave it to future work to examine these possibilities.

4.3 Performance Comparison

The authors implement LBM simulations on a NVIDIA GTX TITAN (Kepler architecture) in [21]. For D2Q9 model, their performance can reach to 1060 MLUPS in double precision (DP). Although GTX TITAN has higher external memory bandwidth (288.3 GB/s) and FP computing capabilities (4.5 TFLOP), the following reasons prevent LBM simulations from making full use of them: (1) LBM propagation and collision processes have different memory access patterns, which makes it difficult to achieve coalesced memory access during the entire simulation process; (2) unlike conventional lattice cells, the lattice cells in the boundary region have different simulation rules, which causes branch divergences and eventually lead to performance degradation. In addition to use DP data type to increase the simulation accuracy, FPGAs support the arbitrary precision data type, which offers a trade-off opportunity for increasing the simulation accuracy by adopting a more complex LBM model (e.g., D2Q17, D2Q39) with less precision type.

In [15], the authors present an FPGA-based design with an Intel Arria 10 FPGA. They achieve 519.3 GFLOP/s in D2Q9 LBM simulation which is 97.9% of their FPGA board peak performance. Design implementations are based on their own domain-specific language, which requires specific clock-cycles to synchronize computing functions. For different LBM applications, they need to carefully rearrange the scheduling system. On the other hand, our work uses a popular C-based commercial HLS tool. For applications with different LBM models, we only need to make a few changes to the core code, such as the collision rules and boundary conditions.

5 Conclusion

In this work, we present a design and implementation for fluid dynamics simulations on FPGA using the HLS development method. Our design can adjust the simulation performance under the resource constraints of the target FPGA board with two design parameters s_{unroll} and t_{unroll} that utilize both spatial and temporal parallelism of simulations. We specifically discuss the design of data reuse buffers that considers the portability of HLS code. The evaluation results show that using one SLR on the VCU1525 board can achieve 4919 MLUPS or 629.6 GFLOP/s in LBM D2Q9 simulation. Our future work mainly focuses on design automation and routing-aware HLS design optimizations. In addition, applying our design to FPGA clusters is another interesting topic.

Acknowledgments. This work was supported in part by MEXT as Next Generation High-Performance Computing Infrastructures and Applications R&D Program (Development of Computing-Communication Unified Supercomputer in Next Generation), and by JSPS KAKENHI Grant Number JP17H01707 and JP18H03246. The authors would also like to thank Xilinx Inc., for providing FPGA software tools by Xilinx University Program.

References

1. Valero-Lara, P., Pinelli, A., Prieto-Matias, M.: Fast finite difference poisson solvers on heterogeneous architectures. Comput. Phys. Commun. **185**(4), 1265–1272 (2014)
2. Feichtinger, C., et al.: Performance modeling and analysis of heterogeneous lattice Boltzmann simulations on CPUGPU clusters. Parallel Comput. **46**, 1–13 (2015)
3. Sano, K., Hatsuda, Y., Yamamoto, S.: Multi-FPGA accelerator for scalable stencil computation with constant memory-bandwidth. IEEE Trans. Parallel Distrib. Syst. **25**(3), 695–705 (2014)
4. Lewis, D., et al.: The stratix 10 highly pipelined FPGA architecture. In: International Symposium on Field-Programmable Gate Arrays (FPGA), pp. 159–168. ACM (2016)
5. Cong, J., Liu, B., Neuendorffer, S., et al.: High-level synthesis for FPGAs: from prototyping to deployment. IEEE Trans. Comput.-Aided Des. Integr. Circuits Syst. **30**(4), 473–491 (2011)

6. Canis, A., et al.: LegUp: high-level synthesis for FPGA-based processor/accelerator systems. In: The 19th ACM/SIGDA International Symposium on Field Programmable Gate Arrays (FPGA), pp. 33–36. ACM (2011)

7. Chen, S., Doolen, G.D.: Lattice Boltzmann method for fluid flows. Annu. Rev. Fluid Mech. **30**(1), 329–364 (1998)

8. Amati, G., Succi, S., et al.: Massively parallel lattice-Boltzmann simulation of turbulent channel flow. Int. J. Mod. Phys. C **8**(4), 869–877 (1997)

9. Pohl, T., et al.: Performance evaluation of parallel large-scale lattice Boltzmann applications on three supercomputing architectures. In: The 2004 ACM/IEEE Conference on Supercomputing (SC), p. 21. IEEE (2004)

10. Pan, C., Luo, L.-S., et al.: An evaluation of lattice Boltzmann schemes for porous medium flow simulation. Comput. Fluids **35**(8), 898–909 (2006)

11. Obrecht, C., Kuznik, F., Tourancheau, B., Roux, J.-J.: Global memory access modelling for efficient implementation of the lattice Boltzmann method on graphics processing units. In: Palma, J.M.L.M., Daydé, M., Marques, O., Lopes, J.C. (eds.) VECPAR 2010. LNCS, vol. 6449, pp. 151–161. Springer, Heidelberg (2011). https://doi.org/10.1007/978-3-642-19328-6_16

12. Delbosc, N., et al.: Optimized implementation of the Lattice Boltzmann Method on a graphics processing unit towards real-time fluid simulation. Comput. Math. Appl. **67**(2), 462–475 (2014)

13. Wang, Z., et al.: GPU acceleration of volumetric lattice Boltzmann method for patient-specific computational hemodynamics. Comput. Fluids **1**(15), 192–200 (2015)

14. Murtaza, S., Hoekstra, A.G., Sloot, P.M.A.: Cellular automata simulations on a FPGA cluster. Int. J. High Perform. Comput. Appl. **25**(2), 193–204 (2011)

15. Sano, K., Yamamoto, S.: FPGA-based scalable and power-efficient fluid simulation using floating-point DSP blocks. IEEE Trans. Parallel Distrib. Syst. **28**(10), 2823–2837 (2017)

16. Waidyasooriya, H.M., et al.: OpenCL-based FPGA-platform for stencil computation and its optimization methodology. IEEE Trans. Parallel Distrib. Syst. **28**(5), 1390–1402 (2017)

17. Zohouri, H.R., Podobas, A., Matsuoka, S.: Combined spatial and temporal blocking for high-performance stencil computation on FPGAs using OpenCL. In: The 2018 ACM/SIGDA International Symposium on Field-Programmable Gate Arrays, pp. 153–162. ACM (2018)

18. RAM-Based Shift Register (ALTSHIFT_TAPS) IP Core. https://www.intel.com/content/.../ug_shift_register_ram_based.pdf

19. The Xilinx LogiCORE IP RAM-based Shift Register. https://www.xilinx.com/support/.../shift_ram/v12_0/pg122-c-shift-ram.pdf

20. Wittmann, M., et al.: Comparison of different propagation steps for lattice Boltzmann methods. Comput. Math. Appl. **65**(6), 924–935 (2013)

21. Tomczak, T., Szafran, R.G.: Sparse geometries handling in lattice Boltzmann method implementation for graphic processors. IEEE Trans. Parallel Distrib. Syst. **29**(8), 1865–1878 (2018)

High-Level Synthesis in Implementing and Benchmarking Number Theoretic Transform in Lattice-Based Post-Quantum Cryptography Using Software/Hardware Codesign

Duc Tri Nguyen, Viet B. Dang, and Kris Gaj$^{(\boxtimes)}$

George Mason University, Fairfax, USA
{dnguye69,vdang6,kgaj}@gmu.edu

Abstract. Compared to traditional hardware development methodologies, High-Level Synthesis (HLS) offers a faster time-to-market and lower design cost at the expense of implementation efficiency. Although Software/Hardware Codesign has been used in many areas, its usability for benchmarking of candidates in cryptographic competitions has been largely unexplored. This paper provides a comparison of the HLS- and RTL-based design methodologies when applied to the hardware design of the Number Theoretic Transform (NTT) – a core arithmetic function of lattice-based Post-Quantum Cryptography (PQC). As a next step, we apply Software/Hardware Codesign approach to the implementation of three PQC schemes based on NTT. Then, we integrate our HLS implementation into the Xilinx SDSoC environment. We demonstrate that an overhead of SDSoC compared to traditional Bare Metal approach is acceptable. This paper also shows that an HLS implementation obtained by modeling a block diagram is typically much better than an implementation obtained by using design space exploration. We conclude that the HLS/SDSoC and RTL/Bare Metal approaches generate comparable results.

1 Introduction

A threat of quantum computers triggered an effort aimed at designing a new class of cryptographic algorithms, collectively referred to as Post-Quantum Cryptography (PQC) [1]. These algorithms have two common features: (a) there are no known attacks capable of breaking these cryptosystems, even assuming the availability of full-scale quantum computers, (b) all PQC algorithms can be implemented using traditional computing platforms, based on standard semiconductor technology, such as microprocessors and FPGAs. In the standardization process currently run by the National Institute of Standards and Technology (NIST), 26 candidates remain in Round 2 and need to be evaluated from the point of view of their hardware efficiency [1]. A large number of candidates and high

© Springer Nature Switzerland AG 2020
F. Rincón et al. (Eds.): ARC 2020, LNCS 12083, pp. 247–257, 2020.
https://doi.org/10.1007/978-3-030-44534-8_19

complexity of the majority of them make hardware benchmarking extremely challenging. In order to mitigate these difficulties, a new approach based on (a) software/hardware codesign, and (b) the development of hardware accelerators using High-Level Synthesis (HLS) has been proposed [2].

In the traditional RTL approach, a path from developing HDL code to running it on a target device is quite long, since the developer has to create an interface between CPU and FPGA. On the other hand, in the Xilinx SDSoC framework, most of these tasks are performed automatically by the tools.

In the remaining 12 Round 2 lattice-based PQC candidates, 5 use Number Theoretic Transform (NTT) for polynomial multiplication. After software profiling, we decided to implement the NTT hardware accelerators for NewHope and Kyber. Since Kyber has been substantially modified between Rounds 1 and 2, we have decided to compare the implementation efficiencies of these two variants, further denoted as Kyber R1 and Kyber R2.

This paper demonstrates: (a) Advantages of the HLS approach based on block diagrams vs. the HLS approach based on space exploration. (b) Overhead of the SDSoC/HLS methodology over the Bare Metal/RTL approach.

2   Background

2.1   Number Theoretic Transform

Let n be a power of two, and q be a prime modulus. We define a ring $R_q[x] = Z_q[x]/(x^n + 1)$ as the ring of polynomials of degree $n - 1$ with coefficients in Z_q (a field of integers in the range $[0, q - 1]$ with addition and multiplication modulo q). Multiplications in $R_q[x]$ can be performed efficiently in software and hardware using the NTT, which has the complexity of $O(n \cdot log(n))$.

If $\psi^2 = \omega \mod q$ exists, then it is recommended that the input polynomials should be multiplied by ψ^i before Forward NTT instead of supplementing them with n most significant terms equal to zero. As a result, the output of Inverse NTT must be multiplied by ψ^{-i}.

By using NTT, a multiplication in R_q can be computed as follows:

$$C = \mathbf{NTT}^{-1}(\overline{C}) = \mathbf{NTT}^{-1}(\overline{A} * \overline{B}) = \mathbf{NTT}^{-1}(\mathbf{NTT}(A) * \mathbf{NTT}(B))$$

where $\psi^2 = \omega$, $A = (a_0, \psi a_1, \psi^2 a_2, \ldots, \psi^{n-1} a_{n-1})$, $B = (b_0, \psi b_1, \psi^2 b_2, \ldots, \psi^{n-1} b_{n-1})$, $C = (c_0, \psi c_1, \psi^2 c_2, \ldots, \psi^{n-1} c_{n-1})$, and a, b, c are polynomials in $R_q[x]$, with $q = 1 \mod 2n$ [3].

The pseudo-code of the iterative version of Forward NTT is shown in Algorithm 1. The Inverse NTT is similar to Forward NTT but instead of multiplying with ω^i, we multiply with ω^{-i}.

In this paper, we divide the polynomial multiplication into two modes:
(a) **NTT**: Forward (NTT) and Inverse NTT ($INTT$)
(b) **MUL**: Multiplication of the respective coefficients by ψ^i ($PSIS\_MUL$), multiplication of the respective coefficients by ψ^{-i} ($IPSIS\_MUL$), and coefficient-wise multiplication of two polynomials ($COEF\_MUL$).

Modular multiplication can be performed using two primary approaches: Montgomery multiplication (REDC) and the method introduced by Longa et al. in [4] (KRED).

Algorithm 1. Iterative NTT

Require: $F(x) \in R_q[x]$; $ROM[i] = \omega^i$, $\omega^n = 1 \bmod q$
Ensure: $\overline{F}(x) = NTT(F)$
1: $F \leftarrow BitReverse(F)$
2: **for** $s = 0$ to $log_2(n) - 1$ by 1 **do**
3:      $m \leftarrow 2 \ll s$
4:      $\omega_m \leftarrow n/m$
5:      $i \leftarrow 0$
6:      **for** $j = 0$ to $m/2$ by 1 **do**
7:          **for** $k = 0$ to n by m **do**
8:              $u \leftarrow F[k + j]$
9:              $t \leftarrow F[k + j + m/2] * ROM[i]$
10:            $F[k + j] \leftarrow u + t$
11:            $F[k + j + m/2] \leftarrow u - t$
12:          $i \leftarrow i + \omega_m$

---

3 Previous Work

The theory of NTT is summarized in [3]. Previous hardware implementations of NTT were reported in [5,6]. The first hardware implementations of NTT targeted the PQC scheme called Ring-LWE [7]. The most recent efforts aimed specifically at the efficient implementations of the Round 1 PQC candidate NewHope, qualified to the second round of the NIST PQC standardization process [8,9].

Efficient implementations of block ciphers, hash functions, and authenticated ciphers using HLS were reported in [10,11]. In the majority of cases, these implementations closely matched the performance of RTL implementations in terms of throughput and throughput-to-area ratio. The first attempts at the use of HLS for benchmarking of PQC candidates were reported in [2].

4 Block Diagram Versus Space Exploration

There are two major approaches to implementing hardware accelerators in HLS:
(a) SE/HLS: Identify optimal HLS-ready code using design space exploration based on HLS directives. The final hardware architecture is unknown until the best result is achieved.
(b) BD/HLS: Develop block diagram corresponding to the presumed optimal hardware architecture. Write HLS code following this block diagram.

Both SE/HLS and BD/HLS approaches inherit the advantages of HLS: quicker verification and quicker development than in traditional RTL. As shown

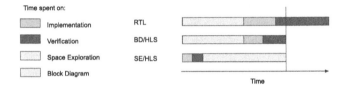

Fig. 1. BD/HLS versus SE/HLS development timeline

Table 1. Results for BD/HLS vs. results for SE/HLS for 1024-point NTT

Work	BRAM 18K	DSP	FF	LUT	Cycles	Cycles reduction
[12]	11.5	10	16,402	21,167	7,597	1.59
[12]	21.5	19	30,498	38,984	5,291	1.10
This work	**10**	**4**	**1,342**	**1,110**	**4,776**	**1.0**

in Fig. 1, in the SE/HLS approach, a small portion of the total development time is spent on writing HLS-ready code and verifying its functionality. The rest of the time is devoted to design space exploration using *pragma* directives. There are over 20 *pragma* directives in the current version of Vivado HLS; their different combinations lead to different architectures. The impact of a particular *pragma* directive is heavily dependent on the code structure and the algorithm. Some directives may have no impact at all, others may dramatically change the speed vs. cost trade-off. Exploring all possible combinations is often unrealistic. Additionally, in many cases, code refactoring may give better results than an optimal choice and placement of directives. As a result, the HLS design by space exploration may lead to the choice of sub-optimal hardware architecture.

In BD/HLS approach, the large portion of the total development time is spent on developing a block diagram and implementing it in HLS-ready C. The rest of the time is spent on verification. Since the exact hardware architecture is known beforehand, space exploration is not required. With the HLS-ready code based on a block diagram created manually by an experienced designer, the BD/HLS approach can significantly outperform the SE/HLS methodology.

In Table 1, the comparison of the NTT implementations according to two approaches, BD/HLS and SE/HLS, is summarized. The BD/HLS approach uses **2x, 5x, 22x, 35x,** and **1.1x** less BRAMs, DSPs, LUTs, FFs and Clock Cycles, respectively. In [12], the authors experiment with multiple combinations of directives, applied to multiple loops. However, the final design outcome is still not as good as in our BD/HLS design.

5   Hardware Design

5.1   NTT Top Level Design

A top-level block diagram of a hardware accelerator for NewHope and Kyber is shown in in Fig. 2. There are 3 main components: *NTT*, *MUL* and *Reorder*.

For NewHope and Kyber R1, the *NTT* unit is responsible for the **NTT** and **MUL** modes of operation, described in Sect. 2.1. In Kyber R2, the *NTT* unit is only responsible for the **MUL** mode. As a result, a dedicated MUL unit must be added. The role of the Reorder unit is explained at the end of the next section.

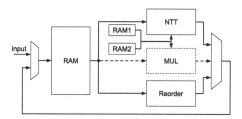

Fig. 2. Top-level block diagram of a hardware accelerator for NewHope and Kyber

Table 2. Selected NTT-based Round 2 PQC candidates investigated in this study. N and q are major parameters of NTT. k and m are used in the Longa-Naehrig modular reduction, and $qinv$ in the Montgomery Reduction.

Candidate	Cat (#NTT)	n	q	2^m	k	k^2	qinv
NewHope	1,5 (1)	512/1024	12,289	2^{12}	3	$2^3 + 1$	$2^{13} + 2^{12} - 1$
Kyber R1	1,3,5 (2,3,4)	256	7,681	2^9	15	$2^8 - 2^5 + 1$	$2^{13} - 2^9 - 1$
Kyber R2	1,3,5 (2,3,4)	256	3,329	2^8	13	$2^7 + 2^5 + 2^3 + 1$	$2^9 + 2^8 + 1$

5.2 Number Theoretic Transform

A block diagram of our NTT implementation, shown in Fig. 3, is based on the design from [6]. One of the improvements is support for both odd and even numbers of NTT layers. When $log_2(n)$ is odd, the signal X is asserted during the *last* iteration to let coefficients A', B', C', D' pass directly to the SIPO unit instead of going through the 2nd NTT layer. On the other hand, when $log_2(n)$ is even, the multiplexers with the select signal X can be eliminated.

Our NTT hardware architecture has a 2×2 butterfly structure, which can process two layers of NTT with two butterfly units per layer. Four coefficients are loaded in each clock cycle and placed into registers A, B, C, D. If KRED is selected as a modular reduction method, the square boxes m_1 and m_2 are KRED and KRED2x, respectively. If REDC Montgomery reduction is chosen, m_1 can be removed and m_2 represent REDC.

When $S = 0$, the circuit operates in the **MUL** mode, used to perform operations *PSIS_MUL*, *COEF_MUL*, and *IPSIS_MUL*. The coefficients in the lines B and D are multiplied by coefficients from RAM1, which are $(\psi^{4i+1}, \psi^{4i+3})$ or (r_{4i+1}, r_{4i+3}) or $(\psi^{-(4i+1)}, \psi^{-(4i+3)})$, depending on the performed operation.

The obtained results are reduced by the function m_2 and stored in B_{save} and D_{save}, which go to SIPO_B and SIPO_D later on. After that, coefficients from lines A and C are switched to lines B and D, allowing them to be multiplied with coefficients from RAM2, reduced by m_2, and directed to SIPO_A and SIPO_C, respectively. When the following outputs of SIPOs: $A1st, B2nd, C3rd$ and $D4th$ become available, they are concatenated and written back to RAM at the index where $A1st$ was loaded from.

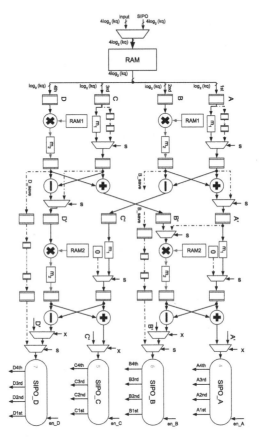

Fig. 3. Block diagram of the proposed hardware architecture for fast polynomial multiplication using NTT. The red lines represent four likely critical paths. (Color figure online)

When $S = 1$, the circuit operates in the **NTT** mode use to perform operations $INTT$ and NTT. Four coefficients go through the 2×2 butterfly structure, and results are written to SIPOs. Coefficients in lines B and D are multiplied with ω_n^i or ω_n^{-i}, depending on whether the circuit computes NTT or $INTT$. When $SIPO_A$ is full, four coefficients available at the outputs $A1st, A2nd, A3rd, A4th$ are concatenated, and stored back to the RAM at the position where $A1st$ was loaded from. After one clock cycle, the same happens with results accumulated in $SIPO_C$, and then $SIPO_B$ and $SIPO_D$.

Shuffle and Reordering. The order of coefficients is changed in the **NTT** mode. Thus, after each NTT operation, one must shuffle and reorder the obtained coefficients. We apply the in-place matrix transposition proposed in [13]. The number of clock cycles for 128-, 256-, and 1024-point NTT is 64, 80, 318 clock cycles, respectively. In particular, for the 1024-point NTT, we use 318 clock cycles vs. 1024 clock cycles in [9].

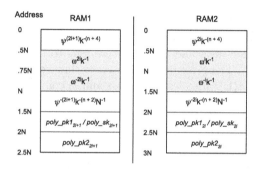

Fig. 4. The memory maps of RAM1 and RAM2, including formulas for values of constants stored in specific memory ranges. $n=log_2 n$, $\omega = \omega_n$, $i \in [0, 1, \ldots, n/2)$ for RAM1 and RAM2, except the gray area of RAM 1, where $i \in [0, 1, \ldots, n/4)$. For the KRED, the value of k is given in Table 2. If the REDC is used, k is assumed to be 1. $poly\_pk$ and $poly\_sk$ are NTT domain preloaded public and secret polynomials.

Table 3. Results of the HLS implementations of KRED and REDC

Candidate	Modular reduction	DSP	LUT	FF	Slice	Max. Freq
NewHope	KRED	1	118	100	28	530
KyberR1		1	125	93	32	507
KyberR2		1	150	112	35	502
NewHope	REDC	1	370	357	85	515
KyberR1		1	387	333	69	512
KyberR2		1	391	382	91	476

For NewHope and Kyber R1, all five operations from Sect. 2.1 are supported by the circuit from Fig. 3. In the case of Kyber R2, $PSIS\_MUL$ and $IPSIS\_MUL$ do not apply. Only NTT and $INTT$ are performed by the NTT unit. The $COEF\_MUL$ is performed by a separate unit. Therefore, the NTT mode of Kyber R2 can be simplified by stripping the dot line and removing multiplexers to save resources and improve maximum clock frequency.

The precomputed values of all constants are stored in the dual-port memories RAM1 and RAM2, of the size $2.5n$ and $3n$ memory locations, respectively. The number of bits stored at each memory location is equal to $log_2 q$. The memory map and formulas for the values of constants stored within each specific address range are shown in Fig. 4.

6   Results

The target device is Zynq UltraScale+ MPSoC ZCU104, with CPU Cortex-A53 running at 1.2 GHz. All results presented in this section are obtained after placing and routing.

Results of the HLS implementation of two alternative reduction methods, KRED and REDC, for the value of q corresponding to investigated candidates, are shown in Table 3. These results demonstrate that compared to REDC, the implementation of KRED uses less resources and is comparable in term of performance. Therefore, KRED is selected as a modular reduction method.

The comparison between HLS and RTL is shown in Table 4. The PQC candidates are compared at the multiple security levels: 1, 3, and 5. The number of BRAMs in HLS is higher than in RTL due to a higher abstraction level description of HLS. In particular, the tool duplicates RAM1 and RAM2 for each MUL

Table 4. Resources Utilization for HLS and RTL

Algorithm	#NTT	DSP	BRAM 36K	LUT	FF	Slice	Freq.(Mhz)
RTL							
NewHope 1	1	4	3	1,040	940	190	476
NewHope 5	1	4	5	842	803	170	476
Kyber R1-1	2	8	2	2,185	2,625	411	500
Kyber R1-3	3	12	3	3,318	3,937	605	500
Kyber R1-5	4	16	4	4,363	5,237	795	500
Kyber R2-1	2	24	5	2,040	3,223	433	500
Kyber R2-3	3	36	8	3,054	5,098	637	500
Kyber R2-5	4	48	10	4,055	6,803	960	500
HLS/RTL							
NewHope 1	1.00	1.00	1.00	1.14	1.49	1.26	0.95
NewHope 5	1.00	1.00	1.00	1.32	1.67	1.29	0.96
Kyber R1-1	1.00	1.00	1.00	1.28	1.03	1.45	0.91
Kyber R1-3	1.00	1.00	1.00	1.27	1.03	1.45	0.91
Kyber R1-5	1.00	1.00	1.00	1.27	1.06	1.54	0.91
Kyber R2-1	1.00	1.00	1.40	1.35	1.43	1.57	0.91
Kyber R2-3	1.00	1.00	1.40	1.40	1.51	1.65	0.89
Kyber R2-5	1.00	1.00	1.40	1.47	1.53	1.67	0.89

Table 5. Comparison of the transfer time & overhead between SDSoC and bare metal

Algorithm	Total transfer size (bytes)		Times	Total transfer time (μs)		Transfer ratio	Transfer overhead	
	In	Out		BM	SDSoC	SDSoC/ BM	BM	SDSoC
ENCAPSULATION								
NewHope 1	2,048	2,048	1	7.91	12.64	1.60	4.51%	7.01%
NewHope 5	4,096	4,096		11.90	19.50	1.64	3.67%	5.87%
Kyber R1-1	1,024	1,536		7.85	9.86	1.26	4.94%	6.12%
Kyber R1-3	1,536	2,048		8.05	11.71	1.46	3.58%	5.12%
Kyber R1-5	2,048	2,560		9.42	13.49	1.43	2.86%	4.04%
Kyber R2-1	1,024	1,536		7.85	9.86	1.26	7.77%	9.54%
Kyber R2-3	1,536	2,048		8.05	11.71	1.46	3.99%	5.69%
Kyber R2-5	2,048	2,560		9.42	13.49	1.43	3.12%	4.40%
DECAPSULATION								
NewHope 1	3,072	3,072	2	15.22	21.57	1.42	8.56%	11.69%
NewHope 5	6,144	6,144		19.81	32.13	1.62	5.93%	9.26%
Kyber R1-1	2,048	2,048		15.15	17.99	1.19	9.35%	10.89%
Kyber R1-3	3,072	2,560		15.90	20.76	1.31	7.02%	8.96%
Kyber R1-5	4,096	3,072		17.91	23.47	1.31	5.39%	6.94%
Kyber R2-1	2,048	2,048		15.15	17.99	1.19	11.36%	13.17%
Kyber R2-3	3,072	2,560		15.90	20.76	1.31	7.53%	9.58%
Kyber R2-5	4,096	3,072		17.91	23.47	1.31	5.78%	7.42%

Table 6. Speed up of the Software/Hardware Codesign vs. Pure Software

Algorithm	Total SW (μs)	Total SW NTT (μs)	%SW NTT	Total SW/HW (μs)		Total Speed-up @Max Freq	
				BM	SDSoC	BM	SDSoC
ENCAPSULATION							
NewHope 1	360.3	199.8	55%	175.2	180.3	2.06	2.00
NewHope 5	737.0	438.1	59%	324.0	332.2	2.27	2.22
Kyber R1-1	389.2	240.9	62%	158.9	161.1	2.45	2.42
Kyber R1-3	582.3	368.3	63%	224.8	228.7	2.59	2.55
Kyber R1-5	826.9	509.4	62%	329.6	334.0	2.51	2.48
Kyber R2-1	328.5	237.8	72%	101.1	103.4	3.25	3.18
Kyber R2-3	533.9	343.0	64%	201.5	205.7	2.65	2.60
Kyber R2-5	785.2	495.4	63%	301.8	306.4	2.60	2.56
DECAPSULATION							
NewHope 1	427.5	273.5	64%	177.8	184.6	2.40	2.32
NewHope 5	895.7	598.0	67%	334.0	347.1	2.68	2.58
Kyber R1-1	483.2	340.8	71%	161.9	165.2	2.98	2.92
Kyber R1-3	710.4	504.2	71%	226.5	231.8	3.14	3.06
Kyber R1-5	992.1	682.4	69%	332.0	338.0	2.99	2.94
Kyber R2-1	429.5	315.5	73%	133.3	136.6	3.22	3.14
Kyber R2-3	667.8	476.8	71%	211.1	216.8	3.16	3.08
Kyber R2-5	950.8	662.9	70%	310.0	316.4	3.07	3.00

component. Thus, the number of BRAMs for Kyber R2 is higher than in RTL. There are two pairs of RAM1 and RAM2 in a single HLS NTT module, instead of just one. The number of LUTs, FFs, and Slices is consistently greater in HLS.

Traditional RTL SW/HW Codesign often uses Bare Metal (BM) to handle transfer between CPU and FPGA. The DMA in BM is often implemented manually. Contrary to that, SDSoC creates an abstraction layer of the interface handler. As a result, switching from software to hardware is very easy. To demonstrate the overhead of abstraction in using SDSoC, the best selected transfer interface in SDSoC is compared with Bare Metal in Table 5. Additionally, the **Transfer Overhead** column is the percentage of **Total Transfer Time** over the **Total SW/HW** in Table 6.

In Table 6, timing results are summarized. The HLS/SDSoC approach generates comparable accelerator speed up for all investigated algorithms. The number of clock cycles of NTT HW acclerator for polynomial multiplication (excluding the transfer time) in Encapsulation and Decapsulation phase for NewHope 1, NewHope 5, Kyber R1, and Kyber R2 are 3300, 6300, 1400, 1300 and 4100, 7900, 2200, 2100, respectively.

The **Total SW** is the software only execution time, the **Total SW NTT** column is the time spent on NTT operations in SW, **%SW NTT** is the percentage of the total execution time in software devoted to NTT, the **Total SW/HW** is the total time after offloading the critical function (NTT) to hardware. The **Total Speed-up @Max Freq** is the ratio between **Total SW** and **Total SW/HW**. This speed-up is roughly equal between the SDSoC and Bare Metal approaches.

7   Conclusions

Using HLS and SDSoC are two promising approaches to benchmarking SW/HW implementations of PQC. With the help of these approaches, the development time is substantially reduced, with the relatively small penalty in terms of the total execution time, HW-SW transfer time, and the total speed-up vs. purely SW implementation. Overhead in terms of resource utilization is more substantial, especially in terms of the number of LUTs, FFs, and Slices. The BD/HLS approach, based on the use of block diagrams, was shown to be substantially more efficient than the approach, SE/HLS, based on applying various pragmas to existing code and letting the tool to infer the best possible architecture.

References

1. NIST Post-Quantum Cryptography Standardization
2. Farahmand, F., Dang, V.B., Nguyen, D.T., Gaj, K.: Evaluating the potential for hardware acceleration of four NTRU-based key encapsulation mechanisms using software/hardware codesign. In: Ding, J., Steinwandt, R. (eds.) PQCrypto 2019. LNCS, vol. 11505, pp. 23–43. Springer, Cham (2019). https://doi.org/10.1007/978-3-030-25510-7_2

3. Chu, E., George, A.: Inside the FFT Black Box: Serial and Parallel Fast Fourier Transform Algorithms. Computational Mathematics Series. CRC Press, Boca Raton (2019)
4. Longa, P., Naehrig, M.: Speeding up the number theoretic transform for faster ideal lattice-based cryptography. In: Foresti, S., Persiano, G. (eds.) CANS 2016. LNCS, vol. 10052, pp. 124–139. Springer, Cham (2016). https://doi.org/10.1007/978-3-319-48965-0_8
5. Pöppelmann, T., Güneysu, T.: Towards efficient arithmetic for lattice-based cryptography on reconfigurable hardware. In: Hevia, A., Neven, G. (eds.) LATIN-CRYPT 2012. LNCS, vol. 7533, pp. 139–158. Springer, Heidelberg (2012). https://doi.org/10.1007/978-3-642-33481-8_8
6. Du, C., Bai, G., Wu, X.: High-speed polynomial multiplier architecture for ring-LWE based public key cryptosystems. In: GLSVLSI (2016)
7. Renteria-Mejia, C.P., Velasco-Medina, J.: High-throughput ring-LWE cryptoprocessors. IEEE Trans. Very Large Scale Integr. (VLSI) Syst. **25**(8), 2332–2345 (2017)
8. Oder, T., Güneysu, T.: Implementing the NewHope-Simple key exchange on low-cost FPGAs. In: Lange, T., Dunkelman, O. (eds.) LATINCRYPT 2017. LNCS, vol. 11368, pp. 128–142. Springer, Cham (2019). https://doi.org/10.1007/978-3-030-25283-0_7
9. Kuo, P.-C., et al.: High performance post-quantum key exchange on FPGAs. Cryptology ePrint Archive 2017/690, February 2018
10. Homsirikamol, E., Gaj, K.: Hardware benchmarking of cryptographic algorithms using high-level synthesis tools: the SHA-3 contest case study. In: Sano, K., Soudris, D., Hübner, M., Diniz, P.C. (eds.) ARC 2015. LNCS, vol. 9040, pp. 217–228. Springer, Cham (2015). https://doi.org/10.1007/978-3-319-16214-0_18
11. Homsirikamol, E., Gaj, K.: A new HLS-based methodology for FPGA benchmarking of candidates in cryptographic competitions: the CAESAR contest case study. In: FPT 2017 (2017)
12. Kawamura, K., Yanagisawa, M., Togawa, N.: A loop structure optimization targeting high-level synthesis of fast number theoretic transform. In: ISQED (2018)
13. Knuth, D.E.: The Art of Computer Programming, Fundamental Algorithms. Addison-Wesley, Boston (1997)

Exploring FPGA Optimizations
to Compute Sparse Numerical Linear
Algebra Kernels

Federico Favaro[1]([⊠]), Ernesto Dufrechou[2], Pablo Ezzatti[2], and Juan P. Oliver[1]

[1] Instituto de Ingeniería Eléctrica, Facultad de Ingeniería,
Universidad de la República, Montevideo, Uruguay
{ffavaro,jpo}@fing.edu.uy
[2] Instituto de Computación, Facultad de Ingeniería,
Universidad de la República, Montevideo, Uruguay
{edufrechou,pezzatti}@fing.edu.uy

Abstract. The solution of sparse triangular linear systems (SPTRSV) is the bottleneck of many numerical methods. Thus, it is crucial to count with efficient implementations of such kernel, at least for commonly used platforms. In this sense, Field–Programmable Gate Arrays (FPGAs) have evolved greatly in the last years, entering the HPC hardware ecosystem largely due to their superior energy–efficiency relative to more established accelerators. Up until recently, the design for FPGAs implied the use of low–level Hardware Description Languages (HDL) such as VHDL or Verilog. Nowadays, manufacturers are making a large effort to adopt High–Level Synthesis languages like C/C++ or OpenCL, but the gap between their performance and that of HDLs is not yet fully studied. This work focuses on the performance offered by FPGAs to compute the SPTRSV using OpenCL. For this purpose, we implement different parallel variants of this kernel and experimentally evaluate several setups, varying among others the work–group size, the number of compute units, the unroll–factor and the vectorization–factor.

Keywords: FPGAs · Sparse linear algebra · SPTRSV · Power consumption

1 Introduction

Many numerical methods in scientific applications entail the solution of sparse triangular linear systems (SPTRSV), e.g. the solution of sparse linear systems by direct methods, or by iterative methods with ILU preconditioners, where the SPTRSV kernel is the most computationally demanding stage [4,12]. This motivates the development of efficient implementations of such kernel, at least for the most commonly used hardware. The efficient parallelization of this kernel is especially difficult. Similar to other sparse linear algebra kernels, the SPTRSV is a memory–bound operation and presents an irregular data access pattern.

© Springer Nature Switzerland AG 2020
F. Rincón et al. (Eds.): ARC 2020, LNCS 12083, pp. 258–268, 2020.
https://doi.org/10.1007/978-3-030-44534-8_20

Additionally, the triangular structure of the nonzero entries is tied to a load imbalance between threads, and data dependencies between equations severely constrain the available parallelism.

Propelled by the popularization of using massively–parallel devices (such as GPUs) for scientific computations, HPC platforms experienced a revolution in the last decade. This, in combination with the tremendous scale of clusters and supercomputers, has led to a growing concern in the HPC community about energy consumption and the efficiency of computing devices [1,2,5,9]. In this context, FPGAs renewed their importance, emerging as a low–energy–consuming alternative to other accelerators. As a result, the former use of FPGAs in highly specialized niches has now expanded to general–purpose problems. One of the major drawbacks that hindered the massive use of FPGAs among the HPC community was the required knowledge on low–level Hardware Description Languages, e.g. VHDL or Verilog. These impose a programming model radically different than that of standard languages, with longer development times and complex debugging. Furthermore, their use requires specialized knowledge of the underlying hardware. To overcome these disadvantages, manufacturers are making efforts to adopt High–Level Synthesis languages like C or OpenCL. Evidence of this is the introduction of SDKs for OpenCL by prominent FPGAs manufacturers such as Intel [3] and Xilinx [20].

OpenCL is an open–source, royalty–free parallel programming standard, which allows describing task parallelism using an abstract model independent of the underlying hardware. It considerably reduces development times and allows portability between platforms. Although this has enabled a greater adoption of FPGAs as hardware accelerators by the software community, there is still much to investigate regarding the performance attainable by OpenCL kernels in FPGAs, the role played by specific platform optimizations, and how much knowledge of the underlying hardware is required.

In this regard, we implement different parallel variants of the SPTRSV kernel for FPGA using OpenCL. Additionally, we perform a deep evaluation of several FPGA optimization techniques.

2   Work Context

Given a (lower) triangular sparse matrix $L \in \mathbb{R}^{n \times n}$ and a vector $b \in \mathbb{R}^n$, the usual approach to obtain $x \in \mathbb{R}^n$ such that $Lx = b$, is the *forward–substitution* procedure, presented in Algorithm 1, where the matrix L is stored in the CSR storage format [8]. The algorithm starts by trivially solving the first equation and then, in each step, it replaces the solved unknowns by their values in the following equations, solving at least one equation per step. To obtain the unknown x_i it is necessary to multiply the sub-diagonal entries l_{ij} of row i by the value of x_j, subtracting the result from b_i and dividing by the diagonal entry l_{ii}. It is clear that if l_{ij} is not zero, the unknown x_j needs to be solved before x_i, which constrains the parallelism of the operation.

Several efforts have addressed the use of FPGAs to process NLA operations, typically considering both performance and energy consumption. Most of these

---

Algorithm 1. Solution of sparse lower triangular systems.

---

1 **Input:** row_ptr, col_idx, val, b
2 **Output:** x
   $x = b$
   for $i = 0$ **to** $n - 1$ **do**
      for $j = row\_ptr[i]$ **to** $row\_ptr[i + 1] - 2$ **do**
         $x[i] = x[i] - val[j] \times x[col\_idx[j]]$
      end for
      $x[i] = x[i]/val[row\_ptr[i + 1] - 1]$
   end for

---

works are focused on dense NLA kernels. Some of the most prominent ones are the Kestur et al. [13,14] that implement some BLAS [6] operations, the [17] for the general matrix–matrix multiplication using OpenCL, and more recently, two efforts for achieving a BLAS version for FPGAs, i.e. fBLAS [15] and Vitis BLAS[1]. In the sparse context, the SPMV (or other solvers based on it) is most the commonly studied kernel. The importance of this kernel and its low level of data dependencies, in comparison with other sparse NLA kernels (e.g. SPTRSV), make this operation attractive to implement in HPC hardware. Some remarkable efforts in this direction are Fowers' article [11], the work of Umuroglu and Jahre [19], and the thesis of Townsend [18].

3 Proposal

In this section we detail our process for the development of the SPTRSV kernels. Our effort is focused on the use of the OpenCL framework. We employ two different OpenCL paradigms, NDRange and Single Work Item Kernels. To the best of our knowledge, this is the first OpenCL implementation of the SPTRSV for FPGAs, excluding our preliminary results in the Power–Aware Computing – PACO2019 [10].

3.1 NDRange Kernels

Intel recommends structuring the OpenCL kernels as *Single Work–Item*, whenever possible, to benefit from the coarse–grained parallelism. However, there may be cases where the explicit definition of concurrent threads of the NDRange model may be beneficial. In particular, when data or memory dependencies prevent achieving pipelined loops with low Initialization Intervals (II). Given the nature of the parallel SPTRSV algorithm, where there is plenty of indirection in memory accesses, we first opted for the NDRange approach. Moreover, we choose, as a starting point, a GPU implementation following a similar model that obtained good results in the past.

---

[1] https://www.xilinx.com/products/design-tools/vitis/vitis-libraries/vitis-blas.html.

We develop two NDRange kernels for the parallel SPTRSV, both based on the level–set approach. One work–group is issued for every row, following the order of the *iorder* vector (array containing the rows ordered by levels). Each work–item enters a for loop where it fetches one element from the matrix and its corresponding x vector element, performs the product and accumulation, and then moves forward *local group size* elements to process another pair. The loop iterates until all the non–zero elements of the row are handled. Before processing a row, the algorithm requires that all its dependencies are resolved. The two kernels resolve this matter differently. In the first variant (NDR$_{wait}$), each work–item reads from memory its corresponding x element and verifies whether it is solved. If it is, it performs the multiplication and sets the corresponding flag. When all the flags in a work–group are set, all work–items move forward to process the next *local work size* elements. Once the entire row has been processed, the accumulated products of each work–item are reduced and subtracted from b, then the x value is obtained dividing the result by the diagonal element.

To verify that x is solved, the array is preloaded with the float representation of *infinite* before executing the kernel. This allows determining whether the x value is ready by checking if it differs from *infinite*. The accumulated products and flags are stored in local memory to be visible by all work–items. Threads within each work–group are synchronized using barriers.

The Intel SDK for OpenCL does not provide reduction functions across work–items, so this operation was implemented based on local memory and barriers. As the order in which work–groups are issued by the scheduler is not defined, it is necessary to maintain a counter, in global memory, to go through the *iorder* vector in the correct sequence. To avoid race conditions between work–groups in the writing of this counter an atomic addition is required.

To simplify the kernel and obtain a better performance, a second version (NDR$_{multi}$) was explored, in which the verification on the x values is avoided. Instead, the kernel is launched once for each level, processing only the rows on that level. As long as the kernels are executed following the order of the *iorder* vector, all dependencies are met for each row. All kernel executions work on the same x vector and, after each run, the x values are updated in global memory. To control which rows are processed on each run, the *ilevels* vector must be used. This vector contains indexes pointing to the first row of each level in the *iorder* vector. By eliminating the verification on the x values, the loops for memory access and computations are simpler and can be partially unrolled. The update of x values in both kernels is made by only one thread per work–group.

3.2   Single Work Item Kernels

For the *Single Work–Item* approach we develop three different versions: SWI$_{simple}$, SWI$_{channel}$ and SWI$_{hash}$.

The SWI$_{simple}$ is a naive implementation that consists of three nested loops, where the outermost iterates over levels, the middle one over the rows in each level, and the innermost over the non–zeros in each row. The latter is where computations are performed. To add parallelism, this loop is partially unrolled.

Memory dependencies among x values prevent this kernel from being fully pipelined with II equal to 1.

For the $\text{SWI}_{channel}$ two kernels are used, one for all global memory transactions, and the other in charge of the calculations. The kernels communicate with each other using channels. These are mechanisms based on FIFO buffers for synchronizing and passing data between kernels with high efficiency and low latency. Three channels are used, one to send the number of non–zero coefficients (nnz) per row, another for exchanging the x values, and the last one for the matrix coefficients. Moving the memory accesses away from the computations allow the kernel to be fully pipelined. The kernel that accesses global memory is structured as three nested loops similarly to the SWI_{simple}. To allow pipelining, this kernel is told to ignore memory dependencies using the $ivdep$ pragma in the middle loop. The outermost loop, which is responsible for issuing the levels one by one, is serialized. This guarantees that dependencies are met for every row.

We improve over this last version by adding a hash to store the solved x. This hash consists of a local memory array that stores a portion of the x values. This allows accessing the x values much faster, as opposed to reading them from global memory. We refer to this last version as SWI_{hash}. We tested two different versions of the SWI_{hash}, one that updates the x in global memory at the same time it is stored in the hash, and another one that impacts all x values from the hash to global memory at the end. This last version proved to be faster.

4   Experimental Evaluation

The hardware employed is a DE10–nano board from Terasic, it is based on a Cyclone V SoC form Intel, that includes a dual–core Cortex–A9 processor, around 110K Logic Elements of programmable logic and 1 GB of high–speed DDR3 memory shared between the processor and the FPGA. The FPGA has 6 MB of on–chip memory that can be used as scratchpad memory and 112 variable precision DSP blocks (capable of a peak performance of 22.4 GFLOPS). We use the Intel FPGA SDK for OpenCL v18.1 to compile our kernels.

To measure power consumption we use a FLUKE 45 multimeter (4.5 digits, accuracy: $0.2\% + 6$). The runtime is obtained by the profiling functions of OpenCL. The runtime results are the average of 10 independent executions.

We select 9 matrices from the SuiteSparse Matrix Collection with similar dimensions, between 17 k and 30 k rows, and large differences in the number of nnz, i.e. between 32 k and 6.76 M. Table 1 summarizes the characteristics of the matrices used.

Considering that the static power consumption of our experimental platform is elevated, in comparison with the dynamic one, in the first stage of the analysis we focus only on the runtime of the different variants.

The first study is for the NDR_{multi} variant. Table 2 presents the runtime attained to solve the different sparse matrices by the NDR_{multi} solver. We explore the use of several OpenCL parameters, particularly: (i) BS: the work–group size, with values of 1, 2, 4 and 16; (ii) CU: the number of compute units,

Table 1. Rows (n), non–zero elements (nnz) and levels of sparse matrices.

Matrix	Called	n	nnz	levels
Bcsstm35	BcsS	30237	32645	6
Chipcool0	ChipC	20082	281150	534
Gyro	Gyro	17361	519260	2796
Godwin_40	GodW	17922	561677	739
TSOPF162	T_{162}	20374	812749	114
Thread	Thread	29736	2249892	1446
TSOPF_RS_b300	T_{300}	28338	2943887	112
Ndk	Ndk	18000	3457658	5621
TSOPF_RS_b2052	T_{2052}	25626	6761100	61

Table 2. Runtime (in ms) for the NDR_{multi} variant of SPTRSV kernel with different optimizations.

BS	CU	UF	VE	ChipC	T_{162}	T_{300}	Gyro	GodW	BcsS	T_{2052}	Thread	Ndk
1	1	2	1	30.6	19.0	23.4	216.9	50.6	1.2	39.1	209.3	946.4
1	1	4	1	30.7	15.5	20.9	211.3	49.1	1.3	36.2	192.7	906.3
1	2	2	1	34.3	14.3	26.5	238.4	54.9	**1.1**	37.2	238.0	1121.8
1	2	4	1	31.4	13.0	22.8	221.7	52.0	1.1	35.0	205.5	995.3
2	2	2	1	31.0	12.5	21.8	205.1	48.4	1.3	39.7	172.7	774.4
2	2	2	2	33.5	22.3	60.5	225.7	54.3	1.1	132.2	230.3	1068.2
2	2	4	1	30.7	**12.1**	**20.8**	194.3	47.6	1.3	35.7	162.6	732.8
4	1	2	1	29.3	13.3	22.5	154.2	41.6	2.5	36.4	128.4	528.4
4	1	2	2	30.3	16.4	30.3	164.0	45.0	1.6	59.1	148.9	603.2
4	1	4	1	**29.5**	12.4	22.2	**150.2**	**41.5**	2.5	**33.3**	124.3	472.5
4	1	4	2	30.7	14.5	29.6	163.1	46.6	1.7	54.8	146.5	537.2
4	2	2	1	30.2	13.0	21.6	169.5	44.1	1.7	34.8	141.6	612.6
4	2	4	1	30.9	12.5	21.2	163.2	46.5	1.8	34.3	135.0	542.1
16	1	2	1	41.9	19.5	32.7	150.8	50.2	15.8	45.8	**112.2**	368.4
16	1	2	2	36.5	15.9	34.4	153.0	46.4	8.6	62.3	126.6	396.2
16	1	4	1	42.9	18.9	30.5	155.9	51.9	16.7	43.8	118.8	**361.9**
16	1	4	2	40.0	16.1	32.3	159.7	50.9	9.5	60.4	135.4	411.6

with values of 1 and 2; (iii) UF: the unroll–factor, with values of 1, 2 and 4; (iv) VE: the vectorization–factor (SIMD), with values of 1, 2 and 4. Note that the vectorization factor must be less than or equal to the work–group size, i.e. $VE \leq BS$. Additionally, our board does not allow many combinations of the optimization parameters due to hardware resource restrictions.

In the first place, the experimental results reached by NDR_{multi} variant show that there is not a single configuration of the optimization parameters that obtains the best results for all the matrices. From the work–group size perspective it seems that the higher the cost of solving the system is, the better it is to have a large BS. For the unroll–factor (UF) it appears that higher numbers are better. Most of the best runtimes occur for an unroll–factor of 4 and a few for a value of 2. The number of compute units (CU), a priori, does not show any recognizable pattern. Finally, the vectorization does not offer any gains, in all cases the variant with a vectorization–factor of 1 outperforms the other options. This is because the compiler is failing to vectorize the memory accesses since these are not contiguous. A similar explanation could be done for the compute unit replication since replicating the pipeline should double the computing capacity, but not necessarily the memory bandwidth. Taking the general behavior of this variant into account, it can be observed that the number of levels strongly affects the performance. Thus, this feature is more important than the number of non-zeros of each matrix. This situation is aligned with other works over the SPTRSV kernel with different hardware platforms, see [7,16].

Table 3. Runtime (in ms) for the NDR_{wait}, $SWI_{channel}$ and SWI_{hash} variants of SPTRSV kernel with different optimizations.

	BS	CU	UF	VE	ChipC	T_{162}	T_{300}	Gyro	GodW	BcsS	T_{2052}	Thread	Ndk
NDR_{wait}	4	1	1	1	**8.0**	15.8	52.5	**52.7**	12.5	4.5	132.5	**51.9**	**143.6**
	4	1	1	2	8.6	18.9	58.0	54.4	13.7	**4.0**	143.2	67.5	144.3
	8	1	1	1	9.7	25.9	86.9	78.2	20.9	7.0	200.3	75.5	162.0
	8	1	1	2	8.6	18.6	**51.3**	89.5	17.5	4.4	**113.6**	57.6	200.3
	16	1	1	1	18.0	36.4	116.2	102.8	29.1	17.9	264.5	99.6	224.6
	16	1	1	2	16.2	18.8	59.7	115.8	30.3	9.3	133.6	65.6	208.6
$SWI_{channel}$	1	1	1	1	**11.3**	12.0	32.3	**20.7**	**11.5**	11.4	66.5	**29.4**	59.6
	1	1	2	1	12.3	**11.7**	**31.4**	21.8	12.4	10.9	**57.3**	31.7	**58.9**
	1	1	4	1	12.4	15.4	47.8	24.5	13.9	12.3	89.2	40.8	72.0
	1	1	8	1	14.1	22.1	64.2	30.6	16.6	15.8	122.6	51.3	96.6
SWI_{hash}	1	1	1	1	**11.8**	22.0	69.1	24.0	12.5	**12.1**	150.5	55.3	99.9
	1	1	2	1	12.7	**11.3**	22.3	**19.9**	**12.4**	13.7	42.2	25.3	46.8
	1	1	4	1	14.0	12.1	**18.1**	20.9	13.4	15.3	**30.6**	**25.1**	**42.2**

The first rows of Table 3 summarizes the experimental results for the NDR_{wait}. The number of compute units, and the unroll–factor, are kept in 1, since incrementing the number of CU did not produce any runtime improvements and the structure of the kernel does not allow to implement unrolling. When comparing the attained performances with the NDR_{multi} counterpart, it is clear that NDR_{wait} version strongly improves the runtime for linear systems with a large number of levels, and it is not a good option for the smallest case and the TSOPF problem family. Additionally, the best parameter configurations in this variant are less scattered. And, more importantly, when this variant outperforms the previous one, the better configuration is in all cases the same (work–group size equal to 4 and a vectorization value of 1). For the Single Work Item Kernels, the OpenCL optimization space is more reduced. Only the unroll–factor is explored with values of 1, 2, 4 and 8. The other differences involve changing the algorithm strategy in each variant, i.e. whether or not a hash is used as cache memory.

Middle rows of Table 3 summarizes the runtime for $SWI_{channel}$ variant. These results reveal that the use of 1 and 2 for the unroll–factor are the best options for all test cases. Also, the differences between both configurations are negligible. Studying the general behavior of this variant, we need to highlight that the runtime differences between the test cases are smaller than in previous kernels. In NDR_{multi} version runtime ranges from 1.1 to 361.9 and in NDR_{wait} from 4.0 to 143.6, while in the current variant the interval is between 10.9 and 58.9. Additionally, it seems that the runtime performance is more related to the nnz value of each matrix.

The runtime results for SWI_{hash} are presented in the last rows of Table 3. First, we can see in the table that the results obtained for the different matrices are closer to each other, even more than in the $SWI_{channel}$ version. This is because the SWI_{hash} variant offers more benefits for matrices with large nnz, i.e. reduced runtime for the most costly test cases. Additionally, the use of the hash in the smallest test cases does not offer any benefits, increasing the runtime only marginally. Finally, in this variant, the optimization configuration (the value for unroll factor) is guided by the nnz of each matrix.

Table 4. Version, optimization configuration and runtime (in ms) for the best variant of SPTRSV kernel for the different test cases.

Matrix	Version	BS	CU	UF	VE	Runtime	Power (W)	Energy (mJ)
ChipC	NDR_{wait}	4	1	1	1	8.0	5.65	45.0
T_{162}	SWI_{hash}	1	1	2	1	11.3	6.60	74.3
T_{300}	SWI_{hash}	1	1	4	1	18.1	6.55	118.3
Gyro	SWI_{hash}	1	1	2	1	19.9	5.45	108.6
GodW	$SWI_{channel}$	1	1	1	1	11.5	5.25	60.3
BcsS	NDR_{multi}	1	2	2	1	1.1	5.50	6.1
T_{2052}	SWI_{hash}	1	1	4	1	30.6	6.80	208.2
Thread	SWI_{hash}	1	1	4	1	25.1	6.15	154.4
Ndk	SWI_{hash}	1	1	4	1	42.2	6.00	253.1

Column 7 of Table 4 consolidates the runtime results. The first observation that can be made from the numerical values is that all versions are the best for at least one case. The NDRange Kernels seem to be the best option for smallest test cases, while the Single Work Item Kernels are the best choice for matrices with large nnz. From the OpenCL optimization configuration perspective, our proposals are neither able to leverage the vectorization nor the use of more than one compute unit (only one of the best cases used 2 as a CU, but the difference is negligible when comparing against the non–replicating version).

On the other hand, the use of different values for the unroll–factor offers some benefits. Concretely, large test cases take advantage of larger unroll factors.

The last study is on energy consumption. In this line, the Columns 8 and 9 of Table 4 offers the Power and Energy consumption corresponding to the different test cases when the best kernel is employed. In Fig. 1 we plot the nnz ($\times 10^3$) processed by mJ of energy consumed for each test case, as the nnz is considered the best estimation of the effort implied by the SPTRSV for a particular sparse system. It should be noted that the cases that require more Power (e.g. the T_{2052} case) are the more efficient from the perspective of this metric.

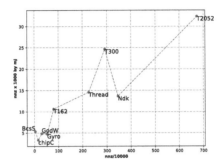

Fig. 1. Thousands of nnz processed by energy consumption (1 mJ).

5 Final Remarks and Future Work

We have studied the performance of several kernels for the solution of sparse tri-angular linear systems (SPTRSV) in FPGAs. In particular, we presented OpenCL implementations for the SPTRSV kernel following two different parallel execution paradigms: the NDRange and a Single Work–Item. Additionally, our study explores the most relevant OpenCL optimization configurations, such as the use of threads, vectorization and unrolling.

The experimental evaluation performed on a low–end FPGA shows that the best method varies from one test case to the other. This situation is aligned with other efforts for the SPTRSV kernel on massively–parallel devices. Additionally, the runtimes achieved by the best configuration of each case are competitive considering those found in the literature and our previous experience, while the energy consumption is lower.

In future work, we plan to address the combination of OpenCL with low–level developments to strongly improve the kernel performance. Also, it would be interesting to evaluate the performance of our solvers in other FPGAs and for a larger number of test cases, particularly including high-end boards and large linear systems. Finally, we will try to advance in the characterization of the FPGA performance and energy consumption of each technique.

Acknowledgments. The researchers were supported by Universidad de la República and the PEDECIBA. We acknowledge the ANII – MPG Independent Research Groups: "Efficient Heterogeneous Computing" with the CSC group.

References

1. The Green500 list (2019). http://www.green500.org
2. Benner, P., Ezzatti, P., Quintana-Ortí, E., Remón, A.: On the impact of optimization on the time-power-energy balance of dense linear algebra factorizations. In: Aversa, R., Kołodziej, J., Zhang, J., Amato, F., Fortino, G. (eds.) ICA3PP 2013. LNCS, vol. 8286, pp. 3–10. Springer, Cham (2013). https://doi.org/10.1007/978-3-319-03889-6_1
3. Czajkowski, T., et al.: From OpenCL to high-performance hardware on FPGAs. In: 22nd International Conference on Field Programmable Logic and Applications (FPL), pp. 531–534. IEEE (2012)
4. Davis, T.: Direct Methods for Sparse Linear Systems. Society for Industrial and Applied Mathematics, Philadelphia (2006)
5. Dongarra, J., et al.: The international ExaScale software project roadmap. Int. J. High Perform. Comput. Appl. **25**(1), 3–60 (2011)
6. Dongarra, J.J., Croz, J.D., Hammarling, S., Duff, I.S.: A set of level 3 basic linear algebra subprograms. ACM Trans. Math. Softw. **16**(1), 1–17 (1990)
7. Dufrechou, E., Ezzatti, P.: Solving sparse triangular linear systems in modern GPUs: a synchronization-free algorithm. In: 2018 26th Euromicro International Conference on Parallel, Distributed and Network-Based Processing (PDP), pp. 196–203 (2018)
8. Erguiz, D., Dufrechou, E., Ezzatti, P.: Assessing sparse triangular linear system solvers on GPUs. In: 2017 International Symposium on Computer Architecture and High Performance Computing Workshops (SBAC-PADW), pp. 37–42, October 2017
9. Ezzatti, P., Quintana-Ortí, E.S., Remón, A., Saak, J.: Power-aware computing. Concurr. Comput. Pract. Exp. **31**(6), e5034 (2019). e5034 cpe.5034
10. Favaro, F., Dufrechou, E., Ezzatti, P., Oliver, J.P.: Unleashing the sptrsv method in FPGAs. In: PACO 2019: 3rd Workshop on Power-Aware Computing (2019)
11. Fowers, J., Ovtcharov, K., Strauss, K., Chung, E., Stitt, G.: A high memory bandwidth FPGA accelerator for sparse matrix-vector multiplication. In: Proceedings of the IEEE International Symposium on Field-Programmable Custom Computing Machines, FCCM 2014, pp. 36–43. IEEE Computer Society (2014)
12. Golub, G.H., Van Loan, C.F.: Matrix Computations. Johns Hopkins University Press, Baltimore (2013)
13. Kestur, S., Davis, J.D., Chung, E.S.: Towards a universal FPGA matrix-vector multiplication architecture. In: 2012 IEEE 20th International Symposium on Field-Programmable Custom Computing Machines, pp. 9–16, April 2012
14. Kestur, S., Davis, J.D., Williams, O.: BLAS comparison on FPGA, CPU and GPU. In: 2010 IEEE Computer Society Annual Symposium on VLSI, pp. 288–293, July 2010
15. De Matteis, T., de Fine Licht, J., Hoefler, T.: FBLAS: Streaming Linear Algebra on FPGA (2019)
16. Naumov, M.: Parallel solution of sparse triangular linear systems in the preconditioned iterative methods on the GPU, NVIDIA Corp., Westford, MA, USA, Technical report, NVR-2011, 1 (2011)

17. Tan, Y., Imamura, T.: Performance evaluation and tuning of an OpenCL based matrix multiplier. In: PDPTA, pp. 107–113. The Steering Committee of The World Congress in Computer Science (2018)

18. Townsend, K.R.: Computing SpMV on FPGAs. Graduate Theses and Dissertations (2016). https://lib.dr.iastate.edu/etd/15227

19. Umuroglu, Y., Jahre, M.: A vector caching scheme for streaming FPGA SpMV accelerators. In: Sano, K., Soudris, D., Hübner, M., Diniz, P.C. (eds.) ARC 2015. LNCS, vol. 9040, pp. 15–26. Springer, Cham (2015). https://doi.org/10.1007/978-3-319-16214-0_2

20. Wirbel, L.: Xilinx SDAccel: A Unified Development Environment for Tomorrows Data Center. The Linley Group Inc., Mountain View (2014)

Architectures

A CGRA Definition Framework for Dataflow Applications

George Charitopoulos[1]($^{(\boxtimes)}$)(iD) and Dionisios N. Pnevmatikatos[2](iD)

[1] School of Electrical and Computer Engineering,
Technical University of Crete, Chania, Greece
gcharitopoulos@isc.tuc.gr
[2] School of Electric and Computer Engineering,
National Technical University of Athens, Athens, Greece

Abstract. Executing complex scientific applications on Coarse Grain Reconfigurable Arrays (CGRAs) promises execution time and/or energy consumption reduction compared to software execution or even customized hardware solutions. The compute core of CGRA architectures is a cell that typically consists of simple and generic hardware units, such as ALUs, simple processors, or even custom logic tailored to an application's specific characteristics. However generality in the cell contents, while convenient for serving multiple applications, comes at the cost of execution acceleration and energy consumption.

This work proposes a novel Mixed-CGRA Definition Framework (MC-DeF) targeting a Mixed-CGRA architecture that leverages the advantages of CGRAs by utilizing a customized cell-array, and FPGAs by utilizing a separate LUT array used for adaptability. Our framework employs a custom cell structure and functionality definition phase to create highly customized application/domain specific CGRA designs. This is achieved through the use of cost functions that use metrics such a resource usage, connectivity overhead, chip area occupied, i.a., and user-defined threshold values. Thus, the framework aids the user in creating suitable designs based on the application's needs and/or design restrictions, energy and/or area constraints.

We evaluate our framework using three applications: Hayashi-Yoshida, Mutual Information and Transfer Entropy and present fully functional, FPGA-based implementations of these applications to demonstrate the validity of our framework. Comparisons with related work show that MC-DeF performs favourably in terms of processing throughput - even when compared with much larger designs, uses fewer resources than most of the compared architectures, while utilizing better the underlying architecture recording the second best efficiency (LUT/GOPs) rating.

Keywords: CGRA · CGRA framework · Reconfigurable computing · FPGA

This research is supported in part by the General Secretariat for Research and Technology (GSRT) and the Hellenic Foundation for Research and Innovation (HFRI).

F. Rincón et al. (Eds.): ARC 2020, LNCS 12083, pp. 271–287, 2020.
https://doi.org/10.1007/978-3-030-44534-8_21

1   Introduction

The dataflow paradigm is a promising and well-established alternative towards customized hardware solutions. Several frameworks that create dataflow graphs (DFGs) and map them on specialized hardware have been proposed [13,24]. Coarse-grain architectures (CGA) have been used to map DFGs on their pre-defined and fixed hardware, and -due to hardware customization- often achieve faster and more energy efficient execution. A key disadvantage of CGAs is the lack of flexibility and versatility in their resources compared to more flexible approaches. A promising solution to this is *Coarse-Grain Reconfigurable Array (CGRA)* architectures, i.e. architectures that feature large reusable units with reconfigurable capacity [9], compared to more flexible approaches, which are highly customizable and tailored to the application's needs and requirements.

A key disadvantage of current CGRA architectures is the mapping process: a single node in the application's DFG is mapped onto a single cell in the array. Additionally CGRA architectures strive to be as generic as possible. This intentional lack of customized hardware leads to sub-optimal designs in terms of offered acceleration and general execution time. We need a CGRA definition framework that is able to: (a) map multiple nodes in one cell and (b) offer customized cell functionality, while maintaining a degree of flexibility.

In this work we propose a novel *Mixed-CGRA Definition Framework (MC-DeF)* couple with a *Mixed-Coarse Grain Reconfigurable Array (Mixed-CGRA)* architecture. The Mixed-CGRA architecture uses both a coarse-grain array and an adjacent reconfigurable LUT array for flexibility, connected with a fast and high bandwidth communication infrastructure. The definition framework uses the application's DFG representation and performs; application analysis in order to decide the CGRA-cell structure and functionality, mapping and routing. Moreover MC-DeF presents to the user area occupancy and energy consumption values based on the created design.

The resulting design can be implemented either as an ASIC, with added flexibility through the use of the adjacent reconfigurable LUT array, or as an overlay to an FPGA. Additionally, by fine-tuning the threshold values used by MC-DeF, the user can perform design space exploration in order to find a suitable hardware solution based on area or energy restrictions. To evaluate our proposed framework and architecture we use three scientific applications, Hayashi Yoshida estimator, Mutual Information of two random variables and Transfer entropy between two processes, and report on their resulting Mixed-CGRA designs as defined by MC-DeF. We also compare MC-DeF with other proposed CGRA architectures and show how our architecture fares against them.

The main contributions in this paper can be summarized as:

- A definition framework to create customized CGRA architectures, through the use of application analysis
- A cell-structure and mapping technique, able to map multiple stand-alone and/or chains of DFG nodes in a single CGRA cell
- A novel technique to unify operand nodes with same functionality and different bit-widths to create a more homogeneous CGRA design.

The rest of the paper is structured as follows: Sect. 2 presents related work on the field of CGRA architectures, MC-DeF and the targeted Mixed-CGRA are described in Sect. 3. Evaluations of MC-DeF and comparisons with other works are in Sect. 4. Finally Sect. 5 concludes our work and presents our final remarks.

2 Related Work

This section presents related work in the field of Coarse-Grain Reconfigurable array architectures. Our main focus is on architectures that have been evaluated using FPGA devices or act as FPGA overlays. Stojilovic et al. present a technique to automatically generate a domain-specific coarse-grained array from a set of representative applications [26]. Their technique creates a shortest common super-sequence found among all input applications based on weighted majority merge heuristic. Using this super-sequence, the framework creates a cell array able to map the application's instructions.

REDIFINE [2] is a polymorphic ASIC in which specialized hardware units are replaced with basic hardware units that can create the same functionality by runtime re-composition. The high-level compiler invoked creates substructures containing sets of compute elements. Paired with REDIFINE, HyperCell [21] enhances the CGRA compute elements with reconfigurable macro data-paths that enable exploitation of fine grain and pipeline parallelism at the level of basic instructions in static dataflow order.

Mapping Dataflow applications on CGRAs is wide research field. Niedermeier et al. present a novel programming paradigm designed to combine the principles of dataflow execution with CGRAs, [22]. The authors present a Haskell-based programming language coupled with a CGRA architecture comprising of reconfigurable cores. Each core includes a functional unit (FU), a register file and a program memory.

Intermediate Fabrics (IF) is an overlay architecture consisting of 192 heterogeneous FUs with an island-style interconnect [7]. The complete CGRA is implemented on an Altera Stratix III FPGA in order to support fully parallel, pipelined implementations of a set of image processing kernels. The DySER architecture consists of a heterogeneous array of 64 functional units interconnected with a programmable network [11,12]. A key disadvantage of DySER is high LUT consumption. Early implementations were only able to fit a 2 × 2 32-bit DySER on the FPGA. Subsequent implementations used DSP blocks as the homogeneous FU, thus achieving larger arrays.

Apart from using heterogeneous customized FUs, several researchers have elaborated on the use of DSP blocks as the CGRA FU. A fully pipelined DSP block based overlay architecture is presented in [17]. The overlay uses the dynamic programmability of the DSP block and maps up to three operations to each node (1 add/sub, 1 mul, 1 ALU op), resulting in a significant reduction in the number of processing nodes required. DECO [18], uses the same principle as [17] but the CGRA is arranged in a cone shaped cluster of DSP-based FUs utilizing a simple linear interconnect between them.

Another type of CGRA architecture is the expression-grained reconfigurable array (EGRA) [3]. The architecture described as a template with each Processing Element (PE) hardware able to be customised prior to fabrication. The authors by analyzing patterns in the application's computations decide on a set of arithmetical/logical units to implement in the PEs.

While MC-DeF bares resemblance to many of the works stated in this section it stands aside as being one of the few works adding LUT array based versatility as well as creating unique CGRA-cells that can be either domain- or application-specific depending on the user's requirements. Contrary to [26] MC-DeF employs a technique that tries to find common sequences of operations within one application. This leads to a more application-specific CGRA with the flexibility added through the use of an adjacent LUT array. MC-DeF and EGRA [3] are the only frameworks able to create an operation/function based CGRA cell based on application analysis. While similar in principle, MC-DeF performs a more detailed application analysis, including in the cell chains of common used functions instead of just the stand-alone functions. In Sect. 4 we evaluate our approach and compare it to *Intermediate Fabrics, Intermediate Fabrics (opt), DySER and DECO.*

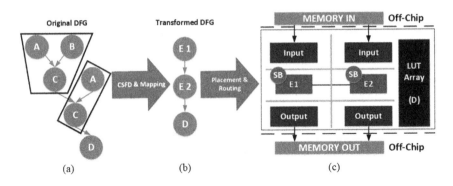

Fig. 1. The major processes carried out by the MC-DeF definition framework.

3   Mixed-CGRA Definition Framework

The problem that motivates this paper is the following: Given the dataflow graph (DFG) (Fig. 1 (a)): find the most suitable set of nodes to implement in a CGRA cell, map the graph nodes according to the cell created and place and route the resulting transformed application DFG in the CGRA architecture shown in Fig. 2. The whole process performed by our framework is shown in Fig. 1. The framework comes along with a novel CGRA architecture that incorporates a diagonal mesh network [15]. Additionally the framework presented in this paper utilizes several techniques that ultimately implement a highly efficient CGRA design in terms of execution time, bandwidth, energy consumption and area occupied.

The framework consists of four phases described in this section:

- **Cell Structure and Functionality**: the process used to decide the structure and functionality of the CGRA cell,
- **Mapping**: the process of mapping the application's computational elements on the CGRA cells and the accompanying LUT array,
- **Routing**: the process of connecting the different cells using switch boxes and the underlying network,
- **Area & Energy Calculation**: the process of calculating the occupied area and the energy consumption of the resulting chip.

In order to have a DFG representation of the target application, MC-DeF has to interface with a High-Level Synthesis framework. The Maxeler Platform, which uses the Dataflow Paradigm to enable massive amounts of hardware acceleration is used as the front-end to our MC-DeF definition framework. Maxeler Technologies is an HPC company that specializes in Multiscale Dataflow Computing (MDC) [23].

During Synthesis, the Maxeler framework produces a .xml file that contains the DFG hardware representation of the application, as well as, the connectivity between different nodes. The nodes of the DFG are simple, high abstraction hardware modules such as adders, counters, multipliers, etc. The DFG nodes are an intermediate representation between the high-level code and the resulting hardware.

3.1 Target Architecture

The architecture we propose, tries to balance the versatility and generality aspects of MC-DeF. The main computational needs of the applications are to be served by the cell-array, however the inclusion of a LUT array structure adds versatility to our architecture. The target architecture for our framework is shown in Fig. 2. It can be characterized as a mixed-coarse-grain reconfigurable array architecture, containing both a cell and a reconfigurable LUT array. The presented architecture can be either coupled as an accelerator core to a processor unit implemented in ASIC or as a standalone FPGA overlay.

The MC-DeF architecture consists of:

- **The Cell Array:** An array of homogeneous cells containing the appropriate, according to the application's needs, compute and memory elements.
- **Input/Output infrastructure** necessary for transferring input and output data to and from the MC-DeF.
- **LUT Array:** A reconfigurable LUT array adding versatility to the MC-DeF.
- **Switch Boxes & Network:** The necessary elements (data lines and connectivity matrices) in order to establish, cell-to-cell, cell-to-LUT array, I/O-to-cell or -LUT array communication. Cell-to-cell communication is handled

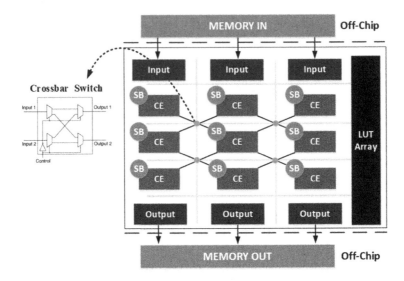

Fig. 2. Structure of the proposed CGRA.

by smaller, faster connections (black coloured lines). Cell-to-LUT array communication is achieved by larger buses (yellow coloured line). I/O nodes are directly connected to cells or LUT nodes.

– **Crossbar Switches:** Logic needed to enable bidirectional communication among cells at the network junctures (green circles).

3.2 Cell Structure and Functionality Definition (CSFD) Phase

Most of the proposed CGRA architectures use a static and pre-defined set of compute elements, soft-core processors or ALU structures coupled with instruction memories. While this approach is flexible and general enough to target a wide range of applications it lacks in terms of application scaling, resource utilization and the total number of operations performed in parallel.

The MC-DeF framework utilizes two novel techniques to create highly customized cells optimized to the target application's characteristics. The *Impact Factor* metric, introduced in [5], denotes the impact a DFG node has on the actual resource utilization of the application, i.e. percentage of LUTs, FIFOs, BRAMs and DSPs used by a node, over the total resource usage of the application. Nodes with high *Impact Factor* are labeled for inclusion in the cell structure.

The next step is to discover frequently occurring sub-graphs, a process similar to identifying frequent chains of instructions [6]. In [5] the authors run a modified version of GraMi [10], an algorithm for extracting frequent sub-graphs from a single large graph. A graph is extracted only if it exceeds a frequency and a resource utilization threshold, thus limiting the search space to sub-graphs that have high occurrence frequency and use the most hardware resources.

During the course of preliminary development of the CSFD phase we observed that nodes with same functionality had different operand bit-widths creating an issue with the homogeneity of the CGRA cells. To address this we design **Node Merging**; an algorithm designed to find whether two nodes with the same functionality should be merged under the same bit-width and what the optimal bit-width for the current application is. By node merging we create a more unified environment for our CGRA, in terms of bit-width. The resulting design is more generic and easier to implement.

The metrics used by Node Merging are: the bit-width difference between the two nodes and the *Percentage Gain*, i.e. the percentage increase in terms of resource utilization gained by a possible merging. By applying threshold values to the two metrics the algorithm is able to decide whether or not two nodes should be merged.

In our work node merging is the process of joining two same-functionality nodes with different bit-widths. There are two ways in which merging is performed in the context of MC-DeF definition framework: (a) perform bit extension on the smaller bit-width node, and (b) map the larger bit-width node in multiple CGRA cells.

The first merging option creates smaller designs but with a computation and communication overhead due to the non-useful extension bits. The second creates designs that use more CGRA cells but are faster in terms of internal bandwidth. The two associated overheads are calculated in order to choose the optimal bit-width. Moreover, in the case of bit-extensions re-adjustments are made to address the issue of arithmetic overflows. Nodes that undergo bit-extension, during the Node Merging process, are tagged and a special overflow circuit is added to their output.

Through the *CSFD phase* the MC-DeF framework ensures that the functionality of the CGRA-cell is beneficial in terms of resources, frequency of occurrence in the DFG and bandwidth achieved among cell communication. The threshold values applied are subject to change according the user needs and design restrictions.

3.3   Node Mapping

Node mapping is the process of assigning an application's DFG nodes in CGRA cells. However, CGRA cells contain chains of nodes and individual nodes as well, making the problem of mapping nodes to cells a difficult algorithmic process.

In order to efficiently allocate the DFG nodes on the CGRA cells, we implement a novel algorithm, *Node Grouping*. To explain Node Grouping, we present the following example: Let us consider an application graph with nodes $N=A$, B, C, D, and a CGRA cell with one node and a sub-graph $E = A \rightarrow C, B$. The desired functionality for Node Grouping, based on the example, is shown in Fig. 1 (b).

However, some nodes do not directly map to CGRA cells, e.g. node D in Fig. 1 (a). The functionality of these nodes is implemented in the adjacent LUT array seen in Fig. 2. The *CSFD phase* ensures that these node are but a small fraction of the total resources used by the application. A large application DFG and a more complex CGRA cell structure increase the graph transformation's complexity. Node Grouping finds and evaluates possible covering/mappings of the DFG using two cost functions:

- Unutilized cell resources: A cost function that measures the amount of unused resources among all the CGRA cells. A CGRA cell consisting of three nodes, with only two of them used will have an unutilized cell resources count equal to one.
- Connections between cells: A cost function that measures wire connections between different CGRA cells. If more than one outputs from one cell are connected to another then the connection is weighted, but still counts as one.

Finally after assigning nodes to cells the *Node Mapping* phase based on the number of cells used decides on the array size. The function responsible opts towards creating a square array, despite the fact that some cells might end up unused. Extra cells might prove beneficial if the user decides to map a different application on the existing array or if the application scales up demanding more resources at a later stage of development.

The implemented cost functions ensure that the resulting mapping is minimized in terms of cell utilization and cell communication complexity. Maximizing cell resource utilization creates compact and power efficient designs. Moreover, a design with few cell connections can achieve high clock frequency resulting in a higher internal bandwidth, while also minimizing wire power dissipation.

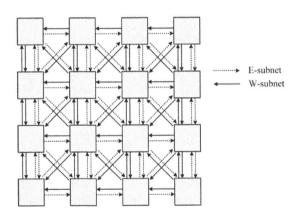

Fig. 3. Topology and links of DMesh.

3.4 Communication Infrastructure

Mixed-CGRA uses a two-level network as its communication infrastructure. The first level is used for local, i.e. cell-to-cell, communication and uses a diagonal mesh network. The DMesh network, presented in [15] and shown in Fig. 3, is the basis of our network. The second level of the MC-DeF network is grid of large bi-directional buses, yellow coloured lines in Fig. 1. This network is used for the communication of the cell-array and the I/O infrastructure with the adjacent LUT array.

We opt towards the DMesh network because experiments show that DMesh offers a 25% reduction of inter-node distance over a classic 2D-Mesh, while using almost double the resources. In our modified DMesh network instead of implementing dedicated N,S,W,E connections we implement a bi-directional crossbar switch at the intersection of the diagonal links reducing the total resource utilization by $\approx 35\%$. The elimination of four connection points does not affect our design since there use is to alleviate network congestion. In our case this is not necessary since very few cell-to-cell connections are bi-directional and also all computations are pipelined.

The *Routing* phase of MC-DeF uses two cost function in order to create designs with low communication overhead: the number and size of synchronization FIFOs used in each cell and the distance of two communicating cells.

Synchronization FIFOs. Dataflow execution dictates that operands arrive at compute nodes synchronized. However, operands from different paths may observe different compute and communication latencies. MC-DeF uses synchronization FIFOs where needed to re-time inputs in each CGRA cell. Synchronizing cell-node inputs could be remedied -but not fully solved- by latency-aware mapping of the cells, however this would lead to increasing the overall latency of all the cell-array. By inserting synchronization FIFOs inside the cells we ensure unobstructed parallel and pipelined execution. After inserting timing synchronization FIFOs, the Routing process continues to record all the connections between Input/Output nodes, cells and the LUT array. The connections found are then translated in connectivity matrices and are stored in the switch boxes.

Cell Distance. Cells are recognised by their position in the array, i.e. vertical and horizontal coordinates. The distance of cell A (0,0) and cell B (2,1) is 2. After calculating cell distance between two connecting cells the synchronization FIFOs are formulated accordingly. Distance between cells and, Input/Output nodes and the LUT array is three since communication is achieved over the slower grid network. Distance between the nodes within the LUT array is not considered.

These cost functions are used for improving the communication infrastructure. The next step of the routing process is to minimize them via traversing the Cell array. For the two cells mentioned before, we move one of them along the axis that shows the largest distance. For example, moving Cell A to the (1, 0) position reduces the distance by 1. After this traversal we need to re-evaluate the cost functions and perform more traversals if necessary. The process is repeated until a local minimum value is found, after a finite number of traversals.

3.5   Area and Energy Calculation

The overall cost of the resulting CGRA architecture is evaluated by measuring the area of the resulting architecture and the energy consumption. Similar to [4] and [25] we estimate the area occupancy of our architecture assuming a 7 nm lithography technology. Thus, a 6T SRAM bit cell unit's size is 30 nm^2, i.e. 38.5 Mb in 1 mm^2. For example a 1 k × 8bit FIFO will occupy approximately 250 μm^2, while the area needed to implement a fused double precision Multiply-Accumulate on 7 nm is 0.0025 mm^2. Additionally, we consider two 19.5 mm^2 Input/Output infrastructures at the top and bottom of the CGRA with 13 mm length and 1.5 mm width. Also, the LUT array area is calculated based on [1,27]. The numbers reported by the area evaluation phase of MC-DeF are: CGRA-only, CGRA+I/O and Total (CGRA+I/O+LUT) Area in mm^2.

Table 1. Energy consumption of electronic circuits used in MC-DeF

Circuit (32-bit double percision)	Energy (pJ)
Node Add/Sub	10
Node Multiply	9
Node Division	13
Logic Gates Nodes	0.5
64-bit read from an 8-KB SRAM	2.4
Data movement between cells	0.115 pJ/bit/mm

Calculating energy consumption of the resulting Mixed-CGRA design is based on the individual computing elements used. Bill Dally in [8] shows how the 64-bit double precision operation energy halved from 22 nm to 10 nm. Additionally in [20] the authors accurately measure the energy consumption of several electronic circuits. The numbers reported in this study are the basis of our energy consumption calculations.

In Tables 1 and 2 we present the area and energy measurements considered by our MC-DeF framework. The system interconnect access requires 1000pj. These values are worst case scenarios so they correspond to highly overestimated scenarios. Additional optimizations at the implementation level would allow for more efficient designs.

3.6   Discussion

The Mixed-CGRA reconfigurable designs produced by MC-DeF are technology agnostic. Two main avenues for the implementation of these designs are (i) on FPGAs, and (b) as custom ASICs. The former option is typical in the CGRA research field and we can take advantage of the FPGA reprogramming and use MC-DeF results as an overlay structure. The overlay, together with the data transfer protocol and framework forms a complete system. The latter option is

Table 2. Area occupancy of electronic circuits used in MC-DeF

Circuit		Area (μm^2)
Node Add/Sub Node Multiply/Divide		2500
FIFO (bits)		
Width	Depth	
<=8	<=1000	250
>8	<=1000	250
<=8	>1000	$\lceil Depth/1000 \rceil^{*}250$
>8	>1000	$\lceil Depth/1000 \rceil^{*}\lceil Width/8 \rceil^{*}250$

to produce a highly optimized, one time programmable accelerator for a specific application domain. However, the certain level of reconfigurability remains in the LUT array and the programmability of the Cell Array switch boxes.

Table 3. MC-DeF metrics, thresholds and cost-functions. Entries annotated with * are used for Communication infrastructure optimization, and with † for CGRA array optimization.

Name	Type	MC-DeF phase
Impact factor†	metric	CSFD application analysis
Utilization of frequently occurring sub-graphs†	threshold	CSFD Sub-graph discovery
Frequency of frequently occurring sub-graphs†	threshold	CSFD Sub-graph discovery
Percentage gain†	metric (threshold applied)	CSFD node merging
Bit-difference†	metric(threshold applied)	CSFD node merging
Connections between cells*	cost function	Mapping
Unutilized cell resources†	cost function	Mapping
Cell distance*	cost function	Routing
Number and Size of Sync. FIFOs*	cost function	Routing

Throughout its execution MC-DeF uses several metrics, thresholds and cost-functions. In Table 3 we list the name, type and MC-DeF phase each of them is used. The parameters used can be divided in two categories: those used to create a more compact and resource efficient array and those used to create a fast and high bandwidth communication framework.

The threshold values applied can be used for design space exploration in order for the user to find a hardware solution tailored to either area or energy restrictions. This feature is also aided by the fast execution and simulation times of MC-DeF averaging below two minutes.

4   Experimental Results

To evaluate our MC-DeF framework we use three scientific applications: Hayashi Yoshida coefficient estimator [14], Mutual Information of two random variables and Transfer entropy between two processes [16]. The characteristics of the three applications, i.e. resource utilization and DFG size, are presented in Table 4. All the results related to the final Mixed-CGRA architecture for the three applications are presented in this section. Additionally in this section we compare the MC-DeF framework and Mixed-CGRA architecture with related work in the field.

4.1   MC-DeF Results

Given the application DFG MC-DeF determines the optimal cell structure and functionality for the CGRA and the contents of LUT array, proceeds to map the nodes of the DFG to cells and specifies the connectivity network of the array. Finally MC-DeF calculates the energy consumption and area occupancy of the design and presents a final report to the user.

For the three applications used, we report their customized CGRA cell, the size of Cell and LUT arrays, clock frequency achieved, total chip area, energy consumption per 20 GB of input data, the average distance/cell and synchronization FIFO size/cell and finally the internal bandwidth recorded. All designs are parallelized and pipelined and can be implemented in either an overlay fashion or as a standalone design following the architecture shown in Fig. 1, in this case the target board for our designs is a Stratix V FPGA. The results are presented in Table 4.

Communication infrastructure configuration for all applications are 32-bit channels. The majority of operations performed by CGRA cells are 32-bit double precision floating-point. For all the applications MC-DeF achieves over 80% utilization using the CGRA cells. The remaining percentage is mapped on the LUT array. In the resulting designs the less utilized CGRA is observed in Hayashi Yoshida averaging 1 output/cell. Transfer Entropy and Mutual Information average 2.5 outputs/cell.

Clock frequency among applications is different due to the critical path observed within the CGRA cell. Since the three applications perform similar computations their energy consumption is also similar. We observed that even though the Hayashi Yoshida CGRA cell-count is larger, a single cell performs two double-precision floating-point operations. Thus, the Hayashi Yoshida application lets us observe the trade-off between floating-point operations per cell and the number of cells in the CGRA and how the two affect energy consumption.

4.2   Comparisons

As presented in Sect. 2, several works propose CGRA designs. Since of the different FPGA fabrics and the different overlay architectures, it is difficult to make fair and direct comparisons. Additionally there are no common application cases between these works and ours. Following the methodology presented in [19], we compare a baseline worst case scenario architecture created by MC-DeF with *Intermediate Fabrics, Intermediate Fabrics (opt), DySER and DECO*. Our comparison are based on generic metrics: clock frequency achieved, total operations

Table 4. MC-DeF Experimental Results

	Hayashi Yoshida	Transfer Entropy	Mutual Information
Resources (LUT, BRAM, DSP)	(3912, 0, 4)	(17677, 2, 4)	(17533, 2, 4)
DFG Nodes	270	199	225
Cell Structure	Equality → And Mul Add/Sub	Add/Sub Mul Div	Add/Sub Mul Div
CGRA dimensions	5 × 5	4 × 4	4 × 4
Clock Frequency	150 MHz	200 MHz	200 MHz
LUT array size	805	2941	2836
Total chip area mm^2	144.70	133.60	133.60
Energy Consumption	22.24 J	22.24 J	22.24 J
Avg. distance/cell	3	5.4	5.6
Avg FIFO size/cell	4	9.4	10.9
Internal Bandwidth	15 GB/s	32 GB/s	32 GB/s

carried out in parallel on the array, peak giga-operations per second on a fully utilized array and resource utilization.

As an additional comparison metric, we use the LUTs/GOPs metric, introduced in [19] in order to have a more quantitative and meaningful comparison between different CGRA designs. This metric represents the interconnect resource used per unit peak throughput, and gives the ability to quantify the area overhead of the overlay interconnect architectures irrespective of the FU/cell implementation.

Table 5 presents how our design fares compared to other related works. The *Intermediate Fabrics* architecture, is implemented in a Altera Stratix III E260 FPGA, *DySER* and *DECO*, are implemented both in a Xilinx Zynq XC7Z020 device. A uniqueness observed in *DECO* is that the cells are arranged in a cone-shape so X, Y array size is not applicable. As a reference design for our comparisons we consider a CGRA size 6 × 6 with 3 ops/cell operating at a maximum *frequency* of 200 MHz. Calculation of the GOPs operations performed is done by multiplying the frequency with the total operations performed by each cell when the CGRA is fully utilized. In all of the cases the cell is considered to perform all available operation per clock cycle.

MC-DeF is able to map multiple operational nodes from the application's DFG in a single cell. Since operations in the cell are parallel and pipelined, the total operations performed in the cell is equal to the number of original DFG nodes in it, e.g. the Transfer Entropy design performs 3 operations/cell at each cycle. As the contents of the cell as defined by our framework matches the needs and structure of the application DFG nodes, both the utilization and the processing throughput of the corresponding circuits within the cell is high. This is an advantage compared to related work where the basis of a cell is a generic large FU/ALU performing at maximum 1 or 2 operations per cycle. This also means that our designs are more compact, thus reducing resource utilization and energy consumption.

Table 5. Quantitative comparison of CGRAs

Resource	IF	IF (opt.)	DySER	DECO	MC-DeF	MC-DeF+DSP
CGRA grid	14 × 14	14 × 14	6 × 6	20 (cone)	6 × 6	6 × 6
Frequency	131	148	175	395	200	200
Total OPs	196	196	36	60	108	108
Peak GOPs	25.6	29	6.3	23.7	21.6	21.6
LUT used	91 K	50 K	48 K	10 K	15 K	13 K
LUT/GOPs	3550	1725	7620	430	694	601

The current implementation of the proposed Mixed-CGRA architecture does not use the maximum amount of DSPs offered by the FPGA. By allocating one DSP per cell we can achieve a better combination of fixed hardware logic and reconfigurable LUTs as is our intention. By doing so we also have a reduction in the LUTs used by the whole architecture. The enhanced design is presented in Table 5 as MC-DeF (+DSPs) and uses 2 K less LUTs, recording 601 LUT/GOPs.

In terms of peak performance (GOPs), compared to the *IF* overlay MC-DeF is outperformed by 1.8x, but the implemented MC-DeF design is 7 times smaller than *IF*. Compared to *DySER*, our design records higher peak GOPs and has a better LUT/GOPs metric. MC-DeF has the second lowest LUT/GOPs metric approaching an almost ideal interconnect area overhead. The best performing design is *DECO*, however the superiority of DECO is mainly due to the high clock frequency achieved, a result of the fact that it is a DSP-only CGRA architecture. It is possible for MC-DeF to increase the number of peak GOPs by including more operations in a single cell thus improving both GOPs and the LUT/GOPs metrics. This is feasible due to the customization performed during the *CSFD* phase of our framework.

We also note that the applications we used to evaluate MC-DeF are larger (in terms of nodes) than the ones used in other works. For example, an FFT graph has ≈40 nodes while the Hayashi Yoshida graph has over 100 nodes.

The above comparisons highlight three key advantages of MC-DeF over related work. First, MC-DeF is able to formulate highly customized cells that match the application computational needs. Moreover, the universality of computations over an application domain allows the user to map and execute other applications on the same array. MC-DeF achieves better LUT resource utilization when compared with same array-sized designs like DySER. Regarding the operations performed, MC-DeF outperforms same array-sized designs in terms of GOPs, MC-DEF is 3.4 times faster than DySER. Finally, compared to much larger designs, i.e. IF, MC-DeF is just 1.18x slower, while using 7 times less resources.

5 Conclusion

In this paper we propose the MC-DeF definition framework, that can create efficient CGRAs customized for specific applications. MC-DeF supports all the required definition and mapping steps to offer a complete and self-contained solution. Through the use of cost functions, threshold values and metrics, the framework can be used for design-space exploration and reach the desired cost and performance targets set by the designer. Furthermore, the use of a small LUT array in parallel with the core compute cell array allows the efficient mapping of irregular computation that does not fit the cell computation features, and also retains a level of general reconfigurability. Our evaluation and comparison to the state of the art shows that MC-DeF performs favourably in terms of GOPs even when compared with much larger designs in terms of CGRA size, uses less resources than most of the compared architectures, and utilizes better the underlying architecture recording the second best LUT/GOPs rating.

In the future we plan to further explore the communication infrastructure of Mixed-CGRA and evaluate alternative network topologies, connectivity, etc. Additionally we want to explore the benefits of adding small amounts of reconfigurability in the cells, so as to be able to use different portions of the cell to map different applications. Finally we want to create a suite of available Mixed-CGRA designs from various benchmark scientific applications.

References

1. Ahmed, E., Rose, J.: The effect of LUT and cluster size on deep-submicron FPGA performance and density. IEEE Trans. Very Large Scale Integr. (VLSI) Syst. **12**(3), 288–298 (2004)
2. Alle, M., et al.: REDEFINE: runtime reconfigurable polymorphic ASIC. ACM Trans. Embed. Comput. Syst. **9**(2), 11:1–11:48 (2009)
3. Ansaloni, G., Bonzini, P., Pozzi, L.: EGRA: a coarse grained reconfigurable architectural template. IEEE Trans. Very Large Scale Integr. Syst. **19**(6), 1062–1074 (2011)
4. Chang, J., et al.: 12.1 A 7nm 256 Mb SRAM in high-k metal-gate FinFET technology with write-assist circuitry for low-VMIN applications. In: 2017 IEEE International Solid-State Circuits Conference (ISSCC), pp. 206–207, February 2017
5. Charitopoulos, G., Pnevmatikatos, D.N.: DARSA: a dataflow analysis tool for reconfigurable platforms. In: 18th International Conference on Embedded Computer Systems: Architectures, Modeling, and Simulation, SAMOS 2018, pp. 65–72 (2018)
6. Clark, N., Zhong, H., Mahlke, S.: Processor acceleration through automated instruction set customization. In: Proceedings of 36th Annual IEEE/ACM International Symposium on Microarchitecture, MICRO-36, pp. 129–140 (2003)
7. Coole, J., Stitt, G.: Intermediate fabrics: virtual architectures for circuit portability and fast placement and routing. In: 2010 IEEE/ACM/IFIP International Conference on Hardware/Software Codesign and System Synthesis (CODES+ISSS), pp. 13–22, October 2010
8. Dally, B.: Challenges for future computing systems. Presentation in HiPEAC Conference (2015)

9. De Sutter, B., Raghavan, P., Lambrechts, A.: Coarse-grained reconfigurable array architectures. In: Bhattacharyya, S.S., Deprettere, E.F., Leupers, R., Takala, J. (eds.) Handbook of Signal Processing Systems, pp. 427–472. Springer, Cham (2019). https://doi.org/10.1007/978-3-319-91734-4_12

10. Elseidy, M., Abdelhamid, E., Skiadopoulos, S., Kalnis, P.: GRAMI: frequent subgraph and pattern mining in a single large graph. Proc. VLDB Endow. **7**(7), 517–528 (2014)

11. Govindaraju, V., et al.: DySER: unifying functionality and parallelism specialization for energy-efficient computing. IEEE Micro **32**(5), 38–51 (2012)

12. Govindaraju, V., Ho, C., Sankaralingam, K.: Dynamically specialized datapaths for energy efficient computing. In: 2011 IEEE 17th International Symposium on High Performance Computer Architecture, pp. 503–514, February 2011

13. Hartenstein, R.: Coarse grain reconfigurable architecture (embedded tutorial). In: Proceedings of the 2001 Asia and South Pacific Design Automation Conference, DAC 2001, pp. 564–570. ACM (2001)

14. Hayashi, T., Yoshida, N.: On covariance estimation of non-synchronously observed diffusion processes. Bernoulli **11**(2), 359–379 (2005)

15. Hu, W.H., Lee, S.E., Bagherzadeh, N.: DMesh: a diagonally-linked mesh network-on-chip architecture. In: Network on Chip Architectures, p. 14 (2008)

16. Iordanou, K., Nikolakaki, S.M., Malakonakis, P., Dollas, A.: A performance evaluation of multi-FPGA architectures for computations of information transfer. In: 18th International Conference on Embedded Computer Systems: Architectures, Modeling, and Simulation, SAMOS 2018, pp. 1–9 (2018)

17. Jain, A.K., Fahmy, S.A., Maskell, D.L.: Efficient overlay architecture based on DSP blocks. In: 2015 IEEE 23rd Annual International Symposium on Field-Programmable Custom Computing Machines, pp. 25–28, May 2015

18. Jain, A.K., Li, X., Singhai, P., Maskell, D.L., Fahmy, S.A.: DeCO: a DSP block based FPGA accelerator overlay with low overhead interconnect. In: 2016 IEEE 24th Annual International Symposium on Field-Programmable Custom Computing Machines (FCCM), pp. 1–8, May 2016

19. Jain, A.K., Maskell, D.L., Fahmy, S.A.: Are coarse-grained overlays ready for general purpose application acceleration on FPGAs? In: 2016 IEEE 14th International Conference on Dependable, Autonomic and Secure Computing, 14th International Conference on Pervasive Intelligence and Computing, (DASC/PiCom/DataCom/CyberSciTech), pp. 586–593, August 2016

20. Keckler, S.W., Dally, W.J., Khailany, B., Garland, M., Glasco, D.: GPUs and the future of parallel computing. IEEE Micro **31**(5), 7–17 (2011)

21. Madhu, K.T., Das, S., Nalesh, S., Nandy, S.K., Narayan, R.: Compiling HPC kernels for the redefine CGRA. In: IEEE 17th International Conference on High Performance Computing and Communications, and 12th International Conference on Embedded Software and Systems, pp. 405–410, August 2015

22. Niedermeier, A., Kuper, J., Smit, G.J.M.: A dataflow inspired programming paradigm for coarse-grained reconfigurable arrays. In: Goehringer, D., Santambrogio, M.D., Cardoso, J.M.P., Bertels, K. (eds.) ARC 2014. LNCS, vol. 8405, pp. 275–282. Springer, Cham (2014). https://doi.org/10.1007/978-3-319-05960-0_29

23. Pell, O., Averbukh, V.: Maximum performance computing with dataflow engines. Comput. Sci. Eng. **14**(4), 98–103 (2012)

24. Sen, M., et al.: Dataflow-based mapping of computer vision algorithms onto FPGAs. EURASIP J. Embedded Syst. **2007**(1), 049236 (2007)

25. Standaert, T., et al.: BEOL process integration for the 7 nm technology node. In: 2016 IEEE International Interconnect Technology Conference/Advanced Metallization Conference (IITC/AMC), pp. 2–4, May 2016
26. Stojilović, M., Novo, D., Saranovac, L., Brisk, P., Ienne, P.: Selective flexibility: creating domain-specific reconfigurable arrays. IEEE Trans. Comput. Aided Des. Integr. Circuits Syst. **32**(5), 681–694 (2013)
27. Xilinx: 7 Series FPGAs Data Sheet: Overview, rev. 2.6, February 2018

Implementing CNNs Using a Linear Array of Full Mesh CGRAs

Valter Mário[1], João D. Lopes[2(✉)], Mário Véstias[3], and José T. de Sousa[1,2]

[1] IObundle Lda/IST, Lisboa, Portugal
[2] INESC-ID/IST, Lisboa, Portugal
joao.d.lopes@tecnico.ulisboa.pt, jts@inesc-id.pt
[3] INESC-ID/ISEL, Lisboa, Portugal

Abstract. This paper presents an implementation of a Convolutional Neural Network (CNN) algorithm using a linear array of full mesh dynamically and partially reconfigurable Coarse Grained Reconfigurable Arrays (CGRAs). Accelerating CNNs using GPUs and FPGAs is more common and there are few works that address the topic of CNN acceleration using CGRAs. Using CGRAs can bring size and power advantages compared to GPUs and FPGAs. The contribution of this paper is to study the performance of full mesh dynamically and partially reconfigurable CGRAs for CNN acceleration. The CGRA used is an improved version of the previously published Versat CGRA, adding multi CGRA core support and pre-silicon configurability. The results show that the proposed CGRA is as easy to program as the original full mesh Versat CGRA, and that its performance and power consumption scale linearly with the number of instances.

Keywords: Convolutional Neural Networks · Coarse Grained Reconfigurable Arrays · Reconfigurable computing · Embedded systems

1 Introduction

During the last few years we have seen extensive developments in Machine Learning (ML), Artificial Intelligence (AI) and the Internet of Things (IoT). These advances increased the complexity of algorithms and the need to lower the size and power consumption of the hardware platforms used to run them. To tackle computational complexity, it is common practice to use dedicated hardware to speed up computations. However, using non-programmable hardware offers poor scalability, prevents updates and upgrades, and increases the cost of design errors. For these reasons, programmable hardware such as GPUs or FPGAs are preferred for these functions but their large size and high power consumption prevents their use in embedded devices powered by batteries.

For embedded applications a more suitable accelerator is the Coarse Grained Reconfigurable Array (CGRA), which is also programmable and can be made small and energy efficient. A CGRA is a collection of programmable Functional Units (FUs) and embedded memories connected by programmable interconnects.

© Springer Nature Switzerland AG 2020
F. Rincón et al. (Eds.): ARC 2020, LNCS 12083, pp. 288–297, 2020.
https://doi.org/10.1007/978-3-030-44534-8_22

When programmed, specialized hardware datapaths are formed in the CGRA, able to execute the target tasks orders of magnitude faster than a regular CPU.

In the last 25 years, CGRAs have become the subject of several research papers [5]. CGRA architectures can be homogeneous [6], using only one type of programmable FUs, or heterogeneous [8], using FUs of different types. As for the programmable interconnections between FUs, direct neighbour-to-neighbour connections or 2D-Mesh networks are the most popular choices [13]. CGRAs can be statically reconfigurable, i.e., they are configured once for an entire application [7], or dynamically reconfigurable [10], that is, they are reconfigured at runtime. Some CGRAs can only be fully reconfigurable [10], whereas others use partial reconfiguration [4,6,12]. The success of any architecture depends crucially on the available tool support [13]. Different types of compilers have been proposed [11] for CGRAs but this is still a critical weakness preventing these architectures from becoming mainstream.

To address the lack of compiler tools, an extreme approach of using a full mesh CGRA called Versat has been proposed in [9]. Being a full mesh, the compilation complexity, namely the need to place and route the designs is removed, and the configurations can even be produced on-the-fly by the application itself. Versat featured self-generated dynamic and partial reconfiguration driven by an external controller unit. The Versat core was good for applications that require a small number of FUs. However, ML applications require a massive amount of parallelism, which was unattainable with the original Versat core. In fact, its full mesh structure cannot scale spatially, creating routing congestion and forcing lower operation clock frequencies.

To target ML applications, this work proposes the use of a multi-core Versat architecture controlled by a simple RISC-V [2] processor. The RISC-V architecture is supported by the GNU toolchain, enabling the development of applications using the C and C++ languages.

2   The Deep Versat Architecture

The multi-core architecture has been called Deep Versat and is organised as a ring of Versat cores. This topology is one of the simplest that can utilise multiple instances, and its ring structure facilitates the reuse of the data left in the accelerator between different configurations.

Each individual Versat core keeps the full mesh topology of the original proposal, for retaining its programmability, but the size of each core is limited to 10 FU output ports. A large number of cores can be added to the ring, depending on the needs of the target application, and the limit is only the device size. A block diagram of this architecture is depicted in Fig. 1.

Figure 1 shows several Versat cores linearly interconnected forming a ring. Since CGRAs are used to accelerate program loops a linear topology can easily exploit loop optimisation techniques such as loop unrolling. The ring topology facilitates the reuse of the data left in any of the Versat cores by the next configuration applied to the array.

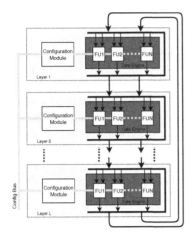

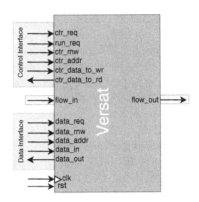

Fig. 1. Deep Versat architecture.   **Fig. 2.** Versat symbol and interface.

In each Versat core, the FUs can select as inputs any FU outputs from the previous core and from itself. Hence, each core can only produce at most 10 output ports so that the number of selection inputs for each FU port does not exceed 20: 10 from the previous core and 10 from the current core. This way, the routing complexity of each core is similar to that of the previous Versat core proposal and independent of the number of cores. The number of Versat cores is only limited by the device size.

The individual Versat cores have been streamlined and simply comprise the Data Engine (DE), which is formed by its FUs, and the Configuration Module (CM), which holds the FU configurations. The interface of each CGRA is represented in Fig. 2 and consists of Control, Data and Flow interfaces. The Control Interface is used to read and write to the Versat registers. The Data Interface is used by the processor or DMA core to read and write data from/to the Versat memories. The Flow Interface consists of the `flow_in` and `flow_out` buses, and it is used to connect two consecutive Versat cores.

3   The RV32 Deep Versat System

To control the Deep Versat core, the picoRV32 open source processor [3] has been adopted. The picoRV32 processor is a RISC-V architecture which can be programmed using the well known `gcc` and `g++`, C and C++ compilers, respectively.

The picoRV32 processor runs the application code and uses the Deep Versat core as an accelerator. For many applications the use of a single picoRV32 core and a Deep Versat core will suffice. Other applications may require a more powerful processor for running the software, for example, a superscalar RISC-V or ARM core. The system shown in Fig. 3 is composed of the picoRV32 processor having as peripherals the Deep Versat core and a UART core.

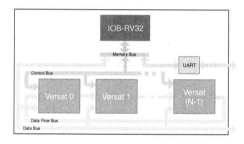

Table 1. Memory map.

Peripheral	Base address
UART module	0×10000000
Deep Versat control bus	0×11000000
Deep Versat data bus	0×12000000

Fig. 3. The RV32 Deep Versat system.

The peripherals are memory mapped as described in Table 1. The picoRV32 system uses a 32-bit address bus where 8 bits are used to choose the peripheral. Hence, there are 24 bits to address Deep Versat. 15 out of these 24 bits are used for internally addressing each Versat core. The remaining 9 bits are used to select the Versat core, so in theory the Deep Versat core may contain as many as 512 Versat cores for achieving maximum parallelism and acceleration.

4   Pre-silicon Configurability

Pre-silicon configurability consists in the ability to choose the set of FUs for the Versat core before the circuit is implemented. This powerful feature enables tailoring and optimizing Versat for different applications. The automatic generation of the FU array has been implemented using Verilog macros and *generate for* statements (e.g. Fig. 4).

```
generate
  for (i=0; i < 'nALU; i=i+1) begin : add_array
    xalu alu (
      .clk(clk),
      .rst(run_reg),
      // Data IO
      .data_bus(data_bus),
      .result(data_bus['DATA_ALU0_B - i*'DATA_W -: 'DATA_W]),
      // Configuration data
      .configdata(config_reg_shadow['CONF_ALU0_B -
                                    i*'ALU_CONF_BITS -: 'ALU_CONF_BITS])
    );
  end
endgenerate
```

Fig. 4. Pre-silicon configuration of the ALU array.

To configure Versat at pre-silicon time, the user sets the types and numbers of FUs to be instantiated using the macros in the main header file. This file can be edited for each specific application. The size of each memory can also be specified, allowing Versat to have memories of different sizes. An obvious future improvement is to replace the macros by Verilog generic parameters, which will allow instantiating multiple and heterogeneous Versat cores.

5   The Deep Versat API

As can be seen in Fig. 1, the Deep Versat hierarchy is the following: Deep Versat is an array of Versat cores, and each Versat is an array of FUs. Modeling hardware with an object oriented language is convenient as the hardware modules can be represented by classes whose methods are used to configure and operate the modules. The Deep Versat API has been written in the C++ object oriented programming language.

To represent the Deep Versat hardware an array of *CVersat* objects is declared. One may ask why the size of this array must be declared if the number of layers is already known from the Verilog code. The reason is that the API makes it possible to work with a virtual Deep Versat core whose size is different from its physical size. This is useful if the application does not need to use all cores or would need to use more cores than the ones actually present. This is called virtual hardware, a feature that is planned but not yet implemented.

After declaring the CVersat object, one needs to populate it with a set of FUs. At the moment, the available FU types are the following: ALU (of 2 different types), Barrel Shifter, 1 multiplier type and 1 new multiply-accumulate (MAC) type. The FU population in each CVersat class has to of course match the FUs in the actual Versat core, and in the future this can be automated so that both the hardware and software are created consistently. The FUs in each Versat core can be operated by the control processor by writing to their configuration registers in the configuration module. There are registers to configure the FU function and connections.

6   The CNN Application: Handwritten Digit Recognition

The chosen application is a handwritten digit recognition program that uses the well known *mnist* dataset [1] and performs Convolutional Neural Network (CNN) inference on a previously trained network (Fig. 5). Each 28×28 image passes through a series of layers in order to be classified. The layers are of the following types: convolutional, pooling, fully connected and softmax. The output represents the most likely classification, from digit 0 to digit 9, and its respective probabilistic value between 0 and 1.

The convolutional layer performs the multiply-accumulate function of each element of the filter by the corresponding pixel of the image. 22 matrix filters of dimension 5×5 are used, which produces a $22 \times 5 \times 5$ tensor. The maxpool layer is responsible for down sampling the largest images, from size 24×24 down to size 12×12, while keeping the relevant information. The process used in this layer is simple: it goes through the 24×24 image and takes the greatest value in each 2×2 region. Hence, the output of the pooling layer is $22 \times 12 \times 12$ tensor. The (fully) connected layer takes the $22 \times 12 \times 12$ tensor produced and again uses a convolutional process to turn it into a 10-element vector, where each position contains the votes for the respective digit. The last layer of the CNN is the softmax layer. It finds the digit with most votes and classifies it as the most likely handwritten digit represented in the image.

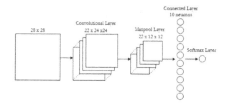

Fig. 5. CNN architecture with a single convolutional layer.

Table 2. Execution time per layer when running on the ARM processor.

Layer	Execution time (μs)	%
Convolutional	32839	88.41%
Maxpool	1300	3.50%
Connected	2998	8.07%
Softmax	5	0.01%
Total	37142	100%

The application is divided in four parts corresponding to the four CNN layers. The time profile of the application is presented in Table 2 for a 667 Mhz ARM Cortex-A9 processor. The table shows that the layer that takes most of the execution time is the convolutional layer, which has been chosen for acceleration. The software code that implements this layer is divided in two parts: (1) the *preparation* of the images for convolution with the filter, which is basically a replication of the data in the memory, and (2) the convolution itself, which is done by the General Matrix Multiply (GeMM) algorithm.

As there are 22 filters of 5×5 coefficients, a matrix B of size 22×25 is created. The input image is prepared, that is, it is transformed into a 576×25 matrix A, where the number of rows is 24×24 and the number of columns is 5×5. It can be shown that the convolution is equivalent to computing matrix $C = AB^T$. The preparation of matrix A, being just a replication of the image data, is not very interesting from the point of view of acceleration. The part that takes most of the execution time and is candidate for acceleration is the GeMM algorithm.

Each Versat core can execute 2 nested loops. Thus, a single Versat core with the new multiply-accumulate FU (MULADD) could be used to run the GeMM algorithm. However, to scale the performance, multiple Versat cores are used by distributing the workload among them using the loop unrolling technique. The inner-most loop of the GeMM, which in this case goes from 0 to 24 is distributed over 5 cores, resulting in a 5-core Deep Versat architecture. Note that this is possible because there are no data dependencies between iterations. The first core computes elements 0 to 4, the second core computes elements 5 to 9 adding its result to the result coming from the first core and so on up to the fifth core. This creates a pipeline structure with 5-cycle latency and a throughput of one result per cycle. Therefore, the execution time of the GeMM is reduced roughly 5 times, which is the expected acceleration for 5 cores running in parallel compared to a single core. For simplicity, only 2 out of the 5 cores are shown in Fig. 6.

As can be seen in Fig. 6, each Deep Versat core uses 1 MULLADD FU and 4 AGU blocks from 4 memory units (shown in blue). Two of the AGUs are used for addressing the MULADD operands, another is used for controlling the MULADD and the last is used for addressing the result from the previous core, which had been stored in a memory of the current core. For a single MULADD,

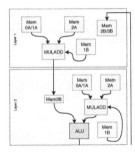

Fig. 6. Two convolutional layers.

2 data memories would be enough but in fact 5 memories per core have been used, because this is the number required by the fully connected layer, which was accelerated in a similar way. Each of the 5 memories can hold up to 8192 data words. If needed 2 MULADDs per core could be used to double the parallelism.

Given the chosen memory sizes, the 14400-word matrix A needs to be stored in 2 different memories. Half the matrix is stored in memory 0 and the other half is stored in memory 1, as shown in Fig. 6. The same happens to the output matrix C, which has 576 * 22 words divided between memories 2 and 3. The Deep Versat API code used to configure layers 1 and 2 of the designed datapath is presented in Fig. 7 to illustrate the process. The `setConf` method, whose details are not explained here due to lack of space, is used to create full configuration of an FU, and the `writeConf` method is used to write the configuration to the configuration registers. The `setStart` method is used to set only one configuration register, the start address of a memory port. Partial reconfiguration is clearly illustrated here: `setConf` configures just one FU and `setStart` configures just one configuration register of an FU. The `versatRun` function runs Deep Versat after waiting for the previous run to finish.

7   Experimental Results

The described system has been run on a Xilinx XCKU040 FPGA of the Kintex UltraScale product family, and compared with 2 other systems running the same application: a RISC-V + single Versat system, and an ARM Cortex-A9 processor + 4 General Matrix Multiply (GeMM) IPs.

Table 3 compares the FPGA resources used and the execution performance in each system. RAM stands for 36kbit RAM blocks, Frequency is the clock frequency, WNS stands for Worst Negative Slack, Time is the execution time and Speedup is the ratio of the execution time on the ARM system over the execution time on each system. Note that the ARM core runs independently at 667 MHz.

The RISC-V + Deep Versat system is around five times larger than the RISC-V + Versat system, which is expected since Deep Versat integrates 5 single Versat cores. It is not possible to make direct size comparisons to the ARM + 4 GeMM

```
void gemmBT( CVersat v1, CVersat v2) {
  int rowsA = 24*24, colsA = 25, rowsB = 22;
  int i;

  //Config MEM2A to read filter weigths (0-110)
  v1.memPort[m2A].setConf(0, 22, 1, 0, 5, 5, 0, 0, 0);
  v1.memPort[m2A].writeConf();
  v2.memPort[m2A].setConf(0, 22, 1, 1, 5, 5, 0, 0, 0);
  v2.memPort[m2A].writeConf();

  //Config MEM1B to control MULADDs
  v1.memPort[m1B].setConf(0, 22, 1, 1, 5, 5, sADDR, -5, 0);
  v1.memPort[m1B].writeConf();
  v2.memPort[m1B].setConf(0, 22, 1, 2, 5, 5, sADDR, -5, 0);
  v2.memPort[m1B].writeConf();

  //Config MEM0A to read 1st half of matrix A (0-7199)
  v1.memPort[m0A].setConf(0, 22, 1, 0, 5, 5, 0, -5, 0);
  v1.memPort[m0A].writeConf();
  v2.memPort[m0A].setConf(5, 22, 1, 1, 5, 5, 0, -5, 0);
  v2.memPort[m0A].writeConf();

  //Config MULADD
  v1.muladd[0].setConf(sMEMA[2], sMEMB[1], sMEMA[0], MULADD);
  v1.muladd[0].writeConf();
  v2.muladd[0].setConf(sMEMA[2], sMEMB[1], sMEMA[0], MULADD);
  v2.muladd[0].writeConf();

  //Pipeline layer 1 - 2
  v2.memPort[m3B].setConf(0, 22, 0, 8, 5, 1, sMULADD_p[0]);
  v2.memPort[m3B].writeConf();

  //AluLite layer2
  v2.alulite[0].setConf(sMEMB[3], sMULADD[0], ALULITE_ADD);
  v2.alulite[0].writeConf();

  //Save 1st part of the result (6336) in v1.MEM2 (1856-8191)
  v1.memPort[m2B].setConf(1856, 22, 1, 20, 5, 1, sALULITE_p[0]);
  v1.memPort[m2B].writeConf();

  //Running layers 1 and 2
  for (i=0; i<rowsA/2; i++) {
    v1.memPort[m0A].setStart(i*colsA+0);
    v2.memPort[m0A].setStart(i*colsA+5);

    //We get 22 results in each run
    v1.memPort[m2B].setStart(1856+rowsB*i);

    versatRun();
  }
}
```

Fig. 7. Code to configure the datapath presented in Fig. 6.

Table 3. FPGA implementation and execution results.

	LUTs	FFs	RAM	DSPs	Frequency (MHz)	WNS (ns)	Time (μs)	Speedup
RISC-V + Versat	7081	3460	62	8	100	0.521	9780	3.36
RISC-V + DeepVersat	40478	14631	196	20	100	0.292	1689	19.44
ARM + 4 GeMM	16706	17715	16	16	100	NA	3961	8.25
ARM	NA	NA	NA	NA	667	NA	32839	1

system, since the ARM processor is a hard macro. However, it should be clear that the ARM + 4 GeMM system is much larger if implemented in a ASIC compared to both the RISC-V + Versat or the RISC-V + DeepVersat systems. This means that combining RISC-V and Versat cores can be very competitive compared to combining standard processors and custom hardware.

As for the execution results, Deep Versat can effectively accelerate this application, and this is true for many other ML algorithms. Even the RISC-V + single

Versat system has a speedup of 3.36x compared to the standalone ARM system. The RISC-V + Deep Versat system is almost 20x faster than the ARM system, and it is faster than the ARM + 4 GeMM IP system by 2.3x. As expected, the RISC-V + Deep Versat is more than 5x faster than the RISC-V + Versat system due to the almost perfect parallelism of the inner loop and some code optimizations that have been done for RISC-V + Deep Versat after the results for the RISC-V + Versat system had been obtained.

8   Conclusions

This paper presents an implementation of a Convolution Neural Network (CNN) using a linear array of full mesh dynamically and partially reconfigurable Coarse Grained Reconfigurable Arrays (CGRAs) called Deep Versat. This design extends the previous single core Versat design by adding spatial scalability: performance scales linearly with the number of Versat cores without impacting the frequency of operation.

The Versat core has been enhanced with the capability of being configured at pre-silicon time. It can be configured with the types and quantities of FUs required. A new Multiply-Accumulate unit (MAC) has been developed, which is useful for the CNN application and others. Additionally, picoVersat, the previous Versat controller, which was only Assembly programmable, has been removed from the architecture which now relies on an external processor for control. A RISC-V open source core called picoRV32 has been adopted for controlling Deep Versat.

The new Deep Versat core is a ring of several new Versat cores created using Verilog generate statements. With the RISC-V processor used for control, which is programmable using the GNU toolchain, a C++ software API for reconfiguring and running Deep Versat has been developed. In essence, Deep Versat retains the programmability of the previous Versat core but can be pre-silicon configured to optimise the size and power consumption of the target application. Like the previous Versat architecture, the new Deep Versat architecture is also dynamically and partially reconfigurable to take advantage of the space and time locality of hardware configurations.

In the CNN algorithm, the neurons are organized in layers and it is important to have as many of them as possible working in parallel. The layers only differ in the activation functions of the neurons, the way they are interconnected or the way they access data from the memories. The chosen application contains the fundamentals of modern AI algorithms for image recognition, and is a perfect fit for CGRA implementation. In this paper, a 5-core Deep Versat instance has been used to accelerate a CNN handwritten digit recognition algorithm. The implementation runs 19x faster compared to an ARM Cortex-A9 processor hard macro in a Xilinx FPGA. If the ARM system is accelerated using 4 GeMM IP cores, the RISC-V + Deep Versat system is still more than 2 times faster.

It is concluded that by using a multi-core CGRA architecture, the system size grows proportionally with the workload and the clock frequency does not degrade with size. Given the preliminary nature of this work, the considered CNN network is not too complex, but the results clearly show that the same methodology can be applied to larger CNNs, serving as a good alternative to FPGAs and GPUs.

Acknowledgments. This work was supported by national funds through Fundação para a Ciência e a Tecnologia (FCT) under projects PTDC/EEI-HAC/30848/2017 and UIDB/50021/2020.

References

1. The MNIST database of handwritten digits. http://yann.lecun.com/exdb/mnist/
2. RISC-V: The Free and Open RISC Instruction Set Architecture. https://riscv.org/
3. PicoRV32 - a RISC-V CPU. https://github.com/cliffordwolf/picorv32 (2019)
4. Baumgarte, V., Ehlers, G., May, F., Nückel, A., Vorbach, M., Weinhardt, M.: PACT XPP - a self-reconfigurable data processing architecture. J. Supercomput. **26**(2), 167–184 (2003). https://doi.org/10.1023/A:1024499601571
5. De Sutter, B., Raghavan, P., Lambrechts, A.: Coarse-grained reconfigurable array architectures. In: Bhattacharyya, S.S., Deprettere, E.F., Leupers, R., Takala, J. (eds.) Handbook of Signal Processing Systems, pp. 449–484. Springer, Boston (2010). https://doi.org/10.1007/978-1-4419-6345-1_17
6. Ebeling, C., Cronquist, D.C., Franklin, P.: RaPiD — reconfigurable pipelined datapath. In: Hartenstein, R.W., Glesner, M. (eds.) FPL 1996. LNCS, vol. 1142, pp. 126–135. Springer, Heidelberg (1996). https://doi.org/10.1007/3-540-61730-2_13
7. Hartenstein, R., Herz, M., Hoffmann, T., Nageldinger, U.: Mapping applications onto reconfigurable kressarrays. In: Lysaght, P., Irvine, J., Hartenstein, R. (eds.) FPL 1999. LNCS, vol. 1673, pp. 385–390. Springer, Heidelberg (1999). https://doi.org/10.1007/978-3-540-48302-1_42
8. Heysters, P.M., Smit, G.J.M.: Mapping of DSP algorithms on the MONTIUM architecture. In: Proceedings of the International Parallel and Distributed Processing Symposium, p. 6, April 2003
9. Lopes, J.D., de Sousa, J.T.: Versat, a minimal coarse-grain reconfigurable array. In: Dutra, I., Camacho, R., Barbosa, J., Marques, O. (eds.) VECPAR 2016. LNCS, vol. 10150, pp. 174–187. Springer, Cham (2017). https://doi.org/10.1007/978-3-319-61982-8_17
10. Mei, B., Lambrechts, A., Mignolet, J.-Y., Verkest, D., Lauwereins, R.: Architecture exploration for a reconfigurable architecture template. Des. Test Comput. **22**(2), 90–101 (2005)
11. Mei, B., Vernalde, S., Verkest, D., De Man, H., Lauwereins, R.: DRESC: a retargetable compiler for coarse-grained reconfigurable architectures (2002)
12. Hemani, A., Shami, M.A.: Partially reconfigurable interconnection network for dynamically reprogrammable resource array (2009)
13. Wijtvliet, M., Waeijen, L., Corporaal, H.: Coarse grained reconfigurable architectures in the past 25 years: overview and classification (2016)

A Block-Based Systolic Array on an HBM2 FPGA for DNA Sequence Alignment

Riadh Ben Abdelhamid[1]([⊠]) and Yoshiki Yamaguchi[2]

[1] Graduate School of Systems and Information Engineering,
University of Tsukuba, 1-1-1 Ten-ou-dai, Tsukuba, Ibaraki 305-8573, Japan
`benabdelhamid@hpcs.cs.tsukuba.ac.jp`
[2] Faculty of Engineering, Information and Systems, University of Tsukuba,
1-1-1 Ten-ou-dai, Tsukuba, Ibaraki 305-8573, Japan
`yoshiki@cs.tsukuba.ac.jp`
`http://www.cs.tsukuba.ac.jp/~yoshiki/eng/`

Abstract. Revealing the optimal local similarity between a pair of genomic sequences is one of the most fundamental issues in bioinformatics. The Smith-Waterman algorithm is a method that was developed for that specific purpose. With the continuous advances in the computer field, this method becomes widely used to an extent where it expanded its reach to cover a broad range of applications, even in areas such as network packet inspections and pattern matching. This algorithm is based on Dynamic Programming and is guaranteed to find the optimal local sequence alignment between two base pairs. The computational complexity is O(mn), where m and n are defined as the number of the elements of a query and a database sequence, respectively. Researchers have investigated several manners to accelerate the calculation using CPU, GPU, Cell B.E., and FPGA. Most of them have proposed a data-reuse approach because the Smith-Waterman algorithm has rather high "bytes per operation"; in other words, the Smith-Waterman algorithm requires large memory bandwidth. In this paper, we try to minimize the impact of the memory bandwidth bottleneck through the implementation of a block-based systolic array approach that maximizes the usage of memory banks in HBM2 (High Bandwidth Memory). The proposed approach demonstrates a higher performance in terms of GCUPS (Giga Cell Update Per Second) compared to one of the best cases reported in previous works, and also achieves a significant improvement in power efficiency. For example, our implementation could reach 429.39 GCUPS while achieving a power efficiency of 7.68 GCUPS/W. With a different configuration, it could reach 316.73 GCUPS while hitting a peak power efficiency of 8.86 GCUPS/W.

Keywords: DNA sequence alignment · Smith-Waterman algorithm · Systolic array · HBM2 · High Level Synthesis · Reconfigurable High Performance Computing

© Springer Nature Switzerland AG 2020
F. Rincón et al. (Eds.): ARC 2020, LNCS 12083, pp. 298–313, 2020.
https://doi.org/10.1007/978-3-030-44534-8_23

1   Introduction

Almost all living cells contain DNA (Deoxyribonucleic Acid) structures that are made of sequences (character strings from the viewpoint of a computer program) based on an alphabet of 4 letters (A, T, G, C). These letters represent four nucleotides, namely, Adenine, Thymine, Guanine, and Cytosine that are the base building blocks of any DNA structure. Over time, DNA sequences are subject to evolution. In fact, some changes, such as deletion or insertion of new letters, are introduced to the original sequence. Therefore, in order to understand how similar a DNA sequence is to another one, or more commonly, in order to quantify how sequences had been changed compared to a common ancestor, scientists resorted to the usage of a technique called sequence alignment to discover and evaluate the similarities between a pair of DNA sequences. This constitutes the most fundamental task in the bioinformatics field. Smith and Waterman invented an algorithm that is guaranteed to find these similarities based on a scoring scheme [17]. Their proposal consisted of computing a similarity score between each pair of sequences, usually called a query and a database, repeating the computation based on the latest pair score and reiterating to the next pair until covering all of the symbols in the two sequences. Using this method, they focused on maximizing the number of matching symbols between the two pairs of sequences. This approach is known as local alignment and is guaranteed to find the optimal one. Nevertheless, this method is extremely demanding in terms of computational resources and effort. To the best of our knowledge, this is the first paper that targets the implementation of the SW (Smith-Waterman) algorithm on an HBM2-enabled FPGA (Field Programmable Gate Array). In this research, we implemented a highly-efficient, block-based systolic array architecture. Then, we applied several micro-architectural optimizations. Finally, we evaluated and compared our proposed implementation to the state of the art. This paper is organized as follows: In the first section, we introduce the background of our research and give an overview of the current work. In the second section, we explain the SW algorithm and its different steps. In the third section, we survey previous attempts that used reconfigurable computing to solve the local sequence alignment problem. In the fourth section, we present architectural details of our proposed block-based systolic array architecture as well as all the architectural and micro-architectural level optimizations. In the fifth section, we illustrate our implementation results. In the sixth section, we discuss those results and compare them to the state-of-the-art, and finally, we conclude this article.

2   The Smith-Waterman Algorithm

The SW algorithm is a famous Dynamic Programming approach to search for pairwise sequence similarity. It consists of 3 steps: First, initializing the score matrix (containing match and mismatch scores), then, computing the similarity matrix between each element of each sequence based on the Eq. (1), and finally backtracking the different directions leading to optimal local alignment, starting from the maximum score in the similarity matrix until reaching a score of 0, or until reaching the first position in the sequence. Unlike the relatively more efficient methods that are based on heuristics, such as BLAST [1], this method is guaranteed to find optimal local alignment between 2 sequences. Originally, The SW algorithm was inspired from an older method called Needleman–Wunsch algorithm [10], that might be used to find optimal global alignment between two sequences, with the difference that the newer algorithm (Smith-Waterman) does not allow negative values inside the similarity matrix and thus, can search for local alignment instead. The SW algorithm is described by the following Eq. (1).

$$S_{i,j} = MAX \begin{cases} (\searrow)\ S_{i-1,j-1} + score(q_j, db_i) : (mis)match \\ (\downarrow)\ S_{i-1,j} - penalty \qquad : gap\ insertion \\ (\rightarrow)\ S_{i,j-1} - penalty \qquad : gap\ deletion \\ 0 \end{cases} \tag{1}$$

Where $score(q_j, db_i)$ is the match score between the jth symbol from the Query and the ith symbol from the Database. $\downarrow$ and $\rightarrow$ denote an insertion of a gap in the database direction and the query direction respectively, therefore a gap penalty is subtracted from the similarity matrix in those directions. Finally, the maximum of all the computed values in Eq. (1) is written to the cell at position (i, j). The 0 in Eq. (1) guarantees that only positive values remain in the similarity matrix. The cells as well as the directions on which the SW similarity score $S_{i,j}$ depends can be seen in Fig. 1.

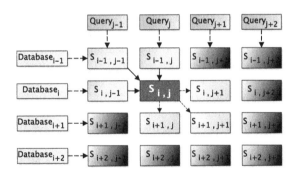

Fig. 1. Dependence scheme between Smith-Waterman similarity matrix cells

Figure 1 shows that for computing the SW similarity matrix at the red cell(i, j), 3 other cells have to be computed beforehand, namely the upper cell(i−1, j), the left cell(i, j−1) and the cell(i−1, j−1) from the diagonal upper-left direction. Furthermore, updating the red cell(i, j) will lead to providing necessary outputs to compute the right cell(i, j+1), the bottom cell(i+1, j) and the diagonal bottom-right cell(i+1, j+1). A simple analysis of this figure shows that all the cells residing on the anti-diagonal have no inter-dependence and hence, can be updated in parallel [4,5]. Understanding these details will allow us to build a linear systolic array, where multiple PEs (Processing Element) are spread across the anti-diagonal and are working concurrently.

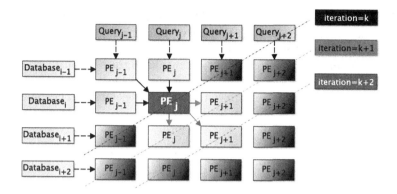

Fig. 2. Mapping the PE dependence onto a linear systolic array

Figure 2 explicitly illustrates the previously described behavior. In fact, it shows that we can map the computation of multiple cells to a linear systolic array, where the multiple PEs are spatially independent, but temporally interdependent. For instance, considering that the number of PEs is equal to the width of the query, all PEs can be mapped to compute the SW similarity cells belonging to the same anti-diagonal. Obviously, all of the cells belonging to the same column in Fig. 1 are updated by the same PE in Fig. 2, across different temporal loop iterations. Each anti-diagonal line represents a new iteration in time. For example, updating the broadcasted values from a single cell towards 3 directions, is spread across 3 iterations. Now, back again to the red cell(i, j), its maximum score will be computed in the first iteration$_k$. In the following iteration$_{k+1}$, the red PE$_j$ (from iteration$_k$) will output the left input of PE$_{j+1}$ as well as the upper input of PE$_j$ at iteration$_{k+1}$. The same red PE$_j$ of iteration$_k$, will output the diagonal upper-left input of PE$_{j+1}$ at iteration$_{k+2}$. Concurrently, after every cell update, the database index is shifted by one position, while the query symbol fed to the PE is kept the same allowing a new comparison against a new DNA symbol. This shift operation is depicted by Fig. 4.

3   State of the Art

Biological sequence alignment is a well researched topic in bioinformatics. In fact, several works to map this algorithm into different hardware platforms such as CPU (Central Processing Unit) [3,12,21] or GPU (Graphics Processing Unit) [9, 15,16] had been proposed and published in the past. Nevertheless, in this section, we mainly focus on reconfigurable hardware implementations targeting FPGA devices. These devices are electronic chips containing a considerable amount of re-programmable logic blocks, switches and memories. They operate in an order of magnitude lower clock frequency when compared to a CPU or GPU, and they certainly have a lower peak performance than those devices. However, their flexibility gives them a metamorphic nature, thus allowing them to take the shape of any specific hardware circuit. Building a targeted specific implementation of a complex algorithm on an FPGA, mostly gives it an edge over a CPU or a GPU in terms of power-efficiency or even sustained computational performance. The SW algorithm is no exception, in fact, thanks to the previously enumerated advantages of FPGAs, an interesting number of works had investigated efficient mapping of that algorithm onto reconfigurable accelerators. The table below gives an overview on some of these works (Table 1):

Table 1. Comparison of the performance of varied single-device implementations of the SW algorithm

Ref	Year	Device	Performance (GCUPs)	Efficiency (GCUPs/W)	Language	Target
[20]	2011	Xilinx XC5VLX330T	129	16	Verilog	Protein
[9]	2013	Nvidia GTX 680	83.3	0.42*	CUDA C++ PTX assembly	Protein
[14]	2016	Altera Stratix V	58.4	0.702	OpenCL	Protein
[14]	2016	Intel Xeon E5-2695 v3	354.8	1.478	OpenCL	Protein
[4]	2017	Kintex Ultrascale	42.47	1.69	OpenCL	DNA
[7]	2017	Intel Arria 10 GX	214	no data	OpenCL	DNA
[5]	2017	Xilinx XC7VX485T	105.9	2.41	Verilog	Protein
[13]	2018	Intel Arria 10 GX	132.43	no data	OpenCL	DNA
[13]	2018	Nvidia GTX1080	250.78	1.39*	CUDA C++	DNA
Ours	2020	Xilinx Alveo U280	429.39	7.68	HLS	DNA

*Computed based on the power specification of the GPU.

4   Implementation Details

In this section we present a top-level description of our proposed block-based systolic array, then we dive into its details, and its architectural and micro-architectural level optimizations. Our implementation is based on the Xilinx SDAccel development flow for FPGA-based acceleration. This flow is based on the OpenCL acceleration model that consists of two sides: the host side(responsible for scheduling and control) and the device or accelerator side(the FPGA in our case). Hence, we propose a block-based systolic approach that is implemented using C++ High Level Synthesis (Vivado HLS C++) and carefully tailored to HBM2-enabled accelerator cards (Xilinx U280).

Figure 3 depicts the way our implementation of the SW acceleration maps to the SDAccel execution model. In fact, our work is split into two main components: the Host and the FPGA. The Host side is responsible for the creation of

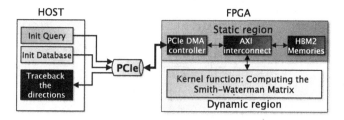

Fig. 3. High-level representation of the computation acceleration model

the acceleration context, command queues, reading and writing memory buffers, and scheduling the execution of the kernel function. In our host code, we fix the width of the query and database sequences, randomly initialize their contents based on the DNA alphabet [A, C, G, T] and then allocate the required host memory resources. The host sends the DNA sequences to the HBM2 memories through PCIe (Peripheral Component Interconnect Express), enqueues the kernel function (the function that computes the SW matrix) in the command queue and waits until its completion. Once the kernel function has finished computing and sending back all of the directions required to traceback the optimal sequence alignment, the host will read these data through the corresponding attached buffers and then starts the traceback process. Finally, the host compares the FPGA-generated results to the software-based simulation outputs and checks the correctness of the hardware design. On the other hand, The FPGA implements the accelerated kernel function. It mainly consists of reading the query and the database inputs from HBM2 memories, storing them into cache buffers (BRAMs), looping over all the required iterations to compute the SW similarity matrix, while shifting the database and storing the traceback data corresponding to each of those iterations in the adequate HBM2 banks, in order to be transferred later to the host side through PCIe.

4.1   A Block-Based Systolic Array Approach

SW algorithm is a Dynamic Programming problem, that is by nature well-adapted to FPGA implementations, due to the data dependency scheme that exists between each iteration of the problem and that complicates the computation process in more conventional hardware architectures such as CPU or GPU. Several reconfigurable hardware implementation of this problem, have been adopting a systolic array architecture [2,6,11,20]. This approach has proved to be very well-suited to Dynamic Programming problems, particularly because it can increase the performance of compute-bound computations, while maintaining similar memory-bandwidth requirements [8]. Figure 4 depicts the details of the proposed block-based systolic array architecture. In fact, The kernel function has only two inputs that are connected to port 0 of HBM2 memory.

These two inputs are useful to load the database and query sequences into the abundant BRAM resources available on-chip. This buffering or input data

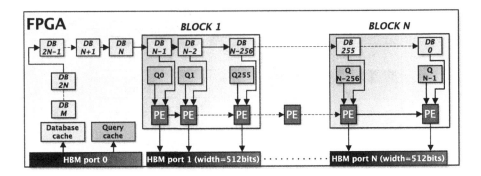

Fig. 4. The proposed block-based systolic array architecture

caching is necessary for increasing the placement step flexibility and leading to timing closure later. Nonetheless, BRAMs are either single-ported or dual ported, therefore they can at most output the contents of two memory locations, in the same clock cycle, hence, it becomes mandatory to partition these memories, either completely or cyclically, using HLS pragmas in order to increase their overall bandwidth. This is very useful for ensuring that the database shift operation can have an initiation interval of 1, meaning that it would be possible to shift a new symbol from the database sequence into the block-based systolic array, in each iteration of the kernel main loop. At startup, each PE is initialized with a fixed query symbol, while a new database symbol is shifted in, in order to be compared against it and generate the local match/mismatch score. Figure 2 suggests that each PE has 3 directional dependences. On iteration$_{k+2}$ for example, PE$_{j+1}$ needs its own output from the previous iteration$_{k+1}$ (Up direction). On the same iteration$_{k+2}$, PE$_{j+1}$ requires the output of PE$_j$, in both iteration$_{k+1}$ and iteration$_k$ (from left and upper-left directions, respectively). This means that in order for all PEs in any anti-diagonal iteration to start their computation, they require all PEs from the previous two anti-diagonals to complete their work and output their computed SW similarity values. The computation flows in the direction of the iterations shown on Fig. 2 in a wavefront manner. The final loop iteration count I of all the iterations required to finish generating all the traceback matrix values, is given by the following equation:

$$I = M + N - 1 \tag{2}$$

Where M is the width of the database sequence and N is the width of the query sequence. Each block of our systolic array, works on a chunk of 256 elements from the query sequence and thus can generate 256 directions in the same iteration. Each direction is encoded into a 2 bits value, therefore each block generates 512 bits, and matches exactly the maximum supported width of one HBM2 memory port. This is very useful because up to 8192 PEs could run in parallel and generate 16384 bits that could be mapped into the 32 HBM2 banks without encountering any memory bandwidth limitation.

4.2   Architectural and Micro-architectural Level Optimizations

In this section we present some of the different optimizations that we had applied and/or investigated in our SW implementation.

Guiding Synthesis Using Pragmas. High-level synthesis is based on configuring hardware using a software programming language. The use of pragma directives is fundamental to ensure generating a near HDL-quality design. Pragmas are special lines of code that convey additional pieces of information to the Vivado HLS compiler [19], in order to efficiently guide the hardware synthesis. Here, we provide the most interesting ones that we used in our implementation.

- **#pragma HLS pipeline II=1:** When targeting high-performance computing, using pragmas for pipelining is a key optimization technique that helps extracting temporal parallelism. This technique allows for more work to be done in every clock cycle, boosts the operational clock frequency and results in shorter execution time. In order for a pipeline to be effective, an II (Initiation Interval) of 1 should always be inferred. This means that the design can process a new input data at every loop iteration.
- **#pragma HLS unroll:** This pragma is equally important as it allows to reach spatial parallelism through unrolling loops. In fact, this is used to create separate, concurrently executing instances of PEs.
- **#pragma HLS array_partition:** The data shared between PEs across iterations are stored into C++ arrays. These arrays are implemented in hardware using the different types of memories available on the FPGA fabric. Obviously, efficient mapping to LUT-based memories is limited to small-sized arrays. Although, Block RAMs provide efficient storage for larger sizes, they offer at most 2 ports to read and write the saved data. Hence, all those data arrays should be stored in a way that allows a parallel access to them in the same clock cycle, whenever required. Here, this pragma facilitates to meet that requirement by splitting the data across multiple memory instances in order to guarantee that more than just 2 memory addresses could be accessed for read and write operations. Unless otherwise specified, this pragma will try to completely partition an array of depth N into N different arrays of depth 1, thus, guaranteeing a minimum of N possible simultaneous reads or writes. Xilinx Vivado sets a maximum size limit of 1024 for an array to be completely partitioned. This limit can be overcome through custom directive file, at the expense of a multiple folds extra compilation time, that is not even guaranteed to successfully complete the partitioning task.

Block-Based Computation and Multi Global Memory Ports. The block-based systolic array is created by decomposing the Input/Output data into chunks of 512 bits width each. We chose this width because it matches the maximum allowed width on HBM2 global memory ports, that maximizes the corresponding bandwidth. In fact, in order to create N processing elements that can compare small portions of the pair sequences in parallel, we divided the query and the database into blocks of 256 elements (512 bits) each. This has indeed two advantages. First, it is way more easier for the HLS tool to synthesize small separate fully unrolled loops (a loop of 256 in each block) rather than to synthesize a fully unrolled loop that is several times larger. Second, each block could be mapped to a separate HBM2 memory port since it generates exactly 512 bits containing 256 elements of the traceback matrix.

Multiple Pairwise Alignment. Another technique, that might seem obvious is combining many symbols from multiple queries into the same PE, in order to make multiple pairwise alignments. This is similar to doing a single alignment on multiple separate compute units or separate kernels. However, using this technique, the same database memory port, cache buffer, control and shift operations are being re-used against multiple queries. Furthermore, there is no overhead of instantiating multiple kernels and more importantly there is a localization of resources inside each PE, that helps avoiding problems such as congestion or negative clock slacks due to long routing paths.

Increasing the Number of HBM2 Memory Banks When Increasing the Query Width. It might seem obvious that the use of HBM2 can speedup the communication between the accelerator global memory buffers and their associated kernel. While this is true to some extent, it tightly depends on the way the access to HBM2 banks is being done. A common mistake is to assume that HBM2 automatically outperforms the bandwidth of DDR4 memories because it is marketed in that way.

Table 2. Global memory resources on Xilinx Alveo U280 Data center accelerator card

Memory	Bank capacity	Number of banks	Total capacity	Bandwidth
DDR4	16 GB	2	32 GB	38 GB/s
HBM2	256 MB	32	8 GB	460 GB/s

For example, Table 2 shows that a Xilinx Alveo U280 acceleration board, embeds 32 banks of on-chip HBM2 (8 GB in total) at a bandwidth of 460 GB/s and 2 banks of DDR4 memory (32 GB in total) at a bandwidth of 38 GB/s [18]. When the total theoretical memory bandwidth is divided by the number of available memory banks, it becomes obvious that a single DDR4 bank has a peak bandwidth of 19 GB/s which outperforms that of a single HBM2 bank (14.375 GB/s). Hence, in memory-bound computing problems targeting this acceleration board, it is possible to solve the DDR4 communication bottleneck, by using more HBM2 banks than the available DDR4 ones. In other words, The number of Input/Output ports of the kernel should contain at least 3 ports mapped to 3 different HBM2 banks to have a higher bandwidth compared to that of a DDR4 memory interface. One relatively minor drawback here, is that the storage capacity of a DDR4 bank is considerably larger than that of a HBM2 bank (16 GB against 256 MB), therefore, while trying to improve a kernel bandwidth, one should carefully plan ahead to avoid rapidly overfilling the allowed memory capacity.

5   Implementation Results

In this section, we present experimental results as well as a description of the deployed hardware (given by Table 3) and the tests carried on it. Later, we compare our findings to previous research. The SP (Sustained Performance) is derived from the kernel execution time T (including all memory transfers to/from global buffers). This performance is measured in billions of cells update per second (GCUPS) and is given through the following equation:

$$SP = 10^{-9} \times \frac{N \times M}{T} \tag{3}$$

Table 3. Environment setup used in the experiments

HOST	Intel(R) Core(TM) i9-9900K CPU @ 3.60 GHz (16 cores, 32 threads, 64 GB RAM)
Operating system	Ubuntu 18.04.1 LTS
Accelerator	Alveo U280 Data Center Accelerator Card [18]
Compiler	Xilinx SDx v2019.1 (64-bit)

Table 4. Resource utilization and performance results for the highest performing single and multiple kernel implementation

N, M, K	LUT (%)	FF (%)	BRAM (%)	GCUPS	GCUPS/W
512, 262080, 6	510774 (46.05)	253655 (11.12)	528 (29.5)	429.39	7.68
2048, 262144, 1	330797 (28.64)	141910 (5.98)	137 (7.62)	316.73	8.86

Figure 5 illustrates the performance obtained from implementing a 2 pairwise alignment on a single kernel function (multi queries) versus implementing 2 kernel functions, each containing a single query sequence (multi kernels). Both implementations are based on a width of 256 for the query and the results are illustrated for varied database width. Figure 5 suggests that a multiple-query-based implementation of the PE tends to be slightly better in terms of GCUPS, than simply duplicating kernels that make use of a single query. Figure 6 shows a trend of a linear increase in performance, for a fixed database width of 262144,

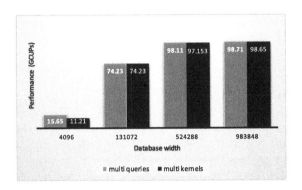

Fig. 5. Performance comparison of a multi-kernel vs multi-query implementation

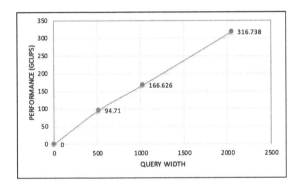

Fig. 6. Systolic array performance trend with a fixed database width of 262144

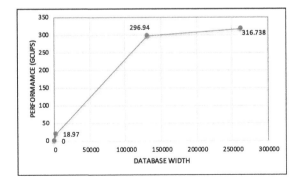

Fig. 7. Systolic array performance trend with a fixed query width of 2048

when increasing the queries width. Whereas, Fig. 7 shows a trend of performance stagnation, for a fixed query width of 2048, when the database width exceeds the threshold of 131072. Table 4 reports the results of the two best performing configurations. The first configuration contains 2 blocks/kernel and the second has 8 blocks/kernel. N, M and K from Table 4 denote the width of the query, the width of the database and the number of compute units (kernels), respectively. For a query width of 512, 512 directions are generated in every iteration, thus, the total number of bits required for the traceback data is equal to 1024 bits in each kernel (2 bits for each direction datum). Thus, the number of systolic array blocks and hence the number of HBM2 ports required is equal to 2 per kernel (512 bits/port). Similarly, for a query width of 2048, the total number of bits required for the traceback data in each iteration step is equal to 4096 bits. Therefore, a total of 8 HBM2 memory ports is required to process a new input and output the related traceback directions, at every iteration.

6   Discussion

Figure 5 suggests that there is a minor gain in performance when implementing a single kernel with multiple query inputs against implementing multiple kernels with a single query input. This means that instantiating a new kernel function is almost done at no additional cost or at a minor overhead. The compute resources of our SW implementation, scale with the increase in problem size (The size of the query). This is called weak scaling and means that it is possible to extract more parallelism along with the increase in the size of the sequences (which translates to an increase in the number of PEs). This is in contrast with strong scaling, which happens when the increase in computational resources, while maintaining the size of the sequences unchanged, still offers more computational performance. Figure 6 suggests a trending linear increase in performance, when increasing the number of PEs. This is explained by the fact that a wider query allows for more parallelism. In fact, since all the PEs reside on the anti-diagonal, they are spatially independent and can consequently update the similarity matrix cells in parallel. Nonetheless, for queries with a length around 4k we noticed the compiler started struggling to place and route the design. This can be explained by issues related to the underlying FPGA architecture. In fact, HBM2 banks are only close to one SLR (Super Logic Region). Since the FPGA has 3 similar-size SLRs, crossing the boundary of 33% resource usage means that communicating with HBM2 banks has to cross an SLR boundary and thus face congestion. Figure 7 shows that for short size databases (less than 16k), the performance of our approach seems to be poor, improves for medium sizes and tends to stagnate when the size is larger than 128k. This is mainly due to the ratio of the computation to the corresponding memory transfers. When investigating the profiling summary reports from SDAccel, we noticed that there are 2 metrics for measuring execution time. The first includes the data transfers to/from global memories and is called kernel execution time, and the second omits the memory transfers and is called compute unit execution time. Based on those two reports, we concluded that our computational performance is in fact independent from the database size. However, when including memory transfers, selecting a database with a small size will result in a drop of the effective memory transfer bandwidth. This, results in turn, in achieving poor performances, and sometimes leads to a memory transfer time that is larger than the effective computation time. Here, we define the theoretical peak performance that depends upon two parameters only: width of the query N and the maximum allowed frequency F_{peak} of the main clock. Thus, the TPP (Theoretical Peak Performance) is defined through the following equation:

$$TPP = N \times F_{peak} \tag{4}$$

This equation is derived from the fact that the number of concurrently operating PEs is equal to the number of symbols in the query. Since each PE updates a single cell in every iteration, multiplying the number of PEs by the operating frequency yields to the performance translated by the number of "Cells Update Per second". This TPP is only achievable when assuming an infinite memory bandwidth, where all the memory transfers between the kernel and its global memory buffers take no time at all. The maximum achievable frequency is 300 MHz because this is the maximum allowed by SDAccel tool flow when implementing HLS based designs. Furthermore, following our block-based systolic architecture, every 256 elements of the query generates 256 traceback directions at every iteration. In order to maintain busy all the 32 HBM2 memory ports, the maximum width of the query should be 8192 (256 times 32). A higher width would impose a memory communication bottleneck, because updating the cells would require waiting for the completion of the memory transfers in every step of the computation. Therefore, the maximum theoretical performance of our accelerator becomes:

$$TPP = 8192 \times 300\,\text{MHz} = 2.475\ TCUPS \tag{5}$$

In practice, this performance is almost non-achievable due to several factors. In fact, the clock frequency decreases, sometimes dramatically when the design size grows, because of the congestion and routing issues. Consuming all the memory banks while requesting the peak clock frequency of 300 MHz will certainly make some paths fail to meet timing requirements (mostly negative slacks and rarely hold violations). In this case, the SDAccel tool would downscale the working frequency to allow proper functionality (only when there are no hold violations). Table 4 hints a new theoretical peak performance based on resource consumption. In fact, the most consumed resource of the best performing implementation is LUTs (Lookup Tables) at 46.05% from the total available at an operating frequency of only 160 MHz. This suggests a new TPP of almost 2 times higher than what we have achieved with the same clock speed. That is around 0.9 TCUPS. Adding more compute kernels can improve the performance but not in a linear way because of the possible decrease in the clock frequency. Increasing the clock speed will linearly improve the achieved performance but remains capped by the previously defined theoretical peak. We are currently working on tweaking our design to reach that level of performance. Using our proposed techniques, our design could reach 429.39 GCUPS and 7.68 GCUPS/W for a query width of 512 using a double block per kernel and 6 duplicated kernels. Our design reached as well, 316.73 GCUPS and 8.86 GCUPS/W for a query width of 2048 using 8 blocks on a single kernel. The highest performing implementation consumes nearly one half of the available resources. When compared to the best reported FPGA implementation, our design could reach 2 times higher performance in terms of GCUPS. Nonetheless, a fair comparison is infeasible since each of the two implementations targets a different FPGA size with a different architecture from a different vendor. On the other hand, our obtained power efficiency 8.86 GCUPS/W, largely outperforms the reported state of the art CPU and GPU implementations (1.47 GCUPS/W and 1.39 GCUPS/W respectively). This work is highly likely to be one of the best performing single-chip implementation of the SW algorithm. Furthermore, thanks to the scalable nature of systolic arrays, our design has the potential to map well and perform even better when targeting next generation HBM2-enabled FPGA.

7   Conclusion

This work provides an efficient block-based systolic array approach that aims to solve the SW local alignment problem. The goal of our approach is to target HBM2-enabled FPGAs, in a way that maximizes the usage of their HBM2 banks and profits efficiently from the available high memory bandwidth. We also investigated combining other approaches such as multiple pairwise alignments. The latter approach did not prove very efficient, because the performance levels almost neared that of a single-query multi-kernel implementation. Nevertheless, our main approach, the block-based systolic architecture, proved extremely efficient and delivered a peak performance that is 1.7 times higher than the best GPU implementation reported in literature and 5.5 times better power efficiency. Furthermore, our design could reach 2 times higher performance in terms of GCUPS, when compared to the best reported FPGA implementation. We are currently continuing our quest towards reaching the theoretical limits that we estimated through our experiments and which should be, at least, nearly 2 times higher than our current achievements.

Acknowledgement. This work was supported in part by MEXT as "Next Generation High-Performance Computing Infrastructures and Applications R&D Program" (Development of Computing-Communication Unified Supercomputer in Next Generation), and by JSPS KAKENHI Grant Number JP17H01707 and JP18H03246. The authors would also like to thank Xilinx Inc., for providing FPGA software tools by Xilinx University Program.

References

1. Altschul, S.F., Gish, W., Miller, W., Myers, E.W., Lipman, D.J.: Basic local alignment search tool. J. Mol. Biol. **215**(3), 403–410 (1990)
2. Chen, P., Wang, C., Li, X., Zhou, X.: Hardware acceleration for the banded Smith-Waterman algorithm with the cycled systolic array, pp. 480–481, December 2013
3. Daily, J.: Parasail: SIMD C library for global, semi-global, and local pairwise sequence alignments. BMC Bioinform. **17**, 81 (2016). https://doi.org/10.1186/s12859-016-0930-z
4. Di Tucci, L., O'Brien, K., Blott, M., Santambrogio, M.: Architectural optimizations for high performance and energy efficient Smith-Waterman implementation on FPGAS using OpenCL, pp. 716–721, March 2017. https://doi.org/10.23919/DATE.2017.7927082
5. Fei, X., Dan, Z., Lina, L., Xin, M., Chunlei, Z.: FPGASW: accelerating large-scale Smith–Waterman sequence alignment application with backtracking on FPGA linear systolic array. Interdisc. Sci. Comput. Life Sci. **10**(1), 176–188 (2017). https://doi.org/10.1007/s12539-017-0225-8
6. Hasan, L., Khawaja, Y., Bais, A.: A systolic array architecture for the Smith-Waterman algorithm with high performance cell design, pp. 35–44, January 2008
7. Houtgast, E., Sima, V., Al-Ars, Z.: High performance streaming Smith-Waterman implementation with implicit synchronization on intel FPGA using OpenCL, December 2017
8. Kung, H.: Why systolic architectures? Computer **15**, 37–46 (1982)
9. Liu, Y., et al.: Cudasw++ 3.0: accelerating Smith-Waterman protein database search by coupling CPU and GPU SIMD instructions. BMC Bioinform. **14** (2013). Article no. 117, https://doi.org/10.1186/1471-2105-14-117
10. Needleman, S.B., Wunsch, C.D.: A general method applicable to the search for similarities in the amino acid sequence of two proteins. J. Mol. Biol. **48**(3), 443–453 (1970)
11. Nurdin, D., et al.: High performance systolic array core architecture design for DNA sequencer. MATEC Web Conf. **150** (2018). Article no. 06009
12. Rognes, T.: Faster Smith-Waterman database searches with inter-sequence SIMD parallelisation. BMC Bioinform. **12** (2011). https://doi.org/10.1186/1471-2105-12-221
13. Rucci, E., et al.: SWIFOLD: Smith-Waterman implementation on FPGA with OpenCL for long DNA sequences. BMC Syst. Biol. **12**, 96 (2018). https://doi.org/10.1186/s12918-018-0614-6
14. Rucci, E., Garcia, C., Botella, G., De Giusti, A., Naiouf, M., Prieto Matias, M.: OSWALD: OpenCL Smith-Waterman on Altera's FPGA for large protein databases. Int. J. High Perform. Comput. Appl. **32**, 337–350 (2016). https://doi.org/10.1177/1094342016654215
15. Sandes, E., et al.: CUDAlign 3.0: parallel biological sequence comparison in large GPU clusters, pp. 160–169, May 2014
16. Sandes, E., et al.: CUDAlign 4.0: incremental speculative traceback for exact chromosome-wide alignment in GPU clusters. IEEE Trans. Parallel Distrib. Syst. **27**, 2838–2850 (2016)
17. Smith, T., Waterman, M.: Identification of common molecular subsequences. J. Mol. Biol. **147**, 195–7 (1981)
18. Xilinx: Alveo U280 Data Center Accelerator Card. https://www.xilinx.com/products/boards-and-kits/alveo/u280.html#specifications. Accessed 8 Dec 2019

19. Xilinx: Vivado HLS Optimization Methodology Guide. https://www.xilinx.com/support/documentation/sw_manuals/xilinx2018_1/ug1270-vivado-hls-opt-methodology-guide.pdf. Accessed 8 Dec 2019
20. Yamaguchi, Y., Tsoi, H.K., Luk, W.: FPGA-based Smith-Waterman algorithm: analysis and novel design. In: Koch, A., Krishnamurthy, R., McAllister, J., Woods, R., El-Ghazawi, T. (eds.) ARC 2011. LNCS, vol. 6578, pp. 181–192. Springer, Heidelberg (2011). https://doi.org/10.1007/978-3-642-19475-7_20
21. Zhao, M., et al.: SSW library: an SIMD Smith-Waterman C/C++ library for use in genomic applications. PLoS ONE 8(12), e82138 (2013)

Comparison of Direct and Indirect Networks for High-Performance FPGA Clusters

Antoniette Mondigo[1(✉)], Tomohiro Ueno[2], Kentaro Sano[2],
and Hiroyuki Takizawa[3]

[1] Graduate School of Information Sciences, Tohoku University, Sendai, Japan
amondigo@dc.tohoku.ac.jp
[2] Processor Research Team, RIKEN Center for Computational Science, Kobe, Japan
{tomohiro.ueno,kentaro.sano}@riken.jp
[3] Cyberscience Center, Tohoku University, Sendai, Japan
takizawa@tohoku.ac.jp

Abstract. As field programmable gate arrays (FPGAs) become a favorable choice in exploring new computing architectures for the post-Moore era, a flexible network architecture for scalable FPGA clusters becomes increasingly important in high performance computing (HPC). In this paper, we introduce a scalable platform of indirectly-connected FPGAs, where its Ethernet-switching network allows flexibly customized inter-FPGA connectivity. However, for certain applications such as in stream computing, it is necessary to establish a connection-oriented datapath with backpressure between FPGAs. Due to the lack of physical backpressure channel in the network, we utilized our existing credit-based network protocol with flow control to provide receiver FPGA awareness and tailored it to minimize overall communication overhead for the proposed framework. To know its performance characteristics, we implemented necessary data transfer hardware on Intel Arria 10 FPGAs, modeled and obtained its communication performance, and compared it to a direct network. Results show that our proposed indirect framework achieves approximately 3% higher effective network bandwidth than our existing direct inter-FPGA network, which demonstrates good performance and scalability for large HPC applications.

Keywords: FPGA cluster · Indirect network · Direct network · Flow control · Scalability · Flexibility

1 Introduction

In addressing the different requirements of HPC applications, various platforms and compute strategies have been considered. Recently, FPGAs are playing a major part in exploring architectural advances, primarily due to the impending end of Moore's law and Dennard scaling. In particular, they excel as efficient hardware accelerators because of their ability to customize algorithms and exploit parallelism in offloaded applications [6,7,18].

© Springer Nature Switzerland AG 2020
F. Rincón et al. (Eds.): ARC 2020, LNCS 12083, pp. 314–329, 2020.
https://doi.org/10.1007/978-3-030-44534-8_24

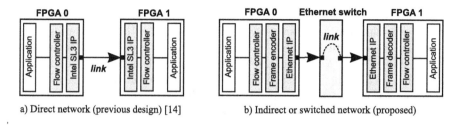

Fig. 1. Connection-oriented links in dedicated FPGA networks

Modern FPGAs have optimized interconnect fabrics, which allow low-latency communication in a dedicated network. Collectively, the networked FPGAs increase their amount of computational resources. With the deployment of FPGA clusters in data centers and cloud services [2,5], large HPC kernels may be mapped into multiple FPGAs, which achieve scaled performance [16,17].

Physically connecting FPGAs through their high-speed transceiver links in a direct network without switches is a straightforward method. However, as the cluster size grows larger, the possibility of utilizing all FPGAs for a particular application decreases. This also requires multiple hop counts to reach a destination, which is inefficient with a large network diameter. In addition, a large-scale FPGA cluster could potentially service multiple applications that can be mapped strategically to maximize resource utilization, which requires network flexibility. Just as customized circuits in FPGAs is the key to performance gains, its network should ideally be scalable and flexible for its target applications.

To address these issues, an indirect network, where FPGAs are connected with switches, seems promising. In this paper, we present a scalable Ethernet-switched FPGA cluster, where the transceiver links are physically connected to ports of high-speed Ethernet switches. With offloaded switching or routing functions, this may mean shorter transmission time for a large network diameter due to lower hop counts. As a long-term standard, Ethernet supports easier migration to higher data rates and has adequate support for FPGAs through intellectual property (IP) cores. With its accelerating momentum towards 400+ Gbps, using Ethernet for our switched network follows the design principle of independence, which facilitates incremental scaling and forward compatibility. However, its upper layer protocols such as TCP/IP are expensive in hardware [11].

For our proposed switched network, we used Layer 2 (L2) Ethernet. By supplying source and destination media access control (MAC) addresses in Ethernet frames, an FPGA could send data to a specified receiver FPGA; thus, providing flexibility without changing physical cabling structures. For some applications such as data-flow stream computing, it is necessary to establish a connection-oriented *link* with backpressure support over the network. For usability, we propose to utilize our own credit-based network protocol with flow control (FC) [14], which was originally intended for a direct network.

This paper aims to know the performance characteristics of our proposed indirect network. By implementing the necessary data transfer hardware on

FPGA, we modeled and obtained the communication performance, and compared it with our existing direct networked FPGA cluster [14], which uses Intel's proprietary Serial Lite III (SL3) protocol [9]. Figure 1 shows the connection-oriented inter-FPGA *links* and the necessary network hardware modules. To demonstrate scalability, we estimated the communication time of a streamed computing case in a large-scale cluster by modeling data stream traversal through a network in a ring connection. The following are our specific contributions:

1. Design and architecture of a connection-oriented network using Ethernet switches for scalable FPGA clusters;
2. Investigation of performance characteristics and performance modeling for a link in the connection-oriented network; and
3. Implementation with Intel Arria 10 FPGAs and performance evaluation for stream computing.

We found that our indirect network with 40 Gbps Ethernet (E40G) has obtained an effective network bandwidth of 4.41 GB/s, which is approximately 3% higher than our existing 40 Gbps SL3 point-to-point FPGA network. This result indicates a good communication performance of applications requiring high-bandwidth and large data transfers. Generally, the scalability and flexibility features of our switched framework provide feasible groundwork for efficient high-level synthesis (HLS) compilers, which target to generate and map customized HPC applications in a large-scale FPGA cluster.

The paper is organized as follows: Sect. 2 shows some related work; Sect. 3 discusses the indirect network framework, protocol, and model; Sect. 4 shows evaluation; and, Sect. 5 presents conclusions and future work.

2   Related Work

Distributed FPGA systems vary in different forms that employ direct interconnects with various topologies that prioritize different requirements. A boxed cluster like BlueHive [11] is a custom 64-FPGA cluster with a full custom interconnect IP, BlueLink, and custom communication protocol with reliability layer. Maxwell [3] has 64 FPGAs on a 2D torus with each link using a single multigigabit transceiver. Cube [13] is a systolic-connected cluster with 512 FPGAs with an $8 \times 8 \times 8$ 3D mesh topology. In [4], 32 FPGAs on eight enclosures are interconnected in different technologies and topologies on a Berkeley Emulation Engine 3 (BEE3) multi-FPGA platform for network exploration. With these direct topologies, most of them are exploring small to mid-scale clusters.

Other works targeting large-scale clusters are typically for heterogeneous computing. Datacenter-scale deployments such as Catapult v1 [15] uses a dedicated direct network for its 48 FPGAs, where they arranged 6×8 2D torus topology. In Catapult v2 [5], they used a "bump-in-the-wire" approach, which accelerates network traffic by routing communication through FPGA. They used a tree topology with top-of-rack servers and used UDP/IP protocol over 40 Gbps Ethernet. Another heterogeneous cloud data center-based FPGA cluster [17] uses OpenStack, a cloud management tool offering several services, to virtualize FPGA utilization with other heterogeneous resources, which involves multiple abstraction layers in its infrastructure implying additional overhead.

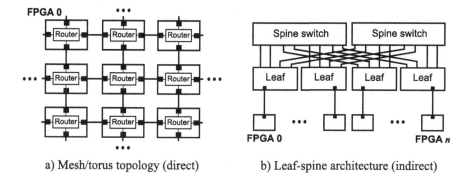

a) Mesh/torus topology (direct)   b) Leaf-spine architecture (indirect)

Fig. 2. FPGA clusters when scaled

Direct networks are common and widely used but to the best of our knowledge, performance characteristics of FPGAs with an indirect network using switches have not been extensively explored, particularly in a large-scale setup.

3   Design and Architecture

This section presents the proposed scalable indirect network framework with its design and architecture, including the custom protocol and model.

3.1   Direct and Indirect Networks for FPGA Clusters

A direct network based on point-to-point connection is popular for inter-FPGA communication because of its practical and extensive features. Since it allows close physical proximity between FPGAs, high-speed and high-bandwidth data transfers are often implied. A fully-connected network is ideal to keep low-latency transfers but unrealistic when scaled with more FPGAs. To minimize the network diameter, high-radix routers are employed but are usually constrained with the limited number of transceiver links. There is also a high-resource penalty for on-chip routers, which reduces FPGA area for application. Figure 2a shows a mesh/torus topology where their routers determine the datapath of a message. In comparison, the absence of a router in Fig. 1a presented a point-to-point connection with a fixed datapath between two FPGAs.

An indirect or switch-based network enables the FPGA fabric to offload the routing or switching functions to a dedicated switch. Using a switch may introduce some additional latency but with a larger network diameter, there will be

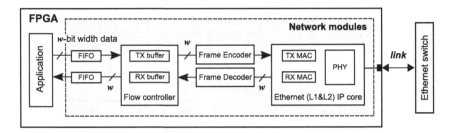

Fig. 3. Network hardware modules for Ethernet protocol

lesser hops to reach a destination compared to a direct network. However, scalability is limited by the number of switch ports. To mitigate this, a multi-stage interconnection network may be constructed by cascading switches such as in a *leaf-spine* architecture [1] shown in Fig. 2b. In this two-layer network topology, FPGAs are connected to *leaf* switches. These switches are then fully meshed to a series of *spine* switches, which allows scaling with more FPGAs and provides better support for increased east-west traffic flows. Unless two communicating FPGAs are in the same leaf switch, this mesh provides a fixed number of hops to a destination regardless of their physical location in the network, thus minimizing latency while keeping it at a predictable level even when scaled.

3.2   Ethernet-Based Connection-Oriented Links and Protocol

To establish connectivity from one FPGA to another in the switched network, we opt to use L2 Ethernet, which involves configuring source and destination MAC addresses on Ethernet frames. For some applications like stream computing, establishing this connection-oriented datapath with backpressure is necessary. However, there is no physical inter-FPGA backpressure channel, which is necessary to propagate receiver availability towards an upstream transmitter. In our previous work [14] with a direct network without backpressure, we implemented our own custom protocol with credit-based flow control mechanism. Here, we tailored this custom protocol to keep high-throughput data transfers through Ethernet, while still keeping it cross-compatible with direct network's SL3 protocol. Figure 3 presents the necessary hardware modules for a single link in an Ethernet-based switching network, which includes the flow controller, frame encoder and decoder, and Ethernet IP core for L2 and Layer 1 (L1) functions.

Ethernet L1 and L2 IP Core: As a standard protocol, there are existing off-the-shelf Ethernet IP cores with different incorporated layers and functionalities available for use. For our proposed indirect network, we selected a low-latency 40/100 Gbps Ethernet IP core with L2 MAC and L1 PHY functions, which follows the IEEE 802.3ba 2010 High Speed Ethernet Standard. This IP core supports frame encapsulation, but without a data link header containing the MAC addresses. It also does not include any upper Ethernet layers, which

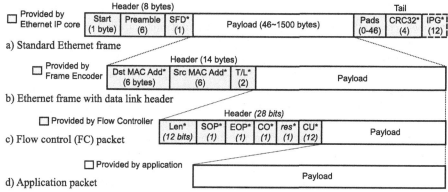

Fig. 4. Protocol layers

is sufficient for our requirements. Figure 4a shows its standard Ethernet frame output.

In the transmit direction, TX MAC accepts a w-bit width input frame and inserts a header and tail, as shown in Fig. 4a. This is then passed to the PHY, which encodes it to serialized data for the FPGA transceiver links. In the receive direction, PHY passes deserialized data to RX MAC, which performs checksum calculations, removes the header and tail, and outputs the rest of the frame.

Frame Encoder and Decoder: The frame encoder and decoder handle the flow of data between the flow controller and Ethernet IP core. Essentially, the encoder's main function is to accept data from the flow controller, inserts the data link header into an Ethernet frame, and passes it to the Ethernet IP core. As shown in Fig. 4b, the encoder inserts the MAC addresses and the type/length (T/L) of the frame. In the receive direction, the decoder strips off the data link header before passing the payload to the flow controller.

This module accepts a maximum payload of 1500 bytes, which is the standard maximum transmission unit (MTU) and can be changed as a parameter. A jumbo frame is also supported, as long as the Ethernet switch ports support handling a payload size greater than the standard MTU. However, when the encoder receives data in the form of a packet, which has start of packet (SOP) and end of packet (EOP) signals, the packet is considered a unit payload and is encapsulated directly with a header without other modifications.

Flow Controller (FC): We utilized our direct network's credit-based FC [14] for the proposed switching network. The main purpose of this module is to provide receiver status awareness between two communicating FPGAs through the exchange of *credits*, which provides transmission reliability. It operates autonomously in either half or full-duplex data transfers. In this paper, we added Ethernet compatibility through frame encapsulations handled by the encoder and Ethernet IP core.

FC receives data from the application, which could be divided into smaller packets composed of *data flits*. A flow control digit, *flit*, is a smaller unit of data from a larger payload size that is sent in one cycle, in which a single flit has (w-bit width)/8 bytes. In each FC packet, a header is inserted. This is also known as a *control flit*, in which other information are embedded in order to reconstruct the original payload in the receive direction. As shown in Fig. 4c, this includes the payload length, SOP and EOP flags, and credit only (CO) flag to indicate a zero-payload packet for half-duplex transfers. The credit update (CU) is also embedded here to update the other FPGA's credit counter, which mimics the backpressure effect of a physical channel.

The CU frequency depends on the FC packet size, which is set as a parameter in this module. In order to embed the payload length in the header, incoming data is placed in a store-and-forward transmitter buffer, FC TX buffer. To minimize induced waiting time for longer payload sizes, CU should be transmitted frequently enough by setting it to every D_{CU} flits. This means that a maximum FC packet sent to the frame encoder is $(D_{CU} + 1)$ flits including the control flit. This is equivalent to:

$$(\text{Maximum FC packet size}) = \frac{(w\text{-bit width})(D_{CU} + 1)}{8} \quad [\text{bytes}], \qquad (1)$$

which should satisfy the encoder's payload size requirements.

Another important parameter is the depth of the receiver buffer, FC RX buffer. In order to operate at a high rate, FC RX buffer allocation must be sufficiently larger the round-trip time plus CU frequency, D_{CU} [10]. Detailed discussion on the FC design parameters and their inter-relationship is in [14].

3.3   Performance Model

In this section, we derive a model to estimate communication time as performance metric, which is dependent on various factors such as communication patterns and the network topology. To simplify and generalize the model, we consider FPGA-to-FPGA communication for both direct and indirect networks. Table 1 lists the parameters affecting network performance.

For any point-to-point connection, a simple model to describe the total transfer time of a message or payload with m bytes is:

$$T_{\text{point-to-point}} = T_L + \frac{m}{B} = t_N + t_{PL} + \frac{m}{B} \quad [\text{s}], \qquad (2)$$

where T_L is the total propagation latency [s] and B is the peak network bandwidth [GB/s], representing latency and streaming factors of a message transfer, respectively. Here, $T_L = t_N + t_{PL}$, where t_N is the node latency [s], also known as start-up latency, which refers to the message handling delays at the sending

Table 1. Parameters for network performance model

Parameters	Description	Unit
m	Message (payload) size	[bytes]
B	Network link bandwidth	[GB/s]
t_N	Node latency (start-up latency)	[s]
t_PL	Physical link latency	[s]
l	Number of physical links	-
s	Number of switch hops	-
t_S	Average switching latency	[s]
T_L	Propagation latency	[s]
T	Total communication time	[s]

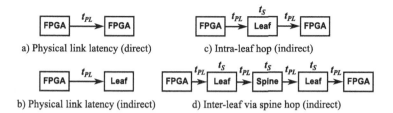

a) Physical link latency (direct)

b) Physical link latency (indirect)

c) Intra-leaf hop (indirect)

d) Inter-leaf via spine hop (indirect)

Fig. 5. Network communication traversal

and receiving nodes, and t_PL is the physical link latency [s], which refers to the time for a node to send and for another node to receive a zero-payload message across a network, as illustrated in Fig. 5a. We also define FPGA as a *node*.

For the switched network, we consider a node-to-node communication time by breaking down the network datapath into parts, as shown in Fig. 5b-d. In an indirect connection, an FPGA is connected to a leaf switch, as shown in Fig. 5b. Figure 5c shows the communication pattern between two FPGAs in a single leaf switch, with its transfer time as:

$$T_\text{intra-leaf hop} = T_\mathrm{L} + \frac{m}{B} = t_\mathrm{N} + 2t_\mathrm{PL} + t_\mathrm{S} + \frac{m}{B} \quad [s], \tag{3}$$

since there are two physical links and the transfer included a single leaf switch hop with a switching latency, t_S, which is included in T_L. Therefore, for an intra-leaf switch data transfer, the communication time is:

$$T_\text{intra-leaf hop} = T_\mathrm{L} + \frac{m}{B} = t_\mathrm{N} + lt_\mathrm{PL} + t_\mathrm{S} + \frac{m}{B} \quad [s], \tag{4}$$

where l is the number of physical links.

Figure 5d presents the FPGA-to-FPGA transfer in separate leaf switches, which involves a spine switch hop. Assuming that we have a fully non-blocking full-bandwidth leaf-spine topology with no contention, then its transfer time is:

$$T_{\text{inter-leaf hop}} = T_L + \frac{m}{B} = t_N + 4t_{PL} + 3t_S + \frac{m}{B} \quad [s], \tag{5}$$

since there are four physical links and three switch hops, assuming the same switching latency for both leaf and spine. To generalize this inter-leaf switch pattern, the communication time is:

$$T_{\text{inter-leaf hop}} = T_L + \frac{m}{B} = t_N + lt_{PL} + st_S + \frac{m}{B} \quad [s]. \tag{6}$$

Consequently, the effective network bandwidth for both network types is:

$$B_{\text{effective}} = \frac{m}{T} = \frac{m}{T_L + \frac{m}{B}} \quad [GB/s], \tag{7}$$

where T is the total communication time.

4   Evaluation

In this section, we investigate the performance characteristics of the switched network and compared it to a direct network. We obtained the resource utilization, latency, and effective network bandwidth of our connection-oriented links. By applying the measured parameters, we used the model to evaluate scalability.

4.1   Implementation

For fundamental evaluation, we implemented the network hardware modules on a Terasic DE5A-NET FPGA board, which includes an Intel Arria 10 FPGA. There are four quad small form-factor pluggable (QSFP+) transceiver ports, but we only utilized two for the experiments. For each port, an instance of the network modules is implemented. For the Ethernet IP core, we used Intel's Low Latency 40 Gbps Ethernet IP core (E40G) [8] to match the tranceiver's 40 Gbps Attachment Unit Interface (XLAUI). As per E40G IP's specification, we used Avalon Streaming (Avalon-ST) interface with a $w = 256$-bit width datapath for the network modules. To complete the network setup, we used a 16-port Mellanox SN2100 Open Ethernet switch [12].

We also prepared two transceiver ports with their own direct network modules on another DE5A-NET board, which includes an FC and a 40 Gbps SL3 IP core per port, as shown in Fig. 1a. For a fair comparison, we used 1-m passive copper QSFP+ transceiver link cables for both network types and utilized the same cross-platform FC design version for both SL3 and E40G setup.

For FC buffer allocations, TX buffer has a depth of 32 flits, where the CU frequency is set to send a credit every $D_{CU} = 32$ flits [14]. Using Eq. (1), the maximum FC packet size sent to the frame encoder is $(256)(32+1)/8 = 1056$ bytes, which satisfies the frame encoder payload size requirements. To fully maximize the network bandwidth, we could increase this to 1500 bytes, with $D_{CU} = 45$ flits and a TX buffer depth of 64 flits, but this would incur additional logic and

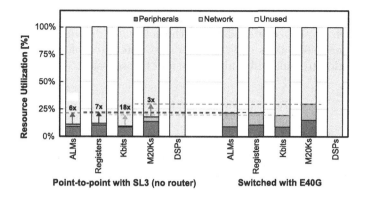

Fig. 6. Resource utilization of SL3 and E40G Ethernet modules

an increase in area. Thus, we chose a 32-flit TX buffer allocation for both SL3 and E40G network to maintain equal FC protocol overhead in this evaluation.

To operate at high data rate, RX buffer depth relies on the link latency [14], in which SL3's RX buffer depth is at a minimum of 512 flits [14]. For the switched network, this is not sufficient due to the additional latency of switch hops; thus, the need to increase E40G's RX buffer depth to a relatively larger size. For E40G network, we set FC RX buffer depth to 2048 flits, while keeping 512 flits for SL3.

Figure 6 shows the resource utilization of adaptive logic modules (ALMs), registers, memory logic array blocks (MLAB Kbits), M20K memory blocks, and digital signal processors (DSPs). As shown in green, point-to-point's network modules consume lesser area, while the switched network's consume about 6x, 7x, 18x, and 3x more ALMs, registers, Kbits, and M20Ks, respectively, than the former. This is due to increased logic and memory needed for the frame encoder, decoder, and FC RX buffer allocation. For the E40G switched network, this is around 70–75% of resources, which is a fair amount considering that we target to map a large application across multiple FPGAs. In addition, it is noteworthy that the SL3 direct network does not include an on-chip router, which when implemented, would imply an increase on its consumption.

4.2   Communication Time and Effective Network Bandwidth

To measure parameters for the performance model in Eq. (6), we setup and used hardware cycle counters for the following cases: (1) point-to-point with SL3, (2) point-to-point with E40G, and (3) a switched network with E40G, as shown in Fig. 7a. Aside from a switched E40G case (3), we also considered a point-to-point connection with E40G case (2) to obtain the average switching latency, t_S.

Table 2 shows the measured values for node latency, t_N and physical link latency, t_{PL} for a zero-payload equivalent, which in E40G, is encapsulated in a minimum-sized Ethernet frame with 46-byte padded payload. For SL3 case (1), t_N only includes FC latency, while for E40G cases (2) and (3), this includes FC, frame encoder, and frame decoder delays; hence, the higher latency of E40G.

Due to IP restrictions on SL3 and E40G IP cores, we could only measure t_{PL} by including their protocol overheads; thus, the noticeable difference of their values. Using the measured values of t_N and t_{PL}, we were also able to verify the RX buffer allocation to maintain a high data rate transmission.

Table 2. Measured latency parameters

Network	Unit	t_N	t_{PL}	t_S
(1) Point-to-point with SL3	[us]	0.245	0.354	N/A
(2) Point-to-point with E40G	[us]	0.336	0.496	N/A
(3) Switched with E40G	[us]	0.336	0.496	0.318

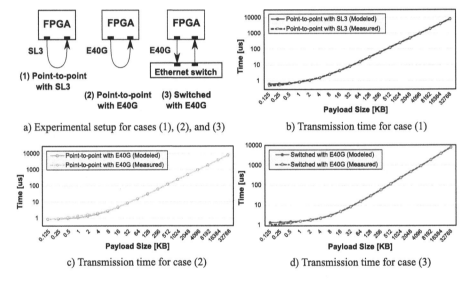

Fig. 7. Modeled vs. measured network communication time

In order to obtain the effective bandwidth, we measured the total communication time by sending various payload sizes and used it in Eq. (7). Case (1) shows the highest bandwidth for smaller payload sizes due to its lower communication latency, as illustrated in Fig. 8. Meanwhile, case (2) shows a lower effective bandwidth than case (1). This is due to the additional protocol overhead of Ethernet and the extra latency of passing through more modules, i.e. frame encoder and decoder, as with case (3). However, the latter shows the lowest effective bandwidth due to a longer communication time via the switch.

For larger payload sizes, we observed that the effective bandwidth for case (1) is 4.29 GB/s with 86% efficiency. For (2) and (3), both reached an effective bandwidth of 4.41 GB/s at 88% efficiency, which is surprisingly about 3% higher than SL3's. This is caused by SL3 protocol's transmission overheads and lane rate calculations [9], where the required network clock frequency derived was 150.813962 MHz, resulting to 4.83 GB/s peak throughput. For E40G IP core, there is no clock frequency requirement. We were able to utilize a 154.99442 MHz clock frequency, which correspondingly results to a higher peak throughput of 4.96 GB/s. Even with Ethernet's additional protocol overhead, a switched network with E40G showed a better effective bandwidth, which is beneficial for large payload sizes since latency no longer dominates transfer time.

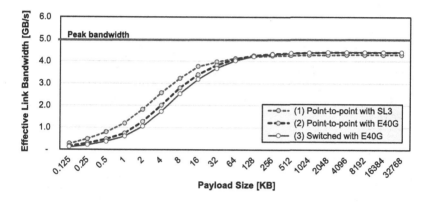

Fig. 8. Effective network bandwidth of SL3 and E40G for cases (1), (2), and (3)

Correspondingly, we also used the measured total communication time to validate the performance model by comparing it with our estimated results. By using the obtained parameters such as t_N and the effective bandwidth, we were able to estimate the transmission time, as shown in Fig. 7b-d. Based on the plotted values, the model closely matches the measured time, which can be used to estimate communication performance in larger FPGA clusters.

4.3   Performance Estimation of Stream Computing on an Indirect Network

In this evaluation, a stream computing case is considered through a single data stream traversal in a ring connection. A direct network is often the typical choice, thus, we investigated its performance in our proposed switching framework. We used two FPGAs in a ring connection to perform fundamental evaluation on a switched network, as shown in Fig. 9a and compared it with its equivalent point-to-point ring connection with SL3. We obtained the total communication time and mapped its effective bandwidth in Fig. 9b. As anticipated, latency prevails in smaller payload sizes, in which the point-to-point connection has higher bandwidth. For larger payload sizes, however, the effective bandwidth of the switched E40G connection saturates at 4.41 GB/s, which still performed better than its direct counterpart at 4.29 GB/s.

Using Eq. (2) for SL3 and Eq. (3) for E40G, we also estimated the communication time by scaling the propagation latency, T_L by a factor of two, since this ring is equivalent to two point-to-point connections. As shown in Fig. 9b, the modeled values approximates the measured points, which is expected since the model only accounts for the network communication without interaction.

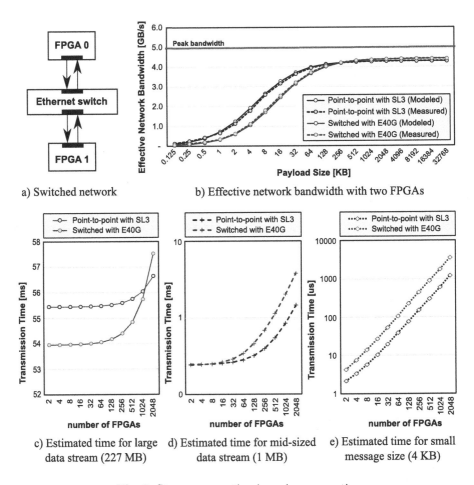

a) Switched network

b) Effective network bandwidth with two FPGAs

c) Estimated time for large data stream (227 MB)

d) Estimated time for mid-sized data stream (1 MB)

e) Estimated time for small message size (4 KB)

Fig. 9. Stream computing in a ring connection

To evaluate scalability, we estimate the communication time of both network connections with a larger cluster setup. We assume a radix-64 switch ($k = 64$), which could accommodate up to $n = 64$ FPGAs. When $n > 64$, we scale using the leaf-spine architecture, where we assume to balance the uplink to downlink ratio (no oversubscription). To build a two-layer, full-bisection bandwidth leaf-spine topology, we could connect up to $n = k \times \frac{k}{2} = 2048$ FPGAs with $a = \frac{2n}{k} = 64$ leafs, and $b = \frac{a}{2} = 32$ spines, which are connected in a full bipartite graph with $\frac{k}{a} = 1$ uplink per leaf to all 32 spines.

In this ring connection, we assume the lowest latency traversal, where an FPGA hops to their neighboring FPGA first via intra-leaf hops (see Fig. 5c), before an inter-leaf hop through the spine (see Fig. 5d). With $n <= 64$, we can scale T_L by n, since there are n FPGA-to-FPGA transfers in the ring through a single leaf ($a = 1$). With $n > 64$, the scaling factor for T_L is $a(\frac{k}{2} - 1)$, since the FPGAs on the edges of the leaf have to perform an inter-leaf transfer. Consequently, an inter-leaf communication's scaling factor for T_L is a, when $a > 1$. By hypothetically assuming the measured parameters in Table 2 and the measured effective bandwidth, we estimated the total time, $T = T_L + \frac{m}{B}$, by accumulating the scaled T_L values for both intra-leaf and inter-leaf hops, which forms the communication pattern of the ring, while increasing the FPGA cluster size.

Figure 9c-e show the transmission time for a large data stream (227 MB), a mid-sized data stream (1 MB), and a small message size (4 KB), respectively. For the large data stream size, we observed a lower latency for E40G up to $n = 1024$ FPGAs, due to the higher effective bandwidth. With $n = 2048$, the data stream size is no longer sufficient and the latency factor catches up, making SL3 perform better. For the mid-sized data stream, the higher effective bandwidth of E40G keeps the time difference at a minimum only for a small FPGA cluster (up to $n = 16$ FPGAs). Meanwhile, the lower latency of a point-to-point connection influences the transfer time, making it perform better for small message sizes.

5   Conclusions

This paper presented the design and architecture of an Ethernet-based switched platform for scalable FPGA clusters, where we established a connection-oriented datapath with backpressure over the network. For usability and to establish connectivity, we utilized our credit-based protocol with flow control over Ethernet and implemented the supporting network modules to achieve high-throughput data transfers.

We investigated the performance characteristics of the connection-oriented links and modeled its communication performance. By obtaining the communication time and effective network bandwidth, we estimated the communication latency of a streamed computing pattern when scaled to a large-sized cluster. With the E40G switched network saturating at a higher effective bandwidth for large data streams in comparison with its point-to-point SL3 counterpart, our proposed indirect framework has demonstrated good communication performance and scalability for applications requiring high-bandwidth and large data transfers, despite its longer network propagation latency.

For our future work, we will evaluate other communication patterns on the switched network to further evaluate its network flexibility. In addition, the performance model needs to be fine-tuned since it only focused on communication time, without considering computation or interaction delays. We are also planning to upgrade the framework using Stratix 10 FPGAs, where their transceiver links support 100 Gbps data rate. Another area of future work is to provide a standard platform for FPGA cluster management, such as mapping of applications and network configurations.

References

1. Alizadeh, M., Edsall, T.: On the data path performance of leaf-spine datacenter fabrics. In: Proceedings - IEEE 21st Annual Symposium on High-Performance Interconnects, HOTI 2013, pp. 71–74. IEEE Computer Society (2013). https://doi.org/10.1109/HOTI.2013.23
2. AWS: Amazon EC2 F1 instances. https://aws.amazon.com/ec2/instance-types/f1/
3. Baxter, R., Booth, S., Bull, M., et al.: Maxwell - a 64 FPGA supercomputer. In: Second NASA/ESA Conference on Adaptive Hardware and Systems (AHS 2007), pp. 287–294. IEEE, August 2007. https://doi.org/10.1109/AHS.2007.71
4. Bunker, T., Swanson, S.: Latency-optimized networks for clustering FPGAs (2013). https://doi.org/10.1109/FCCM.2013.49
5. Caulfield, A.M., Chung, E.S., Putnam, A., et al.: A cloud-scale acceleration architecture. In: MICRO-49 The 49th Annual IEEE/ACM International Symposium on Microarchitecture (2016). https://doi.org/10.1109/MICRO.2016.7783710
6. Fowers, J., Ovtcharov, K., Papamichael, M., et al.: A configurable cloud-scale DNN processor for real-time AI. In: 2018 ACM/IEEE 45th Annual International Symposium on Computer Architecture (ISCA), pp. 1–14. IEEE, June 2018. https://doi.org/10.1109/ISCA.2018.00012
7. Herbordt, M.C., VanCourt, T., Gu, Y., et al.: Achieving high performance with FPGA-based computing. Computer **40**(3), 50–57 (2007). https://doi.org/10.1109/MC.2007.79
8. Intel: Low latency 40-gbps Ethernet IP core user guide. https://www.intel.com/content/www/us/en/programmable/products/intellectual-property/ip/interface-protocols/m-alt-40gb-ethernet.html
9. Intel: SerialLite III IP Solution. https://www.altera.com/solutions/technology/transceiver/protocols/pro-seriallite-3.html
10. Kung, H., Morris, R.: Credit-based flow control for ATM networks. IEEE Network **9**(2), 40–48 (1995). https://doi.org/10.1109/65.372658
11. Markettos, A.T., Fox, P.J., Moore, S.W., et al.: Interconnect for commodity FPGA clusters: standardized or customized? In: Conference Digest - 24th International Conference on Field Programmable Logic and Applications, FPL 2014, pp. 1–8, September 2014. https://doi.org/10.1109/FPL.2014.6927472
12. Mellanox Technologies Ltd.: Sn2100 open Ethernet switch (2019). https://www.mellanox.com/ethernet/switches.php
13. Mencer, O., Tsoi, K.H., Craimer, S., et al.: Cube: a 512-FPGA cluster. In: Proceedings of the 2009 5th Southern Conference on Programmable Logic (SPL), pp. 51–57. IEEE, April 2009. https://doi.org/10.1109/SPL.2009.4914907
14. Mondigo, A., Ueno, T., Sano, K., Takizawa, H.: Scalability analysis of deeply pipelined Tsunami simulation with multiple FPGAS. IEICE Trans. Inf. Syst. **E102-D**(5), 1029–1036 (2019). https://doi.org/10.1587/transinf.2018RCP0007

15. Putnam, A., Caulfield, A.M., Chung, E.S., et al.: A reconfigurable fabric for accelerating large-scale datacenter services. In: ISCA 2014 Proceeding of the 41st Annual International Symposium on Computer Architecture, Minneapolis, MN, USA, pp. 13–24. IEEE (2014). https://doi.org/10.1109/ISCA.2014.6853195
16. Sheng, J., Yang, C., Herbordt, M.C.: High performance communication on reconfigurable clusters. In: 2018 28th International Conference on Field Programmable Logic and Applications (FPL), Dublin, Ireland (2018)
17. Tarafdar, N., Lin, T., Fukuda, E., et al.: Enabling flexible network FPGA clusters in a heterogeneous cloud data center (2017). https://doi.org/10.1145/3020078.3021742
18. Xiong, Q., Skjellum, A., Herbordt, M.C.: Accelerating MPI message matching through FPGA offload. In: 2018 28th International Conference on Field Programmable Logic and Applications (FPL), pp. 191–1914. IEEE, August 2018. https://doi.org/10.1109/FPL.2018.00039

A Parameterisable FPGA-Tailored Architecture for YOLOv3-Tiny

Zhewen Yu and Christos-Savvas Bouganis[(⊠)]

Department of Electrical and Electronic Engineering, Imperial College London,
London, UK
{zhewen.yu18,christos-savvas.bouganis}@imperial.ac.uk

Abstract. Object detection is the task of detecting the position of objects in an image or video as well as their corresponding class. The current state of the art approach that achieves the highest performance (i.e. fps) without significant penalty in accuracy of detection is the YOLO framework, and more specifically its latest version YOLOv3. When embedded systems are targeted for deployment, YOLOv3-tiny, a lightweight version of YOLOv3, is usually adopted. The presented work is the first to implement a parameterised FPGA-tailored architecture specifically for YOLOv3-tiny. The architecture is optimised for latency-sensitive applications, and is able to be deployed in low-end devices with stringent resource constraints. Experiments demonstrate that when a low-end FPGA device is targeted, the proposed architecture achieves a 290x improvement in latency, compared to the hard core processor of the device, achieving at the same time a reduction in mAP of 2.5 pp (30.9% vs 33.4%) compared to the original model. The presented work opens the way for low-latency object detection on low-end FPGA devices.

Keywords: YOLOv3-tiny · FPGA · Object detection

1 Introduction

The object detection technology deals with the problem of detecting instances of objects in images and videos. Applications of this technology can be found in the deployment of advanced intelligent systems like Advanced Driver Assistance Systems (ADAS) and video surveillance. Accurate object classification and identification of the objects' position are often required, as this information forms the basis for further processing and decision making in the rest of the application's pipeline.

Recently, capitalising on the recent advances in machine learning, and more specifically on the development of deep neural networks, researchers and practitioners have developed powerful object detection systems that can provide accurate detection in a number of challenging situations. Furthermore, in cases where low latency of processing is required, work in the area has moved away from scanning the image in multiple positions and applying image classifiers

© Springer Nature Switzerland AG 2020
F. Rincón et al. (Eds.): ARC 2020, LNCS 12083, pp. 330–344, 2020.
https://doi.org/10.1007/978-3-030-44534-8_25

(i.e. casting the problem of object detection to the classification problem over multiple windows) to combining the above distinct steps in a single pipeline, usually based on a deep neural network.

Early works towards this direction include R-CNN [4], Fast R-CNN [3] and Faster R-CNN [15]. These works implement the object detection by two distinct parts, region proposal selecting possible candidates that include an object and a deep neural network responsible for the classification of these regions. As resource sharing between the two parts is limited, the above approach exhibits usually high computational loads and detection latency.

In an attempt to provide object detectors with lower computational requirements and enable object detection in low-power devices, research has focused on the one-step approach, where the bounding boxes around the objects are predicted directly though the DNN rather than having a separate region proposal step [19]. Two of the most popular such frameworks are the Single Shot MultiBox Detector (SSD) [7] and the YOLO (You only look once) [13].

SSD is based on a VGG16 network and has been extended by custom convolution layers in order to generate bounding boxes. SSD uses a set of predefined anchor boxes for detection at various scales impacting the framework's precision and computational load.

The YOLO framework relies on a single DNN, DarkNet, in order to predict both the position of the objects (i.e. bounding boxes) as well as their classification. Early versions of the YOLO approach exhibited low computational loads by trading the classification precision for low latency, which led to their deployment in embedded systems. The most recent version of YOLO is YOLOv3, which adopts a deeper neural network than its predecessors, achieving more accurate classifications. Currently, YOLOv3 demonstrates its advantages of both low latency and high classification precision over other competitors [14].

In cases where the deployment of an object detection system is required in an embedded form for real-time applications, such as an ADAS system, low power and latency considerations have pushed the designers to solutions that are based on low-power FPGA and mobile GPU platforms. Because generic mobile processors usually do not provide the necessary performance under the desired power envelopes.

This work addresses the challenging problem of deploying YOLO in a low-power FPGA device, and more specifically it targets the mapping of YOLOv3-tiny, a variant of YOLOv3 version for embedded systems. The paper's novel contribution is a latency-optimised parameterisable architecture tailored to YOLOv3-tiny workload that can be tuned to the resource availability of any targeted FPGA device. To enable the above, a parameterisable architecture is developed and implemented using Vivado HLS. Performance and resources models are derived that guide the Design Space Exploration (DSE) phase for identifying design points that optimise the latency of the system, meeting at the same time the resource constraints.

To the best of the authors' knowledge, this is the first work that addresses this problem when a low-power and limited resources FPGA device is targeted and use of off-chip memory is required to store the parameters and intermediate results of the network, enabling the deployment of YOLOv3-tiny in scenarios with extremely limited resources.

The rest of the paper is organised as follows. Section 2 describes network architecture of YOLOv3-tiny and challenges in its mapping to an embedded system. Section 3 elaborates the proposed architecture and explains how YOLOv3-tiny is mapped onto the accelerator. Section 4 focuses on the resource and performance models which enable the Design Space Exploration described in Sect. 5. Section 6 introduces the wordlength optimisation used in the architecture, where Sect. 7 provides a discussion on the evaluation of the system. Finally, Sect. 8 concludes the paper.

2   Background

2.1   YOLOv3-Tiny Network

YOLOv3-tiny is a light-weight version of YOLOv3. It exhibits a reduced number of layers compared to YOLOv3, allowing its deployment to resource-constraint devices. The reduced number of layers leads to lower computational load and inference latency with a penalty on the object detection precision.

YOLOv3-tiny accepts an RGB image of 416×416 resolution as input. Contrary to YOLOv3, YOLOv3-tiny predicts bounding boxes at two different scales only. The first scale divides the input image into 13×13 grids, while the second operates on 26×26 grids. The framework generates three bounding boxes in every grid. The network outputs a 3d tensor containing information on the bounding box, the objectness confidence and the class predictions.

The network mainly utilises five types of layers; Convolutional, Max pooling, Route, Upsample and Yolo layer. Route layers are responsible for creating different flows in the network, where Upsampling is used to support multiple detection scales. The Yolo layer is responsible to generate the output vector. Figure 1 shows the dataflow of the network alongside with the number of operations required for convolution.

2.2   Mapping YOLO-Based Networks to FPGAs

Current toolflows for automated mapping of CNNs to FPGAs do not support the specialised computational layers of YOLO [16]. As such, a number of works have focused on customised designs for deploying various versions of the YOLO network onto FPGAs. Some perform a faithful mapping of YOLO while others introduce certain approximations to tailor the hardware. Wei et al. [18] presented an FPGA-based architecture for the acceleration of YOLOv2-tiny, where the parameters of the layers are required to be stored on local memory in advance. In their architecture, the Leaky ReLU activation is replaced with ReLU for reducing the resource consumption. The authors reported a latency per inference of 52 ms on Zynq 7035.

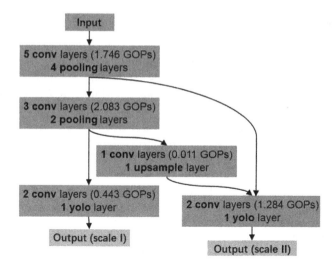

Fig. 1. Dataflow of YOLOv3-tiny

The acceleration of YOLOv2-tiny is also targeted in Liu et al. [6]. Their system combines adjacent layers in order to reduce the communication cost between the host and the device. In their approach, a fixed point number representation is utilised, where the inputs and outputs are kept at 16 bits while intermediate multiplication products are stored at 32 bits. Their system achieves 69.2 fps using Arria 10 GX1150.

Wai et al. [17] also targeted the acceleration of YOLOv2-tiny. In the proposed solution, the batch normalisation and convolution layers are merged together. In their system, the computation of the convolutions is based on a General Matrix-Matrix Multiplication (GeMM) core that has been designed via OpenCL. The proposed design can be parameterised by tuning the multiplication block size. Their work achieves 3.06 fps using Cyclone V PCIe device.

Nakahara et al. [9] proposed a modified version of YOLOv2 which was termed Lightweight YOLOv2. In the proposed network, the convolution layers for feature extraction are replaced with binary multiply-add operations. Furthermore, a Support Vector Machine algorithm (SVM) is responsible for the prediction of the objects' coordinates and classifications. Using a ZCU102 device, their system achieves 40 fps, with a modest drop in accuracy (1.5 pp).

Nguyen et al. [10] proposed Sim-YOLOv2, a quantised version of YOLOv2, and its implementation on FPGA. The proposed architecture focuses on maximising the throughput of the system, and as such each layer of the network is mapped to a dedicated hardware block. Weights are stored on chip to minimise off-chip data transfers. Due to the requirement of on-chip storage, a Virtex-7 VC707 device is targeted. The latency reaches 9.15 ms at the cost of 18.29 W power consumption.

2.3   Challenges and Target

Mapping YOLOv3 or YOLOv3-tiny to an FPGA device brings new challenges. In YOLO and YOLOv2, the networks are trained for VOC [1,2] dataset and are able to address twenty different object classes. YOLOv3 is trained for COCO2014 [5] which instead targets 80 classes, and as such it exhibits higher computational load.

The target of this work is the design of a latency optimised and FPGA-tailored architecture that can be customised to the available FPGA resources in order to accelerate the inference stage of YOLOv3-tiny model. The previously mentioned works are addressing the problem of mapping YOLOv2, and its variants to an FPGA device. To the best of the authors' knowledge, the only work that addresses the mapping of the newest model, the YOLOv3-tiny, is LogicTronix [8], where a Xilinx DPU-DNNDK was used for its acceleration using a ultra96 FPGA device, achieving 30 fps. Even though the work quantises the model, no evaluation or any accuracy result is reported. The proposed framework targets lower-end devices that have considerably fewer resources.

3   Proposed Architecture

The proposed architecture is tailored for the execution of YOLOv3-tiny model, providing as such hardware support for the newly introduced special Yolo layer. The developed accelerator is utilised for the execution of all layers of the network through a run-time parameter setting. The proposed architecture is tailored and compile-time parameterisable in HLS to target low-end FPGA devices with limited resources, and as such no hard constraints on adequate on-chip memory for storing of the data are imposed by the system.

3.1   System Overview

Figure 2 provides a high-level picture of the proposed architecture. The FPGA Hardware Accelerator denotes the proposed FPGA architecture and consists of a three-stage pipeline, where each stage corresponds to a layer of YOLOv3-tiny network. The Accelerator is controlled by the ARM processor who is responsible for the overall control of the system. The data and weights are transferred between the Accelerator and the off-chip memory through DMA interfaces.

The FPGA accelerator consists of a three-stage pipeline. The first stage of the pipeline supports the execution of the convolution layer, whose output is accumulated in the second stage of the pipeline. Depending on the network structure that is executed at a given time, the accumulation results are sent for further processing in the Max pooling, Upsample or Yolo layer.

3.2   Module Design

The FPGA Hardware Accelerator consists of five main computational blocks; the convolution, accumulation, max pooling, upsample and yolo blocks.

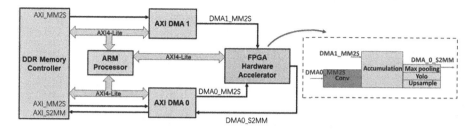

Fig. 2. System-level architecture of this work

Convolution Block: The block performs direct convolutions of N_{in} input channels with the corresponding kernels and produces N_{out} output channels. Internally the block contains three main sub-modules, including an input line buffer, convolution kernels and an output buffer.

The compile-time (synthesis-time) known parameters of the block are

$$\{N^{max}, f_w^{max}, K_c^{max}, p_c\}$$

which define the maximum number of input and output channels, the maximum width of the input feature map, the maximum kernel size, and the number of parallel compute units in the block respectively.

The adopted architecture of the block provides flexibility on trading off resources for performance. p_c provides the option to control the unrolling factor of computing the convolutions, as well as the way that the input and output channels are interleaved. As Fig. 3 shows, p_c can also be expressed as the product of parallelism among output channels ($p_{c,1}$), parallelism among input channels ($p_{c,2}$) and parallelism inside convolution kernels ($p_{c,3}$). The maximum number of input and output channels (N^{max}) depends on the available FPGA resource and DMA bandwidth of the platform. Both p_c and N^{max} are tuned to the targeted device during the Design Space Exploration stage.

During run-time, the operation of the block is tuned by the ARM processor through the following parameters

$$\{N_{in}, N_{out}, f_h, f_w, K, S\}$$

where f_h and f_w are the padded height and width of input feature maps, K is the kernel size, and S is the kernel stride.

Accumulation Block: The block is designed to allow input channels folding (Sect. 3.4), supporting the convolution block. The module accumulates outputs of multiple sub-layers, and is parameterised during the compile time through the parameters

$$\{N^{max}, f_w^{max}, p_a\}$$

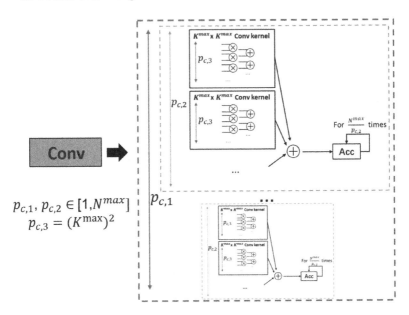

Fig. 3. Parameterisation of the convolution block

which define the maximum number of input channels, the maximum width of the input feature map, and the number of parallel compute units in the block respectively. During run-time, the operation of the block can be customised through the following parameters:

$$\{N_{in}, f_h, f_w, E_{bias}, E_{leaky}\}$$

E_{bias} controls whether the bias is added to the accumulated results. E_{leaky} is a parameter that enables Leaky ReLU activation function.

Yolo Block: The block implements the functionality of the YOLO layer which is mainly composed of sigmoid activation. The sigmoid function is implemented as a fixed point division operation and an exponential module. The compile-time parameters of the block are

$$\{N^{max}, f_w^{max}, p_y\}$$

p_y defines the number of parallel compute units in the block. During run-time, the block is parameterised by setting the following parameters:

$$\{N_{in}, f_h, f_w\}$$

In the proposed implementation, the maximum and average error of the sigmoid implementation are 0.39% and 0.19% respectively.

Max Pooling Block and Upsample Block: These two blocks are responsible for the downsampling and upsampling operations respectively. Two blocks can be parameterised at compile and run-time similar to the Yolo block.

3.3   Network Mapping to FPGA Hardware Accelerator

Given a configuration of the proposed FPGA architecture, the workload of YOLOv3-tiny is mapped onto the accelerator. As computational hardware blocks are time-multiplexed for the successful execution of the workload, certain transformations of the network need to take place in order to schedule the execution of the tasks on the accelerator.

Channels Folding: At synthesis time, the maximum number of channels N_{max} that can be processed by the proposed system is determined. When N^{max} is smaller than N_{in} or N_{out}, the computation of a layer has to be spilt into multiple sub-layers. The computation of a convolution layer having N_{in} input channels and N_{out} output channels can be expressed as:

$$g_j = \sum_{i=1}^{N_{in}} f_i * w_{i,j} + b_j, \quad with \quad j \in [1, N_{out}] \tag{1}$$

f_i is the ith input channel, and g_j is the jth output channel. $w_{i,j}$ and b_j are weights and biases of the convolution layer. When input channels are folded by a factor of $F_{in} = \lceil \frac{N_{in}}{N^{max}} \rceil$, (1) is turned into

$$g_j = \sum_{i=1}^{N^{max}} f_i * w_{i,j} + \sum_{i=N^{max}+1}^{2N^{max}} f_i * w_{i,j} + ... + \sum_{i=(F_{in}-1)N^{max}+1}^{N_{in}} f_i * w_{i,j} + b_j \tag{2}$$

By folding the output channels, g_j is divided into F_{out} sub-layers, with $F_{out} = \lceil \frac{N_{out}}{N^{max}} \rceil$, each containing up to N^{max} output channels.

Kernel Size Padding: The size of the kernels varies across the layers of the network. In this work, the maximum required kernel size (K^{max}) is actually implemented. The computation with smaller kernel sizes is performed by embedding the kernel in the maximum supported kernel. Necessary padding is applied during the process.

Layer Fusion Computation: As the work targets devices with limited resources, the mapping of the network onto the proposed architecture is broken down into smaller tasks that are supported by the proposed architecture. As such, a policy is needed to guide the segmentation of the computational load in smaller chunks such as the system's performance is optimised. The policy that has been adopted in this work is to use the convolution layers as points of boundaries for the division of the network workload into smaller chunks. As such, network layers between two boundary points are bounded together as a batch, which is referred as "**layer batch**" for the rest of this paper.

As such, the original network structure **N** is transformed into a series of layer batches $\mathbf{N}_i$, where for each layer batch i the run-time parameters of the architecture are defined as follows:

$$\mathbf{N}_i = \{F_{in}, F_{out}, N_{in}, N_{out}, f_h, f_w, K, S, \mathbf{E}\},$$

where **E** provides information regarding the activation or not of a specific block inside the accelerator in the current layer batch. During the inference stage, the smallest scheduled task is a layer batch, where the data are streamed in and out of the accelerator. Using the above approach, off-chip memory accesses are omitted between layers inside the same batch.

3.4   System Processing Flow

During the inference stage, the ARM processor acts as a master and controls the inference process. The computation of the network is broken down to smaller components, the layer batches, which are scheduled by the processor and executed sequentially. Figure 4 captures the processing flow for a single layer batch.

More specifically, the ARM processor firstly sets the parameters for each individual block in the hardware accelerator and configures the DMA modules. Then, it initiates the weight loading and input data transfers via DMA streaming onto the Hardware Accelerator. The FPGA Acceleration block starts processing the data and the output data are transferred back to off-chip DDR memory. The necessary invalidation of the corresponding cache region is performed by the processor, ensuring correct data transfer.

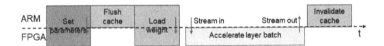

Fig. 4. System processing flow for a layer batch

4   Latency and Resource Estimations

Analytical models have been derived to provide resource and latency estimates of the system under a specific configuration and load. Utilising the derived models, a design space exploration phase is possible for the identification of Pareto-optimal design point in the latency-resource space.

4.1   Hardware Latency Model

As the proposed architecture of the FPGA accelerator has a pipeline structure, the initiation interval II_{sys}, i.e. the number of clock cycles before a new input can be processed, is dictated by the slowest active block. The initiation interval for each individual block is denoted by II_b, where b={*convolution, accumulation, max pooling, upsample, yolo*} and it is a function of:

$$II_b = \max\left(\frac{p_b^{max}}{p_b}, r_b^{OtoI}, OP_b\right) \qquad (3)$$

where p_b^{max} is the maximum number of parallel compute units in theory and p_b is the actual number of units that finally implemented, r_b^{OtoI} is the ratio of output to input data transfer size, and OP_b is the lower boundary of the number of cycles required for operations inside the block.

For a given II_{sys}, the latency of the hardware accelerator for computing a layer batch $T_{batch}^{hardware}$ is:

$$T_{batch}^{hardware} = F_{out}F_{in}(f_h f_w \left\lceil \frac{N_{in} \times WL_{bus}}{WL_q} \right\rceil II_{sys} + T_{communication}) \qquad (4)$$

where WL_{bus} denotes the width of the bus (DMA) in the platform, and WL_q denotes the wordlength of the input. $T_{communication}$ captured the required time for setting up the control parameters via AXI4-Lite and, in the case of a convolution layer, for retrieving weights and biases.

4.2   Software Latency Model

The overall latency of the system depends also on the latency introduced by the tasks executed on the ARM processor. The overall latency model has been refined to account for the above overheads leading to:

$$T_{batch} = T_{batch}^{hardware} + T_{batch}^{cpu} \qquad (5)$$

where T_{batch}^{cpu} models the time spent by the CPU. The actual value of T_{batch}^{cpu} mainly depends on flushing and invalidation of the cache for DMA transfers. T_{batch}^{cpu} can be measured and estimated for each device by experiments.

The overall latency of the system, assuming N layer batches in total, is given by:

$$T_{sys} = \sum_{i=1:N} T_{batch}^i \qquad (6)$$

where T_{batch}^i denotes the latency for executing batch i.

4.3   Resource Estimation

DSP Utilisation: The proposed architecture utilises DSP cores for the computations that are required in the convolution and sigmoid function evaluation. The architecture unrolls fully the computations in the convolution filter resulting in the utilisation of K^2 DSPs for every $K \times K$ kernel. Finally, K takes the maximum kernel size K_c^{max}. For the evaluation of the sigmoid function in the Yolo layer, the fixed point exponential function provided by Xilinx is utilised, requiring the utilisation of 2 DSPs. Given a targeted parallelism factor of p_c and p_y, for the convolution and Yolo layers respectively, the total number of utilised DSP cores of the system under configuration $\mathbf{P}$ are:

$$DSP_{sys}(\mathbf{P}) = (K_c^{max})^2 p_{c,1} p_{c,2} + 2p_y \tag{7}$$

Memory Utilisation: On-chip memory is utilised mainly as convolution weights buffer and input buffer. For the weights buffer, the storage size (in words) is the product of the number of input channels (N_{in}), the number of output channels (N_{out}), and the dimensions of kernels (($K_c^{max})^2$). As N_{in} and N_{out} are capped at N_{max}, the weights buffer needs to have a maximum capacity of $N_{max}^2 (K_c^{max})^2$ words.

The proposed architecture adopts input line buffers for sliding windows in convolution and max pooling layers. For a layer with kernels of size $K \times K$, the line buffer has K lines. K should be K_c^{max} and K_p^{max} for convolution and pooling respectively. (8) captures the overall number of the BRAMs required by the architecture.

$$BRAM_{sys}(\mathbf{P}) = \left\lceil \frac{N_{max}^2 W L_q}{BRAM_{size}} \right\rceil (K_c^{max})^2 + \left\lceil \frac{N_{max} f_w^{max} W L_q}{BRAM_{size}} \right\rceil (K_c^{max} + K_p^{max}) \tag{8}$$

f_w^{max} denotes the maximum width of the input feature map, where $BRAM_{size}$ denotes the size of the BRAM in bits. The first term of (8) captures the memory requirements for storing the kernel weights, where the second term is the necessary number of BRAMs for the input buffers.

5   Design Space Exploration

A key advantage of the proposed framework is that it can tailor the architecture of the system to the resource availability of the targeted device. Moreover, the proposed framework can be deployed to any FPGA device without having hard constraints on the targeted resource availability such as the requirement of having enough on-chip memory for storing the parameters of the whole network on-chip.

The problem of mapping YOLOv3-tiny to an FPGA device targeting latency-sensitive applications is cast as an optimisation problem as follows:

$$\min_{\mathbf{P}} T_{sys}(\mathbf{P})$$
$$s.t.\ DSP_{sys}(\mathbf{P}) \le DSP_{avail} \tag{9}$$
$$BRAMs_{sys}(\mathbf{P}) \le BRAMs_{avail}$$

where $\mathbf{P}$ is the compile-time known parameter vector of the system.

As such, given a set of resources, the proposed framework automatically searched the parameter (i.e. configuration) space $\mathbf{P}$ with the help of analytical models, in order to identify a design point that optimises the latency of the system.

6   Wordlength Optimisation

YOLOv3-tiny only reduces the structure of the network compared to Yolov3, where the parameters of the network are left as floating point numbers. The work investigates the robustness of the network when reduced precision network parameters are utilised in order to achieve a reduction on the required resources and off-chip memory accesses.

The quantisation process is guided through the Weight loss metric $Wl(q)$, that measures the impact of quantisation on the representation of the network parameters using a quantisation process q (10).

$$Wl(q) = \sum_{i,j} \frac{(w_{i,j} - \hat{w}_{i,j})^2}{w_{i,j}^2} \qquad (10)$$

$w_{i,j}$ represents the original floating point weight, where $\hat{w}_{i,j}$ represents its quantised version under quantisation process q. Two quantisation schemes that have been investigated are 8-bit and 16-bit wordlength, where half of the wordlength is allocated for the fractional part. In both schemes, linear quantisation is used. Table 1 shows the impact of each configuration to the Wl metric across convolutional layers of the network. The results led to the adoption of 16-bits wordlength for the system. Tested on COCO val5k [5], the 16-bit version achieves 30.9% mAP50, compared with 33.4% of the original floating point network, indicating a small loss in detection precision.

Table 1. Weight loss of fixed point quantisation

Layer index	1	2	3	4	5	6	7	8	9	10	11	12	13
Wl @ 8 bit(%)	7.81	2.68	3.37	11.01	24.26	48.40	7.30	70.91	17.85	6.35	1.36	60.33	3.00
Wl @ 16 bit(%)	0.00	0.01	0.01	0.05	0.11	0.26	0.03	0.56	0.08	0.03	0.01	0.44	0.01

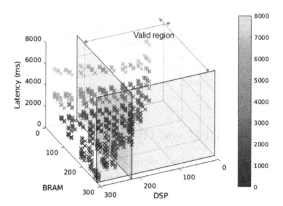

Fig. 5. Design space exploration between resources and latency, valid region is given by resources constraints

7   Evaluation

A Zedboard development kit with Xilinx XC7Z020 SoC and 512 MB DDR3 is used for the evaluation of the proposed framework. The clock frequency of programmable logic and processing system is 100 MHz and 666.7 MHz respectively.

Targeting the utilisation of the whole device, the Design Space Exploration stage identifies a number of design points that meet the constraints imposed by the available resources and predicts a latency figure for each point. The traversed space is depicted in Fig. 5. The best performing design achieved a latency of 532 ms per inference (measured on the board) requiring 185 BRAMs, 160 DSPs, 25.9k LUTs and 46.7k FFs. The measured power consumption is 3.36 W.

7.1   Performance Model Evaluation

The accuracy of the performance and resource model was investigated by producing design points under various resource constraints. The deviation on the predicted resource utilisation and achieved latency was derived by deploying the designs on the actual hardware platform. Figure 6 shows the accuracy of the derived performance models as well as the impact of including the software latency model.

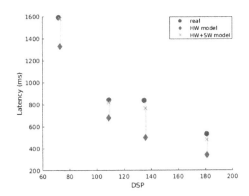

Fig. 6. Latency model evaluation across various resource targets. "real" refers to the measured performance on the board.

7.2   Comparison with CPU and GPU

Redmon et al. [14] deployed floating point YOLOv3-tiny on a Pascal Titan X achieving a 220 fps, leading to a power efficiency of 2.03 GOPS/W [11]. The proposed solution is 1.53 times more power efficient. Also, an ARM (ARM-Cortex A9 at 667 MHz) based-only implementation of the system was developed and compared against the proposed solution. The results showed that the proposed system is 290 times faster.

7.3   Comparison with Existing FPGA Implementations

Even though FPGA implementations of YOLOv3 have not been reported in the literature, the system is positioned with work that targets the previous version of YOLO, which is a less computationally demanding model (Table 2).

Table 2. Target networks comparison of the proposed design with previous works

	[18]	[12]	[9]	[10]	This work
Target network	FPGA YOLO	Tincy YOLO	Lightweight YOLOv2	YOLOv2 tiny	YOLOv3 tiny
Data type	–	1-8b	1-32b	1-6b	16b
Test platform	Zynq7035	XCZU3EG	ZCU102	Virtex-7 VC707	Zedboard
BRAM18k	787	–	1706	1026	185
DSP	409	–	377	168	160
LUT	47k	–	135k	86k	25.9k
FF	40k	–	370k	60k	46.7k
GOPS	–	71.04	610.93	464.7	10.45
Latency (ms)	52	63	25	9.15	532
Power (W)	7.518	6	4.5	18.29	3.36
DSE					✓

8   Conclusion

In this paper, the first latency-driven, scalable, framework for mapping YOLOv3-tiny to an FPGA device is presented. The key feature of the framework is the lifting of any assumptions on on-chip memory capacity for storing the model parameters and intermediate results, making possible the deployment of the YOLOv3-tiny object detector with limited resources. Targeting a Zedboard, the proposed system achieves a frame rate of 1.88 fps and the throughput of 10.45 GOPS. Tested on COCO val5k, a reduction in mAP of 2.5 pp (30.9% vs 33.4%) is achieved under 16bit fixed point implementation without any retraining step. The presented work opens the way for low-latency object detection on low-end FPGA devices. The source code of the framework is available in github[1].

References

1. Everingham, M., Van Gool, L., Williams, C.K.I., Winn, J., Zisserman, A.: The PASCAL Visual Object Classes Challenge 2007 (VOC2007) Results. http://www.pascal-network.org/challenges/VOC/voc2007/workshop/index.html

---

[1] https://github.com/Yu-Zhewen/Tiny_YOLO_v3_ZYNQ

2. Everingham, M., Van Gool, L., Williams, C.K.I., Winn, J., Zisserman, A.: The PASCAL Visual Object Classes Challenge 2012 (VOC2012) Results. http://www.pascal-network.org/challenges/VOC/voc2012/workshop/index.html

3. Girshick, R.: Fast R-CNN. In: The IEEE International Conference on Computer Vision (ICCV), pp. 1440–1448, December 2015

4. Girshick, R., Donahue, J., Darrell, T., Malik, J.: Rich feature hierarchies for accurate object detection and semantic segmentation. In: IEEE Computer Society Conference on Computer Vision and Pattern Recognition, pp. 580–587, June 2014

5. Lin, T., et al.: Microsoft COCO: common objects in context. CoRR abs/1405.0312 (2014). http://arxiv.org/abs/1405.0312

6. Liu, B., Xu, X.: FCLNN: a flexible framework for fast CNN prototyping on FPGA with OpenCL and Caffe. In: 2018 International Conference on Field-Programmable Technology (FPT), pp. 238–241, December 2018

7. Liu, W., et al.: SSD: single shot multibox detector. In: Leibe, B., Matas, J., Sebe, N., Welling, M. (eds.) ECCV 2016. LNCS, vol. 9905, pp. 21–37. Springer, Cham (2016). https://doi.org/10.1007/978-3-319-46448-0_2

8. LogicTronix: Yolov3 tiny tutorial: Darknet to caffe to xilinx dnndk (2019). https://logictronix.com/wp-content/uploads/2019/08/Yolov3-Tiny-Tutorial-Darknet-to-Caffe-Conversion-and-Implementation-on-Xilinx-DNNDK_August12_2019.pdf

9. Nakahara, H., Yonekawa, H., Fujii, T., Sato, S.: A lightweight YOLOv2: a binarized CNN with a parallel support vector regression for an FPGA. In: 2018 ACM/SIGDA International Symposium, pp. 31–40, February 2018

10. Nguyen, D.T., Nguyen, T.N., Kim, H.: A high-throughput and power-efficient FPGA implementation of YOLO CNN for object detection. IEEE Trans. Very Large Scale Integr. (VLSI) Syst. 27(8), 1861–1873 (2019)

11. Nvidia: Geforce gtx titan x user guide (2014). https://www.nvidia.com/content/geforce-gtx/GTX_TITAN_X_User_Guide.pdf

12. Preußer, T.B., Gambardella, G., Fraser, N., Blott, M.: Inference of quantized neural networks on heterogeneous all-programmable devices. In: 2018 Design, Automation Test in Europe Conference Exhibition (DATE), pp. 833–838, March 2018

13. Redmon, J., Divvala, S., Girshick, R., Farhadi, A.: You only look once: unified, real-time object detection. In: 2016 IEEE Conference on Computer Vision and Pattern Recognition (CVPR), pp. 779–788, June 2016

14. Redmon, J., Farhadi, A.: YOLOv3: an incremental improvement, April 2018. https://pjreddie.com/media/files/papers/YOLOv3.pdf

15. Ren, S., He, K., Girshick, R., Sun, J.: Faster R-CNN: towards real-time object detection with region proposal networks. IEEE Trans. Pattern Anal. Mach. Intell. 39, 1137–1149 (2015)

16. Venieris, S.I., Kouris, A., Bouganis, C.S.: Toolflows for mapping convolutional neural networks on FPGAs: a survey and future directions. ACM Comput. Surv. 51(3), 56:1–56:39 (2018). https://doi.org/10.1145/3186332. http://doi.acm.org/10.1145/3186332

17. Wai, Y.J., bin Mohd Yussof, Z., bin Salim, S.I., Chuan, L.K.: Fixed point implementation of Tiny-Yolo-v2 using OpenCL on FPGA. Int. J. Adv. Comput. Sci. Appl. 9(10), 506–512 (2018)

18. Wei, G., Hou, Y., Cui, Q., Deng, G., Tao, X., Yao, Y.: YOLO acceleration using FPGA architecture. In: 2018 IEEE/CIC International Conference on Communications in China (ICCC), pp. 734–735, August 2018

19. Zhao, Z.Q., Zheng, P., Xu, S.T., Wu, X.: Object detection with deep learning: a review. IEEE Trans. Neural Netw. Learn. Syst. 30, 3212–3232 (2019)

Hardware/Algorithm Co-optimization for Fully-Parallelized Compact Decision Tree Ensembles on FPGAs

Taiga Ikeda[1]($\boxtimes$), Kento Sakurada[1], Atsuyoshi Nakamura[1], Masato Motomura[2], and Shinya Takamaeda-Yamazaki[3]

[1] Hokkaido University, Sapporo, Japan
{ikeda.taiga.zm,k_sakurada,atsu}@ist.hokudai.ac.jp
[2] Tokyo Institute of Technology, Yokohama, Japan
motomura@artic.iir.titech.ac.jp
[3] The University of Tokyo, Bunkyo, Japan
shinya@is.s.u-tokyo.ac.jp

Abstract. Decision tree ensembles, such as random forests, are well-known classification and regression methods with high accuracy and robustness, especially for categorical data that combines multiple weak learners called decision trees. We propose an architecture/algorithm co-design method for implementing fully parallelized fast decision tree ensembles on FPGAs. The method first produces compact and almost equivalent representations of original input decision trees by threshold compaction. For each input feature, comparisons with similar thresholds are merged into fewer variations, so the number of comparisons is reduced. The decision tree with merged thresholds is perfectly extracted as hard-wired logic for the highest throughput. In this study, we developed a prototype hardware synthesis compiler that generates a Verilog hardware description language (HDL) description from a compressed representation. The experiment successfully demonstrates that the proposed method reduces the sizes of generated hardware without accuracy degradation.

Keywords: Random forest · FPGA · Compression

1 Introduction

Various machine learning methods based on decision trees (DTs) have been proposed, and they achieve high interpretability and discrimination ability. A DT ensemble, such as random forest (RF), is a well-known classification and regression method with high accuracy and robustness that combines many weak learners of DTs. A computation flow of RF repeatedly compares input data with the threshold predetermined by learning and deciding on an inference result. Thus, RF requires many comparisons between input data and thresholds. In point of hardware implementation, such comparisons require comparator circuits. Therefore, reducing the number of comparators can improve computing

© Springer Nature Switzerland AG 2020
F. Rincón et al. (Eds.): ARC 2020, LNCS 12083, pp. 345–357, 2020.
https://doi.org/10.1007/978-3-030-44534-8_26

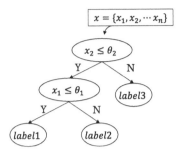

Fig. 1. Decision tree algorithm

performance and hardware resource efficiency. In this study, we propose an architecture/algorithm co-design method for implementing DT ensembles on FPGAs. To achieve high throughput on FPGAs, we focus on the fully parallelized architecture that extracts all DTs in RF. However, such a fully parallelized approach usually requires intense hardware resources, because every DT is realized as an actual circuit. This restricts the number and the size of implementable DTs. To overcome this problem, we employ the threshold compaction method that merges similar threshold values of branching nodes in DTs into fewer variations. Therefore, the number of comparison operations is reduced, and the hardware resources of comparator circuits can be reduced. We developed a prototype hardware synthesis compiler that generates a fully parallelized accelerator design in Verilog hardware description language (HDL) from pre-learned DT ensembles. A generated accelerator executes the inference process of trees in a parallel manner. This study mainly focuses on the evaluation of the compaction method in relation to the hardware resources. Based on the prototype compiler, we evaluate the impact of the threshold compaction method by using standard CAD tools for FPGAs. We then discuss an improved approach to reduce the hardware resources based on the evaluation results.

2   Random Forest

2.1   Decision Tree and Tree Ensemble

In recent years, deep learning has attracted attention in various applications. It is an algorithm that uses large amounts of data for learning and creates a complex model with enormous parameters. Such high-performance machine learning utilizes the term strong learner. On the other hand, RF is one of the ensemble learning algorithms [3]. Ensemble learning is an algorithm that creates many weak learners and unifies their prediction results. The learning of weak learners can be computed at less cost than strong learners, so learning time and learning data is less. Since individual week learners have low performance, a predictor with high accuracy can be obtained by combining weak learners.

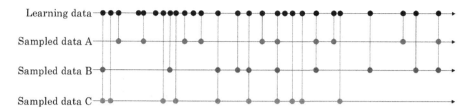

Fig. 2. Bagging

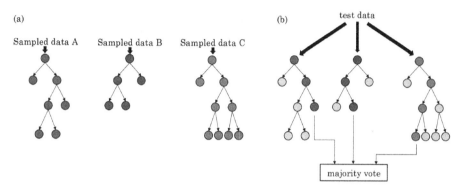

Fig. 3. (a) Learning process of RF, (b) Inference process of RF

RF uses a DT as a weak learner and performs classification and regression by voting or averaging the outputs. Popular learning algorithms of DT are CART and C5.0. It divides the data by the mechanism shown in Fig. 1. A DT has branching nodes where input data is divided and leaf nodes where a specific label is indicated. In inference calculation, data is sorted by branching conditions until reaching the leaf node. The learning process of a DT generally creates a condition at each branching node by sorting each feature value in input data and finding the appropriate feature and threshold to divide the input data with a low impurity. The term impurity denotes a criterion of label variation in the data and generally is employed Gini impurity or entropy. These divisions are repeated and a tree structure is produced. If the depth of the tree is increased, the learning data will overfit, so it is necessary to adjust the tree's size. The decision forest creates a combination of small DTs to avoid overfitting. An individual DT predicts with low accuracy, but a merged forest has high prediction accuracy.

In addition, the random sampling of the learning data of each DT is performed by a method called bagging in RF [2]. Bagging is a learning method that employs bootstrap sampling, and this sampling allows for obtaining different datasets from the same input data as shown Fig. 2. This method provides each DT with versatility and further improves accuracy. Figure 3 shows the learning and inference process of RF when bagging is performed tree times. In the leaning process, bagging is employed for the number of trees and creates DTs of various sizes. In inference, the output is determined by a majority vote of each tree

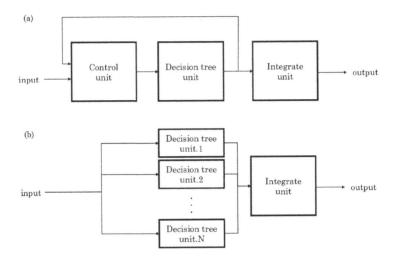

Fig. 4. (a) Tree serial architecture, (b) Tree parallel architecture

created by various samples. However, as the number of trees increases, the calculation time increases. Therefore, this study provides a hardware implementation method for accelerating the inference calculation.

2.2 Hardware Implementation of Random Forest

Various methods of implementing a RF have already been proposed. The learning process is accelerated by the implementation methods in [4,5]. On the other hand, the inference process is accelerated in [12,13], and we paid attention to this study. There are two main implementation approaches. First, Fig. 4(a) shows an architecture that uses one DT unit repeatedly and reuses by the number of trees and aggregate. This method handles various sizes of decision forests with small resources. However, Fig. 4(b) shows an architecture that arranges multiple trees and computes each tree in parallel. The computation effort is reduced due to a decrease in the number of reused DT units, although it consumes more resources.

Similarly, in the DT unit, there is a method of reusing one node unit and unrolling the entire DT on a circuit. In [8], several DTs are implemented by a combinational circuit composed of comparators and multiplexers, and pipeline processing is performed to increase operational speed. However, this method requires intense memory resources because a register is inserted between trees.

In this study, we adopt a method of unrolling the entire decision forest and unrolling each node of the DT by a combinational circuit. We propose the architecture that full nodes are unrolled in Fig. 5. One branch node is composed of a comparator and a multiplexer. A comparator outputs 0 or 1 by comparing

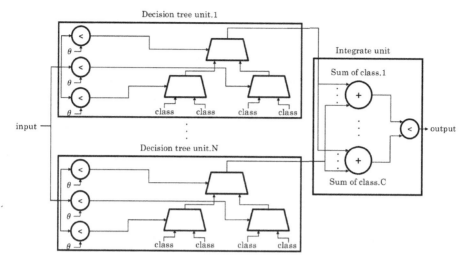

Fig. 5. Fully parallelized decision forest architecture

the input data of a specific dimension with threshold decided by learning. A multiplexer selects one of two inputs by the output of the comparator. Thus, it performs DT inference calculation and obtains a majority vote in the integrated unit.

In this method, since labels are maintained with one-hot signals in the flip-flops, values must be stored in the memory and each calculation does not require memory access. The ultra-high-speed RF hardware is realized as registers with intermediate value are unnecessary. Conversely, the circuit becomes larger when the size of the RF is larger. Therefore, it is not a realistic assumption to consider actual circuit resources. The advantages of this method are related to sharing the outputs of several comparators. The condition for sharing is the comparison with the same dimension and threshold. Further, if two nodes connect to the same comparator and branch to the same labels, a multiplexer can be shared. This way, the circuit size can be reduced by creating compressed trees with the same function. Therefore, by compressing the DT using the method described in the next section, we aim to store a large RF that otherwise would not suffice in the supply circuit resource.

2.3   Algorithm for Reducing Branching Conditions

This section introduces the DT compression algorithm used in this study. Generally, DT compression is obtained by adjusting the learning parameters or reforming the tree structure. The learning parameters are depth, maximum leaf number, minimum number of samples in a node, and so on. To reform the tree structure, pruning is popular and various methods are proposed [10, 14]. However, these methods can reduce prediction accuracy. Therefore, caution is considered to use these compression methods (Fig. 6).

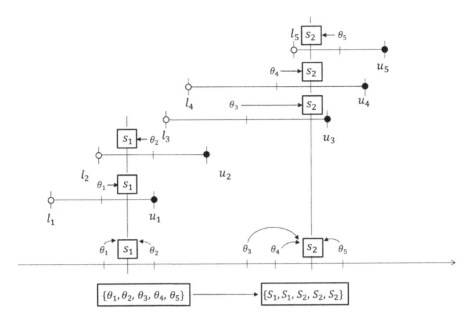

Fig. 6. Algorithm for reducing branching conditions

The algorithm shown in [11] obtains the compressed DTs without loss of accuracy. This algorithm reduces the number of distinct thresholds that are the branching conditions of the nodes. The calculation method is:

1. At each branching node with condition $x_i >= \theta_i$, find the ranges $[l_i, u_i)$ of θ_i where the branch path of any learning data does not change.
2. Sort the lower limit values of the ranges in the ascending order
3. Group the thresholds in the order based on the condition that the minimum value of the upper limits in the current group is smaller than the lower limit in the next range
4. Replace the original thresholds for the average value S_j between the maximum value of the lower limits and the minimum value of the upper limits

This method unifies several thresholds into one value and reduces the number of distinct thresholds. In [11], a mathematical proof is provided to ensure the method minimizes the number of distinct thresholds. The threshold range can be obtained from the learning data sampled by bagging during RF learning. In the normal learning process, thresholds are chosen based on the center of the boundary feature values of the divided datasets minimizing impurity or entropy. However, when the DT is used only for classifying the learning data, no threshold between the boundary feature values of the divided datasets changes the output of the DT. Therefore, if the thresholds change another value in the range, prediction accuracy is not lost.

Table 1. Datasets

Dataset	#instances	#features	#classes
Iris [7]	150	4	3
Breast [7] cancer	569	30	2
Blood [15]	748	4	2
Robot [7]	5456	24	4
Parkinson [9]	195	22	2
Wine quality white [6]	4898	11	11
Epileptic [1]	11500	28	2

Table 2. Accuracy and #thresholds when branching conditions are reduced

Dataset	Prediction accuracy [%]		#distinct thresholds	
	Original	Reduced branching conditions	Original	Reduced branching conditions
Iris [7]	96.67	97.00	104.5	43.4
Breast cancer [7]	97.02	97.02	1442.3	603.7
Blood [15]	77.07	77.00	153.6	79.8
Robot [7]	99.40	99.40	9510.0	3010.0
Parkinson [9]	93.08	92.56	1042.5	405.5
Wine quality white [6]	68.22	68.26	7188.0	1356.0
Epileptic [1]	69.62	69.46	75542.8	23505.4

Subsequently, we examine the effect of the algorithm on prediction accuracy and the number of distinct thresholds. For this, we use seven datasets shown in Table 1 from the standard University of California Irvine (UCI) Machine Learning Repository database [7] and others [1,6,9,15]. Table 2 indicates the changes in the number of branching conditions and the prediction accuracy when this algorithm is employed. We use the RF classifier from the Scikit-learn library and set the number of trees to 100. The value in the table is the average of the values obtained after 10 simulations.

Initially, we did not tune the parameters of the RF classifier with the Scikit-learn library, so the original accuracy is not high. Although, parameter tuning is important to avoid overfitting, in the designed model it was not performed as it was not necessary to achieve the objectives of this study. In this algorithm, since the threshold value is adjusted without changing the branch path of the learning data, the accuracy is not lowered. However, the threshold variation is reduced to 20%–50%. The reduction rate depends on the complexity of the dataset and the number of features. Therefore, we investigate the benefits of this method in hardware implementation from the next section.

3   Exploration of Hardware-Aware Optimizations

In this section, we simulate the quantization of input data and thresholds for hardware implementation. Then we employ the reducing branch conditions algorithm from the previous section.

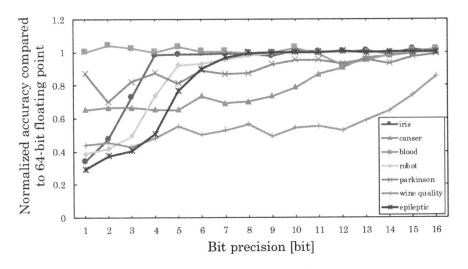

Fig. 7. Accuracies for varied quantization bits

3.1   Quantize Bit Precision

In software simulation, the RF calculation is performed with a 64-bit floating-point. When implementing hardware, the circuit size is large, so quantization is necessary. Appropriate quantization must be performed for each data set since the accuracy decreases due to quantization.

Figure 7 indicates the accuracy when the bit-precision is changed for several tasks. By changing the precision of an integer, the vertical axis represents the ratio when the accuracy at the 64-bit floating-point is 100%. This shows that the accuracy increases as the bit precision is increased although there is low fluctuation. In the case of the iris, the precision is 97.8% with 4-bit, and the accuracy of almost 64-bit values can be reproduced. This is because the iris is a simple classification task. Nevertheless, the number of bits required increases for datasets that are difficult to classify.

In Fig. 7, the accuracy for each bit number is shown in seven datasets. Although the accuracy transition varies in each the data set, the accuracy decreases as the bit number are reduced. Therefore, quantization is effective in reducing the circuit size although the accuracy is decreased.

3.2   Reducing Branch Conditions

We examine the decrease in accuracy when the number of thresholds is reduced using the algorithm of Sect. 2.3. Figure 8 shows the transition from the accuracy shown in Fig. 7 when the algorithm is employed. It indicates almost no decrease in accuracy, and there are examples where the accuracy has increased. However, the accuracy decreased as the number of bits increased, and a significant decrease in accuracy was observed in some datasets. This considered that quantization causes a misclassification by shifting a threshold appropriately determined by the threshold reduction algorithm.

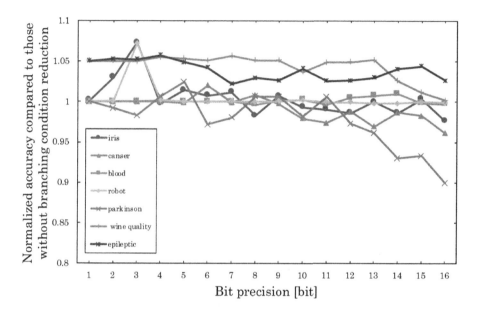

Fig. 8. Accuracies for varied quantization bits with branching condition reductions

Table 3. Estimate of logic utilization (#Adaptive Logic Modules)

[Bit]	1	2	3	4	5	6	7	8	9	10	11	12	13	14	15	16
Iris	175	248	345	437	475	453	489	562	550	579	479	505	599	509	669	631
Cancer	603	773	610	786	781	775	775	870	967	900	1114	1085	1302	1320	1588	1460
Blood	97	138	141	206	363	373	424	484	637	800	1167	1661	1969	2557	2330	2238
Robot	2132	2728	3709	4379	4712	5857	6484	7794	8434	9985	10465	12127	12966	15364	14961	15174
Parkin	454	506	488	570	531	566	660	684	687	734	910	844	900	1061	1107	1205

Further, the quantization method can be considered as another cause for accuracy decrease. The threshold value distribution is not considered because of quantization at equal intervals between the maximum and the minimum values of the thresholds. Therefore, it seems that the accuracy is improved by performing quantization according to the threshold distribution of each dimension.

4 Experiments

We implement a random forest classifier trained with Scikit-learn library in hardware using a combinational circuit and evaluate its performance. We create a prototype compiler that converts the results from Scikit-learn into a hardware description language and evaluated it with Quartus Prime ver.15.1. This compiler automatically generates the Verilog HDL-style code based on the method proposed in Sect. 2.2.

Table 4. #Comparators after reduced branching conditions

[Bit]	1	2	3	4	5	6	7	8	9	10	11	12	13	14	15	16
(a)#comparators before reduced branching conditions (b)#comparators after reduced branching conditions (b) divided by (a) [%]																
Iris	7	11	15	22	42	60	79	100	94	90	82	75	91	87	104	83
	7	11	13	21	31	40	41	50	47	43	42	41	44	46	48	42
	100	100	86.67	95.45	73.81	66.67	51.90	50	50	47.78	51.22	54.67	48.35	52.87	46.15	50.60
Cancer	31	34	38	49	60	78	119	166	222	219	337	404	498	583	680	625
	31	34	38	49	59	70	88	109	150	154	202	230	267	293	346	343
	100	100	100	100	98.33	89.74	73.95	65.66	67.57	70.32	59.94	56.93	53.61	50.26	50.88	54.88
Blood	4	6	10	18	28	39	55	58	63	71	70	77	10	5136	155	148
	3	6	10	16	27	29	34	33	35	40	42	52	68	83	80	77
	75	100	100	88.89	96.43	74.36	61.82	56.90	55.56	56.34	60	67.53	64.76	61.03	51.61	52.03
Robot	30	76	164	330	604	1069	1775	2897	417	35671	6894	8364	8615	9780	8989	8706
	30	76	157	275	436	717	1122	1724	2180	2584	280	63042	2971	3180	2995	2890
	100	100	95.73	83.33	72.19	67.07	63.21	59.51	52.24	45.57	40.70	36.37	34.49	32.52	33.32	33.20
Parkinson	22	26	29	36	46	76	91	130	156	183	223	243	27	9349	420	450
	22	26	28	34	43	53	67	78	76	83	100	107	131	164	194	202
	100	100	96.55	94.44	93.48	69.74	73.63	60	48.72	45.36	44.84	44.03	46.95	46.99	46.19	44.89

First, Table 3 shows the transition of the circuit size when quantizing bit precision as in the previous section. In this study, we estimate the circuit size based on the number of Adaptive Logic Modules (ALMs) by analysis and synthesis. ALM is a logic unit on some FPGAs made by Intel Corporation and mainly composed an adaptive lookup table and some registers. This table shows that the lower the number of bits, the smaller is the circuit size. For example, according to Fig. 2, the iris classifier has comparable accuracy of 16-bit precision with 4-bit precision. Conversely, the circuit with 4-bit is 69%, the size of one with 16-bit precision. Thus, quantization has the effect of reducing the circuit size, although we must adjust the bit precision for the required accuracy.

We investigated the effect of the algorithm of Sect. 2.3 in each quantized bit. Table 4 shows the change in the number of comparators after the branching conditions are reduced. From the results, the number of comparators was reduced in all conditions. This indicates that the sharing ratio of the output of the comparator increased. This is because comparison operations at the same value increase by reducing the branching conditions. However, the reduction rate is lower than the software simulation. The result indicates that quantization reduces some distinct thresholds. In comparison with the comparator reduction by quantization, the reduction by the proposed algorithm is lower, although the prediction accuracy reduction is unnoticeable.

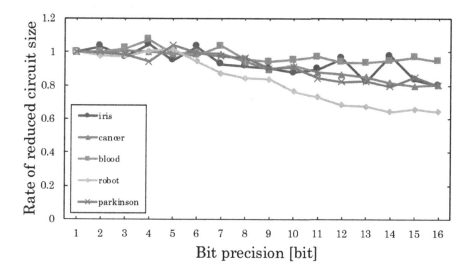

Fig. 9. Hardware performance when reduced branching conditions

Figure 9 shows the changes in the overall circuit size. It can be confirmed that the circuit size is reduced by reducing the number of comparators. However, the reduction rate is low with low bit precision because the quantization reduces the number of distinct thresholds without using the algorithm. Namely, in the proposed method, the circuit size can be reduced especially with high bit precision.

From these experiments, we understand what conditions CAD tools optimize the circuit. The conditions are:

1. If there are comparison operations with the same threshold and dimension, unifying comparators and output of a comparator are shared.
2. The multiplexers prepared just the required number of bits.
3. If both children nodes of the branching nodes are leaf nodes, using the output of comparators as indicating the labels after branching and multiplexers are deleted.

To reduce the circuit size further, optimization by considering these conditions is necessary. The first condition was the focus of this study and succeeded in reducing the number of comparators. Subsequently, the multiplexer of a certain branching node employs enough bit precision to deal with the number of distinct labels of leaf nodes in the deeper layer than the branching node since labels are one-hot signals. Therefore, if two distinct labels in a deeper layer than a branching node, the branching node is implemented as a 2-bit multiplexer. Ultimately, when there is only one type of label, the multiplexer is deleted because branching is not necessary. Finally, if the branching result of a certain node is both leaf nodes, it is clear which labels will be selected at the node. Then, the multiplexer is reduced by connecting the output of the comparator, or its inverted signal, to appropriate the bit of multiplexer in the upper layer.

We must explore other optimization to meet these conditions. In addition to sharing comparators output by the proposed method, many circuits are shared by creating the sub-trees that have the same branching nodes and leaf nodes. If the same sub-trees exist in RF, CAD tools recognize the equivalent circuits. Therefore, circuit size can be further reduced by sharing sub-tree circuits including multiplexers and comparators. However, it is difficult to decide which sub-trees are most efficient to shared. Then, we will compress an RF by optimization with a restriction like a hardware size.

Subsequently, we proposed the fully-parallelized architecture composed of comparators and multiplexers in this study, and other architectures may reduce the circuit size further. In fully-parallelized architecture, there are two main methods of implementation. One of the methods is circuits based on multiplexers—label exploration of direction to be shallow depth from leaves. The other is label exploration of direction to be deep from roots and propagate a flag to one leaf. Thus, we will experiment with various architectures and explore the circuits optimized for hardware.

5   Conclusion

The purpose of this study is to reduce the inference calculation time of random forest (RF). We used an algorithm to reduce the branching conditions to implement the hardware of RF. The algorithm reduces the threshold variation without reducing accuracy. Accordingly, the results of analysis and synthesis indicate that the number of comparators was reduced to 30%–50%. We tested various quantization bit precisions, and results indicate that the circuit size was reduced with high bit precision. For example, a circuit size of the implementation with 16-bit precision was reduced to 80%–90%. Therefore, we demonstrated that by using the proposed algorithm, a small circuit can be achieved without reducing accuracy.

Furthermore, to reduce the circuit size further, other perspectives are necessary. From the perspective of hardware implementation methods and software simulation algorithms, we must try to increase equivalent circuits that would produce s small circuit size of RF with no accuracy degradation.

References

1. Andrzejak, R.G., Lehnertz, K., Mormann, F., Rieke, C., David, P., Elger, C.E.: Indications of nonlinear deterministic and finite-dimensional structures in time series of brain electrical activity: dependence on recording region and brain state. Phys. Rev. E **64**, 061907 (2001). https://link.aps.org/doi/10.1103/PhysRevE.64.061907
2. Breiman, L.: Bagging predictors. Mach. Learn. **24**(2), 123–140 (1996). https://doi.org/10.1007/BF00058655
3. Breiman, L.: Random forests. Mach. Learn. **45**(1), 5–32 (2001). https://doi.org/10.1023/A:1010933404324
4. Cheng, C., Bouganis, C.: Accelerating random forest training process using FPGA. In: 2013 23rd International Conference on Field Programmable Logic and Applications, pp. 1–7, September 2013
5. Cheng, C., Bouganis, C.: Memory optimisation for hardware induction of axis-parallel decision tree. In: 2014 International Conference on ReConFigurable Computing and FPGAs (ReConFig 2014), pp. 1–5, December 2014
6. Cortez, P., Cerdeira, A., Almeida, F., Matos, T., Reis, J.: Modeling wine preferences by data mining from physicochemical properties. Decis. Support Syst. **47**(4), 547–553 (2009). https://doi.org/10.1016/j.dss.2009.05.016
7. Dua, D., Graff, C.: UCI machine learning repository (2017). http://archive.ics.uci.edu/ml
8. Jinguji, A., Sato, S., Nakahara, H.: An FPGA realization of a random forest with k-means clustering using a high-level synthesis design. IEICE Trans. Inf. Syst. **E101.D**(2), 354–362 (2018)
9. Little, M.A., McSharry, P.E., Roberts, S.J., Costello, D.A., Moroz, I.M.: Exploiting nonlinear recurrence and fractal scaling properties for voice disorder detection. BioMed. Eng. OnLine **6**(1) (2007). https://doi.org/10.1186/1475-925X-6-23. Article no. 23
10. Mansour, Y.: Pessimistic decision tree pruning based on tree size. In: ICML 1997 (1997)
11. Nakamura, A., Sakurada, K.: An algorithm for reducing the number of distinct branching conditions in a decision forest. In: European Conference on Machine Learning and Principles and Practice of Knowledge Discovery in Databases (ECMLPKDD) (2019)
12. Struharik, R.: Decision tree ensemble hardware accelerators for embedded applications. In: 2015 IEEE 13th International Symposium on Intelligent Systems and Informatics (SISY), pp. 101–106, September 2015
13. Struharik, R.: Implementing decision trees in hardware, September 2011
14. Kulkarni, V.Y., Sinha, P.K.: Pruning of random forest classifiers: a survey and future directions. In: 2012 International Conference on Data Science and Engineering (ICDSE) (2012)
15. Yeh, I.C., Yang, K.J., Ting, T.M.: Knowledge discovery on RFM model using Bernoulli sequence. Expert Syst. Appl. **36**(3), 5866–5871 (2009). https://doi.org/10.1016/j.eswa.2008.07.018

Applications

StocNoC: Accelerating Stochastic Models Through Reconfigurable Network on Chip Architectures

Arshyn Zhanbolatov, Kizheppatt Vipin$^{(\boxtimes)}$ (ID), Aresh Dadlani (ID),
and Dmitriy Fedorov

Department of Electrical and Computer Engineering, Nazarbayev University,
Nur-Sultan 010000, Kazakhstan
{arshyn.zhanbolatov,vipin.kizheppatt}@nu.edu.kz

Abstract. Spreading dynamics of many real-world processes lean heavily on the topological characteristics of the underlying contact network. With the rapid temporal and spatial evolution of complex interconnected networks, microscopic modeling and stochastic simulation of individual-based interactions have become challenging in both, time and state space. Driven by the surge to reduce the time complexity associated with system behavior analysis over different network structures, we propose a network-on-chip (NoC) based FPGA solution called StocNoC. The proof of concept is supported by the design, implementation and evaluation of the classical heterogeneous susceptible-infected-susceptible (SIS) epidemic model on a scalable NoC. The steady-state results from the proposed implementation for the fractions of susceptible and infected nodes are shown to be comparable to those acquired from software simulations, but in a significantly shorter time period. Analogous to network information diffusion, implementation of the SIS model and its variants will be beneficial to foresee possible epidemic outbreaks earlier in time and expedite control decisions.

1 Introduction

Epidemic modeling is an effective mathematical tool widely adopted in many domains to quantify the spreading dynamics of processes intertwined with large-scale networks [21]. It serves as a viable framework for analyzing information diffusion in social networks [8], cascading failure in power grids [14], secure routing in communication networks [7], and digital virus spreading in wireless mobile networks [23]. Dynamical models at the network scale can be broadly classified into two types: *deterministic* and *stochastic*. In deterministic models, the network is divided into smaller groups, each representing a specific stage of the epidemic. Such models, often formulated as differential equations (in continuous time) or difference equations (in discrete time), abstract what happens on the average at the network level. In contrast, a stochastic model is formulated as a stochastic process which in turn, is a set of random variables, $X(t; \varpi) \equiv X(t)$,

© Springer Nature Switzerland AG 2020
F. Rincón et al. (Eds.): ARC 2020, LNCS 12083, pp. 361–375, 2020.
https://doi.org/10.1007/978-3-030-44534-8_27

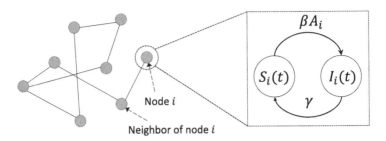

Fig. 1. Schematic of the SIS model where A_i denotes the direct neighbors of node i in the network adjacency matrix A.

defined as $\{X(t;\varpi)|t \in T$ and $\varpi \in \Omega\}$ where T and Ω represent time and a sample space, respectively. The solution of a stochastic model is a probability distribution for each of the random variables. Such models allow follow-up of each node in the network randomly [4,5].

Evolution of natural and man-made networks in both scale and complexity has triggered interdisciplinary research on characterizing the dynamics of stochastic processes spreading over them. Similar to the spreading of pathogens in biological systems, the virulence of spreading processes depends not only on the infection rate of each node, but also on the connectivity of the underlying network structure [20]. Increase in computational power over recent years has revealed the existence of heterogeneous and multi-faceted relations in the description of various diffusion processes [16]. The time taken to project the spreading pattern is important in devising effective countermeasures to prevent any potential outbreaks.

We propose a network-on-chip (NoC) model supported on a reconfigurable platform called StocNoC to accelerate the epidemic projection of the spreading model. Due to its inherent parallelism, hardware implementation may significantly outperform pure software implementation especially due to the concurrent friendly nature of the model. The model is easily scalable to support larger network sizes, only limited by the resource availability of the target FPGA devices. Recent introduction of FPGA-accelerators in the cloud environment is especially encouraging in this regard, where users can choose the target device and scale it based on their computing requirements [17]. Since the cloud-model charges users based on the target platform type and their running time, accelerated computation can significantly reduce the cost of computation. With minor modifications, the proposed platform can be used for hardware acceleration of other epidemic spreading models as well as spreading dynamics in contact networks in general.

The remainder of this paper is organized as follows. Section 2 discusses the background of epidemic models and related works. Section 3 presents the detailed architecture of the proposed hardware platform. Section 4 discusses the hardware implementation results and the comparison with corresponding software implementation and Sect. 5 finally concludes the paper and gives future research directions.

2 Background and Related Works

Epidemic models are used to predict the progression of infectious diseases in a given population and the likely outcome of an epidemic. The classical susceptible-infected-susceptible (SIS) model depicted in Fig. 1 serves as the basis for many extended models, wherein $S_i(t)$ and $I_i(t)$ denote the probability of node i being in the susceptible (S) or the infected (I) state, respectively, in a network of size N [21]. Nodes that recover from the infection immediately transition to being susceptible again. The discrete-time node-level SIS epidemic model has the following form:

$$S_i(t) = \beta S_i(t-1) \sum_{j=1}^{N} a_{i,j} p_j(t) - \gamma p_i(t), \tag{1}$$

satisfying the condition $S_i(t) + I_i(t) = 1$ for all t values. Here, β denotes the rate at which node i gets infected, γ is the recovery rate, p_i is the probability of i being infected at time t, and a_{ij} is any element in the adjacency matrix A corresponding to the network defined as:

$$A = \{a_{ij}\} = \begin{cases} 1, & \text{if nodes } i \text{ and } j \text{ are connected neighbors} \\ 0, & \text{otherwise.} \end{cases} \tag{2}$$

Advancements in network science led to the revival of several unique recurring patterns inherent in networks which essentially drive the spreading pattern of processes. The Erdös-Rényi (ER) model was the first to be used for generating typical random networks [10]. An ER network of N nodes, wherein a link is included independent of other links with probability p, has a mean link count of $\binom{N}{2}p$, mean degree of $(N-1)p$, and binomial degree distribution. Such networks manifest low degree heterogeneity (most nodes have the same degree), low clustering coefficient (probability that two neighbors of a node are also neighbors), and short average path length. While ER networks are highly robust against deliberate attacks, they lack the large degree of transitivity witnessed in reality. To overcome this shortcoming, the Watts-Strogatz (WS) model was proposed to generate random graphs with small-world properties by rewiring the links of a lattice with some given probability [2]. This model is built on the interpolation between a standard ER random graph and a network with maximal clustering. The Barabási-Albert (BA) model was then developed to generate random scale-free networks with high degree heterogeneity. Based on the concept of preferential attachment or "the rich gets richer", the network initially begins with at least two nodes where a newly added node is most likely to connect to nodes with higher degrees. This results in the formation of a few highly-connected nodes in the network. The resulting network degree distribution has no characteristic scale as they have power law tail. Unlike ER networks that exhibit an average distance of $\log(n)$, scale-free BA networks are ultra small-world networks with a sub-logarithmic small diameter proportional to $\log(\log(n))$ and thus, are particularly robust against random node failures.

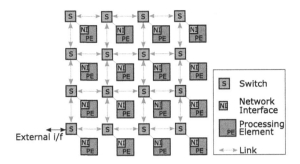

Fig. 2. Proposed NoC-based platform with mesh topology showing switch interconnections and network interfaces.

Except for a few, most of the existing simulation tools support deterministic modeling of simplified processes. EpiModel [12] is an R package to analyze stochastic individual and network-level epidemic models. A stochastic simulator for generalized epidemic modeling known as GEMFsim [18] has been reported and made available in MATLAB, R, Python, and C programming platforms. These simulators however, demand longer running time as the scale and complexity of the network increases.

In this work, we propose to emulate the SIS process on an NoC platform. NoC is an interconnect approach that helps different subsystems in a system to communicate with each other in a scalable manner [9]. In this approach, each processing element (PE) is connected to a switch and multiple switches are interconnected to form a network. They follow packet switched communication paradigm which makes them highly scalable. In the past, NoCs have been successfully used in many applications including image and signal processing [13], neural networks [11], multi-processor systems [3], and virtual machines [15]. To the best of our knowledge, this is the first application of NoCs for accelerating stochastic models.

Due to the inherent similarity in architecture, NoCs appear to be ideal candidates for mapping different network models encountered in spreading models. In the past, FPGAs in general and NoCs in particular have not been explored for modeling stochastic network models. The overall aim of this work is to introduce the FPGA community the possible application of FPGA-based NoCs in accelerating dynamics of spreading models. It is not limited to epidemics but to other spreading networks including social media.

3   Architecture

StocNoC follows mesh topology with each processing element (PE) along with its network interface (NI) representing a *node* in the contact network. Nodes are interconnected with the help of switches and bi-directional physical links as shown in Fig. 2. The NoC configuration and inter-node communication are supported via packet switching. The bottom left switch acts as the communication

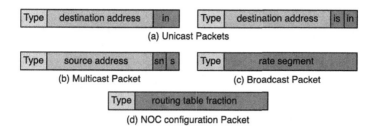

Fig. 3. Different packet formats to support network configuration and data communication.

interface with external world, through which configuration packets are sent as well as the network status is monitored. An external host such as a server computer configures the NoC for the target network and monitors the network status as time progresses. By analyzing the packets received from the network, the host can determine the specific nodes that are infected, nodes that have recovered, and the overall spreading pattern of the process.

3.1 Packet Formats

StocNoC manages configuration as well as inter-node communication using the different packet formats shown in Fig. 3. It supports unicast, multicast and broadcast packet transmissions based on the packet *type*. Unicast packets are used for node configuration (at zero epoch or at $t = 0$) by an external host. The target node address (X and Y coordinates of the node) is stored in the *destination address* field and the configuration data are carried in the *input number (in)* and *initial status (is)* fields. The *input number* configures the number of neighbors (number of nodes connected to this node based on the adjacency matrix) and the *initial status* configures whether the node is infected or susceptible at zero epoch.

Multicast packets are used for inter-node communication, where each node updates all its neighbors with its status after each epoch (each discrete time in simulation). Rather than sending the same packet to each of its neighbors, each node injects a single packet to the NoC and the unique router design duplicates the packets close to the target nodes. This considerably reduces the network routing congestion and improves the overall latency. The packet carries the address of the injecting node in the *source address* field and the status (infected/susceptible) in the *status (s)* field. Due to the packet switched nature of the NoC, it is possible that packets are delivered out-of-order to the destination nodes. To manage this, each multicast packet carries a *sequence number (sn)* field, which specifies the discrete simulation time. Every packet in the network originating at the same discrete simulation time will have the same sequence number.

Since all nodes in the network share the same infection (β) and recovery rates (γ), this information is broadcasted across the network at the beginning

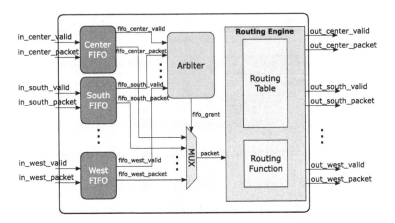

Fig. 4. The NoC switch architecture with store-and-forward functionality and support for unicast and multicast routing.

of the simulation. Again, the router design and the routing algorithm enables injecting a single packet from the external host and the packet being replicated and delivered to each node. The *rate segment* of the packet initializes a portion of the pseudo random binary sequence (PRBS) generator used in the network interface discussed in Sect. 3.3. Since the current implementation uses a 100-bit long PRBS and the rate segment is only 10-bits wide, 10 configuration packets are required to initialize them. NoC configuration packets are special broadcast packets that configure the routing tables (RTs) inside the switches. Each packet configures a portion of an RT and multiple packets are required to configure the entire network.

3.2 Switch

The overall architecture of the StocNoC switch is depicted in Fig. 4. The switch follows store and forward architecture with each interface (from 4 neighboring switches and the node) connected to an input FIFO. Every switch interface follows AXI4-Stream protocol [22]. To limit resource utilization, output FIFOs are omitted in the design. An arbiter chooses one of the input FIFOs for packet transmission based on their requests following a round-robin scheme. This avoids resource starvation and minimizes packet queueing delays. The *fifo_grant* signal from the arbiter drives the output of a multiplexer which selects the appropriate FIFO output for packet transmission.

The selected packet is forwarded to the routing engine (RE). The RE logic first checks for the packet type. Unicast packet (PE configuration packets) routing is managed by a routing function (RF) and multicast packet (PE status packets) routing is managed by a routing table (RT). The RF logic implements the traditional dimension-ordered XY routing by comparing the destination address embedded in the packet with the switch's address [6].

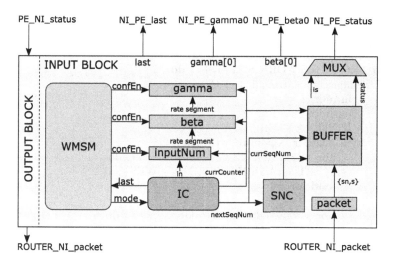

Fig. 5. Network interface architecture.

Multicast routing scheme is deployed for status packets to reduce the network congestion and latency. This method also frees nodes from storing the RTs thus, making their design relatively simple. A node sending its status puts only its source address into the packet and injects to the corresponding switch, unaware of the packet's ultimate targets. Each entry in the RT used for multicast routing is 5 bits wide and the RT depth is same as the overall network size (number of nodes in the network).

The source address embedded in the multicast packets serves as the RT entry number. Each bit in a table entry determines the directions in which a packet originating from the corresponding address will be forwarded. The broadcast could be to one or more of the neighboring switches as well as the to the node interfaced with the switch. By appropriately configuring the RTs, packets from any node can be broadcasted to any given subset of nodes within the network. The routing path taken by each packet is similar to *tree routing*, where the root of a tree is the source node and the destination nodes are located at the tree branches and leaves. If the destination nodes are located along the tree branches, intermediate switches perform forward-and-absorb operation. Traditional tree routing suffers from the possibility of deadlocks [19] in the intermediate nodes, but combining it with XY routing circumvents this possibility.

The content of each RT is determined offline by an application based on the network adjacency matrix. For a network with $NETWORK\_SIZE$ nodes, aspect ratios X and Y, and adjacency matrix $adjacencyMatrix$ $[NETWORK\_SIZE]$ $[NETWORK\_SIZE]$, each table entry i corresponding to each switch j is generated based on Algorithm 1. The entire RT is injected to the network through the bottom-left switch as NoC configuration broadcast packets. This approach is taken to keep packets sizes small, as packets do not carry information regarding router and RT address. From the received broadcast packets, each switch

Algorithm 1. Routing Table Generation

```
1: Clear all RT entries.
2: for j =0; j<NETWORK_SIZE; j=j+1 do
3:     for i =0; i<NETWORK_SIZE; i=i+1 do
4:         if adjacencyMatrix[j][i]==1 then
5:             inAddr=i;
6:             outAddr=j;
7:             RT[i][j][CENTER] = 1;
8:             if outAddr [X]> inAddr [X] then
9:                 for x=outAddr[X]; x>inAddr[X];x=x-1 do
10:                     RT[outAddr[Y]×XSIZE+x][j][WEST]=1
11:                 end for
12:             else
13:                 for x=outAddr[X];x<inAddr[X];x=x+1 do
14:                     RT[outAddr[Y]×XSIZE+x][j][EAST]=1
15:                 end for
16:             end if
17:             if outAddr[Y]>inAddr[Y] then
18:                 for y=outAddr[Y];y>inAddr[Y];y=y-1 do
19:                     RT[y×XSIZE+inAddr[X]][j][SOUTH]=1
20:                 end for
21:             else
22:                 for y=outAddr[Y];y<inAddr[Y];y=y+1 do
23:                     RT[y×XSIZE+inAddr[X]][j][NORTH]=1
24:                 end for
25:             end if
26:         end if
27:     end for
28: end for
```

selects only the portions corresponding to its RT and transmits the entire table to the neighboring switch to its right. Switches along the first column of the NoC transmits these packets to the neighboring switches in the north direction as well. The switch's knowledge about its own address and an internal packet counter enables this configuration strategy. Each packet carries only a fraction of the table (10-bits or 2 entries) and may require thousands of packets for complete configuration.

3.3   Network Interface (NI)

The NI module manages the communication between a switch and the corresponding PE. Moreover, it also implements the logic to control the state of the node after each discrete simulation time. Its detailed architecture is depicted in Fig. 5. The *working mode state machine* (WMSM) manages the operating mode of a node, which may be either in *configuration state* or in *running state*. When the network is in the configuration state, WMSM routes the configuration packets received from the switch interface to appropriate destination registers.

The contents of the unicast packet specifying the number of neighbors of the node is stored in the *inputNum* register.

The discrete time probabilities required to decide the state of a node (whether infected or susceptible) are implemented by the *gamma* and *beta* PRBS generators. Both are linear feedback shift registers (LFSRs) composed of 100 flip-flops with the last stage feeding back to the first stage. In order to implement a specific rate (infection or recovery), the corresponding probability is multiplied by 100 and the LFSR is initialized with a random binary pattern with number of ones equal to the result of multiplication. For example, to achieve a β value of 0.3, the 100 flip-flops in the *beta* LFSR are initialized with a random binary pattern with 30 ones and 70 zeros. The initialization values for the two PRBS generators are received as broadcast packets from the external host. Since the size of PRBS generators is much larger than the packet size, multiple configuration packets are required to initialize them. The *Input Counter (IC)* logic specifies the index number of the PRBS generators to which the incoming configuration packet values are written.

After initialization, the LSFRs freely run and the least significant bit (LSB) is used for achieving the required rate. Due to the initialization pattern, the probability of the LSB becoming one will be same as the required rate. This is similar to finding a number between 0 and 1 from a uniform distribution and checking whether its value is less than the required rate. This software approach is emulated in hardware through the said mechanism. The initialization patterns are generated offline through a software application and broadcasted to the nodes through multiple packets as discussed before. Although same initialization packets are broadcasted to all the nodes, due to the inherent latency in packet switching, each LFSR will have a different initialization pattern at epoch zero but representing the same rate.

Once the WMSM receives the unicast packet carrying the initial node status, it is transferred to the PE and is switched to *running state*. When a PE receives its initial status, it is immediately broadcasted to its neighbors. Thus, some PEs may possibly receive packets from its neighbors before the end of the configuration. Moreover, due to path length differences and different congestion levels along different paths, out-of-order packets may arrive even at running state which may result in a node receiving a status from one of its neighbors for the next discrete time before receiving all status for the current time.

To overcome the out-of-order status delivery, PEs embed a sequence number into the status packets. The sequence number indirectly represents the current discrete time. When status packets are received, they are initially stored in a buffer with logical partition for each sequence number. Each partition can store NETWORK_SIZE number of status and each entry is just one 1 bit wide (to represent infected or susceptible). Each partition maintains its own counter which counts the number of status that have already arrived and to which entry the next status will be updated. In running mode, the status are extracted from a partition specified by the *sequence number checker* (SNC) one at a time and transferred to the PE. The status are sent to the PE only after receiving the

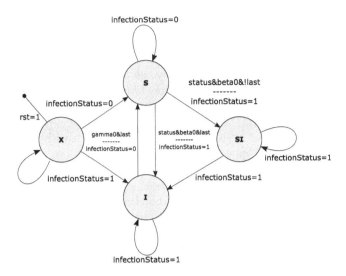

Fig. 6. SIS state machine

status from all its neighbors, whose number is specified in the *inputNum* register during configuration. Once all status are sent, the SNC is incremented to select the next partition. Since each PE generates a status packet only after receiving the status from all its neighbors, it could be proven that two sequence numbers are enough to distinguish between different discrete times. Thus, the size of the buffer is $2 \times$ NETWORK_SIZE bits to support two partitions.

3.4   Processing Element (PE)

Each PE runs the SIS state-machine, similar to the one shown in Fig. 6. The initial infection status is received from the NI during the configuration stage. Once the NI receives status from all the neighbors for a discrete time, it transfers the status one at a time to the PE. If the PE is in susceptible state and receives an infected status from one of the neighbors, it checks the output of the *beta* PRBS generator. If the PRBS output is high, the PE state is switched to *infected*. Further status received from the neighbors are ignored for the current epoch since, in the SIS model, a node cannot change its state more than once in any discrete time. If the PE is in *infected* state, it checks the output from *gamma* PRBS generator after receiving status from all neighbors. If the PRBS output is high, the state is switched to *susceptible* and the status of the neighbors play no role in this state transition. In all cases, the status of the PE after a discrete time is sent to the NI module which is then multicasted to all its neighbors.

The SIS state-machine is relatively simple, but due to the modular design approach any other model can be easily incorporated by modifying this state-machine alone. In future, as cloud FPGA instances start supporting partial reconfiguration (PR), models can be dynamically updated by only reconfiguring the PE module which substantially reduces the design and configuration time.

3.5   Simulation Steps

The host computer executes the following steps for StocNoC-based SIS model simulation:

Table 1. Resource utilization of the proposed architecture for 16×16 implementation when targeting Xilinx Ultrascale+ VU9P

Module name	Slice LUTs	Slice regs	Memory block
Network interface	322	251	0
Processing element	7	7	0
Switch	299	351	0
Total per node	628	609	0
Total network	**159710**	**156290**	**0**

- Inject the NoC configuration broadcast packets to configure the routing tables (Fig. 3d).
- Inject the broadcast packets to configure β and γ (Fig. 3c).
- Inject the unicast packets to configure the number of neighbors to each node (Fig. 3a).
- Inject the unicast packets to configure the initial status of each node (Fig. 3a).
- Receive packets from the NoC and monitor the network status. Once status packets are received from all nodes, increment the discrete time step and log the number of infected and susceptible nodes.

4   Results and Discussion

The proposed platform is designed with Verilog HDL and implemented on a Xilinx Ultrascale+ VU9P device targeting Amazon AWS cloud-based FPGA instances. Module-wise utilization for important building blocks and the overall utilization for a 16×16 network (256 nodes) is given in Table 1. The implementation consumes about 8% LUTs and 3% of flip-flops on the target device. At this rate, a network of 3000 nodes can be supported on this device after reserving enough resources for the communication infrastructure (AWS shell infrastructure). FPGA architecture-dependent resources such as BRAM/URAM tiles of DSP slices are not utilized making the design highly portable to other platforms such as the Microsoft Azure or on-premises implementations. Due to the heavily pipe-lined implementation, the platform can support to up to 260 MHz clock frequency, but is restricted to 250 MHz due to the PCIe-based host system interface.

We first verified the validity and the functional correctness of the proposed platform by comparing its output with corresponding software-based implementation of the discrete SIS model. Tests were conducted for three different network sizes (10×10, 16×16, and 32×32) for three β and γ values and three different topologies, thus giving a total of 27 test cases. Results from each test case were averaged over 10 runs to avoid outliers. Software and hardware test outputs corresponding to a 10×10 implementation (network with 100 nodes) with different rate and topology configurations shown in Fig. 7. It reveals that the steady state behavior and the number of discrete steps required to reach the steady state are similar in both cases which validates the functional correctness of the platform.

Table 2 compares the total run-time of software and the corresponding NoC-based implementations for modeling 100 discrete time steps for different network models and sizes. The software runs on an *AWS EC2 a1.xlarge* cloud compute instance with 4 vCPUs and 8 GB RAM. The NoC runs on an *AWS f1.2xlarge FPGA* at 200 MHz clock frequency. The FPGA run-time includes the time required for configuring the RT each time before starting the simulation. In a practical scenario, this could be avoided as long as the network topology remains intact. The run-time for 10×10 and 16×16 are very similar for NoC implementation since the 10×10 implementation is physically a 16×16 implementation mapped using appropriate adjacency matrix. This also shows the flexibility of the NoC architecture where a sub-network with any topology can be mapped to a mesh architecture using appropriate adjacency matrix. It is evident from the data that hardware outperforms software by an order of 2 to 3. Considering the hourly rate of 0.102 USD for a1.xlarge instance and 0.76–1.65 USD for (based on subscription type) for f1.2xlarge instance, hardware acceleration can provide considerable financial benefits to users.

One of the main limitations of NoC-based implementation of network models is the size of the supported network size. Even with modern FPGAs with multi-million equivalent gate capacity, networks with a few thousand nodes can be supported. Modeling large networks such as social media will require implementation of networks with millions of nodes. In a cloud environment, multiple FPGAs can be combined to simulate larger networks. Communication between the FPGAs will be managed by the cloud communication infrastructure. Two other approaches can be used for overcoming this limitation for resource constrained FPGAs. Using partial reconfiguration, FPGA resources can be time multiplexed and portions of the network can be simulated during different time instances and results can be combined to determine the total network performance. Another method is through structural reconfiguration, where portions of the network is configured through modifying network parameters such as the PE address. Intermediate result for each configuration is stored in external memory and broadcasted to the network after reconfiguration.

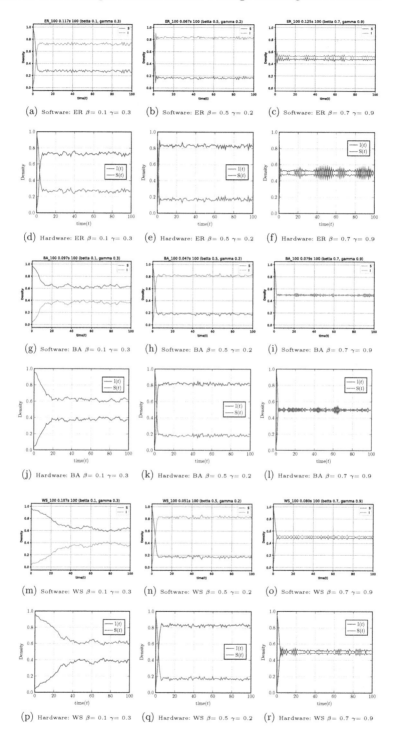

Fig. 7. Comparison of software simulation and hardware simulation outputs for different β and γ values in a 10×10 network.

Table 2. Wall clock time required for simulating 100 discrete time steps in software and proposed implementation

Topology	Run time (ms)	Network size		
		100	256	1024
WS	Software	107	312	1297
	NoC	0.213	0.232	2.81
BA	Software	97	242	1130
	NoC	0.215	0.248	2.78
ER	Software	117	473	4408
	NoC	0.217	0.262	3.67

5 Conclusion and Future Work

In this paper, we discussed the design, implementation and performance evaluation of StocNoC, a network on chip based solution for stochastic modeling. Experimental results show that the proposed architecture can accelerate the spreading model by many orders compared to software implementation on cloud-infrastructure and can provide significant financial benefits to users. The proposed model can be easily adapted to other scenarios such as social information diffusion, wireless malware propagation and viral marketing. It is shown that a hardware-based solution can significantly outperform software simulation in terms of run-time and at the same time, provide scalability due to the NoC-based architecture.

As future work, partial reconfiguration and structural reconfiguration will be evaluated for modeling large scale networks. We intend to extend and demonstrate the effectiveness of the platform in modeling multiple competitive processes in multi-layered networks. We believe that modeling of spreading dynamics will provide new research directions to the hardware accelerator research community. For generating research interest, the HDL implementation and the dataset used for evaluation are available as open source from the following git repository [1].

References

1. StocNoC Git repository (2019). https://github.com/dsdnu/sisNoC
2. Barabasi, A.L.: Network Science. Cambridge University Press, Cambridge (2016)
3. Bertozzi, D., et al.: NoC synthesis flow for customized domain specific multiprocessor systems-on-chip. IEEE Trans. Parallel Distrib. Syst. **16**(2), 113–129 (2005)
4. Brauer, F., Catillo-Chavez, C.: Mathematical Models in Population Biology and Epidemiology. Springer, New York (2001). https://doi.org/10.1007/978-1-4757-3516-1
5. Britton, T.: Stochastic epidemic models: a survey. Math. Biosci. **225**(1), 24–35 (2010)

6. Chawade, S.D., Gaikwad, M.A., Patrikar, R.M.: Review of XY routing algorithm for network-on-chip architecture. Int. J. Comput. Appl. **43**, 20–23 (2012)
7. Cheng, S., Chen, P., Lin, C., Hsiao, H.: Traffic-aware patching for cyber security in mobile IoT. IEEE Commun. Mag. **55**(7), 29–35 (2017)
8. Dadlani, A., Kumar, M.S., Maddi, M.G., Kim, K.: Mean-field dynamics of inter-switching memes competing over multiplex social networks. IEEE Commun. Lett. **21**(5), 967–970 (2017)
9. Dally, W., Towles, B.: Principles and Practices of Interconnection Networks. Morgan Kaufmann, Burlington (2003)
10. Erdős, P., Rényi, A.: On the evolution of random graphs. In: Publication of the Mathematical Institute of the Hungarian Academy of Sciences, pp. 17–61 (1960)
11. Furber, S.B., et al.: Overview of the SpiNNaker system architecture. IEEE Trans. Comput. **62**(12), 2454–2467 (2013)
12. Jenness, S.M., Goodreau, S.M., Morris, M.: EpiModel: an R package for mathematical modeling of infectious disease over networks. J. Stat. Softw. **84**(29731699), 8 (2018)
13. Joshi, J., Karandikar, K., Bade, S., Bodke, M., Adyanthaya, R., Ahirwal, B.: Multicore image processing system using network on chip interconnect. In: Proceedings of Midwest Symposium on Circuits and Systems, pp. 1257–1260, August 2007
14. Korkali, M., Veneman, J., Brian, B., Tivnan, F., Bagrow, J., Hines, P.: Reducing cascading failure risk by increasing infrastructure network interdependence. Nat. Sci. Rep. **7**, 44499 (2017)
15. Mathias, G., Kent, K.: An embedded Java virtual machine using network-on-chip design. In: Proceedings of IEEE International Workshop on Rapid System Prototyping (2006)
16. Newman, M.: Networks: An Introduction. Cambridge University Press, Cambridge (2014)
17. Patel, P.: FPGA-based accelerated cloud computing with AWS EC2 F1 and SDAccel (2018)
18. Sahneh, F.D., Vajdi, A., Shakeri, H., Fan, F., Scoglio, C.: GEMFsim: a stochastic simulator for the generalized epidemic modeling framework. J. Comput. Sci. **22**, 36–44 (2017)
19. Samman, F.A., Hollstein, T., Glesner, M.: Adaptive and deadlock-free tree-based multicast routing for networks-on-chip. IEEE Trans. Very Large Scale Integr. (VLSI) Syst. **18**(7), 1067–1080 (2010)
20. Van Mieghem, P.: Performance Analysis of Complex Networks and Systems. Cambridge University Press, Cambridge (2014)
21. Vynnycky, E., White, R.: An Introduction to Infectious Disease Modeling. Oxford University Press, Oxford (2010)
22. Xilinx Inc.: UG761: AXI Reference Guide, March 2011
23. Yang, L., Yang, X., Tang, Y.Y.: A bi-virus competing spreading model with generic infection rates. IEEE Trans. Netw. Sci. Eng. **5**(1), 2–13 (2018)

Implementation of FM-Index Based Pattern Search on a Multi-FPGA System

M. M. Imdad Ullah[(⊠)], Akram Ben Ahmed, and Hideharu Amano

Department of Information and Computer Science, Keio University, Yokohama, Japan
fic@am.ics.keio.ac.jp

Abstract. Pattern matching is a versatile task which has a variety of applications including genome sequencing as a major application. During the analysis, short read mapping technique is used where short DNA sequences are mapped relative to a known reference sequence. This paper discusses the use of reconfigurable hardware to accelerate the short read mapping problem. The proposed design is based on the FM-index algorithm. Although several pattern matching techniques are available, FM-index based pattern search is perfectly suitable for genome sequencing due to the fastest mapping from known indices. In order to make use of inherent parallelism, a multi-FPGA system called Flow-in-Cloud (FiC) is used. FiC consists of multiple boards, mounting middle scale Xilinx's FPGAs and SDRAMs, which are tightly coupled with high speed serial links. By distributing the input data transfer with I/O ring network and broadcasting I-Table, C-Table and Suffix-Array with the board-to-board interconnection network, about 10 times performance improvement was achieved when compared to the software implementation. Since the proposed method is scalable to the number of boards, we can obtain the required performance by increasing the number of boards.

1 Introduction

String matching is a task of searching for patterns in a long string. While it has a wide range of applications, the major one is in bioinformatics, particularly in genome sequencing. In genome sequencing, a short read alignment technique is used where matching of short strings (popularly known as "reads") against a reference genome is performed. This operation involves millions of pattern matching making it highly computationally intensive. Different data structures are discovered over the times for solving string matching problems. Out of all, FM-index [5] is a remarkable algorithm for solving computationally intensive string matching problems. Its highly efficient data structure makes it perfectly suitable for short read alignment.

FM-index stands for Full-text index in Minute space. It efficiently searches for occurrences of a pattern within a compressed text, and also locates the position of each occurrence. The compressed text is based on the *Burrows-Wheeler Transform* (BWT), which is a technique for lossless data compression. It can be efficiently computed from *Suffix-Array*. Powerful features of the *BWT* and

© Springer Nature Switzerland AG 2020
F. Rincón et al. (Eds.): ARC 2020, LNCS 12083, pp. 376–391, 2020.
https://doi.org/10.1007/978-3-030-44534-8_28

Suffix-Array have paved the way for the development of FM-index. FM-index inspired several software based DNA sequencing tools such as Bowtie [7], SOAP3 [9] and BWA [8]. These tools achieved some orders of magnitude faster execution than other tools using classical hash table like indices. To further speed up the DNA sequencing process, several hardware based accelerators have been proposed. Among them, FM-index based hardware accelerator on FPGAs has become popular because of its high performance per power [1,2,4].

However, most of them are implemented on a single board with a single or small number of FPGAs. Since FM-index has a high level of parallelism, the performance can be increased by using a number of searching modules in parallel. Here, we used a multi-FPGA system called *Flow in Cloud* (FiC) consisting of 24 boards, each of which mounts a mid-range cost efficient Xilinx's Kintex UltraScale. The final goal of FiC is building a multi-FPGA system in a cloud providing more than 100 boards. They are tightly connected with 9.9 Gbps high speed serial links directly, as well as an I/O board connected with a host through the PCIe bus.

Here, our target is to search for a pattern on the input reference sequence and also find the location of the pattern in the sequence. First, *BWT*, *I-table* and *C-table* are computed in software and broadcasted to the FPGA boards. Then we perform the search operations on our architecture. The evaluation results showed that the performance is almost 10 times faster than the software implementation even with a single board, and almost scalable performance improvement can be achieved.

2   BWT and FM-Index Data Structure

BWT is a reversible transformation invented by Michael Burrows and David Wheeler in 1994 [3]. Although it does not compress strings, it is frequently used for prepossessing of various compression algorithms. BWT is computed by sorting the cyclic rotations of a given string. Suffix-Array is a sorted array of all suffixes of a string. As BWT is the sorted cyclic rotation of the given string, we can efficiently compute BWT from the Suffix-Array. Suffix-Array will also help us to find the location of the pattern in the original string that we will describe later. Table 1 shows Suffix, Sorted Suffix, Suffix-Array and BWT for a random input string "TATGCTGATCAT".

After computing BWT, we move forward to constructing the FM-index data structure. FM-index data structure is composed of two tables, *I-table* and *C-table*.

- **I-Table**: It is also called as the frequency table. $I(x)$ is the number of characters in the BWT format that are lexicographically smaller than 'x'. For example, for character 'C', $I(C) = 4$. There are three 'A' and one '$' character in BWT, that are lexicographically smaller than 'C'. Thus, the *I-table* can be constructed as shown in Table 2.
- **C-Table**: It is also known as the occurrence table. $C(x)@index$ is the number of occurrences of 'x' in the BWT between the range *[0, index-1]*.

Table 1. Suffix, Sorted Suffix, Suffix-Array and BWT

Index	Suffix	Sorted Suffix	Suffix-Array	BWT
0	TATGCTGATCAT$	$	12	T
1	ATGCTGATCAT$	AT$	10	C
2	TGCTGATCAT$	ATCAT$	7	G
3	GCTGATCAT$	ATGCTGATCAT$	1	T
4	CTGATCAT$	CAT$	9	T
5	TGATCAT$	CTGATCAT$	4	G
6	GATCAT$	GATCAT$	6	T
7	ATCAT$	GCTGATCAT$	3	T
8	TCAT$	T$	11	A
9	CAT$	TATGCTGATCAT$	0	$
10	AT$	TCAT$	8	A
11	T$	TGATCAT$	5	C
12	$	TGCTGATCAT$	2	A

Table 2. I-table

A	C	G	T
1	4	6	8

Complete *C-table* is shown in Table 3. For example, $C(G)@6 = 2$ because there are 2 occurrences of 'G' between the range $[0, 5]$.

3   Pattern Search Using FM-Index

In this section, the pattern search procedure using FM-index is introduced. This pattern search technique is based on the *I-table*, *C-table* and *Suffix-Array* that we computed in the last section. The FM-index search procedure iterates through each character of the search pattern by two pointers, namely *top* and *bottom* pointers. The indices between the *top* and *bottom* pointers are the *Suffix-Array* indices. To search a pattern, we go through each of the character of the pattern beginning from the last character. One character is processed at a time by computing *top* and *bottom* pointers. The following formula is used to compute *top* and *bottom* pointers respectively for character 'x'.

$$top\_new = C(x)@top\_current + I(x) \qquad (1)$$

$$bottom\_new = C(x)@bottom\_current + I(x) \qquad (2)$$

To begin the process, we initialize the *top* and *bottom* pointers with first and last indices of the *C-table* respectively. Iteration starts from the last character

Table 3. C-table

Index	Suffix-Array	BWT	A	C	G	T
0	12	T	0	0	0	0
1	10	C	0	0	0	1
2	7	G	0	1	0	1
3	1	T	0	1	1	1
4	9	T	0	1	1	2
5	4	G	0	1	1	3
6	6	T	0	1	2	3
7	3	T	0	1	2	4
8	11	A	0	1	2	5
9	0	$	1	1	2	5
10	8	A	1	1	2	5
11	5	C	2	1	2	5
12	2	A	2	2	2	5
13	Total		3	2	2	5

of the search pattern. The *top* and *bottom* pointers move to different indices according to the current character being processed. If *bottom* pointer points to an index that is less than or equal to an index pointed by *top* pointer, then the pattern does not exist in the text and the search process is terminated. If the above condition does not occur throughout the iterations for all characters, then the search pattern exists in the text. Next is to locate the position of the pattern in the text. As *top* pointer points to an index of the *Suffix-Array* where a specific pattern is first located, the *Suffix-Array* element that corresponds to the final *top* pointer index is the location of the pattern in the text. As we can realize from the description that FM-index based search iterations are solely dependent on the size of search pattern rather than the size of the input text, it is highly efficient searching method for very large text.

In the following, we have shown the search process iteration in details with both exist and non-exist patterns.

3.1 Search Method (Exist)

Figure 1 depicts an example of a search method where the pattern exists in the text. We will search for pattern "CTGA" in the reference text "TATGCTGAT-CAT".

At first we initialize the *top* and *bottom* pointers to '0' and '13' respectively. Then we begin the search iteration with the last character 'A' of the search pattern. Next, we computed the *top* and *bottom* pointers at each iteration by the formula mentioned above. We go through four iterations for four characters. As the index of the *top* pointer is less than the *bottom* pointer throughout the

1st Iteration (for A)	
top_new = C(A)@top_current + I(A) = 0+1 = 1	bottom_new = C(A)@bottom_current + I(A) = 3+1 = 4
2nd Iteration (for G)	
top_new = C(G)@top_current + I(G) = 0+6 = 6	bottom_new = C(G)@bottom_current + I(G) = 1+6 = 7
3rd Iteration (for T)	
top_new = C(T)@top_current + I(T) = 3+8 = 11	bottom_new = C(T)@bottom_current + I(T) = 4+8 = 12
4th Iteration (for C)	
top_new = C(C)@top_current + I(C) = 1+4 = 5	bottom_new = C(C)@bottom_current + I(C) = 2+4 = 6

Fig. 1. Search iterations (exist)

iterations, the pattern exists in the text. At the last iteration, the value of *top* and *bottom* pointers are '5' and '6' respectively. The value of *top* pointer will provide the location of the pattern in the text. If we look for *Suffix-Array* value at index '5' in the Table 3, we get the value of '4'. This means that the pattern is located on the 4th position in the text.

3.2 Search Method (Not-Exist)

Figure 2 represents an example of search method where the pattern does not exist in the reference text. We search for the pattern "TACG" in the reference text. At first we initialize the *top* and *bottom* pointers as before. Then we begin the search iteration with the last character 'G' of the search pattern. The search process is terminated at the second iteration as the *top* and *bottom* pointer values are equal. This example shows that the search process is terminated as soon as it finds the mismatch. Consequently, we do not have to go through all the characters of the pattern when the pattern does not exist in the reference text.

1st Iteration (for G)	
top_new = C(G)@top_current + I(G) = 0+6 = 6	bottom_new = C(G)@bottom_current + I(G) = 2+6 = 8
2nd Iteration (for C)	
top_new = C(C)@top_current + I(C) = 1+4 = 5	bottom_new = C(C)@bottom_current + I(C) = 1+4 = 5

Fig. 2. Search iterations (not-exist)

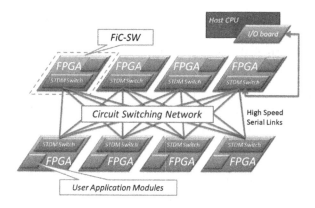

Fig. 3. Flow-in-Cloud

4 FiC System

4.1 FiC Prototype Overview

The current prototype of FiC system consists of multiple *FiC-SW* boards connected with each other and with the I/O board by high-speed serial links illustrated in Fig. 3. Although the figure shows an example with 8 boards, the current system has 24 FiC-SW boards that are connected to form a 6×4 torus network. For the serial links, we employ the cost-efficient *Firefly^{TM} Micro Flyover^{TM}* system by Samtec [11]. Each of the serial links offers four bi-directional channels to one destination, so this design choice introduces a restriction that four channels must be connected to the same destination together. Hereafter, we call such a set of four bi-directional channels a *bundle*. Logically, the network is shared with Static Time Division Multiplexing (STDM), a method for keeping a constant latency and bandwidth between multiple communications [6]. Additionally, in the prototype of FiC system, there is a control server connecting an I/O board using Xilinx KCU1500. The I/O board is connected to the host via *PCI Express Gen3.0x8* and FiC-SW boards by two bundles (eight channels) for data exchange between FiC-SW boards and the control server. For the board management purpose, each FiC-SW board equips with an on-board *Raspberry Pi 3* (RPi3) single-board computer, connected to a management network by Ethernet and offers remote management features.

4.2 FiC-SW Prototype Board

Figure 4a shows the block diagram of FiC-SW. We employ a middle-class Xilinx's Kintex UltraScale XCKU095 FPGA mounted on the board which supports up to 64 of GTH high-speed serial transceivers for the FiC interconnect network. Although the maximum bandwidth of the GTH serial ports is 16.3 Gbps, we regulated the transfer speed to 9.9 Gbps for the sake of easy implementation.

To provide enough bandwidth, it delivers up to 32 channels per board at the current design, supporting various network topologies connecting hundreds of boards. Although FiC-SW board provides 32 bidirectional channels, 4 channels are bundled and connected through a *Firefly^{TM}* cable. Here, we call 4 channels in a cable a lane. That is, 8 lanes, *Lane* 0 to *Lane* 7 are provided on each board. In the current prototype with 24 boards, *Lane 0* to *Lane 3* are used for board-to-board interconnection to form 4×6 torus network, *Lane 5* to *Lane 7* are employed for IO network introduced later, and *Lane 4* is kept for future usage. Each board provides two of 16 GB DDR4-SDRAM for data storage or buffering. The RPi3 daughter board is also mounted as a board management controller and connected to the FPGA by GPIO ports.

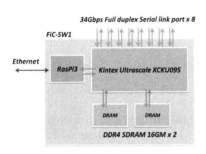

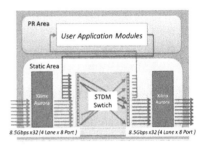

(a) Block diagram of FiC-SW

(b) Static and Partial Reconfiguration area

Fig. 4. Block diagram & PR area of FiC system

The FiC-SW FPGA logic is illustrated in Figure 4b. They are divided into two regions: (1) static region (hereafter, we call it *shell*) which includes the STDM (Static Time Division Multiplexing) network switch and peripheral controller logic, and (2) partial re-configurable (PR) region for user generated logic, designed with HLS [12]. The FM-index serach module proposed in this paper is implemented in this region. In the PR region, several HLS modules are connected with each other using the AXI stream interface, and form a group wrapped with a standard HDL module to connect the static region. Since all HLS modules use the same AXI stream interface to the shell, it can be replaced without stopping the communication between other boards. Only a routing table in the STDM is changed when new circuits are needed for new application programs. Four ports of the STDM switches are directly connected to the PR region, and 85 bit data are transferred with 100 MHz clock. That is, each PR region can input and output data with 34 Gbps bandwidth in total. To control the HLS modules, we defined standard application reset/start/done signals: *ap_rst, ap_start, ap_done* and data input/output signals. All signals are mapped to control registers in the *shell* region, and it is accessible from software on the RPi3. When an HLS module uses DRAM, a full AXI-4 bus is optionally provided in the static region to connect the PR region and the DDR4 DRAM controller. Table 4 summarizes the hardware specifications of the current prototype.

Table 4. Specifications of current FiC system prototype

System scale	24 FiC-SW board and an I/O board (KCU1500)
FPGA	Kintex UltraScale XCKU095-FFVB2104
Clock freq.	100 MHz
STDM switch	4 × 4 (9 × 9 at maximum)
Serial links	32 channels bundled into 8 lanes
Effective speed	8.5 Gbps (9.9 Gbps at a link)
Total exchange bandwidth	272 Gbps
Total throughput for the HLS modules	34 Gbps
Pass through latency	550 μs
Max latency of the system	1710 μs
DRAM	16 GB DDR4 DRAM (200 MHz) × 2
On-board controller	Raspberry Pi3 Model B (BCM2837 ARM Cortex-A53 Quad 1.2 GHz)

5 Single Board Implementation

5.1 FM-Index Search Module

The parallel execution of FM-index search itself is simple, since we can distribute the search pattern to a number of FiC-SW boards and execute the FM-index search for each pattern independently. First, we explain our implementation of FM-index search in each FiC-SW board. We design the FM-index search module (fm_search) using High Level Synthesis (HLS). HLS is a design process where the designer describes the desired behavior of the algorithm and generates the hardware description language format that implements the behavior. Moreover, HLS tools also provide *pragmas* that can be used to further optimize the design. Different kinds of optimizations such as reducing latency and area, improving throughput performance can be done using the *pragmas*. In our implementation, we used *Vivado HLS* which synthesizes our C++ specifications to RTL. The functional behavior of our design has been simulated on the C++ level through test bench simulation, then executed on the real FiC-SW board.

The block diagram of *fm_search* module is shown in Fig. 5. Our HLS design takes *I-Table, C-Table, Suffix-Array* and search pattern as inputs, and returns the search results as the output. As the generation of *I-Table, C-Table and Suffix-Array* from the input text is required only once, we make these computations on software and send the data to the HLS module. We take an input string of length 60001 (including the '$' sign) for our implementation. For the search

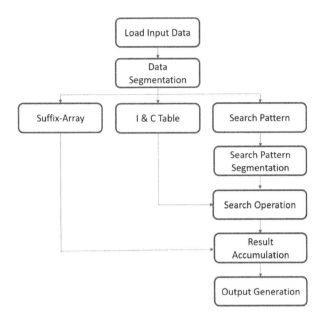

Fig. 5. Block diagram of *fm_search* module

pattern, we set the length of each search pattern to 16 and the maximum search
pattern count to 512. Our input data size is shown in Table 5a. We use '$' sign
to separate each type of the data from the data streaming. For the output, we
return whether the searched pattern exists or not in the input text, and also
the location of the pattern in the input text, if the pattern exists. As mentioned
later, our IO communication requires 128 bit data transfer, we define 128 bit
width for the input and output of our HLS module. To better utilize the 128 bit
data width, we try to fit as much data as possible for both input and output.
Inside the HLS module, we optimized our design by pipelining and loop unrolling.
After the completion of HLS of *fm_search* module, we instantiate our design in
the partial reconfiguration area of the FiC system.

Table 5. HLS input data & resource utilization

(a) Input Data for HLS module

Data	Size (Byte)
I-Table	16
C-Table	960032
Suffix-Array	240004
Search Pattern	32768

(b) Resource Utilization

	BRAM	DSP	FF	LUT
Used	1432	3	112195	72520
Allowed	1680	768	1075200	537600
Utilization (%)	85.24	0.39	10.43	13.49

5.2   Implementation Results

After the completion of the HLS, we synthesized, and place&routed the design with Vivado. The used tools shown in Table 6 are the standard ones for implementing applications on the FiC system. The resource utilization after the implementation for a single board is shown in Table 5b. Note that the presented values are the resources used in the partial reconfigurable region. Since the FM-index module uses a lot of BRAM, we can not implement multiple modules in a single FPGA. However, we rely on the performance of parallel execution with multiple boards here.

Table 6. Design tools

HLS	Vivado HLS Version 2018.3 (Xilinx)
Implementation	Vivado Version 2018.3 (Xilinx)
FPGA	Kintex UltraScale XCKU095-FFVB2104 (Xilinx)
Frequency	100 MHz

The execution time of FM-index based pattern search implementation on each board was evaluated and compared with software implementation. The host computer used here is Intel(R) Xeon(R) CPU E5-2680 v2 @ 2.80 GHz. Note that, parallel execution using OpenMP directives for enhancing a single FM-index module is not efficient. Like our parallel implementation shown later, the input-string level parallel implementation can achieve scalable performance improvement even with using multiple cores on the host. Thus, we used the single core execution results for the comparison. The obtained results are summarized in Table 7. As we can see from the table that we have achieved approximately 15 times faster execution on HLS compared with the software execution on the host. However, the execution time of the single board ignores the data transfer time from the host computer which is a major challenge of the implementation, as explained later.

6   Multi-board Implementation

6.1   The FiC I/O Communication

The multi board implementation requires two types of data: (1) *I-Table, C-Table and Suffix-Array* broadcasted to all boards when the computation starts, and (2) 16 × 512 search patterns. Both types of data are transferred from the host computer, and in order to guarantee a high performance implementation, we must design the I/O system without the bottleneck.

For the IO communication, the current FIC-IO board is implemented on a Xilinx general purpose KCU1500 board which is attached to the host via *PCIe Gen3.0x8.* Two small original extension boards are attached on the GTH

Table 7. Results comparison

Type	Software	Single board
Time (m. sec)	79.1	5.9
Time per search	0.15	0.01

channels of KCU1500, and they are connected to one of FiC-SW boards through *Firefly*^{TM} cables just like the interconnection between FiC-SW boards.

Figure 6 shows the I/O communication diagram when FiC-SW00 - FiC-SW03 boards are connected via a ring network with *Lane 6* and *Lane 7* to transfer data and control from/to host. *Lane 5* of FiC-SW00 is used to establish the connection with the FiC-IO board. As previously mentioned, in the FiC system, an individual IO network is provided for each board so that the communication with the host server does not interfere with the regular data communication between FiC-SW boards during computation.

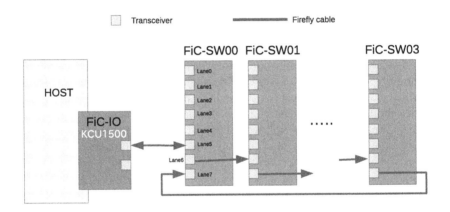

Fig. 6. I/O communication overview

The input data handling mechanism is shown in Fig. 7. In FiC-SW00, *fic_io_ctrl* receives data/control from FIC-IO through *Lane 5*, and either passes it to the local *fm_search* module or forwards it to other FiC-SW boards through the I/O ring. Similarly, the *fic_io_ctrl* in FiCSW01-FiCSW03 receives the data/control from the I/O ring and performs the necessary computations to route them to the proper FiC-SW destination.

As mentioned earlier, FiC-SW receives 170-bit data packet from FiC-IO. The 170 bit packet is used for the I/O data in the ring network, and the first 128 bits are the actual payload that is to be processed by the HLS module. While sending data targeting for the HLS module, we divide our input data into two categories, i.e. "Common Data" and "Specific Data". As, *I-Table, C-Table and Suffix-Array* are same for all FiC-SW boards, we categorize these data as "Common Data".

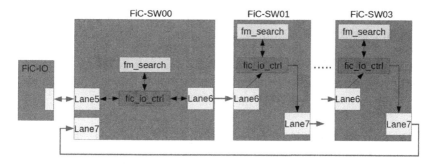

Fig. 7. Data handling mechanism

These data is broadcasted to all boards. On the other hand, the search pattern data which is different from one board to another is categorized as "Specific Data". The search pattern data is sent to a given board by configuring the packet destination ID. In our implementation, we sent 512 search patterns to each of the FiC-SW boards.

The maximum bandwidth of *PCIe Gen3.0x8* is 7.9 GByte/s almost matches to the maximum bandwidth of FiC-IO (9.9 Gbitx4x2), and there is no performance bottleneck in the initial design. However, the DMA mechanism of the current FiC-IO is under debugging, so the maximum bandwidth is severely limited at the path between the host and FIC-IO. Therefore, when the current FiC-IO is used with *Programmed IO* (PIO), about 98% of the total execution time was occupied by the I/O transfer. So, we developed FiC-IO emulation system and evaluated the performance on it.

6.2   FIC-IO Emulation

The objective of this emulation is to find out the exact data processing time of our *fm_search* module when assuming optimal I/O data transfer. For this emulation, we setup a system shown in Fig. 8. Here, the FIC-IO behavior is emulated

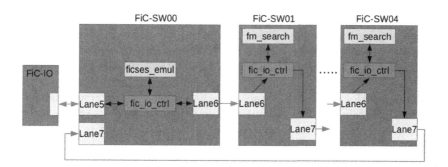

Fig. 8. FIC-IO emulation with FIC-SW00

with FIC-SW00. We design one additional HLS module called *ficses_emul* for FIC-SW00. Now, FIC-SW00 will send preloaded 170 bit data packet from the host to other FIC-SW boards. For FICSW01-FICSW04 boards, the scenario is the same as before. Also, the FIC-SW00 broadcasts the data for initialization: *I-Table, C-Table and Suffix-Array* by using the board-to-board interconnection network which is not needed for the computation.

6.3   Performance Evaluation on Multiple FiC Boards

First, the time for broadcasting on the FiC system from FiC-SW00 is evaluated. The STDM switch used in FiC can naturally broadcast the data just by selecting an input register in a specific time slot as shown in Fig. 9a. The data in *S1* is transferred to several output ports according to the pre-loaded table in the same slot *S2*. By using this method, we can send the same data to all boards with only 5 hops in a 4×6 torus system. Figure 9b shows the time for broadcasting all data sets used in FM-index based pattern search module. The total time is increasing related to the number of boards, but it is less than 5.38 ms even with 24 boards. Since the board-to-board network used for the broadcasting is independent with the FiC-IO ring network, overlapping of the data transfer can be done for the next data sets if needed.

(a) Data multicast with the STDM switch

(b) The time for data broadcasting from FiC-SW00

Fig. 9. Data multicast and time for data broadcasting

Then, we implemented the proposed search module from FiC-SW01 to FiC-SW04, as represented in Fig. 8 using FiC-SW00 as FiC-IO emulator. We evaluated the execution time in each FiC-SW board by the hardware timer embedded in the design. The execution time is increased compared with the one without the communication overhead (5.9 ms), but it is still about 10 times faster than the software execution. The execution time is increased constantly by 0.08 ms for a board (Table 8). This is corresponding to the overhead to pass through the input data. Without this small overhead, scalable performance is achieved. However, it is also shown that the execution time is estimated to be 9.70 ms with 24 boards. It is 8.1 times faster than the software execution with 23 cores.

Table 8. Execution time by using FiC-SW00 as FiC-IO emulator

Board	Exec time (m. sec)
FIC-SW01	7.94
FIC-SW02	8.02
FIC-SW03	8.10
FIC-SW04	8.18

7   Related Work

There are a lot of recent researches on FPGA based acceleration of short-read mapping. Since the evaluation basis is different, it is difficult to fairly compare the proposed method with previously proposed ones. In [2], a simple measure "bases aligned per second (baps)" was proposed:

$$baps = readsize \times readcount/processtime$$

Table 9. Performance comparison with *baps*

Design	Platform	Freq (MHz)	Devices	baps
SOAP3 [9]	NVIDIA GTX580	900	1 × 512	3.84
Design in [2]	Xilinx Virtex-6 SX475T	150	1 × 3	13.5
Design in [2] (estimated)	Xilinx Virtex-6 SX475T	150	8 × 1	108
Design in [10]	Xilinx Virtex-6 SX240T	250	8 × 8	112
Proposed design	Xilinx Kintex Ultrascase XCKU095	100	1 × 24	24

Table 9 compares the different approaches presented in [2] with ours. Since our design in this paper focuses on the scalable performance improvement on a large scale multi-FPGA system, the single core implementation uses Vivado-HLS, and the optimization is not enough. In order to obtain comparable performance to the design in [10], we need to provide more than 100 boards. Also, they achieved much better results with the recent implementation using Intel's Stratix-V FPGAs [1]. We must improve the implementation of the single core to follow such competitive results.

8   Conclusion

In this paper, we proposed a hardware implementation of FM-index based pattern searching on a multi-FPGA system FiC. By distributing the input data transfer with I/O ring network and broadcasting *I-Table, C-Table and Suffix-Array* with the board-to-board interconnection network, about 10 times faster performance compared to the PC software and almost scalable performance improvement was achieved.

The current implementation is based on the emulation of I/O transfer until DMA in the FiC-IO board is available. Our future work is to confirm that similar results can be obtained when the DMA is used on the real FiC-IO board. The implementation by using 24 boards is under going. We must finish it to confirm that the real scalable results are obtained. The current FiC system provides only a FiC-IO board for 24 boards. It might not be enough for IO dominant implementation like the search module implemented here. We are planning to increase the number of FiC-IO board and use multiple ring networks to increase the performance. Finally, in order to follow the competitive work, we must optimize the single core design.

References

1. Arram, J., Kaplan, T., Luk, W., Jiang, P.: Leveraging FPGAs for accelerating short read alignment. IEEE/ACM Trans. Comput. Biol. Bioinform. **14**, 668–677 (2017)
2. Arram, J., Tsoi, K.H., Luk, W., Jiang, P.: Hardware acceleration of genetic sequence alignment. In: Brisk, P., de Figueiredo Coutinho, J.G., Diniz, P.C. (eds.) ARC 2013. LNCS, vol. 7806, pp. 13–24. Springer, Heidelberg (2013). https://doi.org/10.1007/978-3-642-36812-7_2
3. Burrows, M., Wheeler, D.J.: A block-sorting lossless data compression algorithm. Technical report (1994)
4. Fernandez, E., Najjar, W., Lonardi, S.: String matching in hardware using the FM-index. In: 2011 IEEE 19th Annual International Symposium on Field-Programmable Custom Computing Machines, pp. 218–225, May 2011
5. Ferragina, P., Manzini, G.: Opportunistic data structures with applications. In: Proceedings 41st Annual Symposium on Foundations of Computer Science, pp. 390–398, November 2000
6. Hironaka, K., Doan, N.A.V., Amano, H.: Towards an optimized multi FPGA architecture with STDM network: a preliminary study. In: Voros, N., Huebner, M., Keramidas, G., Goehringer, D., Antonopoulos, C., Diniz, P.C. (eds.) ARC 2018. LNCS, vol. 10824, pp. 142–150. Springer, Cham (2018). https://doi.org/10.1007/978-3-319-78890-6_12
7. Langmead, B., Trapnell, C., Pop, M., Salzberg, S.L.: Ultrafast and memory-efficient alignment of short dna sequences to the human genome. Genome Biol. **10**(3), R25 (2009)
8. Li, H., Durbin, R.: Fast and accurate short read alignment with Burrows-Wheeler transform. Bioinformatics **25**(14), 1754–1760 (2009)
9. Liu, C.-M., et al.: SOAP3: ultra-fast GPU-based parallel alignment tool for short reads. Bioinformatics **28**(6), 878–879 (2012)
10. Olson, C., et al.: Hardware acceleration of short read mapping. In: IEEE 20th International Symposium on Field-Programmable Custom Computing Machines (FCCM), pp. 161–168 (2012)

11. Samtec, Inc.: Micro Flyover On-Board Optical Engine, FireFly. https://www.samtec.com/optics/optical-cable/mid-board/firefly
12. Yamakura, M., Hironaka, K., Azegami, K., Musha, K., Amano, H.: The evaluation of partial reconfiguration for a multi-board FPGA system FiCsw. In: Proceedings of the 10th International Symposium on Highly-Efficient Accelerators and Reconfigurable Technologies, HEART 2019, pp. 15:1–15:4 (2019)

Reconfigurable Accelerator for On-Board SAR Imaging Using the Backprojection Algorithm

Rui P. Duarte📙, Helena Cruz$^{(\boxtimes)}$📙, and Horácio Neto📙

INESC-ID/IST-UL, Lisboa, Portugal
{rui.duarte,helena.cruz}@tecnico.ulisboa.pt, hcn@inesc-id.pt

Abstract. Synthetic Aperture Radar is a form of radar widely used to extract information about the surface of the target. The transformation of the signals into an image is based on DSP algorithms that perform intensive but repetitive computation over the signal data. Traditionally, an aircraft or satellite acquires the radar data streams and sends it to be processed on a data center to produce images faster. However, there are novel applications demanding on-board signal processing to generate images. This paper presents a novel implementation for an on-board embedded SoC of an accelerator for the Backprojection algorithm, which is the reference algorithm for producing images of SAR sensors. The methodology used is based on a HW/SW design partition, where the most time consuming computations are implemented in hardware. The accelerator was specified in HLS, which allows to reuse the code from the original implementation of the algorithm in software. The accelerator performs the computations using floating-point arithmetic to produce the same output as the original algorithm. The target SoC device is a Zynq 7020 from Xilinx which has a dual-core ARM-A9 processor along with a reconfigurable fabric which is used to implement the hardware accelerator. The proposed systems outperformed the software-only implementation in 7.7× while preserving the quality of the image by adopting the same floating-point representations from the original software implementation.

Keywords: FPGA · Synthetic Aperture Radar · DSP · Backprojection · Zynq · SoC · Reconfigurable accelerator

1 Introduction and Motivation

Remote sensing technologies such as Synthetic-Aperture Radar (SAR) have been widely used monitor the surface of the Earth, in particular, ships and oil spills tracking at sea, ice-caps and sea level, terrain erosion, drought and landslides, deforestation, fires, and other types of natural disasters. The main strength of SAR is that it operates even in the presence of clouds, smoke and rain and without a light source, making it a very attractive method of monitoring Earth.

The original version of this chapter was revised: the missing funding information was added. The correction to this chapter is available at https://doi.org/10.1007/978-3-030-44534-8_30

© Springer Nature Switzerland AG 2020, corrected publication 2020
F. Rincón et al. (Eds.): ARC 2020, LNCS 12083, pp. 392–401, 2020.
https://doi.org/10.1007/978-3-030-44534-8_29

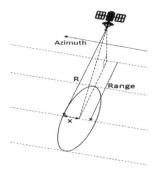

Fig. 1. Illustration of SAR operation and its physical parameters.

A SAR sensor can be mounted on-board flying platforms such as satellites, aircrafts and drones. Moreover, with the advancements in the technology and signal processing methods, there are increasing business opportunities for satellites and drones equipped with lightweight, small, and autonomous systems for on-board processing and generation of SAR images and subsequent broadcasting them, avoiding the time-consuming processing data at the receivers. However, its implementation in low-power embedded systems is limited to simplified implementations of the algorithm. While they are able to reduce the processing time, they sacrifice the image quality.

At the moment, the reference algorithm for SAR imaging is Backprojection (BP), which computes the contribution of each reflected pulse for each pixel on the resulting image. This process is time consuming as the projections all of the received pulses have to be computed for all pixels in the image. Figure 1 illustrates the parameters involved in the operation of a SAR mounted on a moving platform.

Recent radiation tests [4] on System-on-Chip (SoC) Zynq devices from Xilinx have shown that they provided a good performance under a harsh environment, therefore there is an increasing interest in adopting such systems on-board aircrafts. These devices have a dual-core ARM A9 CPU along with a reconfigurable fabric which is capable of implementing a hardware accelerator to alleviate the computations from the CPU and speedup the overall execution time.

This work introduces a novel accelerator architecture for SAR imaging using the Backprojection image generation algorithm and its evaluation on a SoC device.

This paper is organized as follows. Section 2 presents the background on BP algorithm and existing accelerators. Section 3 is dedicated to the profile of the algorithm, which determines which parts of the implementation require more processing time, and thus be the candidates for hardware acceleration. Section 4 details the implementation of the hardware accelerator using High-Level Synthesis (HLS). Section 5 presents the HW/SW system design, and its performance and resources are discussed in Sect. 6. Section 7 concludes the paper with the final remarks.

2   Background

2.1   Backprojection

The following nomenclature related to the Backprojection algorithm is adopted in this paper:

- R - Differential range from platform to each pixel at the center of the swath.
- x_k, y_k, z_k - Radar platform location in Cartesian coordinates.
- x, y, z - Pixel location in Cartesian coordinates.
- r_c - Range to center of the swath from radar platform.
- $f(x, y)$ - Value of each pixel (x, y).
- θ_k - Aperture point.
- r_k - Range from pixel $f(x, y)$ to aperture point θ_k.
- ω - Minimal angular velocity of wave.
- $g_{x,y}(r_k, \theta_k)$ - Wave reflection received at r_k at θ_k (calculated using the linear interpolation in Eq. 2).
- $s(n)$ - Wave sample in the previous adjacent range bin.
- $r(n)$ - Corresponding range to the previous adjacent bin.

As aforementioned, the BP algorithm computes the contribution of each reflected pulse for each pixel on the resulting image. The BP algorithm takes the following values as input: number of pulses, location of the platform for each pulse, the carrier wave number, the radial distance between the plane and target, the range bin resolution, the real distance between two pixels and the measured heights. For each pixel and each pulse, the BP algorithm, performs the following steps:

1. Computation of the distance from the platform to the pixel:

$$R = \sqrt{(x - x_k)^2 + (y - y_k)^2 + (z - z_k)^2} - r_c \tag{1}$$

2. Conversion of the distance to an associated position (range) in the data set (received echoes).
3. Obtain the samples at the computed range via linear interpolation, using Eq. 2 [5].

$$g_{x,y}(r_k) = g(n) + \frac{s(n+1) - s(n)}{r(n+1) - r(n)} \cdot (r_k - r(n)) \tag{2}$$

4. Scales the sampled value by a matched filter to form the pixel contribution. This value is calculated using Eq. 3 [5]. dr is calculated using Eq. 1 [5].

$$e^{i\omega 2|\vec{r_k}|} = \cos(2 \cdot \omega \cdot dr) + i \sin(2 \cdot \omega \cdot dr) \tag{3}$$

5. Accumulates the contribution into the pixel. The final value of each pixel is given by Eq. 4 [5].

$$f(x, y) = \sum_k g_{x,y}(r_k, \theta_k) \cdot e^{i \cdot \omega \cdot 2 \cdot |\vec{r_k}|} \tag{4}$$

The pseudocode to compute the aforementioned steps is shown in Algorithm 2. k_u represents the wave number and is given by $\frac{2\pi f_c}{c}$, where f_c is the carrier frequency of the waveform and c is the speed of light, a_k refers to the position of the pixel, and v_p, corresponds to the platform position. The complex exponential $e^{i\omega}$ is equivalent to $\cos(\omega) + i\sin(\omega)$ and, therefore, a cosine and sine computation is implied in the calculation of each pixel, represented in Eq. 4.

Algorithm 1. Backprojection algorithm pseudocode, from [1].

1: **for all** pixels k **do**
2:      $f_k \leftarrow 0$
3:      **for all** pulses p **do**
4:          $R \leftarrow ||a_k - v_p||$
5:          $b \leftarrow \lfloor (R - R0)/\varDelta R \rfloor$
6:          $w \leftarrow \lfloor (R - R0)/\varDelta R \rfloor - b$
7:          $s \leftarrow (1 - w) \cdot g(p, b) + w \cdot g(p, b + 1)$
8:          $f_k \leftarrow f_k + s \cdot e^{i \cdot k_u \cdot R}$
9:      **end for**
10: **end for**

2.2 FPGA Accelerators for Backprojection

There are several accelerators for the BP algorithm, however they often target High Performance Computing (HPC) systems for real-time generation of images. The work in [3] uses OpenCL to program 16 GPUs (with 2048 cores each), receives all signals in 17.7 s and takes 1 to produce an image. There are also some implementations of accelerators on FPGA of variations of the BP algorithm such as fast-BP [6] or factorized-BP [7]. Even though they perform faster than the complete BP algorithm the image quality is degraded, therefore they are not useful for comparison with the proposed architecture. Previous work on implementing the BP algorithm targeting SoC devices can be found in [2]. However, the authors focused on acceleration by distributing the load on the two CPU cores and introducing a lightweight software-only fault tolerance mechanism.

3 Algorithm Profiling

The profiling of the BP algorithm running on a single core of the A9 ARM processor of the target Zynq device was required to determine which parts of the algorithm should be accelerated. The implementation of the BP algorithm adopted is available in [1]. The obvious functions to be accelerated in hardware are the square root and the sine and cosine functions from the inner loop. Nevertheless, in this algorithm there is a final accumulation operation at the end of the inner loop, which can be seen as a reduce operation, and thus a scale down in the number of data transfers required.

In the profiling, an image of 512×512 pixels was generated from 512 pulses, with 512 samples for pulse. 512 complex floating-point samples produce a single complex floating-point result, which results in reduction of required throughput.

Table 1 summarizes the processing times of the most time consuming mathematical operations in the BP algorithm. All times are in nanoseconds and were measured for 1000 repetitions of the execution of each operation on the ARM processor, compiled with -O3 compiler optimization.

Table 1. Execution times for the operations in the implementation of BP.

Operation	Time [ns]	% Execution time
Sqrt	50	1.3%
Sin+Cos	3108	84.3%
Misc	530	15.4%
Total	3688	100.0%

4   SAR Backprojection Accelerator

The accelerator targeted the most time consuming operations of the BP algorithm, and was specified using Xilinx HLS. Using HLS and maintaining the floating-point representation allows to reutilize parts of the source code and guarantees that the images produced will have the same result as the original implementation of the BP algorithm. The accelerator was implemented as a single IP core, where it receives the range values and samples for 512 pulses. The range values are double precision floating-point values whereas the samples are complex single-precision floating-point values. The operations implemented on the accelerator correspond to line 9 of Algorithm 2.

In this specification, it is noteworthy the separation of the computations between two loops in the HLS specification. The first loop obtains the data for the range values from the streaming interface, computes their product to serve as input to trigonometric functions and stores the result in local memories. The second loop receives the pulse samples also via the streaming interface, performs the complex multiplication and writes the result to the output streaming interface. Figure 3 illustrates the sequence diagram of the relations between the building blocks of the accelerator.

Table 2 summarizes the FPGA resources required to implement the BP accelerator from the specification. The HLS tool produced a circuit design capable of operating at 100 MHz, resulting in an IP core which requires a minimum of 60 clock cycles in latency, of which 24 cycles are required by the CORDIC IP (Fig. 2).

Table 2. Estimate of resources required to implement the BP accelerator reported by Vivado HLS.

Resource	Utilization	% Total on Zynq-7020
BRAM18K	2	1%
DSP48E	34	15%
LUTs	13986	26%

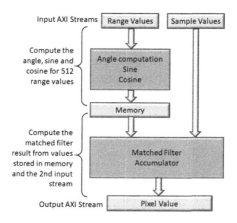

Fig. 2. Organization of the accelerator.

Algorithm 2. HLS accelerator specification.

1: **for all** pulses p **do**
2:    $input \leftarrow inStream.read()$
3:    $R \leftarrow input.data()$
4:    $angle \leftarrow 2.R.Ku$
5:    $s, c \leftarrow hls :: sincos(angle)$
6:    $mem\_sin[p] \leftarrow s$
7:    $mem\_cos[p] \leftarrow c$
8: **end for**
9: **for all** pulses p **do**
10:    $input \leftarrow inStream.read()$
11:    $sample.re \leftarrow input.data()$
12:    $sample.im \leftarrow input.data()$
13:    $matched\_filter\_result \leftarrow (mem\_cos[p] + imem\_sin[p]) \cdot sample$
14:    $acc \leftarrow acc + matched\_filter\_result$
15:    $outStream.write(acc)$ ▷ pixel_val
16: **end for**

5   HW/SW Project

The HW/SW project of the BP algorithm follows the partition created for the accelerator of the algorithm. The accelerator was integrated by establishing a connection to the CPU via AXI streaming interface, which is connected through Direct Memory Access (DMA) controller. Figure 3 illustrates the Vivado project containing the hardware blocks. On the software-side, the accelerator is used issuing data transfers between the DMA controller and the memory.

The Listing 1.1 shows the simplified code running on the ARM A9 CPU. The initial part of the code corresponds to the initialization of constants [1]. The loops for all pixel computations were changed so that only the range computations are performed in software and the rest of the algorithm in the hardware accelerator. Moreover, the original loop which iterated all the pulse samples was removed as they are computed by the accelerator. The interaction with the accelerator happens through the DMA, before instructing to transfer input values of range and sample values from the DDR to the accelerator, is programmed to wait for the computation of a row of pixels.

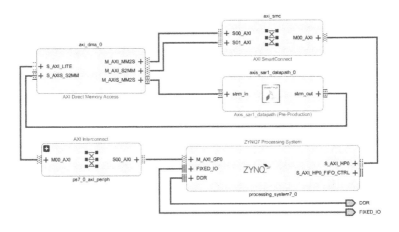

Fig. 3. Hardware project design on Vivado.

Listing 1.1. Backprojection code

```
void Backprojection () {
    sar_constants_calculation ();
    for (iy = 0; iy < BP_NPIX_Y; ++iy)       {
        const double py = (-BP_NPIX_Y/2.0 + 0.5 + iy) * dxdy;
        DMA_Transfer(image + iy*row_offset); // ACCL 2 DDR image row
        for (ix = 0; ix < BP_NPIX_X; ++ix)          {
            // calculate pixel contribution
            DMA_Transfer(range); // DDR 2 ACCL
            DMA_Transfer(samples); // DDR 2 ACCL
        } // x
    } // y
} // func
```

6   Results and Discussion

The proposed system was implemented on a Zynq-7020 device installed on a Pynq-Z2 from TUL. The system was tested with two images, a synthetic one provided in the Perfect Suite [1] and a real one from the AFRL dataset, in Fig. 4. The software was compiled with the -O3 compilation option.

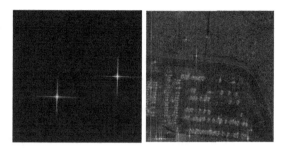

Fig. 4. Synthetic SAR image from the Perfect benchmark suite (left) and real SAR image from the AFRL dataset (right).

6.1   Processing Time

From the original algorithm profiling, it was found the algorithm required 487.5 s to generate of a 512×512px image. The processing times for the computations made by the accelerator in software, corresponding to line 9 of the pseudocode, required 1667.3 us, whereas the same computations in the accelerator required only 37.31 us, a reduction of 44.68×. Comparing the total processing times for a 512×512 image, between the original and the accelerated version, the accelerated is 7.7× faster.

6.2   Hardware Resources

The resources required to implement the accelerator on the reconfigurable fabric of the device are dominated by the Digital Signal Processing (DSP) blocks which consume about 64% of the total available on the device. Table 3 summarizes the resources required to implement the accelerator on the Zynq device.

6.3   Energy Consumption

The current consumption was measured using a UM24C USB power meter, connected between the host computer and the Pynq-Z2 FPGA board. Figure 5 shows the power consumption measured, which details the consumption for power-on, configuration of the device and execution of the algorithm with the reconfigurable accelerator. The average power consumption of the whole system is 1.796 W. The power estimate from Vivado provides insight on the on-chip power consumption,

Table 3. Summary of resource utilization to implement the accelerator on a Zynq-7020.

Resource	Utilization	% Total on Zynq-7020
LUT	11517	21.65
BRAM	4	2.86
DSP	141	64.09

which is 1.584 W. The difference between the measurement and the estimate is around 200 mW (12%) and is attributed to other components present on-board which are not taken into account by Vivado. Figure 6 shows the details of the power consumption, where 86% of power is consumed by the CPU (PS7).

The software-only implementation consumes on average 1.72 W. Even though the system with the hardware accelerator requires more 76 mW, finishes 7.1 min earlier than the software-only implementation. In comparison with the original execution on the CPU, which consumed 241.5 mWh (772.2 J), the system with the hardware accelerator requires 30.4 mWh (109,55 J), which represents 14.18% of the total energy consumption.

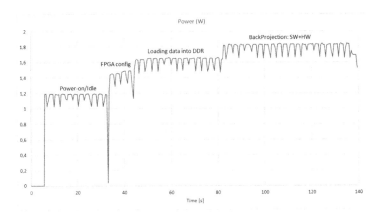

Fig. 5. System current consumption during the different stages of the experiment.

Dynamic:	1.445 W	(91%)	
Clocks:	0.035 W	(2%)	
Signals:	0.045 W	(3%)	
Logic:	0.031 W	(2%)	
BRAM:	0.001 W	(<1%)	
DSP:	0.079 W	(6%)	
PS7:	1.254 W	(86%)	
Device Static:	0.139 W	(9%)	

Fig. 6. On-chip power consumption distributed across the different elements.

7   Conclusions

The work presented proposes a novel HW/SW implementation of the BP algorithm on an embedded SoC platform for on-board processing of SAR imaging. The creation of the accelerator was facilitated by the adoption of HLS to migrate sets of arithmetic operations from software to hardware. The proposed architecture was able to achieve a speedup of 7.7× over the software-only implementation while preserving the quality of the image. Future work will focus on moving other operation of the BP algorithm into hardware to further improve the performance of the accelerator.

Acknowledgement. This work was supported by national funds through Fundação para a Ciência e a Tecnologia (FCT) with references UID/CEC/50021/2019 and PTDC/EEI-HAC/31819/2017 (SARRROCA). HC would like to acknowledge Fundação para a Ciência e a Tecnologia for the support through grant SFRH/BD/144133/2019.

References

1. Barker, K., et al.: PERFECT (Power Efficiency Revolution For Embedded Computing Technologies) Benchmark Suite Manual. Pacific Northwest National Laboratory and Georgia Tech Research Institute, December 2013. http://hpc.pnnl.gov/projects/PERFECT/

2. Cruz, H., Duarte, R.P., Neto, H.: Fault-tolerant architecture for on-board dual-core synthetic-aperture radar imaging. In: Hochberger, C., Nelson, B., Koch, A., Woods, R., Diniz, P. (eds.) ARC 2019. LNCS, vol. 11444, pp. 3–16. Springer, Cham (2019). https://doi.org/10.1007/978-3-030-17227-5_1

3. Gocho, M., Oishi, N., Ozaki, A.: Distributed parallel backprojection for real-time stripmap SAR imaging on GPU clusters. In: Proceedings - IEEE International Conference on Cluster Computing, ICCC 2017, September, pp. 619–620 (2017). https://doi.org/10.1109/CLUSTER.2017.64

4. Lentaris, G., et al.: High-performance embedded computing in space: evaluation of platforms for vision-based navigation. J. Aerosp. Inf. Syst. **15**(4), 178–192 (2018). https://doi.org/10.2514/1.I010555

5. Pritsker, D.: Efficient global back-projection on an FPGA. In: 2015 IEEE Radar Conference (RadarCon), pp. 0204–0209, May 2015. https://doi.org/10.1109/RADAR.2015.7130996

6. Song, X., Yu, W.: Processing video-SAR data with the fast backprojection method. IEEE Trans. Aerosp. Electron. Syst. **52**(6), 2838–2848 (2016). https://doi.org/10.1109/TAES.2016.150581

7. Wielage, M., Cholewa, F., Riggers, C., Pirsch, P., Blume, H.: Parallelization strategies for fast factorized backprojection SAR on embedded multi-core architectures. In: 2017 IEEE International Conference on Microwaves, Antennas, Communications and Electronic Systems (COMCAS), pp. 1–6. IEEE, November 2017. https://doi.org/10.1109/COMCAS.2017.8244770

Correction to: Reconfigurable Accelerator for On-Board SAR Imaging Using the Backprojection Algorithm

Rui P. Duarte🆔, Helena Cruz🆔, and Horácio Neto🆔

Correction to:
Chapter "Reconfigurable Accelerator for On-Board SAR Imaging Using the Backprojection Algorithm" in:
F. Rincón et al. (Eds.): *Applied Reconfigurable Computing*, LNCS 12083, https://doi.org/10.1007/978-3-030-44534-8_29

The funding information was missing from the originally published chapter. This was corrected and the funding information was added.

The updated version of this chapter can be found at
https://doi.org/10.1007/978-3-030-44534-8_29

Author Index

Printed in the United States
By Bookmasters